Luther's Ecumenical Significance

Luther's Ecumenical Significance

An Interconfessional Consultation

edited by
PETER MANNS and HARDING MEYER

in collaboration with
CARTER LINDBERG and HARRY McSORLEY

FORTRESS PRESS   PHILADELPHIA

Published by Fortress Press, Philadelphia, Pennsylvania
and Paulist Press, New York/Ramsey.

Eight of the ten essays (and half the responses and summaries) in this book are translations of the corresponding materials in the companion German volume edited by Peter Manns and Harding Meyer, *Oekumenische Erschliessung Luthers. Referate und Ergebnisse einer internationalen Theologenkonsultation*, copyright © 1983 by Verlag Bonifacius-Druckerei Paderborn and Verlag Otto Lembeck Frankfurt am Main.

COPYRIGHT © 1984 BY FORTRESS PRESS

All rights reserved. No part of this publication may be reproduced, stored in a retrieval system, or transmitted in any form or by any means, electronic, mechanical, photocopying, recording, or otherwise, without the prior permission of the copyright owner.

Library of Congress Cataloging in Publication Data

Oekumenische Erschliessung Luthers. English.
  Luther's ecumenical significance.

  English ed. of: Oekumenische Erschliessung Luthers.
  Papers presented at an international consultation sponsored by the Institute for Ecumenical Research, Strasbourg, and the Institute for European History, Mainz, held in the Maria Rosenberg Academy of the Diocese of Speyer, on October 12–15, 1982.
  1. Luther, Martin, 1483–1546—Congresses. I. Manns, Peter. II. Meyer, Harding. III. Institute for Ecumenical Research. IV. Institut für Europäische Geschichte (Mainz, Rhineland-Palatinate, Germany) V. Title.
BR325.O37 1983   230′.41′0924   83-48001
ISBN 0–8006–1747–9 (Fortress)
ISBN 0–8091–2576–5 (Paulist)

K362F83   Printed in the United States of America   1–1747

Contents

Foreword   ix
    James R. Crumley, Jr.

Foreword   xiii
    John R. Roach

Preface to the German Edition   xv
    Peter Manns and Harding Meyer

Preface to the English Edition   xix
    Carter Lindberg and Harry McSorley

Contributors   xxi

Abbreviations   xxiii

1. The State, Method, and Ecumenical Relevance of Catholic Luther Research   1

   The Validity and Theological-Ecumenical Usefulness of the Lortzian Position on the "Catholic Luther"   3
       Peter Manns

   The "Lutheran" Luther—A Catholic Possibility? An Attempt at an Understanding of "Historical Luther Research" and "Systematic-Theological Luther Interpretation"   27
       Otto Hermann Pesch

   Responses   47
       Marc Lienhard   47
       Erwin Iserloh   54
       Gottfried Maron   57
       Peter Bläser   61

   Summary   65
       Harding Meyer

CONTENTS

2. Luther's Theology and the Formation of Reformation Confessions — 69

    The Importance of Luther's Writings in the Formation of Protestant Confessions of Faith in the Sixteenth Century — 71
    Gottfried Seebass

    Luther's Theology in Its Significance for Church Confession — 81
    Wenzel Lohff

    Responses — 93
    - Brian Gerrish — 93
    - Hans-Jörg Urban — 96
    - Stephen W. Sykes — 99

    Summary — 105
    Heinz Schütte

3. The "One Holy Christendom": Luther's Double-Faceted Concept of the Church — 109

    The Church as Spiritual-Sacramental *Communio* with Christ and His Saints in the Theology of Luther — 111
    Vilmos Vajta

    "A People of Grace": Ecclesiological Implications of Luther's Sacrament-Related Sermons of 1519 — 123
    Hans-Werner Scheele

    Responses — 137
    - Metropolitan John of Helsinki — 137
    - Geoffrey Wainwright — 139
    - Tuomo Mannermaa — 150

    Summary — 155
    Georg Kretschmar

4. Luther's Motif *simul iustus et peccator* as an Approach to the *Novus Homo* and to the *Nova Creatura* — 159

    Justice and Injustice in Luther's Judgment of "Holiness Movements" — 161
    Carter Lindberg

CONTENTS

Luther's Significance for Contemporary Theological Anthropology ... 183
   Martin Seils

Responses ... 203
   James F. McCue ... 203
   Calvin Augustine Pater ... 207
   John S. Oyer ... 215
   Hans Martensen ... 221

Summary ... 225
   James R. Crumley, Jr.

5. Authority, Authenticity, and Relevance of Christian Witness in Light of Luther's Understanding of Scripture and the Word ... 227

"No Other Gospel": Luther's Concept of the "Middle of Scripture" in Its Significance for Ecumenical Communion and Christian Confession Today ... 229
   Inge Lønning

The Diversity of Christian Witnessing in the Tension Between Subjection to the Word and Relation to the Context ... 247
   Douglas John Hall

Responses ... 269
   Gerhard Heintze ... 269
   Henry S. Wilson ... 273
   Yoshikazu Tokuzen ... 277

Summary ... 281
   David W. Preus

Summary of the Consultation ... 285
   Reinhard Frieling

Foreword

JAMES R. CRUMLEY, JR.

It is readily apparent that 1983 is a significant year for Lutherans around the world as they celebrate the 500th anniversary of the birth of Martin Luther and study with renewed intensity his life and work. That Christians of many denominations find common ground with Lutherans in celebrating the event is still somewhat surprising.

The Strasbourg Institute for Ecumenical Research on October 12-15, 1982, sponsored an International Consultation of Theologians in the Maria Rosenberg Academy of the Diocese of Speyer located in the village of Waldfischbach-Burgalben, which held creative and new possibilities for those who were present. Its theme, "Disclosing Luther's Ecumenical Significance," pointed to an interest in the Luther Jubilee year that would go far beyond the Lutheran family. To read the important papers presented by scholars in several traditions and to note that participants included members of the Roman Catholic, Orthodox, Reformed, Anglican, Mennonite, and Methodist churches as well as the United Church of Canada convinces one that Christians in many communions around the world see themselves as having a vital stake in understanding the ecumenical potentials and problems occasioned by Luther.

What has caused the change in attitude? What has happened that the man who in former times was often denounced as "heretic" becomes for many a "father in the faith"?

For one thing, we must not underestimate the tenor of our times. A sure mark of the Spirit's leading, for many of us, is that Christian people today are anxious to express the unity that they have in Christ Jesus rather than clinging to the issues that have divided them so often in the past. Ecumenical concerns are a priority. On every side the search is on for the common theological themes that all of us can affirm and confess as central to our faith.

In that search, the contribution made by Martin Luther is newly appreciated. Lutherans themselves have developed a different perspective. In their celebration of the 450th anniversary of the Augsburg Confession in 1980 they gained an appreciation for the ecumenical and catholic intention of that document. It is understood that the signers of the confession were anxious to affirm that they were not sectarians nor schismatics but that they held the one, true, catholic, and apostolic faith. To claim the teaching of this document as one's own, then, is to assert that one must be ecumenical, that one must recognize the catholicity of teaching in other confessions as well and accept as true brothers and sisters those in every church who confess Jesus Christ as the foundation of all true teaching. Many Lutherans have found a new appreciation for a confession that does not lead them away from the other members of the Christian family but declares unity with them.

Christians other than Lutheran have discerned the same renewing and reforming principles in Luther's thought. The appropriate questions are: Does Luther's teaching properly reflect the Word of God? Does it adequately take into account the history and the tradition of the church? Is it consonant with truth, even though it never claims to be the perfect truth?

There is no question that Luther's life, his personality, his problems, as well as his living in the first half of the sixteenth century, influenced his theology. No one thinks and teaches in a vacuum. Some have made the mistake, however, of searching for a psychological or emotional explanation for Luther's teaching. Much research has been done with the intention of exposing the weakness and the strengths of the man. Much of that work has given interesting results, of course, and a sense of kinship with Luther has been growing on the part of many people. Understandably, that identification comes as much through his less-than-admirable words and actions as in his personal strength. One who insisted that the Word of God and not his own goodness was the foundation of his righteous cause illuminated the way to a strength and courage available to every person. To know God in faith is to possess a new life, one that is constantly supplied by God's grace and not through a person's achievement.

To repeat: we must focus on the teaching of this man. Luther witnesses as a pastor and teacher in the church, relevant not only to his day but also far beyond his own time. The issue of the faithfulness of God's people to the calling and mission that God himself gives them is never relegated to only one moment of history. Nor is the issue to be confined to only one denomination, one church among many. It is the perennial and the burning issue for all of us. What does God ask in our day? Where are we failing in our witness? Luther continues to teach us to follow him in the gospel of God's justifying grace. He also instructs us by his mistakes and excesses, showing where we should follow him with caution or part company.

For Luther, the questions were not theoretical ones, to be relegated to the ivory tower, but questions to be answered in the midst of daily struggle and pilgrimage. They are matters of faith. One does not search for the truth about God in order that one may write laudable tomes. Rather, God reveals himself in Christ. As we know Christ as Lord and Master, we find him to be the truth for us and for all people. Thus we can only proclaim his gifts that have made us new creatures, and his mandates that require our discipleship. Luther knew God, and, even at the risk of martyrdom, he lived out of that relationship.

FOREWORD

These papers, presented in preparation for the Luther Jubilee year, examine Luther and his work in this light and from this perspective. They illustrate how the thought and teaching of this sixteenth-century professor and pastor of the church are of significant ecumenical importance for today.

James R. Crumley, Jr.
Bishop, Lutheran Church in America

Foreword

JOHN R. ROACH

Not only for Lutherans but also for Roman Catholics, Martin Luther remains a figure of historical and contemporary significance. The names of other reformers may not be readily identifiable by many Catholics, but it is hard to imagine a Catholic who would not instantly recognize Luther's name. He continues to be a vivid presence in the Catholic story.

A notable transformation has taken place by stages in the picture of this man presented by Catholic scholarship. A polemical view still predominated at the beginning of this century, when in 1904 Heinrich Denifle, O.P., published *Luther und Luthertum in der ersten Entwicklung*. Attention was tightly focused on Luther's personality, seen as turbulent, and on his subjective role in bringing about a division among Christians for which he was held largely responsible. This psychobiographical or psychohistorical approach also marked the more subtle scholarship of Hartmann Grisar, S.J. How limited and even misleading this viewpoint was, is apparent from the conclusion expressed by Grisar in the preface to his 1925 study *Martin Luther, His Life and Work:* "Luther is regarded by present-day Protestants more and more as a purely historical phenomenon. According to the acknowledgement of Protestant leaders, the present age has in general passed beyond his influence, and the little group which still professes his peculiar doctrines is diminishing." It is evident in the 500th year of Luther's birth that this judgment is quite wide of the mark.

Nearly all would agree that a turning point in Luther scholarship among Catholics was the work of Joseph Lortz, whose history of the Reformation (*Die Reformation in Deutschland*) appeared in 1939/40. It effectively widened the scope of scholarly inquiry to take into account the negative factors in the life of the church in the Middle Ages, thus demonstrating the urgent need for reform. Lortz's work was complemented by that of other renowned Catholic scholars such as Hubert Jedin, who studied the history which led to the Council of Trent. As readers of this volume will see, Lortz's influence is still felt today. Some contemporary scholars offer further research as a defense and extension of his groundbreaking work; others propose corrections and substantial additions to his insights.

If the first shift in the Catholic view of Luther was from a polemical judgment to a wider historical view, which to a greater or lesser extent excused him in light of the distortions in Christian life in his day, there came next a renewed appreciation of the elements of Catholic life and understanding which Luther retained and defended. Thus there emerged a "Catholic" Luther with whom positive links could be maintained, as well as a "heretic" with whom it was impossible to contemplate dialogue. At the present stage of Luther research among Catholics, attention is focused on the issues Luther raised precisely as a reformer: to what extent and in what way were his teachings a departure from Catholic tradition, and to what extent, even when new, may they find a rightful place within that tradition?

As this volume also makes clear, Catholic scholars do not work in isolation from others in addressing this question. They now form one community of scholars with their Lutheran counterparts and those from other churchly traditions. The contributors to the present collection offer us an opportunity to see at first hand a cross-section of the work in progress, and to appreciate its vigor and seriousness.

This scholarly work is a most challenging and demanding task, not least because of the differences of thought structure and language which appear when one seeks possible contact points. Writing in 1970, Warren Quanbeck described the situation in a way that remains pertinent:

> We are embarrassed to discover how vain and fruitless many exercises of traditional *Kontroverstheologie* have been in comparing incomparables, in assuming identity of meaning because the same words are used, or in missing common concerns beneath divergent theology. It is one of the great theological assets of our time that historical-critical method has equipped us with means to realize the variety of theologies with which the New Testament expounds the mystery of God's activity in Christ, the number of different theological methods used through the centuries of the church's existence to communicate this message to the world, and the variety of vocabularies and images which are available to articulate theologies in our time. We are given a new theological situation. We are not imprisoned forever in the fruitless repetition of old quarrels, but by the use of new methods accessible to us can find areas of agreement where formerly discord reigned, and move on to the discussion of questions which are genuinely significant. When we are realistically modest about our theological achievements, we recognize that the problems are not solved, but still waiting for solutions which may emerge from constructive dialogue. (Afterword to *Catholic Scholars Dialogue with Luther,* J. Wicks, ed., Loyola, 1970.)

With each passing year evidence mounts that this goal will be reached, even in our own time. Thus we can hope today not only for the solution of problems from our past, as great a blessing as that would be for the church, but also for a fuller and richer life together.

The Most Reverend John R. Roach
Archbishop of Saint Paul and Minneapolis
President, National Conference of Catholic Bishops

Preface to the German Edition

The Institute for Ecumenical Research (Strasbourg), the Johann-Adam-Möhler-Institut (Paderborn) and the Institut für Europäische Geschichte, Abteilung Abendländische Religionsgeschichte (Mainz), in collaboration with the Konfessionskundliche Institut des Evangelischen Bundes (Bensheim) and the Institut Supérieur d'Etudes Oecuméniques (Paris), called together Luther scholars and bishops of various churches for an International Consultation of Theologians designed to serve the mutual concern for "disclosing Luther's ecumenical significance."

We wish to take the opportunity here to express our gratitude for the generous financial support from the Evangelical Church in Germany and the Association of German Dioceses. The Consultation itself took place at the Maria Rosenberg Academy of the Diocese of Speyer, near Kairserslautern. The participants in the Consultation were theologians and Luther specialists from North America, Scandinavia, Asia, France, and East and West Germany. They came from major churches that from their origins have been dependent on dialogue with Luther, or which out of ecumenical motivation have for decades been concerned with him.

The episcopacy was represented by the Lutheran bishops Gerhard Heintze, formerly bishop of the Evangelical Lutheran Landeskirche in Braunschweig and Catholica-Representative of the United Evangelical Church of Germany, James R. Crumley, Bishop of the Lutheran Church in America and member of the Executive Committee of the Lutheran World Federation, and David W. Preus, Bishop of the American Lutheran Church and Vice-President of the Lutheran World Federation; by the Orthodox Metropolitan John of Helsinki; and by the Roman Catholic bishops Hans Martensen, Bishop of Copenhagen and representative of the Secretariat of Christian Unity, and Paul-Werner Scheele, Bishop of Würzurg and chairman of the Ecumenical Commission of the German Bishops' Conference.

We are now in the position of offering the results of this Consultation to the public. The organizers and authors wish to thank the publishers, Bonifacius-Druckerei of Paderborn and Otto Lembeck of Frankfurt am Main, without whose commitment this publication would not have been possible.

For understandable reasons the publishers wished to limit the size of this publication; therefore the abbreviation and reworking of some of the individual contributions was unavoidable. In particular this concerned the con-

Translated by Carter Lindberg

PREFACE TO THE GERMAN EDITION

tributions of Peter Manns, Otto Hermann Pesch, Vilmos Vajta, and Carter Lindberg. In spite of this unfortunately necessary abbreviation, we think that the essential results of the Consultation are reproduced by the lectures, position papers, and discussion reports published here. In spite of a certain delay due to translation of the English contributions into German, this volume still appears in good time to be a meaningful contribution to the work being carried on for the Luther Anniversary.

The extent to which Luther's theology impedes or may be able to advance contemporary interconfessional dialogue and understanding among the churches is assessed by means of five themes:

1. The present state of Catholic Luther research, in terms of both its positive ecumenical significance and also the remaining problems, is sharply defined in comprehensive contributions and in a series of shorter, clarifying commentaries.

2. Luther's significance for the formation of the Reformation confessions, and therefore for the Reformation movement growing into a church, is a question common to Lutherans, Reformed, Anglicans, and Catholics, which at the same time relates the Luther Anniversary to the important discussions and insights of the recent Anniversary of the Augsburg Confession.

3. The growing significance of ecclesiological questions in the ecumenical dialogue calls for a new consciousness of Luther's understanding of the church, which is discussed by the Orthodox and Methodists as well as the Catholics and Lutherans.

4. The Lutheran *simul iustus et peccator* contains the key problem for the relationship between Lutheranism and the Anabaptist or Holiness Movements of the sixteenth century and those churches which derive from or are in connection with them.

5. Finally, the question of Holy Scripture is one which is fundamental for all Christians and which runs through all the churches and is sharply felt today in the tension between scripturally bound and contextually related Christian witness. This theme is dealt with and considered in light of Luther's understanding of Scripture and the Word.

Each of these five themes appears in manifold elucidations, and the discussion reports show the course of the discussions.

In the opinion of the organizers the result of the Consultation may be characterized above all under two viewpoints:

First of all it is clear that the difficulties which stand in the way of a disclosure of Luther's ecumenical significance may not be minimized. Luther's spiritual and theological heritage must be opened up not only for those churches originally hostile to him but also for his own church, for whom in many respects he has become a "stranger." Now as before, the determination of the genuine "reformatory element" causes particular difficulties. One, to some extent very critical, attitude exists openly above all on

PREFACE TO THE GERMAN EDITION

the side of those Christian communities who as descendants of the so-called Anabaptists—or better, sixteenth century Holiness Movements—feel misunderstood in their concerns by Luther up to today. But this also holds for those churches which have not yet worked out the burden of the history of division and to whom Luther, moreover for the most diverse reasons, appears to be an unacceptable or an extremely difficult partner.

The Consultation, however, produced another perspective by which the striven-for "ecumenical disclosure" of Luther, in spite of the suggested difficulties (which certainly are to be taken very seriously), may be characterized as a whole as a thoroughly possible and extraordinarily fruitful task.

This holds above all for the Lutheran-Catholic dialogue on Luther, the surprisingly positive results of which became visible during the anniversary of the Augsburg Confession (1980) and are confirmed in the mutually recognized "agreement in the central truths of the faith" (John Paul II). These positive results can also be of significance for the Lutheran-Orthodox dialogue which is underway. However, the encounter of the Anglican and Methodist churches with Luther is also positive and ecumenically effective; as is, not least of all, the illumination of the actual and "transconfessional" problematic of contextually related theology and proclamation in light of Luther's understanding of the Scriptures and the Word.

In these and other places it is clear that we must in no way fall back from Luther into paralysing controversies but that, on the contrary, we are experiencing from him exceedingly strong ecumenical impulses and are able to overcome ecumenical stagnation on important points.

Everything depends upon allowing ourselves with Luther to be continually led back to the way of the faith, and that we with him also endure on this way to the end, when we—led by the Lord—go where we do not will.

In closing we express gratitude to all those who, like Dr. André Birmelé, the secretaries, the translators, and the Sisters of Maria Rosenberg, made possible through their efforts the smooth development of the Consultation.

Strasbourg/Mainz, Invocavit 1983

Peter Manns
Harding Meyer

Preface to the English Edition

Little need be added to the Preface by Harding Meyer and Peter Manns except to thank Fortress Press for its initiative in making available to English readers the proceedings of this multi-national, genuinely ecumenical conference designed to highlight the problems as well as the positive possibilities that arise when Luther is listened to today with openness by theologians from the various Christian churches. For the volume to appear during the quincentennial year of Luther's birth, the translators of the papers originally presented in German had to comply with unusually short deadlines. Wherever possible Luther citations from the Weimar Ausgabe are correlated with the American Edition of *Luther's Works*. The effort to provide references to the English translations of secondary sources was limited by the constraints of time.

This English edition could not have been completed without the special help of the following: Professor Harry McSorley assented to make room for editorial and translating assistance in the midst of an already busy sabbatical year in Strasbourg. Georges Herzog, doctoral candidate at Boston University, interrupted his writing on Geiler of Kaisersberg, and Patricia M. Williams, Institute for Ecumenical Research, devoted long weekends and late nights in order to help us meet our deadline; their gracious response to the plea for help in translation is deeply appreciated.

Carter Lindberg, Boston University
Harry McSorley, University of Toronto

Contributors

Prof. Dr. Peter Bläser (Catholic)
Johann-Adam-Möhler-Institut,
Paderborn,
Federal Republic of Germany

The Rev. Dr. James R. Crumley, Jr.
Bishop of the
Lutheran Church in America,
New York

Dr. Reinhard Frieling (Lutheran)
Konfessionskundliches Institut,
Bensheim,
Federal Republic of Germany

Prof. Dr. Brian Gerrish (Reformed)
Divinity School, University of Chicago

Prof. Dr. Douglas John Hall
(United Church of Canada)
Faculty of Religious Studies,
McGill University, Montreal, Canada

Bishop (retired) Dr. Gerhard Heintze
(Lutheran)
Stuttgart,
Federal Republic of Germany

Prof. Dr. Erwin Iserloh (Catholic)
Catholic Theological Faculty,
Westfälischen Wilhelms-Universität,
Münster,
Federal Republic of Germany

Metropolitan John of Helsinki
(Orthodox)
Orthodox Diocese of Helsinki,
Finland

Prof. Dr. Georg Kretschmar (Lutheran)
Evangelical Theological Faculty,
Ludwig-Maximilians-Universität,
Munich,
Federal Republic of Germany

Prof. Dr. Marc Lienhard (Lutheran)
Protestant Faculty of Theology,
University of Strasbourg, France

Prof. Dr. Carter Lindberg (Lutheran)
School of Theology,
Boston University, Boston

Prof. Dr. Wenzel Lohff (Lutheran)
Prediger- und Studienseminar,
Pullach, Federal Republic of Germany

Prof. Dr. Inge Lønning (Lutheran)
Theological Faculty, Oslo University,
Oslo, Norway

Prof. Dr. Tuomo Mannermaa (Lutheran)
Theological Faculty,
Helsinki University, Helsinki, Finland

Prof. Dr. Peter Manns (Catholic)
Institute for European History,
Mainz, Federal Republic of Germany

Prof. Dr. Gottfried Maron (Lutheran)
Evangelical Theological Faculty,
Kiel University, Kiel,
Federal Republic of Germany

Bishop Hans Martensen (Catholic)
Copenhagen, Denmark

Prof. Dr. James F. McCue (Catholic)
School of Religion, University of Iowa,
Iowa City, Iowa

Prof. Dr. Harding Meyer (Lutheran)
Institute for Ecumenical Research,
Strasbourg, France

Prof. Dr. John S. Oyer (Mennonite)
Goshen College, Goshen, Indiana

Prof. Dr. Calvin A. Pater (Reformed)
Knox College, University of Toronto,
Toronto, Canada

Prof. Dr. Otto Hermann Pesch (Catholic)
Evangelical Theological Faculty,
Hamburg University, Hamburg,
Federal Republic of Germany

The Rev. David W. Preus (Lutheran)
Bishop of the
American Lutheran Church,
Minneapolis, Minnesota

Prof. Dr. Hans-Werner Scheele
(Catholic)
Bishop of Würzburg,
Federal Republic of Germany

Prof. Dr. Heinz Schütte (Catholic)
Catholic Theological Faculty,
Bonn University,
Federal Republic of Germany

CONTRIBUTORS

Prof. Dr. Gottfried Seebass (Lutheran)
Evangelical Theological Faculty,
Ruprechts-Karls-University,
Heidelberg,
Federal Republic of Germany

Prof. Dr. Martin Seils (Lutheran)
Evangelical Theological Faculty,
Friedrich-Schiller-University, Jena,
German Democratic Republic

Prof. Dr. Stephen W. Sykes (Anglican)
University of Durham,
Durham, England

Prof. Dr. Yoshikazu Tokuzen (Lutheran)
Japan Lutheran Theological College/
Seminary, Tokyo-Mitaka, Japan

Dr. Hans-Jörg Urban (Catholic)
Johann-Adam-Möhler-Institut,
Paderborn,
Federal Republic of Germany

Prof. Dr. Vilmos Vajta (Lutheran)
Alingsas, Sweden

Prof. Dr. Geoffrey Wainwright
(Methodist)
Union Theological Seminary,
New York

Prof. Dr. Henry S. Wilson
(Church of South India)
Serampore College, Bangalore, India

Abbreviations

ARG	*Archiv für Reformationsgeschichte*
Barge	Hermann Barge, *Andreas Bodenstein von Karlstadt*, 2 vols. (1905; reprint, Nieuwkoop: De Graaf, 1968)
BC	Theodore G. Tappert, trans. and ed., *The Book of Concord* (Philadelphia: Fortress Press, 1959)
BSLK	*Die Bekenntnisschriften der evangelisch-lutherischen Kirchen* (Göttingen: Vandenhoeck & Ruprecht, 1963)
DS	H. Denzinger and A. Schönmetzer, eds., *Enchiridion Symbolorum: Definitionum et Declarationum de Rebus Fidei et Morum* (Freiburg: Herder, 1963)
EA	*D. Martin Luther's sämmtliche Werke* (Frankfurt and Erlangen, 1826–57)
Franz	Günther Franz, ed., *Thomas Müntzer, Schriften und Briefe*, Kritische Gesamtausgabe (Gütersloh: Gerd Mohn, 1968)
Freys-Barge	*Verzeichnis der gedruckten Schriften des Andreas Bodenstein von Karlstadt* (Reprint. Nieuwkoop: De Graaf, 1965)
Hertzsch	Erich Hertzsch, ed., *Karlstadts Schriften aus den Jahren 1523–1525*, 2 vols. (Halle [Saale]: Niemeyer, 1956–1957)
Kähler	Ernst Kähler, ed., *Karlstadt und Augustin: Der Kommentar des Andreas Bodenstein von Karlstadt zu Augustins Schrift De Spiritu et Litera* (Halle [Saale]: Niemeyer, 1952)
KT	Karlstadt, *Von Abtuhung der Bylder*, ed. Hans Lietzmann Kleine Texte 74 (Bonn, 1911)
KuD	*Kerygma und Dogma*
LR	*Lutherische Rundschau*
LThK	*Lexicon für Theologie und Kirche*
LuW	*Lutheran World*
LW	*Luther's Works*. American Edition. ed. J. Pelikan and H. Lehmann (Philadelphia: Fortress Press; St. Louis: Concordia, 1955) (cited by volume: page)
MQR	*Mennonite Quarterly Review*
MS	*Mysterium Salutis*, ed. J. Feiner and M. Löhrer (Einsiedeln-Zurich-Köln, 1967)
NO	*Die Neue Ordnung in Kirche, Staat, Gesellschaft, Kultur*
ÖR	*Ökumenische Rundschau*
RD	Joseph Lortz, *Die Reformation in Deutschland*. 5th ed. 2 vols. (Freiburg-Basel-Wien: Herder, 1962)

ABBREVIATIONS

RG	Joseph Lortz, *The Reformation in Germany*, trans. Ronald Walls. 2 vols. (New York: Herder & Herder; London: Darton, Longman & Todd, 1968)
RR	*Reformata Reformanda. Festgabe für Hubert Jedin*, 2 vols. ed. E. Iserloh & K. Repgen (Münster, 1965)
SM	*Sacramentum Mundi. Theologisches Lexikon für die Praxis*, ed. K. Rahner, et al. (Freiburg-Basel-Wien, 1967)
SvTK	*Svensk Teologisk Kvartalskrift*
TCT	*The Church Teaches* (St. Louis: B. Herder, 1954)
ThLz	*Theologisches Literaturzeitung*
ThPh	*Theologie und Philosophie*
TThZ	*Trierer Theologische Zeitschrift*
WA	*Luthers Werke*. Kritische Gesamtausgabe (Weimar, 1883) (cited by volume: page: line)
WA Br	*Luthers Werke, Briefwechsel* Kritische Gesamtausgabe (Weimar, 1930) (cited by volume: page)
WA TR	*Luthers Werke, Tischreden*, Kritische Gesamtausgabe (Weimar, 1912–1921) (cited by volume: page)
WNM	Martin Schmidt, *Wiedergeburt und Neuer Mensch, Gesammelte Studien zur Geschichte des Pietismus* (Witten: Luther, 1969)
ZThK	*Zeitschrift für Theologie und Kirche*

Luther's Ecumenical Significance

THE STATE, METHOD, AND ECUMENICAL RELEVANCE OF CATHOLIC LUTHER RESEARCH

The Validity and Theological-Ecumenical Usefulness of the Lortzian Position on the "Catholic Luther"

PETER MANNS

The intelligibility of this greatly abbreviated lecture is enhanced if I summarize the deleted parts in two concise remarks.

The first remark concerns the thoroughgoing change of the hermeneutical situation in Luther research in the last two decades. A thorough study of the following lecture by Pesch discerns right away that the Lortzian position on the "Catholic Luther" appears to have virtually completely lost its ecumenical significance in the mid-sixties. Pesch, the leading representative of a new "ecumenical-theological breakthrough," advocates a deepened systematic-theological statement of the question for ecumenical dialogue with Luther by which the Lortzian position allegedly "will definitively be surpassed." Above all, A. Brandenburg, another representative of the new orientation, in the pose of the victors, proclaimed that the formula of the "Catholic Luther" "is no longer justifiable." Even my all too polemical and impassioned plea for the historical-theological orientation of my teacher and his school—which in no way fundamentally denies the justification of the new formulation of the question—was not able to change the new situation taking place. But my effort cannot have been entirely in vain if Pesch himself thinks it expedient to deliver his lecture in the setting of this Consultation in the form of a "late answer" to the questions I had formulated at that time. I regret all the more that the structure of my lecture made impossible a thorough response to the very important substantive issues of his "answer," and that the attempt of at least suggesting a response fell victim to abbreviation. Nevertheless, the new round of discussions with Pesch, to be taken up as soon as possible, is qualified in a very positive sense, if I include—at least in general at this point—the question: How will the events of the last two decades beginning as a controversy between two "fine brothers" over the allegedly unsuitable orientation of the old master of Catholic Luther research and continuing as a dialogue between friends and "brothers in arms" be brought to a good end? In order to suggest the depth and extent of change, I do not shrink from the reference that the reproach leveled then against Pesch by Jedin is expressed against me in a more intensified form by Jedin's student, Bäumer.

The answer to the question can only be suggested here in catchwords. The point of departure under the postulate "beyond Lortz" does in fact lead within Catholic Luther research to a considerable deepening and differentiating of the theological dialogue with the Reformer; a result from which, nevertheless, Lortz and his students

Translated by Carter Lindberg

should not be excluded. It is different with regard to the ecumenical hope associated with this point of departure. The development leads—certainly not without the complicity of theological promoters—into a bottleneck, in which the movement appears to founder on the veto of the ecclesial teaching office. Pesch, underestimating the official position of Evian (1970) on Luther as the "common teacher of faith and love," formulates in the face of the stagnation which is setting in the warning and exhorting question: Are we regressing behind Lortz? A revival of hope at first came from the plan elaborated by the theologians Pfnür and Ratzinger for a "Catholic recognition of the Augsburg Confession," which after its reception by representatives of the Lutheran World Federation and agreement by the Secretariat for Unity grew into a great ecumenical project. As far as Luther is concerned, however, this plan was significant in that it was clearly directed against Luther as developed by its Catholic promoters. This was the occasion for my protest—"ecumenism at the expense of Luther?"—that after the most vehement reaction initiated a new turn. The understanding means that the Augsburg Confession is to be interpreted from Luther and Luther from the Augsburg Confession. Just how serious and justified my apprehension was became apparent not least in the position taken by leading Catholic theologians to the frontal attack launched against Luther by a hitherto unknown author in the new edition of his book (Th. Beer, *Der fröhliche Wechsel und Streit. Grundzüge der Theologie Martin Luthers,* Einsiedeln: Johannes Verlag, 1980). No less than Hans Urs von Balthasar, in an advertising prospectus for this book, openly put this question whether contemporary "ecumenical dialogue" really still can and should be referred back to the "authentic Luther." If the "Protestant side" in this connection recommends the renunciation of Luther, then it is rather obvious by whom he should be replaced; namely, by Melanchthon, and through him the Augsburg Confession. It was certainly not the least danger in this project that Melanchthon's discussions in Augsburg could be played up in distinction to Luther's dogmatism as the model for modern ecumenism. Now, after these things, it may be thankfully observed that the feared crisis not only could be overcome by mutual effort but could be made fruitful for a new turn to Luther and the disclosure of his ecumenical significance. Typical for this new situation is not least the position of the pope. The recognition of a fundamental consensus on the basis of the Augsburg Confession does not diminish in the least his interest for ecumenical dialogue with Luther. Thereby the change is sufficiently suggested that also renews the engagement with the Lortzian position on the "Catholic Luther" and allows it to appear as ecumenically significant.

The second remark has to do with the attempt of a self-critical assessment of more distinct narrow directions in the Lortzian presentation. What is meant here are the often-cited pointed propositions of the author which limit Luther's merit to a mere "rediscovery of Catholic truths" or appear to challenge in general a "heretical rediscovery by itself." The danger of these propositions is that with their help the much-prized Lortzian orientation may revert in no time to the old heretic-abuse of a Denifle. It is not for nothing that Bäumer advanced his abuse of Luther during the time of the papal visit to Germany by reference to Lortz, and afterwards—with particularly pointed reference to me and my presentation of the Lortzian position—sought to justify his position by an abundance of further "propositions." What these "propositions" do, in addition to the problem, is the incontestable fact that Lortz—as he accordingly explains in the fourth edition of his work in 1962—explained that corresponding corrections were unnecessary. Nevertheless this in no way means that the author, in the course of his further work on Luther up to his death in 1975, did not decisively revise and deepen the positions in question. Even more, it is not difficult to show that the pointed propositions lose their apparent unequivocal sense if one takes into account the tenor of the entire judgment. As the Herder Publishing House requested me to write an Afterword to the sixth edition of the *Reformation in Deutschland* (1982), it held me to be qualified, as the co-worker for many years with my deceased teacher, to take up the meaning of his original and later considerably deepened orientation with regard to its criticized narrow and misleading directions. The concerns of the Lortzian orientation are done justice only if the paradoxicality of its simultaneity of the "Catholic" and "heretical" Luther was and is taken into account. Whereby I am already indicating here an analogy to Luther's motif *simul iustus et peccator*, which I shall establish in my lecture.

THE LORTZIAN POSITION IN ITS ORIGINAL FORM

The best entree to Lortz's formulation of the question is found in his reflections over the causes of the Reformation in their broadest sense or presentations of the abuses of the ecclesial situation of the sixteenth century in the view of Luther. At the same time it is advisable and permissible to interpret the scholarly and exacting statements of *The Reformation in Germany*, because they were inhibited by the "censor," from the theses by which Lortz first developed his statement of the problem. These occur in the form of course lectures and addresses since 1934 which comment on the ecumenical situation. We are referring here to *Die Reformation als religiöses Anliegen heute. Vier Vorträge im Dienste der Una Sancta*.[1] The title already indicates a theological-ecumenical program. For how could we "today" take up and realize anew in purified form "the concerns of the Reformation"—which for Lortz were always primarily and essentially "the concerns of Martin Luther"—if we are not engaged in them as "possibilities of our own faith"?

It is above all in the introductory chapter, "The Causes of the Reformation," that Lortz reflects on the preparatory causes and preconditions of the Reformation.[2]

First of all there is the view of a "wandering and sinning Church." Although Lortz does not use this expression the description is of the church as the "bride of the Song of Songs" "simultaneously beautiful and filthy"[3] whose disintegration in the "Middle Ages" produces the basic principles and fundamental forms which "cause" the Reformation.[4] From this perspective it is above all the "universal papacy" with its false claim to lordship which leads the church to Avignon, the Western Schism, and into the crisis of Conciliarism and the Renaissance.[5] Thereby Lortz arrives at the thesis, hardly acceptable for the normal Catholic, that the Reformation was "a well-nigh absolute necessity" due to the failures of the church.[6] The offense of this thesis was not lessened when Lortz stated, clearly for reasons of self-defense, that the Reformation was *"historically* necessary."[7] This sad "necessity" is described for all areas of the church's life: from the failures of the papacy, the curia, the bishops with their cathedral chapters, parish clergy, liturgy, preaching, and piety to the continually deplored "theological unclarity," "religious weakness," and the life-endangering "obscuration of the Catholic idea."[8] Lortz did not shrink back from confessing that at that time *dogmatically* self-evident "lordship of the church as a *historically* recognizable condition . . . was for the most part simply no longer extant; that is, if the expression is permitted, had become *historically* invisible."[9] This is not only an impressive thesis as Lortz formulated it, but it is a comprehensive church-historical judgment of great theological moment. For what is affirmed here of the cause of the sixteenth-century Reformation can continually recur as momentous failure in the life of the church.

The explosive effect of this judgment is not in the least lessened when Lortz continually distinguishes in this connection "cause" and "guilt"—for the ancient church as well as for Luther.[10] For the "objective cause" without "subjective" and "personal guilt" refers all the more strongly to the causes which lie in the area of the "institutional" or the "structural."[11] But the objective and historical causes do not of course exclude the accusation of guilt in individuals, for instance in individual popes or figures such as Eck or even Luther himself, groups of persons and even the church. In this connection, Lortz speaks expressly of a "Catholic complicity,"[12] a complicity of the church which because of its ecclesiology is basically more momentous than the guilt of an individual.

Nevertheless for Lortz, theological justification of this in no way follows without further ado from the demonstrable historical causation of the Reformation by the failure of the church in the sense of "Catholic complicity." The Reformation was in this sense indeed historically necessary; the situation without doubt did affect and stimulate the Reformer and thus within certain limits excuse him. Nevertheless on the other hand, Luther is the essential cause of the Reformation.[13] Thereby he objectively bears the responsibility and guilt for the concrete formation of the Reformation program and indirectly also for its historical effects. Now insofar as Luther in this very crisis-laden situation rediscovered the truth "versus the church" and asserted it against her in pointed theses, Lortz from his presuppositions can take no other position than this: Luther is a "revolutionary" and "heretic"[14] who is all the more dangerous to the church laboring under a thousand crises the nearer he comes to that "center" from which that crisis proceeds as the centrally caused disorder of the entire life of the church.

Here it should be carefully presented how very much Lortz sought to present the condition of the church in relation to the Reformation not only "theologically," but proceeding from the image of the "body," sought to present it primarily "organicalogically" and as a "disturbed organism." From this perspective Lortz used medical analogies[15] and categories such as "power" and "weakness,"[16] or the continually posed question of the "tendency"[17] in the sense of understanding a living movement. In this connection the occasionally disagreeable and embarrassing working categories "fully" and "not fully"—as "fully a believer," "fully Christian," "fully Catholic," "full hearer," "full restitution," etc.[18]—are meaningful. Even more important is that Lortz also thinks "organically" in a far-reaching way about the determination of the "truth." From this perspective he protests, for instance, against the "foolish opinion" of some (certainly no longer today) influential "handbooks of philosophy and theology" according to which the truth may be stated "abstractly" so that it is the same "today as in the thirteenth century."[19] Thus for Lortz the statement of the truth in historical context and in relation to changing situations is something which is very living. But what holds good for "abstract presentation" in timeless formulae also holds good, according to Lortz, for *dogma*: through dogma there must be "a recognizable and clearly stated truth." But this does not mean that a "dogmatic formulation" might be able to capture and as statement give binding expression to the fullness of the divine.[20] Lortz speaks expressly of life where the truth to be recognized is just the "life of history," which can be grasped according to its essence only as "unity in tension and opposition" because quite simply there can be "no kind of one-sided reality." "The truth is expressed then," so Lortz declares from this perspective, "when I have taken into consideration all sides."[21] Lortz speaks of life in this connection above all at that point where he desires to see the dialogue with Luther and the Lutherans conducted under an uncompromising prohibition of "dogmatic tolerance"[22] and renunciation of every "dogmatism" out of consciousness of "service to the truth." The "objective possibility" of such a position is grounded for Lortz in (and now follows the reference to life) "that dogma while indeed unimpeachable truth is so in such a way that this truth is and remains living, and does not become a rigid and foreshortened letter."[23] It is not by chance that Lortz refers to "Christian diversity with the Catholic position,"[24] which "is manifest even today in the context of continuing organic development."[25]

The meaning of this understanding of the "living truth" must be shown for Lortz's total judgment in connection with the organic conception of the church.

In this connection Lortz's often misunderstood and also misunderstandable formulation of the "truth question" loses its apologetic narrowness. In the final analysis for Lortz this concerns the "mysterium" of truth which allows genuine development or alienation of its knowledge through history. This is threatened not only by "error" but just as much by "weakness," by an "insufficient supply of blood"[26] in the sense of "correctness." Which thus admits beyond Vincent of Lerins a development of dogma,[27] which is seen precisely in light of the question of the "fully Catholic,"[28] finally as the *complexio oppositorum* in Cusanus's sense[29] which Lortz grasps as the possible position for dialogue leading to unity.[30]

Thereby, at the same time, the setting is defined in which according to Lortz there can be a theologically important and goal-oriented dialogue. In this setting Luther appears in no way as a "revolutionary" and "heretic" but rather as the "positive power" which produces the Reformation,[31] and from which the "Church of the Reformation" lives or should live, and which also makes dialogue with Luther ecumenically fruitful.[32]

Here it should again be shown through self-critical reflection that Lortz as it were in his first "dialogue-round" did not nearly take advantage of the possibilities of his own position. The recognition of Luther as "a person of prayer," *homo religiosus* and "religious genius"[33] certainly far surpassed the negative image of Luther in Cochlaeus's anathema but it nevertheless still suffers from considerable fixations. There is the Occamism thesis of the "overpowering of an un-Catholic Catholicism"[34] which in itself is to Luther's merit but which nevertheless is an achievement only in the setting of a "tragic misunderstanding" and for which at best Luther is "excused" by reference to the actual theological confusion of the time.[35] There is the unfortunate thesis of subjectivism[36] which is indeed not fundamentally false but which, in spite of its bizarre contradictory exegesis in the sense of a "subjective objectivism" or an "objective subjectivism,"[37] leads to a dangerous error in false judgment[38] which Lortz himself then must continually be correcting. There is finally the attempt to derive and the desire to clarify all of Luther's aberrations from the erroneous and exaggerated thesis of the "exclusive efficacy of God."[39]

But as unsatisfactory as the results of this first "dialogue round" with Luther may be in its particulars, the position already evident in his early work carries the dialogue further than what was achieved in the first encounter. For the orientation already suggests the possibility of an encounter which Lortz in the state of his knowledge at that time was not yet fully able to realize and which in the situation of 1939/40 also did not yet dare to realize. Nonetheless the possibility is seen substantively to understand and theologically to appreciate Luther's development, concerns and struggle as the situation of one in a, to a large extent, "sick" and very disturbed church and on the background of a likewise "organically" understood truth.

From Lortz's analysis of the "sick church" it is, for example, immediately obvious, often without express reference, that it was not the outrageously massive abuses which very much threatened ecclesial life[40] but rather the inner struggles of the best orientations against one another.[41]

But, according to Lortz, what holds for ecclesial renewal in a general and comprehensive way also holds in particular for the reform striven for by Luther. The growing program of reform,[42] completely unintentionally and as a result of a life and death struggle, acquires its explosive power not by reason of a conscious and willfully carried out anti-ecclesial revolution but rather by the painfully and seriously undertaken attempt to renew the church precisely in its life-endangering disturbed core from the depths of the biblical message. From this perspective Lortz clarifies directly the paradoxical effectiveness of this renewal striven for by Luther. In its basic concerns it emphasizes its very fundamental orientation to the Scriptures and the power of the Word, but nevertheless at the same time from and in its situation it receives by exaggeration and foreshortening a heretical character and effectiveness.

The great significance and immense aporia of the Lortzian position, which from this viewpoint also remains fundamentally the orientation of his students, resides in his emphasizing equally both aspects and by their connection leads to an opposition-in-tension[43] which Lortz himself does not always by any means maintain. Where Lortz correctly criticized heresy in Luther and explained it by Luther's one-sided "selection" or by his psychologically conditioned inability for "full hearing," the otherwise strongly emphasized perspective of opposition-in-tension breaks down. But, according to Lortz, he who holds the view that the "fundamentally true" is identical with the "Catholic" retains also in connection with the heretical exaggeration and foreshortening of Luther his orientation to the whole and his legitimating, living, and renewing power. This is immediately obvious in the first conception of his position where Lortz concretizes Luther's thinking and the uniqueness of his theology in the sense of the *theologia crucis* which with the Word of the cross is in fact taken up as the "perspectival means" (W. v. Loewenich) by which every individual truth is included in the whole of an unmistakable and determining conception.

It certainly may be granted that Lortz often again obscures this demonstrated possibility when from the delight of the apologete in clear delimitations and not least from delight in the play with polishing formulations he obscures the laboriously discovered structure. This occurs above all where he too quickly distinguishes "Catholic" structural formulae such as the *et—et* and "synthesis" from the "reformatory" *sola* and *simul* formulae.[44] Also the early Lortz clearly finds it difficult to apply the already-recognized necessity of advancing theological knowledge to the formulation of "fresh dogma"[45] and thus to Luther. Thus Lortz occasionally attempted hastily to qualify the "new" as "innovation," which then awakens the impression that he, as Pesch criticizes, is fundamentally fixated "backwards" with regard to treating the truth question.

Nevertheless I am convinced that the doubtless existing unclarity does not affect the fundamental possibilities of the Lortzian position.

Surely the early form of the position is definitely open to the following possibilities:

First of all within this framework it is thoroughly possible to disclose and fully accept statements of the partners which previously were fought over and considered heresy, as for instance the *simul iustus et peccator*, by an understanding listening to their essential intention and as genuine and fruitful possibilities. In addition it is possible so to present positions in connection with the *theologia crucis* which previously appeared unacceptable, for example, the sacrifice character of the mass or especially the office of ministry, that the partner may not only accept them but grasp them finally as theologically better and consequently as a fulfillment of their own basic concerns. It is also possible to permit contrasts (*Gegensätze*) to exist which arise from differing accents or grow from the spirituality of centuries in so far as they are clearly not based on contradictions (*Widersprüchen*).

The only thing that is impossible in this framework is to put aside or to neutralize another's clearly opposing confession or doctrinal statement by illicit relativizing. From this point of view Lortz believed that he must remain hard for the sake of the truth, and he believed this with express and irrefutable reference to Luther's "dogmatic intolerance."[46] Like Luther, Lortz would rather take the risk of putting individuals and erroneous teachings under anathema than do violence to the truth for the sake of love and unity.[47]

Although there were these above-mentioned possibilities which Lortz used for the deepening of his own position, what also became clear in the course of his development is that which Pesch not incorrectly identified in his research report: Lortz initiated a new epoch of engagement with Luther but at the same time he also marked the "limits" of an epoch which naturally provoke and even impel "stepping beyond" them.

Nevertheless, Lortz remained indefatigably on the track of his position which certainly urgently needs correction and improvement in more than trivial ways but which in the paradoxicalness of his basic concerns tolerates no ortho-praxy and action-related transformation. We are grateful to the old master for this exemplary and strong perseverance which, according to my conviction, is still worthwhile today in the endeavor to deepen the old position in the coming years with regard to the contemporary significance of our theme.

THE POSITION ON THE "CATHOLIC LUTHER" IN THE LATER LORTZ

It seems appropriate here with regard to the deepening of a special position to deal with those works of history and church history in the broad and comprehensive sense to which Lortz devoted himself in his Mainz period. The dialogical character of his thinking is clear as he carries on the conversation with Luther precisely where Luther speaks only indirectly of the issue, as in the question of the essence of church history and its legitimate consideration or in his church historical investigation itself.

Important here is his 1952 answer to H. Jedin, "Nochmals: Zur Aufgabe des Kirchengeschichtsschreibers."[48] The controversy, as friendly as it was decisive, was over the difference between the two great church historians on understanding church history as a theological discipline and its fundamental ecumenical engagement. The former difference was so insignificant, at least in the consciousness of church historians, that the first congress of colleagues in the discipline was structured on the theme of church history and theology as a memorial to the recently deceased old master, Jedin.[49] The difference of judgment on Luther and ecumenism remained. R. Bäumer must be aware of this for in his article on Lortz's Luther critique he continually mentions that Jedin reserved for himself the "Luther" article for the *Lexicon für Theologie und Kirche* while he was ready to allow the "old master of Catholic Luther research" only the article on "Reformation."[50] In fact it is very impressive to see with what caution Jedin opposed "the Catholic Luther" of his colleague while he thoroughly affirmed ecumenism in the engagement with E. Bizer's "Luther."

It is to Lortz's merit that he never lost sight of the "historical method" and the facts of church history in his theoretical and methodological concern for the writing of church history. Thus in deepening his critique of the ecclesial abuses of the late Middle Ages[51] or in inquiring of the unity of Christendom upon the background of its most turbulent history and in view of the Reformation, he sought to follow J. H. Newman rather than Vincent of Lerins in understanding the truth question.[52]

The success of these endeavors is seen in Lortz's effort to issue a completely reworked edition in 1964 of his *Geschichte der Kirche—In Ideengeschichtlichen Betrachtung*.[53]

In the Introduction the old master not only testifies to my collaboration[54] but he testifies at the same time that—in spite of retaining the original subtitle, the *Ideengeschichtliche Betrachtung*—he has long been absorbed in a "theological" deepening by which the Church historian does not just accept (like Jedin) the authorized "dogmatics" but rather endeavors to bring forth a theologically independent report instead of a "historically illustrated dogmatics."[55] In the chapter on Luther and the Reformation there is a series of new insights which not unessentially deepens the old position in spite of remaining fixations. He speaks not only of "love" for Luther as an essential presupposition for understanding,[56] but demonstrates the knowledge won in the meantime that the "reformatory" in Luther is by no means without further ado "heretical";[57] that Luther as a whole is much more "Catholic than we knew," so that present-day Catholic research must question and "permit itself to be genuinely questioned" by the Reformation.[58] Moreover, what is new is the important knowledge that, next to faith in Luther's theology, love is of the greatest, most underestimated significance[59] and that the Catholic "and" may very well be open to the reformatory *sola* and *simul*.[60] Also, Lortz ever more precisely formulates the distinction between "concerns" and "formulations" as a method for interpreting the Luther text.[61] Not least, Lortz frankly grants that the "Catholic reform" is to be examined, notwithstanding its own uniqueness, as a "consequence" of the Reformation,[62] that without Luther there would have been no Council of Trent,[63] and that the Council—by its conscious renunciation of a formal condemnation of Luther—leaves open the possibility of a positive valuation of his theology.[64]

Lortz's engagement with the Council of Trent gave rise to a small study in which he, far beyond Jedin, presented the "reformatory" in Council Fathers such as Seripando, Pole, and Bonuccio.[65] A lecture which Lortz as the "old Germanist" gave in Rome on the *Germanicum* in service to the Counter-Reformation also belongs in this area.[66]

How far Lortz, like Luther, is determined in his statements by the dialogue and the expected contradiction from the partner is shown above all by his highly readable address to the anniversary of the Corpus Catholicorum in Mainz on "Wert und Grenzen der katholischen Kontroverstheologie in der ersten Hälfte des 16. Jahrhunderts."[67]

Lortz measures the controversial theologians by the question of whether they substantively understood the "reality" of the Reformation, that is, "as we by research gradually learn to see it," and "not as the fighters for the church considered it at that time," whereby, by way of introduction, the "view of that time" is pointed out as false.[68] What at first glance appears to be a completely unhistorical question results in an eminent historical consideration of the total complex.

How did the contemporary theologians react to the phenomenon of the Reformation? Not a few of them saw and deplored, like Contarini, the abundance of abuses in the area of the official teaching office. Joh. Hoffmeister openly denounced "our scandalous teaching" and lamented that we have made Christ a prisoner in order that he do what we will. The "reformatory" is not recognized right away by a long shot. The radical theses of the programmatic writings themselves, and even the "De servo arbitrio," are without further ado held to be "un-Catholic." The church and its teaching are even to a large extent no longer self-evident and uncontestably great.[69]

The Reformation itself is ambiguous. It is an "attack" on the church; but at the same time it is "proclamation" and "calling." What the "reformatory" is—to its followers as well as to its opponents—is not unequivocally clear. The accepted meaning in both camps since 1555 that the "reformatory" is "faith-dividing" and then "church-separating" is right for the original circumstances. Lortz referred to this unclarity, which exists up to our own day, in 1963 in Helsinki.[70] This unclarity holds above all for Luther himself. He was much more difficult to understand for his contemporaries than for us.[71]

The question which Lortz formulates in the form of "theology pushing church history" is more pressing and completely unusual: How shall this deviating from its guidelines be judged in the church? Is it simply to be rejected juridically and by anathema? Or should the church first of all show understanding? And then Lortz formulates the question which for him in light of contemporary controversial theology is the "vital question": Would the official church and its defenders inquire about the Christian concerns of those who are "protesting"?

But Lortz goes further, addressing the question to the defenders as to how "fully Catholic" their answer essentially is, examining it by the Bible, the liturgy or even by the teaching office.[72] And Lortz calls attention here to the profound change which has grasped our thinking. The earlier matter of the confrontation of "Catholic truth" on the one side and "heresy" on the other side has taken another attitudinal position. Today in the sense of Vatican II no one any longer speaks of "heresy" and "heretics." But then what do we do with all the controversial theology of yesterday?

And then Lortz asks the colleagues and friends of the Corpus Catholicorum what only he, the first collaborator with J. Greving in the Corpus Catholicorum and the uncontested authority in the field of Catholic engagement with the Reformation, could ask: "Which theological and fruitful sense" of the publications of the Corpus Catholicorum in the various scientific series, apart from interest, "existing" with reference to "theological-historical" development have to be made more readable?[73]

Lortz's severe but fair critique of the Catholic controversial theology contains at the same time the fair standard of a "negative" instruction for the dialogue with Luther. If one follows up the instructions for this dialogue in its particulars then a deepening of the original position is certain which does not remain stuck in cosmetic corrections but rather pushes forward into new territory insofar as the above-mentioned possibilities are now realized.

There the discourse of the dialogue is conducted in another manner than the inquisitorial procedure of the controversial theologians; it is neither "arrogant" nor "self-opinionated," "uncomprehending," and "small-minded" (in the knowledge of the Scriptures and the theology of the Fathers). What is intended is a dialogue which does not remain stuck, as was the case with the "pig-headed nay-sayers" Eck and Cochläus, in self-defense, justification, and provocation in the condemnation of errors. Rather, what is intended is a conversation in which one is open for the challenge of the opponents' position; in which Luther with all his concerns is granted expression; in which one allows himself to be "questioned," "learns," and even is responsible for his own wrong, lack of fullness and even errors. Above all what is intended is a dialogue which considers the mysterium of the *truth*; in which, above the identity in change, the adventure, the scandal, and the problems of a change of everything in history are not forgotten but taken totally seriously. On the other hand Lortz, of course, remains severe here on the question of the truth. Applied to Luther, it reads: "There is *only one* truth of revelation, and thus there can be no discussion about whether Luther if he *were* a representative of a doctrine contradictory to the Catholic position could be fully received by the Church."[74] The relevant presumptions and strategies of ecumenically engaged theologians in one's own camp are then, not without sharpness, rejected as "innovative Catholic elucubrations" and as "endangering Christian doctrine" because they destroy the concept of the "one truth" and canonize "relativism."[75]

This does not mean, as Pesch thinks, that Lortz, any more than I, is fixated upon a verification *"backward"* in the determination of what is "Catholic." I believe I have shown by the above that this does not follow. What I have presented shows that his position is such that his entire critique of the controversial theology of the past is oriented *"forwards,"* that is, from our modern knowledge of the "authentic Luther" and the fundamentally changed statement of the question by Vatican II.

The remarkable thing about the deepened formulation of the Lortzian position seems to me to lie exactly in his overcoming the "backward-fixation" to which his conception of the truth occasionally adheres when he remains too close to Vincent of Lerins. In the conception at issue, however, the Lortzian maxim runs: Only the orientation "forward" and the standpoint characterized by this allows the discovery and disclosure in the case of Luther of what is a genuine possibility in him which, mistaken and distorted by his contemporary opponents and friends, has not achieved historical reality up to today. This and nothing else is what Lortz intends by his demand to once again grasp the Reformation's concerns in the changing situation. The simultaneously expressed Luther critique, that namely his Christian and ecumenically highly significant concerns need reinterpretation in order to lose their historical misunderstanding, does not diminish in the least the expressed recognition of them. Lortz demonstrates in his lecture how little this continuing method of a cautious distinction between concerns and formulations is "cunning" and disgraceful by referring to the identical idea given to the Council by John XXIII.[76]

It seems to me that this not only aptly characterizes essentials of the deepening achieved by Lortz but also presents at the same time the ecumenical usefulness of the position.

What has up to now been set forth in the working area of church historical studies, which only indirectly concerns Luther now leads into the area of that investigation in which Lortz is directly engaged with Luther himself. It should be noted that the publications at hand here make visible only the smallest part of his immense endeavor concerning Luther. The greatest amount of his work was in his Luther seminar which was a masterfully directed research program of his department and in his immense lecture activity which extended undiminished up to the last year of his life. The goal of his endeavor was twofold: First of all, it was the comprehensive presentation of a "theology of Luther," a task which he more and more entrusted to me. Second, it was an ecumenical presentation of the whole history of the Reformation.[77]

In a Luther seminar which I held together with my teacher, Lortz first of all engaged himself very intensively with Luther's *Lectures on Romans*[78] as the access to the Reformer's theology, the "primal religious concern" of which was held valid for Luther's total theological production.[79] By means of this important source Lortz comes to an impressive presentation of the *theologia crucis*[80] in which framework Luther's understanding of "justification,"[81] inclusive of the *simul iustus et peccator* and the *peccatum manens* in the context of the question of "pure love"[82] which so concerned him, is lighted up as equally "Catholic" and "reformatory." With regard to the *simul iustus et peccator* Lortz refers to corresponding positions which he finds represented among the Fathers at Trent, especially by Cardinal Pole,[83] but also by Bernard of Clairvaux,[84] but as I see it, he harmonizes unduly with Thomas Aquinas. This position on the "Catholic Luther" leads Lortz to the insight that the "Catholic" is preserved "even in the later reformatory Luther,"[85] a perception which occasionally even comes to light in Trent.[86] Lortz took up again the theme of "the reformatory and the Catholic in the young Luther" in the Festschrift for W. v. Loewenich[87] where the tendency throughout is to comprehend and disclose the "reformatory" as a "Catholic possibility."

In this sense Lortz advances into the area of ecclesiology with further questions to Luther. In fact, in the area of ecclesiology today there are a number of special studies which will continue to stand in the way of full ecclesial community unless they are reworked. Here we are referring to the essays in the Festschrift for M. Schmaus, "Zum Kirchendenken des jungen Luther,"[88] and in the *Lutherjahrbuch 1969*, "Sakramentales Denken beim jungen Luther."[89] What Lortz presents here with regard to genuine possible community is confirmed and expanded by V. Vajta's contribution to this volume. Lortz's initial restriction to the "young Luther" is later relaxed or transcended to the degree in which our common work extends to the "old Luther" and his "great Genesis commentary."[90] In the 1965 Festschrift for H. Jedin,[91] Lortz concerned himself with Luther's "spiritual structure" (*geistige Struktur*), and in the *Kleinen Reformationsgeschichte*, edited together with E. Iserloh in 1969,[92] Lortz focused on the "reformatory fundamentals, above all Lutheran theology."

These are certainly the most important but by no means all of Lortz's works on Luther. In the context of our reflections a detailed evaluation of them is not necessary; the total results basically rest on the deepening of the Lortzian position presented above.

In sum I repeat: the deepening of Lortz's position is in no way limited to cosmetic corrections dealing only with misunderstandings, but it extensively realizes the possibilities of the original position and thus demonstrates its theological and ecumenical usefulness.

Lortz's limitation is that he cannot help referring to the heretical in Luther. Nevertheless, this negative judgment does not in the least hinder him from also recognizing without reserve the "Catholic Luther." Both judgments are not torn apart from each other but rather both are bound together in what is certainly a paradoxical totality. The full intention of his position can only be understood by keeping this in mind. In this union the "Catholic" is the stronger and decisive element over against the "heretical." Indeed, the latter is a real reduction of the former. However, on the other hand the "Catholic" is allowed to correct the "heretical" whereby the fullness of the fundamental concern is achieved. I am trying to elucidate here the position of my teacher by a comparison which he did not use. But this comparison means that the person who finds it conceivable that the Christian can be sinner and righteous at the same time should not easily reject as an antinomy the thesis "heretic and reformer at the same time."

THE DEEPENING OF THE POSITION IN THE LORTZ-SCHOOL

I am now at the final reflection which is just as important as it is difficult. It is important in view of the exhaustive treatment of the theme. It is difficult because I cannot treat, for reasons of space, the works of all the representatives of the Lortz-school. At the moment I have no better solution than the following: since the existing common ground among the most different representatives of the "Lortz-school" is much greater than the concerned observer thinks, I am going to sketch the achieved deepening, with all caution and the necessary reservations, in the motifs of my own work.

If I see correctly, the Lortzian position is differentiated and deepened above all by the following points:

The Significance of the Agape Motif

That Luther replaces love by faith and apparently legitimates driving love from its pre-eminence by Scripture and tradition, *loco charitatis posuimus fidem*,[93] has been held by theologians since the sixteenth century to the present either as a specifically "reformatory position" or as an unprecedented "heretical innovation." Nevertheless it may be shown that neither evangelical "praise" nor Catholic "anathema" meets Luther's true concern.[94] For Luther never emphasized, in the sense of Nygren's thesis, faith alone in the relationship of the person to God while banishing love in the sense of the works of love to the realm of interpersonal relationships. Rather, love to God remains for Luther a demand throughout one's life by which the Law convicts us of our inability to fully and spontaneously love God as we ought and in this way drives us into the arms of Christ. Here we are not only pardoned by reputative participation in Christ's righteousness and more loving fulfillment of the Law to a life *coram Deo*, but where we then in reality *sola gratia* and *sola fide* live by love for God and our neighbor. From this point it is evident that fundamentally all the central concepts of Luther's theology can be correctly understood only from their negative or positive relationship to agape. This holds true for faith as well as for righteousness and justification, sin, *peccatum manens, peccator fieri, simul iustus et peccator* and also for the life of the *novus homo*, its realization by grace and its sanctification up to the *Libertas Christiana*. It is by this that Luther's doctrines of God and grace, his soteriology and anthropology recover that convincing and attractive power which they have lost for the modern Christian in the clichés of antiquated orthodoxy or the most recent Luther interpretation.

However, not only is the motivating source of his theology thereby found, but at the same time the question which motivated his spiritual (*geistliches*) struggle from the monastic period to the end of his life may be plausibly explained however much he himself continually clouded and jeopardized this by covering the primary sources with the explanation in the "legend" of his later "reminiscence."

However, the significance of this insight is far from exhausted. It bears in its consequences much more than I originally, by way of an adventurous detour through Fénelon's *amour pur* and Bernhard's *De diligendo Deo*, and then together with Lortz, was able to realize. The most important consequences, which in fact pushed "beyond Lortz" and which I therefore can express only as my own responsibility, are first perceived in the work for my Luther biography.

The first consequence concerns Luther research and says that the search for the *"reformatory"* and the moment of his discovery is virtually senseless if the question which for Luther both spiritually and theologically set everything in motion lies in the sphere of the agape motif.

A second, very significant consequence which this time relates directly to Luther's ecumenical significance is that Luther, if my thesis is correct, would be driven and motivated by a position which was neither "Catholic" (in the sense of the contemporary faith) nor "reformatory" (in the sense of the rejection of the "Catholic" in its concrete form). If, as I am emphasizing, the quest for the *amor purus* was Luther's essential motivating concern, then he follows a position of which it may be said at the same time that neither the "Catholic" nor the "reformatory faith" can legitimately and in the long run escape. Thus finally a position is thereby found through whose development Luther grows into in fact an *"ecumenical authority"* as against both churches whose spiritual heritage they have yet to discover because till today they both stand against these concerns.

A final, more professional consequence is that with this thesis the Lortzian theses of Occamism and subjectivism may be given up or reduced to their core. All in all a very significant insight which indeed I shall have to substantiate beyond the given evidence but which nevertheless I can substantiate because they may be conclusively shown from the earliest to the latest work of Luther.

The Understanding of Ministry, Eucharist, and Church

a) First of all the question of Luther's understanding of ministry deserves particular mention. Also, in this connection there is up to now nearly a "consensus" in both churches on the incompatibility of the Lutheran and Catholic positions on the question of ministry. That is why even the last consensus paper of the Lutheran-Roman Catholic Joint Commission carefully steered clear of Luther.[95] In fact, it is not to be denied that Luther's discovery of the "priesthood of all believers" in the writing of 1521, together with the echo which just this discovery finds in the programmatic writings of the same year, appears to dissolve and to abandon the clerical office mediated by ordination into the "priesthood of all believers." Now I have attempted to prove in "Amt und Eucharistie in der Theologie M. Luthers,"[96] a study critically dependent upon the preparatory work of an all-too-prematurely deceased colleague, W. Stein,[97] that Luther—even in this transitional phase with its apparently conclusive expressions to the contrary—in no way gives up this particular ecclesial office. I have also attempted to prove that not only Melanchthon agrees with the proviso of the sacramental understanding of ordination but that even Luther in this matter consistently represented the same conception. Even more important is the conviction shared with W. Stein that Luther, since the *"De instituendis ministris"* (1523) at the latest, represented a conception which grounds and demands the right of "emergency ordination," analogous to "emergency baptism," on the necessity of the ecclesial office for the proclamation and existence of the church.[98] The proposal formulated already at that time to investigate[99] the concept of "emergency ordination" has unfortunately still not been grasped by systematicians. In revision of a presentation which I gave together with H. Meyer at the Luther-Akademie, Ratzeburg, I shall once more set forth the same idea, attempting to show that Luther's "emergency ordination" appears justified not only from the situation of 1523 but that even in the contemporary situation of the church such a demand and praxis could be justified. Only in this way is the charismatic depreciation of the ecclesial office avoidable, which exactly now E. Schillebeeckx[100] seeks to pursue with reference to the same position even if with a completely untenable foundation from historical theology.

If I am correct on this it is truly astonishing that exactly from Luther, and indeed without any violation of the truth, the solution offers itself for a problem; and this in spite of the numerous seriously intended attempts which for the sake of the truth have held till today that the problem is insoluble.

b) In addition, following the Lortzian attempt at a solution, I think without presumption that the problem of the eucharist can be solved or set on the way toward a resolution.

To forestall the expected protest of my friend E. Iserloh on this point, it is emphasized loud and clear that of course for me also the full ecclesial and eucharistic community remains impossible without a preceding real unity with regard to the sacrifice character of the mass. Only it appears to me that an answer convincing for both sides can be found relatively easily here in Luther. I point out that the conception of the mass as sacrifice can be found, or in this context without inner impossibility can be represented, throughout the early sermons and tracts on the eucharist. I further presuppose that Luther's 1522 denial of the sacrificial character of the mass is not against the sacrifice as such but rather against the uncontested "misuse of the mass" and its foundation with reference to the sacrifice. What is more, after denial of the sacrificial character of the mass Luther must substantiate the sacrificial devotion of Christians which necessarily follows from the living community with the crucified and from the Christ-conformity of Christian existence henceforth without direct connection to the cross of Christ and without being set in the *memoria passionis*.[101] One proceeds now from a deepened and chastened understanding of the sacrifice of the mass, which according to Iserloh's investigation is fully reached by neither Eck nor Trent, up to the problem so that a reinterpretation of the entire issue appears possible which can present and establish the sacrifice-character of the mass on the basis of the essential concerns of Luther.

The denial of the *transsubstantiatio* in favor of *consubstantiatio* is not a real major problem either for Luther's understanding of the eucharist or its rejection by the Council of Trent (as Pesch thinks). The same holds for the concerns of a mere *praesentia ad usum* or for the *ubiquitas* teaching as theologumenon which shall explain the "how" of the real presence.

c) A real deepening of the Lortzian position also appears possible to me in the question of Luther's ecclesiology or his "conception of the church." Luther's late writings, going beyond the positions of the "young Luther," are of great importance, for instance, "On the Councils and the Churches" or the "Large Genesis Commentary."

This holds above all for Luther's battle against the papacy under the catchword of the "Antichrist." I have attempted to show in my Luther biography[102] what the discovery of this word really means in the battle against the papacy. In any case it is not primarily an "invective" serving to enrich his insufferably coarse anti-papal polemic. The accusation rather is the application of the knowledge won from 2 Thess. 2:1–4 which Luther, independent of its accuracy, believes must be applied to the papacy for a profusion of not simply challenging reasons. The most important elements forcing putative knowledge upon Luther are the following: The "Antichrist" must come; and he comes not from the sects but forcibly enters the "true church" because only from this position, and indeed without fundamentally changing the institutional structures of the church, can he effect the universal defection; a defense against the "Antichrist" is impossible for us; only the Lord himself can end his rule. Luther did not right away grasp all the consequences of this knowledge. Undoubtedly the most difficult and contradictory insight for him was that even the desired "Reformation" could no longer be grasped as a real defense. The orientation toward a positive understanding with the papal Church is clear in his writing addressed to two, by the way Catholic, pastors: "Concerning Rebaptism."[103] It speaks against the here illuminating possibility of an agreement that Luther was unable to realize as long as he was of the factually erring certainty that with the pope the "Antichrist" has taken over the lordship in the church. It was this certainty of conviction that enabled Luther to declare without justification his final malevolent polemic against "the papacy instituted by the devil." One comes closer to Luther if one considers that he would certainly not have attacked and reviled in this way a papacy represented by popes like John XXIII or John Paul II.

For the time being I leave it at these references to an issue which has remained controversial till today; a theme in which if we could proceed from Luther and achieve a meeting it would be an essential enrichment for both sides beyond mere agreement.

The Question of the Truth

Although I am heartily certain of the approval and recognition of my friends from the Lortz-school, it seems to me more honorable and modest if I report on the thesis of the deepening of the Lortzian position also in the treatment of the truth question for the time being at my own risk.

A step beyond Lortz seems first of all to be visible in my move in the last years, to the amazement of not only my Catholic friends, to characterize Luther as a "father in the faith." This serious, theologically demanding title in the sense of 1 Cor. 4:14ff. arose in the course of my engagement with Luther's exegesis of Abraham and his self-understanding of being "another Paul."[104]

"Father in the faith"—not "father of the faith," as not only R. Bäumer paraphrases it—presupposes not only a highly personal relationship of faith experience to Luther but above all it means that without such "fatherhood" there is no life in the church, and that above all in the ecumene the "becoming-a-witness" ("Gezeugt-Werden") by the word of the gospel takes the lead over every "creedal persuasion" in the sense of knowledge.

Thereby I am going, if you will, at first glance, decisively "beyond Lortz." However, seen from within and out of the experience of the development already touched upon, I do not understand this step as essentially "overstepping" him.

In fact this new title merely deepens the paradoxical tension which I attempted to show above as the certainly "aggravating" but essential quality of the Lortzian position. For to the great disappointment of so many friends I too am not in the position to answer the question "Martin Luther—heretic or father in the faith?" in the sense of an inciting word or a smooth formula which single-mindedly and quickly leads out of the ecumenical dilemma.

Rather, with Lortz, I must maintain that Luther was in a special sense a "heretic" and that the contemporary church, precisely because it was deeply distorted in its relationship to the truth, was only insufficiently able to perceive the truth and had to differentiate itself from him. On the other hand, bracketing both statements in the sense of *simul hereticus et Pater in Fide* intensifies not only the paradoxical tension but also the urgent possibility of solution. For it is evident here that Luther is a heretic for the sake of the truth whereby the concept of heresy, analogously to the concept of sin in the *simul*, without doubt receives a new quality. Correspondingly the possibility and urgency thus arise of transcending the exaggeration and foreshortening of the two poles of the *simul* by fulfillment in the gospel of the "father in the faith."

I must grant in spite of this, as it appears to me, observable deepening of the positions, that he is radically disappointing by his paradoxicality to the expectations not only of an "easy ecumenism" but also of a "serious ecumenism" in its legitimate expectations of a greater striving toward the goal for, at first glance, he is unable to offer any help. The position on the truth question adopted and adhered to by Lortz certainly does not sentence ecumenism to quietistic passivity and certainly not at all to a lack of ideas or sterile conformism to the "ecclesial-official ecumene," but in a decisive point does confine or "paralyse," however, even our initiative. Precisely because it concerns Luther's ecumenical significance it makes no sense to dodge the issue that there can be no ecumenism on the authority of Luther by which we would, as it were, be the owners of a building qualified "to construct" the desired unity "from the ground up."[105]

Rather, from Luther's perspective it is absolutely certain that as impossible and contrary to God as it is to fabricate out of our own power and on our own account the *iustitia propria* or *iustitia domestica*, so it would be according to him impossible and contrary to God if we desire to set ourselves up as unauthorized architects of ecclesial unity.

NOTES

1. Joseph Lortz, *Die Reformation als religiöses Anliegen heute. Vier Vorträge im Dienste der Una Sancta* (Trier: Paulinus, 1948), 9ff. (hereafter cited as *Anliegen*). In terms of his ecumenical objective, Lortz refers to his friendship with M. J. Metzger, the virtual founder of the German "una Sancta" movement who was later executed by the Nazis. At the beginning of the war Lortz's theses on the Reformation were presented, at Metzger's encouragement, as "an aid to ecumenical dialogue," to be published (Meitingen o. J.). But publication was not permitted. In retrospect it is not without interest that Hans Urs von Balthasar brought them out in 1949 and in further editions from the Johannes Verlag, Einsiedeln. Translator's note: Unfortunately, the English translation by John Dwyer, S.J., *The Reformation: A Problem for Today* (Westminster, MD: Newman Press, 1964) (hereafter cited as *Problem*) does not include this "Foreword." It is also unfortunate that "Anliegen" was translated as "Problem."
2. *RD* 1:1–19; *RG* 1:3–21.
3. Cf. *S. Bernardi Opera* (Rome, 1957), 1:25,4–5, 165f.; 26,1–2, 169f.; 28,1–13, 192–202; 29,9, 209; 2: 38,5, 17f.; 61,7, 152f. Cf. Y. Congar, "Die Ekklesiologie des Hl. Bernhard," in J. Lortz, ed., *Bernhard von Clairvaux, Mönch und Mystiker* (Wiesbaden, 1953), 85f.
4. *RD* 1:7; *RG* 1:8.
5. *RD* 1:8, 22ff.; *RG* 1:8, 23ff.
6. *RD* 1:12; *RG* 1:12f.
7. *RD* 1:4; *RG* 1:4; Cf. *Anliegen*, 101f; *Problem*, 93f.
8. Cf. Lortz's presentation of the grievances in the pre-Reformation Church: *RD* 1:69–138; *RG* 1:78–157. Cf. *Anliegen*, 34–105; *Problem*, 23–96.
9. *RD* 2:296; *RG* 2:332.
10. Cf. *RD* 1:4, 192; *RG* 1:4, 217f.; *Anliegen*, 103; *Problem*, 94f.
11. In this sense Lortz criticizes the contemporary papacy and the curia, the bishops and their cathedral chapters, the clerical proletariat and the decadent orders as well as above all the life-endangering failure in the areas of preaching, administration of the sacraments, and above all doctrine. The sharpness of his critique is not in the least diminished when Lortz refers to the "historical form" of these structures and accepts the "essential-structure."
12. Cf. *Anliegen*, 99f., 102; *Problem*, 91f. 94f.
13. Cf. *RD* 1:19; *RG* 1:21.
14. Cf. *RD* 1:3, 10f.; *RG* 1:3, 11f.; *Anliegen*, 110; *Problem*, 100.
15. Cf. *Anliegen*, 83f.; *Problem*, 74f.
16. Ibid.
17. *Anliegen*, 70; *Problem*, 62.
18. *Anliegen*, 69, 75f.; *Problem*, 61, 66ff.
19. *Anliegen*, 16; *Problem*, 4.
20. *Anliegen*, 27; *Problem*, 15.

21. *Anliegen*, 25f.; *Problem*, 13.
22. *Anliegen*, 28; *Problem*, 15.
23. *Anliegen*, 29; *Problem*, 16f.
24. Ibid.
25. *Anliegen*, 30; *Problem*, 17.
26. *Anliegen*, 53; *Problem*, 44.
27. *Anliegen*, 54; *Problem*, 45.
28. *Anliegen*, 54f.; *Problem*, 45.
29. *Anliegen*, 64; *Problem*, 55.
30. Ibid.
31. *RD* 1:19, 192; *RG* 1:21, 217f.
32. This holds in particular for Luther's position with regard to the question of truth. Cf. *Anliegen*, 111f.; *Problem*, 102.
33. For these terms, cf. *RD* 1:388; *RG* 435; *Anliegen*, 147, 124, 112; *Problem*, 137f., 114, 102.
34. The harsh thesis (*RD* 1:176; *RG* 1:200) still lingers in the lectures (*Anliegen*, 115f., 134, 136; *Problem*, 105f., 125ff.) but is already qualified here in a certain sense.
35. *Anliegen*, 136; *Problem*, 126.
36. The original thesis (*RD* 1:161ff., 409; *RG* 1:183ff., 458) is maintained in the lectures (*Anliegen*, 131, 134, 136; *Problem*, 121ff.) before reaching an observable modification (*Anliegen*, 154; *Problem*, 145).
37. *Anliegen*, 155; *Problem*, 145.
38. Cf. the sharp critique by L. Grane, *Contra Gabrielem* (Gyldendal, 1962), 29.
39. Cf. *RD* 1:384f.; *RG* 1:431f.; Lortz, "Zum Menschenbild Luthers," in *Das Bild vom Menschen, F. Tillmann zum 60, Geburtstag* (1934), 60.
40. Cf. *RD* 1:69–111; *RG* 1:78–126.
41. Cf. *RD* 1:119f.; *RG* 1:135f.; J. Lortz, *Zur Problematik der kirchlichen Missstände im Spätmittelalter* (Trier: Paulinus Verlag, 1950).
42. Cf. *Anliegen*, 125; *Problem*, 115f.
43. Cf. *RD* 1:192, 431ff.; *RG* 1:217f., 482ff.
44. This occurs above all where he appears to deny Luther the basic competence for "synthesis" (*Anliegen*, 119, 134; *Problem*, 109, 124) or where he understands "the Catholic 'and'" simply in opposition to the "evangelical 'alone'" (*Anliegen*, 235; *Problem*, 221f.). Other formulations, for instance on "the blunt Catholic 'both—and'" (*Anliegen*, 235; *Problem*, 221) or on the synthesis as "radical unity" (*Anliegen*, 241; *Problem*, 227) show however that the *et—et* may also be understood in the sense of *simul*.
45. *Anliegen*, 54; *Problem*, 45.
46. Cf. *Anliegen*, 220; *Problem*, 208, where Lortz qualifies the Reformer as a "proponent of the most absolute dogmatic intolerance," who understood Christianity as "a doctrine susceptible of only one interpretation . . . binding for all times." From this viewpoint Lortz can then formulate in reference to Luther: "Christianity in its complete form has been given us once and for all in revelation; so true is this that there can be no development properly speaking." *Anliegen*, 219; *Problem*, 207.
47. Recall his pitiless sharp rejection for instance of Karlstadt but also his criticisms of "mediators" like Melanchthon or Bucer, and his stance in the case of the

"Wittenberg Concord." As far as Lortz is concerned this is of little significance for dialogue with Luther; but what is more meaningful is the "distinction" he opens between the original religious concerns of Luther and the Reformation on the one hand, and the theological conclusions that were drawn from them on the other hand (*Anliegen*, 222; *Problem*, 210). It is typical for Lortz to ask in this connection whether it is "possible that theological considerations and conclusions have widened the gap unnecessarily? Was the Reformation . . . too theological . . . ?" (*Anliegen*, 223; *Problem*, 211).

48. *TThZ* 61 (1952): 317–327. Jedin's essay is ibid., 65–78.

49. Internationales Symposion der Kirchenhistoriker zum Thema: "Kirchengeschichte als historische Theologie," Rom Campo Santo Teutonico, 24–27 June 1981.

50. R. Bäumer, "Luther-Kritik bei Joseph Lortz," Beilage "Theologisches" zur *Offertenzeitung für die kath. Geistlichkeit Deutschlands* (June 1982): 4672.

51. Lortz, *Zur Problematik der kirchlichen Misstände im Spätmittelalter* (Trier: Paulinus Verlag, 1950).

52. Lortz, *Einheit der Christenheit. Unfehlbarkeit und lebendige Aussage* (Trier: Paulinus-Verlag, 1959).

53. Vol. 1. *Alterum und Mittelalter;* Vol. 2, *Neuzeit* (Münster: Aschendorff, 1962, 1964).

54. Cf. ibid., 1:xi.
55. Ibid., v f., ix f.
56. Ibid., 2:75.
57. Ibid., 80.
58. Ibid., 128.
59. Ibid., 93.
60. Ibid., 122.
61. Ibid., 115, 127.
62. Ibid., 73.
63. Ibid., 170.
64. Ibid., 166.

65. Cf. Lortz, "Zur Zielsetzung des Konzils von Trient," in A. Dänhardt, ed., *Theologisches Jahrbuch* (Leipzig, 1964).

66. "Germanikum und Gegenreformation," *Korrespondenzblatt für die Alumnen des Collegium Germanicum et Hungaricum* (Rome, n.d.).

67. *Katholisches Leben und Kirchenreform*, 27/28 (Münster, 1968), 9–32.

68. Ibid., 9f.
69. Ibid., 10.
70. Ibid., 11.
71. Ibid., 12.
72. Ibid., 13.
73. Ibid., 14.
74. Ibid., 31.
75. Ibid.
76. Ibid., 30.

77. Cf. the address by Lortz on the occasion of the dedication of the newly restored Old Jesuit University on 17 January 1953: *Drei Reden* (Mainz, 1953), 58.

78. Lortz published the findings of the seminar in two articles: "Luthers Römerbriefvorlesung—Grundanliegen," *TThZ* 71 (1962), 129–153; 216–247. For my collaboration, cf. the introductory remarks, 129.
79. Ibid., 139.
80. Ibid., 149ff.
81. Ibid., 222ff.
82. Ibid., 225ff.
83. Ibid., 140f.
84. Ibid., 131.
85. Ibid., 140.
86. Ibid., 134.
87. Lortz, "Reformatorisch und Katholisch beim jungen Luther (1518/19)," in *Humanitas-Christianitas. W. v. Loewenich zum 65. Geburtstag* (1968), 47–61.
88. L. Scheffczyk, ed., *Wahrheit und Verkündigung. Festschrift für M. Schmaus zum 70. Geburtstag* (Paderborn, 1967), 2:947–986.
89. *Lutherjahrbuch 1969*, 9–40.
90. Cf. J. Lortz, "Luther und wir Katholiken heute," in *Kirche und Staat in Idee und Geschichte des Abendlandes. Festschrift zum 70. Geburtstag von F. Maass, S.J.* (Wien-Munich: Herold, 1973), 176 n. 16.
91. *RR* 1: 214–246.
92. J. Lortz and E. Iserloh, *Kleine Reformationsgeschichte. Ursachen—Verlauf—Wirkung* (Freiburg-Basel-Wien: Herder, 1969).
93. *LW* 26: 129; *WA* 40 1:228, 27–28.
94. Cf. P. Manns, "Fides absoluta—Fides incarnata. Zur Rechtfertigungslehre Luthers im Grossen Galater-Kommentar," in *RR* 1:288–312.
95. *Das Geistliche Amt in der Kirche* (Paderborn & Frankfurt a.M., 1981).
96. P. Manns, "Amt und Eucharistie in der Theologie M. Luthers," in P. Bläser, ed., *Amt und Eucharistie* (Paderborn, 1973), 68–173.
97. W. Stein, *Das Kirchliche Amt bei Luther* (Wiesbaden: Veröffentlichungen des Instituts für Europäische Geschichte, Bd. 73, 1974).
98. Cf. *LW* 40:36f.; *WA* 12:191,16ff.; and Stein, ibid., 144–166.
99. Cf. Manns, "Amt und Eucharistie," 100f.
100. E. Schillebeeckx, *Das kirchliche Amt* (Düsseldorf: Patmos, 1981). The author not only interprets the documentary evidence as he would like (cf. 78ff., 81f.), whereby he makes the contradiction of the historical-critical method the foundation of his hermeneutic (cf. "Kurzes hermeneutisches Intermezzo," 152ff.), but also gives sources for his thesis—for instance, Mansi 2:469 (126)—which clearly say the opposite to his emphasis.
101. Cf. the instructive evidence from "Concerning the Ministry" (*LW* 40:28f.; *WA* 12:185, 16–36) where "sacrifice," as the fifth task of the "universal priesthood," is specified in the sense of Rom. 12:1 and sharply distinguished from Christ's sacrifice on the cross as "the sacrifice of our bodies." The sacrifice of our bodies "slaughtered and butchered by God's Word" is the "only sacrifice in the Church."
102. Cf. P. Manns, *Martin Luther* (Freiburg-Basel-Wien: Herder), 119.
103. *LW* 40:227–262; *WA* 26:144–174.
104. Cf. H. Feld, "Lutherus Apostolus. Kirchliches Amt und apostolische Verant-

wortung in der Galaterbrief-Auslegung Martin Luthers," in *Wort Gottes in der Zeit, Festschrift K. H. Schelkle* (Düsseldorf, 1973), 288–304. Here is Luther's extraordinarily packed statement about "Abraham, father in the faith" which occupied him throughout his life in exegesis and preaching.

105. Instead of many references, cf. the Lectures on Romans, *LW* 25:136f; *WA* 56:158, 10–14.

The "Lutheran" Luther—
A Catholic Possibility?
An Attempt at an Understanding of
"Historical Luther Research" and
"Systematic-Theological
Luther Interpretation"

OTTO HERMANN PESCH

I would like to appeal to James's injunction, "Let every man be quick to hear, slow to speak, slow to anger" (James 1:19), but I am afraid such virtue is lacking when from the outset today I develop my theme as a response to Peter Manns's 1967 frontal attack launched against me and my work (and that of a few colleagues) in Luther research. I am referring to his small but substantial article "Lutherforschung heute: Krise und Aufbruch,"[1] which is still recommended reading for it is more than just a pleasure to read.

The occasion for Manns's attack was my two 1966 reports[2] on the state of Catholic Luther research and evaluation of Luther. He designates the content of these essays as a "manifesto," a "new program," a "research program," a "new orientation," a starting shot for a "break with the system" (v, ix, xiii, 2, 3, 5, et al.). This is a dramatization of the content which will certainly astonish the impartial reader. All the same, Manns has continually returned to the theses of his polemic with well-formulated side-swipes; and the same is true for me.[3] The opening theme of this Consultation provides the opportunity to attempt a somewhat more detailed answer.

A CONCILIATORY PREFACE

The answer must begin with reference to the fact that it takes place under totally different conditions than those at the time of the attack. At that time Peter Manns and I had only just become acquainted. Now we have been personal friends for over a decade. In addition, and this is more important, the actual context of contemporary Luther research has changed since 1967.

This lecture, translated by Carter Lindberg from the version written for the Consultation, is only an abbreviated version of the major points of discussion. The complete text, which is a detailed answer to Peter Manns, is in O. H. Pesch, *Gerechtfertigt aus Glauben. Luthers Frage an die Kirche* (Freiburg i. Br. 1982), 3. Studie. The author and editors thank Herder-Verlag for gracious permission for reproduction.

The common concern not to let Catholic Luther research regress must have absolute priority over all particular controversies. Manns publicly stated this earlier, as I might have expected in the face of my stiff-necked silence, and he had distanced himself from his previous style of attack in a manner which embarrasses me because I consider every kind of "apology" entirely unnecessary in this case. After all I have sufficient reason to apologize before the friends and colleagues of the "Lortz-school," and to say: *Patres Fratresque, peccavi!* Above all: *Patriarcha, peccavi!*

But my apology, like that of Peter Manns, concerns above all the style—verbal blows, many implicit things and continual allegations which produce mistrust—not the substantive issues. These latter *must* be openly discussed. In what follows I shall attempt this as far as possible with the use of examples so that it will be clear exactly where the differences are, or in any case where I think they are.

THE CONTROVERSIAL ISSUES—
AND AN ANSWER

The substantive problems which Manns takes up in his polemic belong without doubt to the most difficult problems of theological methodology. With one fresh approach after another he seeks to bring them "exactly to the point." And in the notes he enters into details and side themes with such intensity that in many of them something of his own theme is once again promoted. At the proper time and place we will look into this expanded abundance of material and return to portions of it. Here it is neither possible nor fruitful to respond with the same obsession with detail. I raise two complexes of questions which encompass everything for Manns. The two most recent summaries on the subject of our conflict by Manns himself[4] prove that I am not mistaken.

The Theological-Historical and Historical-Theological
Significance of the "Lortz-School"

Of these questions, the first, which Manns also poses for debate, might be the simplest. Frankly, I confess that I had and have not yet sufficiently read the works of the "Lortz-school," not only those of the "old master" himself but also those of his students. From the wealth of his long work together with Lortz, Manns continually draws my attention in his notes to publications which at that time I didn't even know the titles of, and even today I have not yet been able to read everything.

On the other hand, it is a misunderstanding when Manns imputes to me (and my colleagues of the so-called "systematic" school) that I (or we) had announced an "exclusive claim" to the only ecumenically productive interpretation of Luther (e.g., vi, xii, 3, et al.) and had "dismissed" the works of prior Catholic Luther research as insufficient and false (38). Manns also recognizes in a few places that I have not written this, rather, he deduces it as the consequence of my formulations (e.g. 5 n.9, 7 n.13). My language, "definitely excessive" *inter alia,* which I now regret because it is unclear and in addition unfair, was meant differently—and I think my text also allows this to be inferred.[5] And even if it were as Manns supposes, this in no way means that, to begin with, much has not been learned from the "excessive" position and may still continue to be learned—which is what I claim for myself.

The following banal reference may lead closer to the true circumstances and thereby to the origins of my Lortz-critique: a person who writes a research report, if he has developed only a spark of literary ambition, would like to present more than just an annotated list of the literature. He would like to present "lines of development" and "trends"; to relate statements of the problems to one another, to expose the directions in which the research is moving. So he seeks to unite the indispensable chronological factual-substantive elements into a plausible classification. Now if it concerns Catholic Luther research since 1945, then it begins with a flashback to Lortz (and a few others). While on the other hand "twenty years" is a small period of time, naturally overlapping chronologically the established substantive new orientations. The result is a classification which sharpens the forced demarcations more than corresponds to reality. *That* is the banal reason for what Manns regards as the "premature laurel wreaths" (vi).

In addition there is a much more serious reason. Very early it surprised me that Catholic Luther scholars and in general open-minded Catholic theologians praised Lortz and, contrary to their evangelical dialogue partners, quite proudly called attention to the "breakthrough" he achieved, while evangelical Luther scholars recognized the Lortzian picture of Luther as indeed the only one worth serious discussion but at the same time strongly opposed it on all those decisive points which the Catholic critics clung to as exactly the "breakthrough."[6] Now this does not imply anything at all for the oft-cited "truth question": also in no case have I simply applauded this criticism, and I surely do not at all feel guilty of "ecumenical opportunism" (14). But the evangelical criticism of Lortz must nevertheless be permitted the occasion to ask to what extent it is correct; this of course is not to be decided on the basis of contemporary ecumenical desires but rather only by the study of Luther itself.

So much for the origins of my criticisms of Lortz. Is it now in the meantime, thanks to receiving better instruction, irrelevant? The "majesty of the facts" commands the historian familiar with them to state the following:

Fact 1: From a particular time on (Catholic) Luther studies were written which immediately come to "the point" and then relinquish it to shift the investigated teaching of Luther into the connection of biographical or personally conditioned factors. Investigations of Augustine, Bonaventure,

Thomas, or Duns Scotus are also written this way without at the same time invariably including the biographical background. Lortz, in comparison, who was still writing at the time of my research report and in later articles about Luther's "spiritual structure," thus held, even if of course not expressly and naturally with good reasons, this problem to be illuminating in relation to Luther's theology.[7] At the same time his two most important students, Erwin Iserloh and Manns himself, still hardly paid attention to it.[8] Manns after all, in his polemic (26), approvingly endorsed the well-known "subjectivism" thesis of his teacher, but later in the Afterword to the new edition of the *Reformation in Deutschland* notes that it is in need of correction.[9] And in his recent fascinating biography of Luther, Manns reduces the biographical and personal factors to those which concern the *specifically reformatory*, i.e., to Luther's "Lutheran" theology. This is reduced so much to common factors and by constraint of the material and misunderstandings that it is simply unbelievable to a representative of the "hermeneutical-systematic orientation."[10] Luther the theologian remains at the same time a passionate and vigorous, to-be-canonized, absolutely unsuspicious, confessing Catholic—only the circumstances were not so.

Fact 2: Lortz understands Luther against the background of Occamist theology. This statement of the problem which then in the "Lortz-school" was driven and carried further with great energy, above all by Erwin Iserloh, is as such not at all typical for this because it is simply essential for Luther research. Two characteristics are however typically "Lortzian": the negative valuation of Occamism on the one hand, and its abiding impress on Luther even in the process of his overcoming of it on the other hand. In his Afterword, Manns expressly maintains the negative valuation in discussion with the post-1939 Occam research; the continuing influence is not disputed or is passed over in silence.[11] Manns has reproached me (9 n.32) for not having sufficiently seen that already Lortz and, all the more, Iserloh attributed the overcoming of this "uncatholic" Occamism to Luther's encounter with the Bible and especially with Augustine; I do not contradict that— but perhaps I have expressed it too awkwardly. In general in relation to both characteristics of the "Lortz-school," I tend, on the basis of the insights which I have been able to get up to now of the state of the research, toward the interpretation of the Lortz-critics.[12]

Fact 3: In the case of Lortz himself,[13] even long after 1940, Luther's conception of the "exclusive efficacy" of God, in the event of justification as in general, forms the decisive hindrance to a theological recognition of the "whole" Luther. This being so, what is correctly seen in this conception is not only a particular doctrine among others but the quintessence of the new and different in Luther's thinking. And since on the other hand Catholic theology did not see itself in the situation by any means to accept this difference, it can, *insofar as* it is logical, think only of the rejection of the "whole" Luther. I do not see what there would be to "differentiate" under this presupposition. For the distinction between a true "kernel" and its unacceptable "clothing," between a "fundamental Catholic concern" and its exaggerated, therefore "one-sided" formulation, even apart from its epistemological and linguistic-philosophical difficulties, cancels exactly that "wholeness" of Luther without which Luther is no longer Luther. Thus I completely agree with Manns and his description of the Lortzian position that here the "Catholic" and the "heretical" lie side by side. But then what can it mean "to speak theologically" with Luther? Can one learn from him when the "Catholic fundamental concern" is freed from this "wholeness" and affirmed as that which is "freed"? Is there not here a posthumous "differentiating" of *Luther* brought about by learning, and indeed in just the same way as it was already also attempted at that time and as Luther exactly thought, *no* more may be learned? In any case it is indisputably a step "beyond Lortz" when one as a Catholic no longer has *any* particular problem with the "exclusive efficacy" of God, in any case is not disconcerted by it—as well or as poorly as one establishes this. The fact of the matter is that this step has been taken, and indeed it appears to give possibilities of "differentiation" which even without the "paradoxicalness" of the "Catholic" and "heretical" Luther at the same time, allows him to be the whole Luther, accepts him as such, regards him as a "Catholic possibility," and nevertheless simultaneously remains capable of being able to criticize him. I am aware that such possibilities and attempts are ordinarily as little perceived by the Lutheran side as is Lortz's picture of Luther, although for different reasons.[14] They certainly want that other orientation which Manns characterizes and condemns as "hermeneutic" "in contradiction to the historical facts." I will return to this.[15]

Fact 4: This is related to what was said above. Where does Lortz (and the "Lortz-school") articulate not only a so-to-speak "stylistic," external-formal, but rather a *theological* critique of the Council of Trent? It must in no way be agreed that such a critique is necessary or permissible; also, the prerogative of Lutheran critics of Trent such as Hanns Rückert, Peter Brunner, Wilfried Joest, Heiko A. Oberman, Albrecht Peters, et al.,[16] must in no way be given in advance. At least in this point there may remain a complete accord between Lortz and Hubert Jedin, in contrast to their otherwise different interpretations of Luther.[17] But on the other hand it is a step further when this since about 1960—here and there—occurs,[18] and indirectly even in relation to the Second Vatican Council.[19] To be sure Trent will not be declared non-obligatory for a long time yet. I had these facts in mind when in 1966 I said less tactfully that Lortz's interpretation of Luther may with such steps be "finally surpassed." This judgment was and is not meant absolutely, but is valid for just this researcher: if they have taken the above-mentioned steps, *they* will exactly for that reason no longer return to the position they left. Personally, I think they may take such steps; but this must still be substantiated. All in all, I am afraid that I cannot agree even today that I have so radically misunderstood and indeed "caricatured" the position of Lortz and his "school" as Manns has accused me of and in fact, as shown by his most recent statements, still claims. Perhaps all of this may become clearer if I turn now to the second complex of questions.

Historical and Systematic Luther Interpretation

I am completely in accord with Manns that the one and, to us, all-binding transcendent truth of God is recognizable to us only in historical form and thereby also in foreshortened historical perspective. Hence I will forego picking up here once more individual, brilliantly formulated theses (for example, and above all, 48: ". . . under the call of 'historicity' it flees from history . . .") to ask whether they really meet what I (and others) have really meant. I agree with him on the indispensability of research in church history and historical theology for systematic-theological work. On the other hand, Manns may not contradict when I also consider necessary systematic-theological conversation with *contemporary* Lutheran theology in its relationship to Luther. It cannot displace study of the sources, which indeed I have never asserted, but it can make this study more fruitful by putting to it its concrete research questions, by mediating motivations, even by having warnings in store for it.

I totally agree in the "brotherhood in arms,"[20] as Manns calls it, where it is concerned to protect or respectively to win back Luther's theology as a spiritual and intellectual power of Christendom from all evangelical "Luther forgetfulness" and Catholic "Luther phobia," or as I formulated it at that time with certainly a somewhat different nuance: to comprehend Luther "as a proper possibility of theological thinking and existing."[21] In general I affirm the common interest, which was never lost in the controversy, as Manns recently registered it.[22] In addition, it is also for my sake, other than Manns fears,[23] the question of Luther's "heresy" is in no way superfluous. I have always emphasized that with my "orientation" there is no way that may be decided a priori. For even according to my understanding, controversial theology is the dispute over heresy.[24] If I place the word "heresy" or "heretic" with respect to Luther in quotation marks this is not in order to leave undecided *in principle* the question of heresy in Luther, but rather only to leave undecided the *conventional assumptions* which end the conversation on all points. What is more, this being the case, the church publicly tolerates and in fact must tolerate heresy in its ranks—today this is called "partial identification with the church"![25]—raising, essentially with regard to the logical literal sense of the concept, the question of which heresies with regard to the faith are and must be Church-dividing and which are not. It is not entirely so certain to me that those listed by Manns[26] in close connection to conventional conceptions contain the essentially neuralgic points: sacraments, church, papacy, honoring of the saints.

What still remains to be discussed after so much agreement? Manns, right up to his most recent expressions on the matter, has continually rejected the critique that Lortz and the "Lortz-school" compared Luther only to the theological tradition *before* him (e.g., Occamism), thereby measuring his orthodoxy by this criterion rather than the *genuine* Catholic tradition. It may be a false interpretation to impute to Lortz that he considered as "Catholic" only the Luther who in breaking through the "uncatholic" Occamism rediscovered the genuine Catholic tradition, and accordingly considered "heretical" that Luther who after rediscovering the Catholic tradition nevertheless still went beyond it. It is true, I have and even recently still said this.[27] Certainly it is incorrect to say that I had thereby imputed to Lortz the intention of a "clever apologetic" (20) which swiftly misappropriates and reclaims as an essentially never squandered heritage that which Luther had rediscovered against the church of that time.[28] Why should it then be a terrible "apologetic" and not rather a most legitimate proclamation of one's own church, thereby pointing out in addition that Luther—in many cases—contrary to his own view of things on the issues forced an open door and this essentially could have been noted?

Now I need not again emphasize that already the comparison between Luther and the tradition before him has as such its topicalness. For in this respect, exactly along the line of Lortz, Luther *also* becomes a witness to the tradition of the church and, in addition, a powerful expression of it. In spite of this I am still not able to see how my evaluation and analysis of the Lortzian valuation of Luther would be upset. I willingly confess that I have underestimated the "paradoxical" way by which Lortz sees in the one Luther the "Catholic" and the "heretical," and believes to be able to have the "Catholic heritage" by Luther only *in* the "onesided false interpretation," the "objectively false presentation,"[29] not outside of and divided from it. Only the question of the *degree of difference* is not thereby answered, or with respect to the given answer—the standardness of the pre-Occamist tradition—still adds no new element. Moreover, reference may be made here to the fact that quite recently no less than Iserloh expressed a valuation of Luther which when interpreted in a nasty way gives exactly a three-part division of Luther: there is the young Luther whose reformatory discovery is not church-dividing; there is the early-reformatory Luther who, without compelling theological reasons but rather from his own stubbornness and lack of readiness to learn, abandons the essential positions of the church's faith and praxis and thereby was rightly condemned; and finally there is the older Luther, who in the course of the dispute with the fanatics re-appropriated to himself the previously sacrificed church convictions even if not sufficiently, especially in his understanding of the church and ministry.[30] But what Manns means is illustrated in spite of all safeguards by an unequivocal quotation:

> There can only be talk of a Catholic "consensus" with Luther if the theologically and substantively determined agreement of the historical Luther with the contemporary teaching of the church may be shown. The fact that this recognition is possible only now clearly refers to historical limitation and to the historic openness of theological knowing. But this goes to prove a twofold insight that first of all the recognized consensus with respect to the historical Luther today means that his essential content also possesses validity for the faith consciousness of the present; and that, secondly, the historical source of Reformatory theology at the same time receives normative significance over against the "modern" Luther of the inner-reformatory development and thus is to be guarded as the costly "heritage" just for the disclosure of his ecumenical significance (43f.).

I would subscribe entirely to these sentences except for the little word "only" in the first sentence. But Manns places this word with care; the quoted sentences are a "solemn" summary of his position (two lines prior: "We hold fast therefore . . ."). Why should I then be shot for a misunderstanding when I emphasize that the comparison, which the question of a harmony between Luther and Catholic doctrine should clarify, occurs in the "Lortz-school" by a "move backwards"? For the "contemporary" teaching of the church is indeed according to the consistent conception of the Lortz-students not Occamism—which is indeed "uncatholic"—but rather the pre- and extra-Occamistic ecclesial tradition in its even at that time continuous effects. Thus Manns can no longer perceive any sense, indeed it may be an offense, when he asks me: "Then what does 'Catholic teaching' still mean for Pesch when he has the conception that today 'Catholic' could be 'what at that time (that is, in the period of Luther and Trent) was uncatholic'?" (42).[31] In this possibility which I consider, Manns sees danger to "the preservation of the simple contents of faith statements which alone may finally justify a 'consensus'" (42 n. 139). A short time later Manns received all the help conceivable for buttressing his position—I of course also received the desired confirmation of my judgment—from the mouth of the "old master" himself when he turned against "the modern Catholic elucubrations" who are still seeking to receive Luther where he contradicts genuine Catholic teaching: "They are canonizing relativism."[32]

Now I have never challenged the contemporary significance of consensus between Luther and the valid Catholic teaching of his time. What I have disputed is solely the "only" in the sentence quoted of Manns. Thus the kernel of the controversy over "historical" and "systematic-ecumenical"

Luther interpretation is in point of fact in the question whether today "Catholic" could be what at that time was "uncatholic" and in what sense: to that end a simple question and a just as simple illustration.

It is well-known that in the "Familia Lortziana" it is agreed that not only is it possible that there was uncatholic teaching in the Catholic Church at that time, but that this is an "essential" point. It was Occamism. On the other hand this teaching *was held* at that time as "Catholic." As Peter Manns has shown[33] again just recently, this is accepted not only by evangelical but also by Catholic scholars today as Catholic even if it no longer continues today to be effective. It was assumed in the well-known academic controversy between Heiko A. Oberman and Hanns Rückert over whether the Council of Trent, by consciously differentiating its use of the words *mereri* and *promereri*, might have left room for clearing Luther from the fiercely attacked thesis of Occamism.[34] In any case, at that time Luther had not only completely avoided that conflict with the church but was able to thoroughly regard himself even according to the opinion of other theological schools as a "good Catholic" when he had fallen back (again) upon the position of the *via moderna*. In spite of this Lortz, with Luther, held Occamism to be uncatholic and Luther, insofar as he overcame Occamism by recourse to the Bible and the tradition of the ancient church, to be Catholic, as seen by today, although Luther according to the judgment of that time and even occasionally today—consider Theobald Beer![35]—was, by his attack against Occamism, uncatholic. In this sense there is thus for Lortz and indeed also for Manns the factual finding that what was *valued* then as "Catholic" is today "uncatholic," or at least may be *represented* as "uncatholic"; and this then means, conversely, that insofar as what was "uncatholic" at that time *is acknowledged* today as "Catholic teaching," then at least its claim to the name "Catholic" *cannot be objected to*. The reference that it is after all really concerned "only" with "the ancient Catholic heritage," which was exposed under the fatal superimposition, is cheap, for then it really must be asked: How did it then become possible—this is really not yet so long ago!—to learn to discover the "uncatholic" of Occamism? This is clearly no chance insight but rests on *later* experiences which first of all awakened on the one hand uneasiness with regard to "that valued as Catholic," in this case Occamist theology, and thereby encouraged sharper questions about its implications, its historical origins and its differences from the older, indubitably ecclesial-catholic tradition. Impulses from the specific *present* of historical research, thus questions which by their nature belong to the subject area of systematic theology, lead to revision of *judgments* on the *past*, in this case on the theology contemporaneous to Luther. In other words, because Luther, in comparison with "the present," suddenly looks more favorable than was usual up to now, the comparison with "the past" is able to follow with more favorable results, thus moving toward far-reaching consensus results. But this means the "substantively determined agreement of the *historical* Luther with the contemporary teaching of the church" (43) already implies, and indeed *precedes*, a "substantively determined agreement of the historical Luther" with the Catholic teaching of the *present*, at least the presupposition of such an agreement.

Now by this one does not then slip into, to speak with Lortz, "canonized relativism" when such a systematically induced sharper historical inquiry into Luther is held, of course, in the framework of binding church teaching. This, for a Catholic theologian of course, indisputable foundation must certainly be so understood that he withstands the "majesty" of a few "facts" which may be checked in every Denzinger edition. I am limiting the illustrations to a few straightforward "classical" cases of the history of dogma[36] and select two of the strongest possible examples from Luther's theology.

Luther's teaching that the Christian is "simultaneously righteous and sinner" (*simul iustus et peccator*)[37] was definitely repudiated by Trent.[38] Thus the formula was held as uncatholic at that time not only by a particular theological school but rather by the *official church*. No less than Karl Rahner has declared it impossible as a dogmatic-theoretical thesis,[39] and Albert Bradenburg still held it in 1967 to be a problematic thesis.[40] But already in 1962 Lortz, clearly under the influence of Manns, was thinking differently,[41] and since the mid-60's there are several who grant that Luther's intention, striking exegesis and interpretation, is a Catholic possibility.[42] Even in the "Lortz-school" no one is really any longer able to present this formula—though it is *a* summary of Luther's doctrine of justification!—today as still being church-dividing, even though at the same time it has been shown that in its Lutheran form it does not correspond to Paul.[43] *Thus today there can be accepted as Catholic what at that time was officially condemned as uncatholic in every form.*

Toward an illustration by an entirely different example: The Council of Trent, while condemning all other conceptions, defined the doctrine of transubstantiation to safeguard the eucharistic Real Presence.[44] The Council thereby declared faith in a change of the eucharistic gifts to be indispensably bound to faith in the Real Presence. Luther had fiercely fought against the doctrine of transubstantiation, with whatever degree of justification, as the "second captivity" of the Lord's Supper[45] and, in connection with the concepts of the church fathers, conceived the Real Presence according to the model of the Incarnation. Just as the human nature is preserved when it is united with the Logos, so also is the bread when it becomes the body of Christ.[46] It is of no help to Luther that he, as no other Reformer, affirms the Real Presence of the body and blood of Christ in the Lord's Supper; he is condemned along with the others by Trent because he teaches no change in the elements.

Now in recent years Catholic theologians, in order to interpret the eucharistic Real Presence and get away from the contemporary and sufficiently well-known difficulties concerning the doctrine of transubstantiation, have again fallen back on that analogy to the Incarnation which in Luther's case was not sufficient for the Council of Trent.[47] Trent's position of course cannot be overlooked but it is believed that it can be overcome even if at the price of some "subtlety" (Luther[48]).[49] Thus again: What was at that time uncatholic, can at least today be represented in a Catholic handbook of dogmatics.

How then are such facts *conceivable* in a literal sense? Isn't there something strange going on, which Manns himself in an unguarded moment but with all desirable forthrightness, declared: that "the illusory self-certainty of the post-tridentine view crushes us" (44 n. 147), where however this theology was valued for centuries as just that which "secured" Catholic teaching against the Reformation? The catchword "misunderstanding," as much as it is in order in controversial-theological dialogues, is only of little help here; far less help than with regard, for instance, to themes such as "certainty of salvation" or *fides caritata formata*.[50] In any case the fact that Luther was never contesting but indeed rediscovering forgotten Catholic truth may *not* be illumined nor explained *by means of church history*. Luther's *simul*—aside from suggestions of some saints based not upon the lines of dogmatic reflection but upon emphatic statements of piety—was no "rediscoverable" traditional formula, as for instance was the case with the "righteousness of God by which he makes us righteous," the so-called *iustitia dei passiva*.[51] Luther's *simul* is a clear case of "something new" in Luther's theology which at that time was considered heretical, and is considered today as orthodox or at least *no longer* criticized as heretical. The use of the Incarnation analogy for the interpretation of the eucharistic Real Presence is certainly *no* "novelty" but rather the reappropriation of a patristic concept; although certainly the official church at that time considered this insufficient, it is today no longer so considered. It could be nastily asked which case is more explosive, the *sheer* novelty or the condemned rediscovery. For in the latter case was not just a theological school (e.g., Occamism) but rather even a Council "uncatholic"?

It is in such a context and on the basis of *such* observations that the problem arises of a "systematic" Luther interpretation, of the theological comparison "forwards," the establishment of consensus between Luther's theology—*nota bene:* the theology of the *historical* Luther!—and contemporary Catholic theology, insofar as it may indeed be scientifically contested but not ecclesially criticized and insofar as the contemporary Catholic faith consciousness is reflected in the frame of church teaching. It is just this which I have been attempting for a long time.[52] For the Catholic judgment of Luther has this one consequence, which according to predisposition may be a release or a burden: Luther can no longer be indicted for saying at that time what Catholic theologians also say today, and for placing in question at that time what Catholic theologians also no longer maintain.

As can be seen this has nothing at all to do with how "existential hermeneutic" is understood. Nor all the more with Manns's continually besought *history*. For nothing else is necessary for such a systematic interpretation of Luther than the clear "facts" of the post-Tridentine church and the history of theology. Certainly such things may be held to be legitimate. One could well turn back and easily demand the unconditional return to the formulations of Trent and correspondingly hold every new systematic judgment to be heretical, or at best ecumenical wishful thinking! This of course presupposes a concept of the "historicity" of faith for which the mastering of the alternatives of "relativism" or "truth" does not suffice. This cannot be further treated here, not because it would be impossible but because it would mean to begin a "gargantuan meal."[53] The simple statement of this clearly does *not* exonerate illegitimate changes of judgment from "uncatholic" (at that time) to "Catholic" (today). But it is a release from the difficulty—and exactly *this* was always my meaning in speaking of "going beyond Lortz"—of having to break off the conversation with Luther there where not only the church at that time but also even now the present church believes it must say no. If one who is not a historian of dogma or dogmatic "positivist" has only the argument which in the meantime has dogmatized what was at that time still "open," how can one consider possible that the Catholic proclamation and praxis inclusive of the teaching office concealed genuine Catholic teaching for the sixteenth century which nevertheless before the twentieth century was imagined from the start to be certain, as one must indeed do if the particular boundaries on the part of contemporary Catholic teaching are held to be "inviolable" in principle? Who then can say that a case like the *simul iustus et peccator* could not also be repeated in the future? May we not—especially in view of the last twenty years—today be expectantly curious about where we ourselves may be brought in the thorny field of ecclesiology by the further effects of inquiring of Luther in this connection?[54] Who desires to say today with *final* authoritativeness, after surmounting so much undeniable theological "unclarity" in the early sixteenth century church, how "Catholic" and also how "uncatholic" the "Lutheran" Luther is, that Luther who also had opposed for theological reasons the church under the papacy of that time?

Now all of this in no way means that "pathetic flight into inexpressibility, felt already as a betrayal of the truth when its content is concretely determined and thus is related as standard" (42) which is reproached by Manns. With our limited minds and with the poor words at our command we should and must within the narrow bounds of our contemporary historical situation substantively determine and decisively state what is "Catholic." Even over this we shall continually struggle and continually dispute, and that is good for then we shall not fall into the error of neoscholasticism, saying in principle that we have exhaustive possession of the truth. We also must and may become aware that after another 500 years the question may be how "uncatholic" we have been in thinking about many questions. But no other way is shown to us. And therefore it is worthwhile in this way to carry controversy through to consensus, and where this does not succeed to continue to endure and publicly witness to the fact that God has called us as finite beings with limited minds to the knowledge of his mysteries. Once more: this does not disqualify "substantive" statements and commitments. But it does indeed disqualify hasty readiness for "anathema," which by the use of "substantive" criteria forgets the relativity of the "subject matter" in the double sense of the word: its relatedness to a very definite situation of life and understanding which provides a statement in general about its disclosing and freeing-guiding power, and the perspectival foreshortening thereby inseparably bound to it which makes it impossible to apprehend the total riches of the knowledge of faith.

If desired, *a little* "existentialism" may be perceived in these last sentences. For in, with, and under one another, and if necessary against one another, statements with regard to the subject matter are finally always related to this one: that "existence," thus the person, in his/her historically determined and open to the future situation of God, is thrown in faith into the arms of the God whose "paradoxical" activity is clear to us in the *cross* of Jesus Christ; and just because of this it is valid to say what no less than Thomas Aquinas said as a warning before all exaggerated pathos about unshakable "contents": "The ultimate thing in the human knowledge of God is that we know that we know nothing of God."[55]

PROSPECTS ON OLD AND NEW TASKS

Here the discussion must be interrupted. Therefore I should like in closing first of all to heartily assure Manns of just that "brotherhood in arms" in the work of the disclosure of Luther which he himself already offered and which basically during the entire controversy was never broken. Preferably I would certainly here choose to speak in terms of a musical, "military" image, perhaps of a "dual partnership concertante." Provided that I have clearly enough expressed myself, Manns's catchword (54ff.) of the "multiple-tracked method" should no longer be alarming. No doubt there is still much to do in the historical investigation of Luther's theology. It is astonishing enough that in spite of all the intensely developed refinements of contemporary methods of historical research the assessment of the consequences of consensus and dissent between Luther's theology *at that time* and Catholic theology *at that time* still holds so many unsettled controversial questions. A now-classical school example of this is the different evaluations of Luther's statements on the office of bishop.[56] Under the circumstances it is next to certain that viewpoints of contemporary systematic theology flow into this differing judgment which can be a true help also for historical Luther research if—on a "second track"—*contemporary* Catholic and *contemporary* Lutheran theology discuss their controversial questions and exhaust all possibilities of agreement. It could thereby be discovered once more, to speak with Bonhoeffer, that controversial issues from the past are "no longer genuine"; that Luther is "dated";[57] that Catholic theology can help Lutheran theology by broadening its narrow course which is one of the long-range historical effects of Luther. In any case it may not simply be self-evident that a blind alley in controversial theology and in inter-ecclesial dialogues therefore will be declared insuperable because Luther was involved in their construction. For the same reasons Lutheran theology must—on a "third track"—continually consider its relationship to the historical Luther. On the one hand this is in order not to squander its precious heritage, as has frequently happened when Luther was simply appointed the chief witness for everything prescribed by the Zeitgeist. On the other hand however it is just as necessary to be responsible for Luther's alien nature[58] and thereby continually to bear in mind that Luther, not only according to Catholic but also according to evangelical self-understanding, cannot simply be the *norma normata*, to say nothing of the *norma normans* of the church, but surely may be the powerful witness to the faith who points beyond himself. Finally, contemporary Catholic theology is set right by all these ways over Luther; it has to ask in a more unbiased manner about the *contemporary* consensus with the Luther *of that time* who has already formulated, sometimes in an uncanny way, so much of what is also today self-evident to the Catholic sense of faith. Thereby it will also—to the benefit of the Lutheran Church as well—not make Luther into a "Church Father," and never develop that so-to-speak a priori personal loyalty which in the Lutheran churches and theology even today is still not infrequently observed when he is judged, in a manner of speaking, according to the motto: Luther is always right unless there is clear evidence to the contrary! But it is entirely "preconfessional" and "transconfessional" to read Luther and stimulating to incorporate this into one's own thinking, as also one's "own" classic figures are read, and like Lutheran theology the Catholic tradition does not exclude Thomas Aquinas, reclaiming in the meantime the "heritage of the Fathers."[59]

In such a "concertante team-work" the statements of the problem and the methods—which not only leave personal placing of emphasis to the individual scholar but even demand it!—permit easier interception and correction of the "wavering achievements of historical research work" (14).[60] I confess that in my report this was also an audacious and necessarily offensive word to the historians. But Manns, in light of so many "classical" disputed questions in historical Luther research, may hardly wish to dispute that it has a large kernel of truth!

In view of the so-understood "multi-track method" I prefer to appropriate the beautiful formulation by Manns in dependence on Luther that the Catholic consensus with Luther is truely hidden *sub contraria specia* (42). The fate of Catholic Luther research proves really in point of fact that it is constantly so. The "factual issues" which are continually received from "history"—even this I know better now than in 1966, not solely but also not inconsiderably in relation to the controversial work together with Manns!—are today all the more difficult as in the meantime the headwind of a growing ecumenical indifference blows in opposition to them.

In this context, the question of the "a priori structures" of Lutheran and Catholic thinking is far more than an, if possible still "typically German," intellectual luxury. They exist, as is no longer to be shown here, often enough in the background of conflicts which are not resolvable on the level of individual contents. Even so, they also conceal "under the opposite" substantive statements with regard to the contents of a deep consensus. This above all then when they intensify, under the conditions of a growing indifference in the contemporary ecumenical climate, the question: *What makes a person a Christian?*

Luther never answered this question *against* "the church"—to emphasize anything else would, in view of the historical Luther, be characterized as absurd. But Luther nevertheless did answer this question in such a way that the tension between "the church" and the individual Christian appears to be constitutive for being a Christian. At the latest since Luther it is expressly and so-to-speak "existentially" known; what was never disputed as always "theoretically" known: that a person is a Christian only *in* the church and even only *through* the church, but not by its *conditions*. For faith cannot be delegated to the church; each person can, by God's work, only personally believe for himself. *To recognize just this point is what makes the church the church.* In this sense, therefore, the "article of justification" is the "article with which the church stands and falls." What hinders the Catholic Church from publicly also granting this? It has long been understood as evidenced by the text of the Second Vatican Council, and even if so desired could not be contested. In order to avoid misunderstanding, it must not do this with the words of Luther. But of itself the insufferable controversial questions concerning the institutional conformity of its hierarchical administration must in no way make it impossible to declare: The church is there for the sake of the gospel—and not the gospel for the sake of the church. To say this loudly and clearly would be the most important word of the Catholic Church to the Luther year 1983. For if this were so, one could henceforth appeal to it to settle the reproach raised by all methodological "tracks" of evangelical Luther research that the church places itself between Christ and the believer, indeed puts itself in the believer's place. By nothing else and without any predecision on individual questions to be further discussed, the Catholic

Church could effectively, as far as it lies in its power, help end the much complained about "ecumenical standstill" by actually saying not only to the contemporary ecumenical situation but to the contemporary human situation in general: We are justified by faith—by faith alone!
And therefore free by faith—by faith alone!

NOTES

1. In the series: Veröffentlichungen des Instituts für Europäische Geschichte (Mainz), Bd. 46, Abteilung Abendländische Religionsgeschichte, J. Lortz, ed. (Wiesbaden, 1967). Hereafter the numbers in parentheses refer to the pages of this text.

2. Cf. O. H. Pesch, "Zwanzig Jahre katholische Lutherforschung," LR 16 (1966): 392–406 (hereafter cited as "Zwanzig Jahre"); English: "Twenty Years of Catholic Luther Research," LuW 13 (1966): 303–316; "Abenteuer Lutherforschung: Wandlungen des Lutherbildes in katholischer Theologie," NO 20 (1966): 417–430 (hereafter cited as "Abenteuer").

3. For Manns cf. e.g.: "Amt und Eucharistie in der Theologie Martin Luthers," in P. Bläser ed., Amt und Eucharistie (Paderborn, 1973), 68–173, 172f.; "Zum Vorhaben einer 'katholischen Anerkennung' der Confessio Augustana: Okumene auf Kosten Martin Luthers?" Okumenische Rundschau 26 (1977): 426–450, 442ff.; "Welche Probleme stehen einer 'katholischen Anerkennung' der Confession Augustana entgegen und wie kann man sie überwinden?" in H. Fries et al., Confessio Augustana: Hindernis oder Hilfe? (Regensburg, 1979), 79–144, 82, 96f., 122; "Das Lutherjubiläum 1983 als ökumenische Aufgabe," ÖR 30 (1981): 290–313, 294f.; "Lortz, Luther und der Papst," Afterword in RD, 6th ed. (1982), 2:353–391, 383f. (hereafter cited as "Lortz"); "Katholische Lutherforschung in der Krise?" in P. Manns, ed., Zur Lage der Lutherforschung heute (Wiesbaden 1982), 90–128, 91f., 102–110 (hereafter cited as "Krise"). For me cf. e.g.: "Existentielle und sapientiale Theologie: Hermeneutische Erwägungen zur systematisch-theologischen Konfrontation zwischen Luther und Thomas von Aquin," ThLZ 92 (1967): 731–742, 738f.; "Luthers theologisches Denken—eine katholische Möglichkeit?" NO 23 (1969): 1–19, 15ff.; "Der gegenwärtige Stand der Verständigung (Über Luther)," Concilium 12 (1976): 534–542, 538f.; "'Um Christi willen . . . ' Christologie und Rechtfertigungslehre in der katholischen Theologie: Versuch einer Richtigstellung," Catholica 35 (1981): 17–57, 33 n.43; "'Ketzerfürst' und 'Vater im Glauben': Die seltsamen Wege katholischer 'Lutherrezeption'" in H. F. Geisser et al., Weder Ketzer noch Heiliger: Luthers Bedeutung für den ökumenischen Dialog (Regensburg, 1982): 123–174, 133f., 145, 170 n.40.

4. Cf. "Lortz," 383f.; "Krise," 102–110.

5. Manns, here as elsewhere, loves to use the method of splitting quotations. This is amusing enough to read but does not always serve the clarity of the information. Indeed he treats nearly every quotation from both my essays this way so that the quotations appear as parts of a gigantic puzzle which can only be put together with difficulty under the direction of Manns. If you want to know my position *precisely* without the possible influence of Manns, read my two essays. No hard feelings!

6. Cf. "Zwanzig Jahre," 397 (with n. 26f.): "Abenteuer," 423 (with n. 33).
7. Cf. Lortz, "Martin Luther. Grundzüge seiner geistigen Struktur," in *RR*, 214–246; J. Lortz and E. Iserloh, *Kleine Reformationsgeschichte* (Freiburg i. Br.: Herder 1969), 13–26, 310–337 (written by Lortz).
8. The works by Iserloh and Manns—to simplify matters I refer to my report as well as to the additions furnished by Manns in *Lutherforschung heute*, especially 8f., notes 20–22—are interesting for the *theological-historical* connections to Luther's teaching, not so much for the biographical which are self-evident for any theological-historical investigation.
9. "Lortz," 385.
10. Cf. P. Manns and N.H. Loose, *Martin Luther* (Freiburg i. Br., 1982).
11. Cf. "Lortz," 360–370.
12. Cf. Pesch, *Theologie der Rechtfertigung bei Martin Luther und Thomas von Aquin* (Mainz, 1967), 708–714; O. H. Pesch and A. Peters, *Einführung in die Lehre von Gnade und Rechtfertigung* (Darmstadt, 1981), 110–118; Pesch, *Hinführung zu Luther* (Mainz, 1982), "Fachsimpelei" (7).
13. Cf. characteristically Lortz, *RD* 1:436.
14. Cf. Pesch, *Hinführung zu Luther*, "Fachsimpelei" (1).
15. Below under point 2.
16. Pesch and Peters, *Einführung*, 170.
17. I have already recognized for some time what Manns correctly sees in *Lutherforschung heute*, 8 n. 19. Cf. my " 'Ketzerfürst' und 'Vater im Glauben,' " 141f.
18. On justification, cf. St. Pfürtner, *Luther und Thomas im Gespräch. Unser Heil zwischen Gewissheit und Gefährdung* (Heidelberg, 1961), 38–43; E. Schillebeeckx, "Das tridentinische Rechtfertigungsdekret in neuer Sicht," *Concilium* 1 (1965): 452–454; H. Küng, "Katholische Besinnung auf Luthers Rectfertigungslehre heute," in *Theologie im Wandel. Festschrift zum 150 jährigen Bestehen der katholischtheologischen Fakultät der Universität Tübingen 1817–1967* (Munich, 1967), 449–468, 460–468; Pesch and Peters, *Einführung*, 176–208. On the other theme, cf. J. Bielmeier, ed., *Abschied von Trient: Theologie am Ende des kirchlichen Mittelalters* (Regensburg, 1969); E. Schillebeeckx, *Die eucharistische Gegenwart. Zur Diskussion um die Realpräsenz* (Düsseldorf, 1968), 15–57, 66-68; Th. Schneider, "Das Opfer Jesu Christi und der Kirche. Zum Verständnis der Aussagen des Konzils von Trient," in his *Deinen Tod verkünden wir. Gesammelte Studien zum erneuerten Eucharistieverständnis* (Düsseldorf, 1980), 223–238 (written in 1977). The above are only a few selections.
19. Cf. Pesch, *Hinführung zu Luther*, ch. 12.
20. "Lortz," 384; "Krise," 103–106.
21. Cf. "Zwanzig Jahre," 406; "Abenteuer," 430.
22. Cf. "Krise," 106.
23. Cf. Manns, *Lutherforschung heute*, 38f.; "Krise," 105f.
24. Cf. on this R. Kösters, "Zur Theorie der Kontroverstheologie. Wissenschaftstheoretische Reflexionen über Begriff, Gegenstand und Methode der Kontroverstheologie," *ZThK* 88 (1966): 121–161.
25. Cf. on this difficult problem, among others, K. Rahner, *Strukturwandel der Kirche als Aufgabe und Chance* (Freiburg i. Br., 1972), 76–81; F. Haarsma, W.

Kasper, and F.-X. Kaufmann, *Kirchliche Lehre—Skepsis der Gläubigen* (Freiburg i. Br., 1970).

26. "Krise," 105f.

27. Cf. "Zwanzig Jahre," 395–397; "Abenteuer," 423–425; Pesch, "Der Stand der Verständigung," 538f.; "'Ketzerfürst' und 'Vater im Glauben,'" 129, 133, 145.

28. One certainly reads with astonishment that Manns ("Lortz," 383) refers to an "extremely dangerous narrowing" of the Lortzian orientation with the same expression "cunning apologetic." Here one would like to directly support Lortz against Manns. Cf. pp. 383ff.

29. Cf. *RD*, 1:192.

30. Cf. E. Iserloh, "Luther und die Kirchenspaltung. Ist das Reformatorische kirchentrennend?" in H.F. Geisser, *Luthers Bedeutung*, 73–92.

31. With reference to "Abenteuer," 425.

32. Cf. Lortz, "Wert und Grenzen der katholischen Kontroverstheologie in der ersten Hälfte des 16. Jahrhunderts," in A. Franzen, ed., *Um Reform und Reformation. Zur Frage nach dem Wesen des "Reformatorischen" bei Martin Luther* (Münster, 1968), 9–32, 31.

33. Cf. "Lortz," 360–370.

34. Cf. H. A. Oberman, "Das tridentinische Rechtfertigungsdekret im Lichte spätmittelalterlicher Theologie," *ZThK* 61 (1964): 251–282; H. Rückert, "Promereri. Eine Studie zum tridentinischen Rechtfertigungsdekret als Antwort an H. A. Oberman," *ZThK* 68 (1971): 162–194; reprinted in his *Vorträge und Aufsätze zur historischen Theologie* (Tübingen, 1972). For Schillebeeckx's agreement with Oberman, cf. above n. 18. H. McSorley has also criticized Oberman's interpretation of Trent in *Luthers Lehre vom unfreien Willen* (Munich, 1967), 168–172, and more extensively, including a reply to Schillebeeckx, in *Luther: Right or Wrong?* (New York, 1969), 167–179. Oberman maintains his position with new references, but does not take McSorley's critique into account; cf. *Werden und Wertung der Reformation. Vom Wegestreit zum Glaubenskampf* (Tübingen, 1977), 135–139.

35. Cf. Th. Beer, *Der fröhliche Wechsel und Streit. Grundzüge der Theologie Martin Luthers* (Leipzig, 1974; 2d ed. with expansion and major changes, Einsiedeln 1980). For critical reviews, cf. W. Löser in *ThPh* 56 (1981): 565–573; Manns, "Das Lutherjubiläum," 295–298; "Krise," 112–127; Pesch, "'Ketzerfürst' und 'Vater im Glauben,'" 143–146; Iserloh in *Catholica* 37 (1982): 101–114.

36. Cf., however, Pesch, "Kirchliche Lehrformulierung und persönlicher Glaubensvollzug," in H. Küng, ed., *Fehlbar? Eine Bilanz* (Zurich, 1973), 249–279, 253–257.

37. On this formula, cf. Pesch, *Hinführung zu Luther* (Mainz, 1982), 189–202. There also is the controversial theological problematic which of course cannot be developed here.

38. Cf. DS 1528.

39. Cf. K. Rahner, "Gerecht und Sünder zugleich," in *Schriften zur Theologie* (1965) 4:262–276.

40. A. Brandenburg, *Martin Luther gegenwärtig. Katholische Lutherstudien* (Paderborn, 1969), 109.

41. Cf. Lortz, "Luthers Römerbriefvorlesung. Grundanliegen," *TThZ* 71 (1962): 129–153; 216–247, 149ff., 238–247.

42. They are listed in Pesch, *Hinführung zu Luther*, 189-202.
43. Cf. above all W. Joest, "Paulus und das luthersche simul iustus et peccator," *KuD* 1 (1955): 269-320.
44. DS 1651f.
45. WA 6:508,1-512,6.
46. WA 6:511,34-512,6.
47. Cf. the lengthy bibliography in the work of Schillebeeckx, *Die eucharistische Gegenwart*, and in Schneider, "Das Opfer Jesu Christi," 95-205. Schneider makes clear that similar observations can be made on the theme of the "sacrificial character of the eucharist." Cf. above n. 18.
48. Cf. WA 2:749,37.
49. Cf. J. Betz, "Eucharistie als zentrales Mysterium," in *MS* 4/2, 185-313, 306-310.
50. Cf. Pesch, *Hinführung zu Luther*, 116-128, 154-168.
51. Cf. the references and literature in Pesch, ibid., 86f.
52. My latest and prior endeavors are concentrated in *Hinführung zu Luther*. I thank Peter Manns for expressly attesting to me that he has never spoke of Luther-*interpretation (-Deutung)* (35 n. 123; cf. 57). I regard the distinction used by A. Brandenburg to be a bad one because the word "Deutung" is much too more or less arbitrary, in any case does not allow firm verification. The distinction I use ("Abenteuer," 417) between Luther *research* (Forschung) and Luther *interpretation* (Interpretation) refers here to consideration of the differences between historical investigation (Erhebung) of Luther's theology and its comparison with *contemporary* (Catholic) theology; and this comparison must in my sense be supported by documentary evidence.
53. Cf. my essay "Kirchliche Lehrformulierung," 253-257, 272-274.
54. Cf. also my *Hinführung zu Luther*, 217-228.
55. De potentia 7,5 ad 14; cf. Summa Theologiae 1:1,9 ad 3.
56. Now most impressively documented in the Catholic judgment by E. Iserloh, "Von der Bischofen Gewalt," in E. Iserloh, ed., *Confessio Augustana und Confutatio. Der Augsburger Reichstag und die Einheit der Kirche* (Münster, 1980), 473-488; and in the evangelical judgment by B. Lohse, "Die Stellung zum Bischofsamt in der Confessio Augustana," in K. Lehmann and E. Schlink, eds., *Evangelium-Sakramente-Amt und Einheit der Kirche. Die Ökumenische Tragweite der Confessio Augustana* (Freiburg i. Br./Göttingen, 1982), 58-79.
57. Cf. the so-to-speak inevitable but refreshingly unconventional SPIEGEL-book for the Luther year: H. Gumnior, *Vergesst Luther. Der überholte Reformator* (Reinbek, 1982).
58. Cf. G. Beetz, ed., "Der fremde Luther," in *Im Lichte der Reformation* (Jahrbuch des Evangelischen Bundes) 17 (Göttingen, 1974); G. Müller, "Der fremde Luther. Die Last der Tradition im neuzeitlichen Protestantismus," in H. F. Geisser, *Luthers Bedeutung*, 93-122.
59. Exemplary as is well-known, U. Kühn, *Via caritatis, Theologie des Gesetzes bei Thomas von Aquin* (Göttingen, 1965), 11-14; similarly, H. Vorster, *Das Freiheitsverständnis bei Thomas von Aquin und Martin Luther* (Göttingen, 1965), 14-20; further agreement in Pesch, *Theologie der Rechtfertigung*, 5-7.
60. Cf. "Zwanzig Jahre," 406.

Responses

Asterisks to Catholic Luther Research

MARC LIENHARD

It is often and correctly said that Catholic Luther Research is in general one of the most exciting chapters of Luther research. The stages of this research are well-known, especially the significance of the work of Joseph Lortz. Space does not permit us to develop the necessary valuations of these works here. Those by Lortz provoked discussion, first of all among historians, which has not yet ended. Peter Manns, in his Afterword to the latest edition of Lortz's classic work, reminds us of the central points of the discussion: the assessment of Occamism in and of itself and its meaning for Luther, the reality and range of abuses, the reaction of the hierarchy, and the judgments of the Catholic controversial theologians, Erasmus, and so forth. Of course the concern here is also with Luther himself, his concerns, his psychological and thought patterns. Three things may clearly be affirmed with relation to the effects of Lortz's work: First, his theses have not prevailed in all the areas referred to. Second, it is striking that today the fronts often run "crosswise." To give only one example: evangelical scholars share, for instance, Lortz's criticism of Erasmus more strongly than Catholic scholars. Third, in any case however it must be emphasized that Lortz posed abiding questions for research even though research has advanced and Lortz himself in his various writings (between 1948 and 1965) went beyond his own original position in, among other things, a more strongly positive valuation of Luther.

The promising 1966 article by O. H. Pesch[1] can give the impression that the Lortz-phase, as it has been positively assessed by Pesch throughout, will still be surpassed by another phase, namely a stronger turn to basic issues, the attempt to understand Luther as one who also represents a kind of Catholic theology. We stand today before a somewhat paradoxical situation. On the one hand the phase Pesch speaks of is actually occurring as is noticeable in a series of distinguished studies on Luther. On the other hand, it must be carefully asked whether or not there is the dangerous threat here and there to regress back behind Lortz. The question is whether the official church, seen by the formal expression of Cardinal Willebrands in Evian 1970, really affirms and integrates the studies of Lortz and the later phase. Furthermore there is the question of the meaning of "abuse of Luther" by

Translated by Carter Lindberg

which a few Catholic scholars have recently surprised their colleagues and fellow Christians. Consider, for instance, the works by R. Bäumer[2] and Th. Beer.[3] It is difficult in these cases—in comparison to Lortz, for example—not to speak of a "regression." What weight is to be given these publications still remains to be seen. At any rate, the criticism of scholarly colleagues, including Catholics, has not been long in coming. However in my contribution I should like rather to turn to some fundamental problems which are presented in the newer Catholic Luther research.

THE QUESTION OF APPROACH
What is the relationship between Luther the person and the subject matter?

It may be granted that in recent decades Luther the person has been lost sight of in evangelical Luther research—seen from the point of view of popular presentations.[4] On the other hand, Catholic Luther research until most recently was always tempted to confine the subject matter to Luther the person. Lortz's expressions in this connection are well-known: recall only the catchword "subjectivism." In Lortz's final publications this characterization of Luther is indeed placed in the background, however Luther's "spiritual structure" remains in any case important to him.[5] Y. Congar emphasizes Luther's moment of experience: Luther was able to comprehend only what he personally experienced.[6] Several presentations also indicate this by allowing the impression that Luther had so to speak "constructed" his teaching in order to cope with his personal problem of conscience. Thus everything may be explained by Luther's personal development.

I should like to pose three questions which represent respectively three theses:

1. In regard to Luther's development should not the early writings be more strongly interpreted theologically instead of focusing on the so-called "Tower Experience" as a psychological event which anyway is testified to only by later sources (after 1530)?[7]

2. The questions whether Luther interpreted the Scriptures "subjectively" and whether or not he was a "full hearer" of the Scriptures should not be posed from a biographical-psychological perspective, but rather as the hermeneutical question of the central meaning of the Scriptures.

3. Seen historically it cannot be denied that Luther as person exercised a great influence upon Protestantism. However it must be emphasized how little Luther himself forced his personal experience upon his followers. The norm was the Gospel and not his personal experience.

Which categories from the history of religion could be used by contemporary Catholics to characterize Luther's person and activity?

1. For a variety of reasons the category of "saint" is not suitable.[8] The presupposition for the use of this certainly would be the raising of the ban of excommunication.

2. The category of "prophet" is present instead of this. The fact that Luther himself rejected this must not unconditionally be a hindrance for historiography. There have been attempts in this direction throughout Catholic Luther interpretation. Here may be mentioned only the works of J. Hessen[9] and D. Olivier.[10] The latter sees in Luther's conflict with Rome a repetition of the basic tension between prophet and priest. This thesis however has aroused criticism. Thus for instance Louis Salleron has noted that the opposition between prophet and priest would not be insurmountable. Persons such as Catherine of Sienna, Theresa of Avila, and Joan of Arc are proof that critical prophets can be dealt with within the church.[11] Must it then be concluded that the separation of Luther from the Roman institution makes it impossible to use the category of prophet?[12]

3. Even the category of "reformer" appears to be bound up with difficulties. Thus Y. Congar, for example, has continually pointed out that Luther reformed not only the ethics and life of the church but also its doctrine. Thus he brought innovations which went beyond a mere reformation of the church.

4. Peter Manns characterizes Luther as a "father in the faith."[13] This is understood primarily in the sense of Luther's witness of faith corresponding to the Pauline words: "For I became your father in Christ Jesus through the gospel" (1 Cor. 4:15).

5. Now we have reached the final and indeed most far-reaching category: Luther as "teacher of the church." This category emerges—even if still with a certain caution—in Cardinal Willebrands's address to the Lutheran World Federation Assembly in Evian (1970): "In this we could all learn from him that God must always remain the Lord, and that our most important human answer must always remain absolute confidence in God and our adoration of him."[14] In the works of Olivier and Pesch it is still more strongly argued how Luther is to be taken seriously as a theologian of the Roman Church and that he is also a "teacher of the church."[15]

What is the question of the "Catholic" in Luther?

It would be possible to present something like a typology of the efforts to present Luther as far as possible as "Catholic." Already Denifle pointed out that Luther's conception of the *justitia passiva* was essentially a common Catholic position. In recent decades Catholic Luther scholars have endeavored to emphasize the objective-ontological elements of Luther over against an existential interpretation. This is pointed out, for example, with reference to the importance of early Catholic dogma or the sacraments. In this effort by the Catholic side to integrate Luther as much as possible, his works are distinguished according to various periods. Thus in the Lortz school it is customary to let the young Luther remain Catholic as long as possible; through the Lectures on Romans (Lortz in his last work) or the Ninety-five Theses (Iserloh). Naturally this does not mean that everything which is later is heretical but it appears differently, that is, it can no longer be integrated into what is Catholic. In this respect the Reformation writings of 1520 are particularly difficult to deal with, especially the "Babylonian Captivity," whereas Luther's 1522–1525 anti-enthusiast conflict stimulated his conservatism. Thus there is a later rapprochement, for example, in the question of ministry.

Thus problems naturally arise which appear for Luther research in general: Wherein is the unity of Luther's theology? Which writings (and which periods of his activity) shall be valid as criteria? In dialogue with Catholic Luther research I should like to raise here only three questions:

1. Is it methodologically possible to so "split up" Luther that only the objective-ontological or only the "acceptable" texts, for example, on ministry, but not the critical works of 1520, are accepted?

Does not such a playing off of one part against another ignore the true Luther (with his tensions) and also lose the Luther who is fruitful for us today? What is won if Luther is flattened into a particular tradition?

2. Does this not introduce into Luther a theological-ecclesial criterion which hinders really presenting his theology, and instead only seeks agreement and does not engage in the challenges?

3. What is the criterion for Catholic (cf. the question by Pesch): the Thomist tradition, Trent, or still others? Yet as well-known as these sources are they still need interpretation. On the other hand it must be asked whether, on the basis of these authorities, it is forbidding Luther what is definitely allowed contemporary Catholic theologians: for instance, an existential theology or a new interpretation of the sacraments.

THE PROBLEM OF THE SUBJECT MATTER

The turn toward the theological "subject matter"—beyond the concern for Luther's person and the Reformation as a historical event—is without doubt to be considered the decisive breakthrough within Catholic Luther research in the last years. Pesch not only has described this breakthrough but has decisively helped to form it. I should like to limit myself to four problem areas connected to this development.

1. It is important to state that the work of the most recent Catholic Luther research is no longer confined to raising the traditional dogmatic loci where differences exist (ministry, sacraments, etc.) but rather inquires about the a priori structures in Luther's mode of doing theology[16] and compares them with other structures. Pesch's use of the distinction between existential theology (Luther) and sapiential theology (Thomas Aquinas) is well known. As everyone knows this procedure has facilitated the dialogue over justification, in particular over the traditional points of discussion like the *simul justus et peccator* and enabled a far-reaching rapprochement with respect to

agreement. It is important to recognize that both thought structures may be demonstrated to be legitimately Christian, indeed Catholic.[17]

Is it a false impression that next to this search for a priori thought structures there is also another line which indeed does not concentrate upon individual points of controversy but nevertheless intends to be able to present a fundamental theological difference between Luther and the Catholic tradition? If I see this correctly, here above all should be mentioned the doctrine of God's exclusive efficacy in the process of salvation (from Stakemeier to Bläser). Congar, in a famous, but in the meantime self-corrected, essay focused on the problem of God's exclusive efficacy on the level of Luther's Christology. I pose the simple question: Do we see today in the Lutheran adherence to God's exclusive efficacy in the salvation process a remaining fundamental difference or not?[18]

2. There is furthermore the question of the mode of how justification and ecclesiology are united. Proceeding on the assumption that there is far-reaching agreement in relation to justification, it should be asked how this affects ecclesiology.

Where were the priorities for Luther himself? Must not the recent emphasis that the most essential and important concerns of Luther were in his battle against the pope be vigorously opposed?[19] Certainly the inner connection between justification and ecclesiology must be more forcefully shown than before. Also, Luther's soteriological-theological concerns in his critique of the papacy must be distinguished from their mythological expressions.[20] Without doubt we have the responsibility not to remain standing at the agreement on justification but to move on to inquire about its ecclesiological consequences, that is, of the subordination of the church under the Word and understanding of ministry determined by this. Pesch grants that "in Catholic Luther research the critical ecclesial point of justification by faith alone is hardly articulated."[21]

But have not the Lutheran-Catholic dialogues of the last years on "Gospel and Church," "Lord's Supper," and "Ministry" already set the course which leads from justification to ecclesiology, even if the question of the papacy—aside from the dialogues in the U.S.A.—has not yet been explicitly dealt with.

3. Naturally Pesch's question whether the Catholic positions are unquestionably and once-for-all given is of great relevance. By this is raised not only the above mentioned problem of criteria: Thomas Aquinas? Trent? and so forth. The more explosive question is: Can what was Catholic in the sixteenth century be characterized today as uncatholic and vice-versa? Examples for this would be not only Occamism but also statements of Trent (for example, the rejection of the *simul justus et peccator*). If such a vision could prevail and be applied in the area of ecclesiology a powerful breakthrough without

doubt would occur which would be of great significance not only for Luther research but also for the ecumenical movement as a whole.

4. Catholic reception of Luther sees itself confronted today not only with Luther as a historical phenomenon *sui generis* but with the fundamental question of unity and plurality. Is it possible the bounds will be further stretched today than in the sixteenth century? Where in the contemporary Catholic view does the heretical begin in Luther? Would a greater plurality in theology and spirituality be conceivable today within a one way or another unified Christendom than in the past? The reflections of G. Kretschmar and R. Laurentin in relation to the honoring of the saints, for instance, point in this direction.[22]

TOWARD THE RECEPTION OF CATHOLIC LUTHER RESEARCH IN THE EVANGELICAL REALM

Nostra res agitur! We as evangelical Luther scholars and also as evangelical churches are not merely interested spectators but rather directly concerned by Catholic Luther research. Only a few of the impulses which emanate from it today may be named:

1. It has—beginning with Denifle—forced Protestant Luther research to take up important historical tasks such as, for instance, the relationship of Luther to the late Middle Ages or to the Scriptures.

2. It poses the often uncomfortable questions of Luther and his church.

a) To begin with, Catholic Luther research was once instrumental in keeping alive, that is, reawakening, interest in Luther in the Lutheran churches (not only in the scholars). "Forgetfulness of Luther" is indeed a well-known problem of contemporary Protestantism.

b) Catholic Luther research however also poses for us the question of our continuity with Luther. For evangelical Christians it appears to be obvious that they would stand by Luther. However in reality there is the "nasty grave" of history, and contemporary Protestantism is often determined more forcefully by later developments than by Luther, for example, by Pietism and the Enlightenment (cf. Troeltsch on this). Thereby it has also often departed from the common Christian heritage, for instance, from the Church Fathers.

3. It helps us to see Luther in connection to history. Instead of an absolute placement of Luther it provides a critical reception in a double sense: Luther must be measured by the Scriptures, and Luther's intention must be distinguished from the historical conditionedness of its expression (language, historical context, etc.).

Certainly there has been criticism of Luther also in the evangelical churches—for instance since the seventeenth century. Among other things this has been concerned with Luther's coarseness or his relationships against the Jews and in socio-political questions. But on the other hand Luther has been to a large extent received uncritically, as for instance in the sense of

Pesch's formulation: "Unless there is clear evidence to the contrary Luther is always right."

Luther's importance, in spite of all forgetfulness of Luther, apparently remains greater in the Lutheran churches than that of Thomas Aquinas in the contemporary Catholic Church. Precisely because of this it is important to have an approach to Luther's reception which is conscious, critical, and only thereby fruitful. In this regard also must be brought up the narrow guidance (Engführungen) which Pesch in his address characterizes as "the long range historical effect." Various things can be thought of in this regard, for example, the typical tendency (which subsequently develops in the Lutheran Church Orders) which structured the worship service mainly along instructional-educational lines. (Or should only Melanchthon be charged with this?) The question of church government as well as the other already mentioned socio-political question areas must also be tackled.

There is no doubt that evangelical Luther research needs the contribution of Catholic Luther research, not least of all their critical questions.

NOTES

1. O. H. Pesch, "Twenty Years of Catholic Luther Research," *LuW* 13 (1966): 303–316; "Abenteuer Lutherforschung: Wandlungen des Lutherbildes in katholischer Theologie," *NO* 20 (1966): 417–430.

2. R. Bäumer, "Das Zeitalter der Glaubensspaltung," in B. Kötting, ed., *Kleine deutsche Kirchengeschichte* (Freiburg, 1980).

3. Th. Beer, *Der fröhliche Wechsel und Streit. Grundzüge der Theologie Martin Luthers* (Einsiedeln, 1980). Cf. the critical reviews by J. Wicks in *Theologische Revue* 78 (1982): 1–12, and E. Iserloh in *Catholica* 36 (1982): 101–114.

4. Cf. H. Bornkamm, "Probleme der Lutherbiographie," *Lutherforschung heute. Referate und Berichte des 1. Internationalen Lutherforschungskongresses* (Berlin, 1958), 15–32. More recent works by Protestant Luther scholars have turned anew to Luther as person. Cf. H. Bornkamm et al., *Martin Luther in ders Mitte seines Lebens* (Göttingen, 1979); M. Brecht, *Martin Luther. Sein Weg zur Reformation 1483–1521* (Stuttgart, 1981).

5. J. Lortz, "Martin Luther. Grundzüge seiner geistigen Struktur," in *RR* 1: 214–246.

6. Y. Congar, *Une vie pour la vérité. Jean Puyo interroge le Père Congar*, (Paris: Centurion, 1975), 62.

7. Cf. L. Grane, *Modus loquendi theologicus. Luthers Kampf um die Erneuerung der Theologie (1515–1518)* (Leiden, 1975).

8. Cf. the eloquent title of the book: *Weder Ketzer noch Heiliger. Luthers Bedeutung für den ökumenischen Dialog* (Regensburg, 1982).

9. J. Hessen, *Luther in katholischer Sicht* (Bonn, 1949).

10. D. Olivier, *Le proces Luther 1517–1521* (Paris: Fayard, 1971), 7; English edition, *The Trial of Luther*, trans. John Tonkin (St. Louis: Concordia, 1978).

11. L. Salleron, "L'anniversaire de deux condemnations: Jeanne d'Arc, mai 1431—Martin Luther, mai 1521," *Carrefour* (26 May 1971).

12. Cf. also Lumen Gentium 1:7: "Among these gifts stands out the grace given to the apostles. To their authority, the Spirit Himself subjected even those who were endowed with charisms."

13. P. Manns, *Martin Luther—Ketzer oder Vater im Glauben* (Hannover, 1980).

14. Evian 1970. *Sent into the World. The Proceedings of the Fifth Assembly of the Lutheran World Federation* (Minneapolis: Augsburg, 1971), 64.

15. O. H. Pesch, *Ketzerfürst und Kirchenlehrer, Wege katholischer Begegnung mit Luther* (Stuttgart, 1971); D. Olivier, *La Foi de Luther. La cause de l'Evangile dans l'Eglise* (Paris: Beauchesne, 1978).

16. O. H. Pesch, "Twenty Years of Catholic Luther Research," 316; *Abenteuer Lutherforschung*, 426 (cf. note 1).

17. O. H. Pesch, "Luthers theologisches Denken—eine katholische Möglichkeit?" *NO* 23 (1969): 1–19.

18. Here it should be presented how Luther directly follows the Christology of the ancient church. Cf. on this: M. Lienhard, *Martin Luthers christologisches Zeugnis. Entwicklung und Grundzüge seiner Christologie* (Berlin: Göttingen, 1980) English edition: *Luther: Witness to Jesus Christ*, trans. E. H. Robertson (Minneapolis: Augsburg, 1982). That Christology is church-dividing is also challenged, correctly in our opinion, by O. H. Pesch in his article, "'Um Christi willen...' Christologie und Rechtfertigungslehre in der katholischen Theologie; Versuch einer Richtigstellung," *Catholica* 35 (1981): 17–57.

19. P. Kawerau, *Luther, Leben, Schriften, Denken* (Marburg, 1969). 68.

20. H. Meyer, "Das Papstamt in lutherischer Sicht," in H. Stirnimann and L. Vischer, eds., *Papsttum und Petrusdienst*, (Frankfurt a.M., 1975), 73–90: "Das Problem des Petrusamtes in evangelischer Sicht," in K. Lehmann, ed., *Das Petrusamt* (Munich-Zurich, 1982), 110–128.

21. *Concilium* 12 (1976): 541.

22. G. Kretschmar and R. Laurentin, "Der Artikel vom Dienst der Heiligen in der Confessio Augustana," in H. Meyer and H. Schütte, eds., *Confessio Augustana. Bekenntnis des einen Glaubens* (Paderborn-Frankfurt, 1980), 256–280, esp. 274ff. English: "The Cult of the Saints," in Forell and McCue, eds., *Confessing One Faith* (Minneapolis: Augsburg, 1982), 282ff.

Remarks on Joseph Lortz's Basic Theses Concerning Martin Luther and the Reformation

ERWIN ISERLOH

1. "In his Reformation breakthrough Luther overpowered a Catholicism which was not (fully) Catholic."[1] Luther's opponents, the "pig-theologians,"

Translated by Carter Lindberg

were the Nominalists, for example, Occamists, who represented the position that the person *ex puris naturalibus* can love God above all things and fulfill the law *secundam substantiam facti* even if not *ad intentionem praecipientis*. "For this reason it is plain insanity to say that man of his own powers can love God above all things and can perform the works of the Law according to the substance of the act, even if not according to the intentions of Him who gave the commandment. . . . O fools, O pig-theologians!"[2]

Melanchthon still had these theologians in mind in the "Apology" when he spoke of the "Scholastici." Thus Johannes Mensing could argue that such scholastics could not be met in Augsburg and not represent the side of the ancient church. Leif Grane, Heiko A. Oberman, and others have objected to Lortz's thesis that "This Occamist system is radically uncatholic," arguing "that Occamism as a philosophical and theological system has never been condemned by the Roman Church."[3] It is to be said concerning this that Occam was charged, summoned, and detained in 1324 by the Curia until he fled in 1328 to the court of Ludwig of Bavaria. The trial was so long drawn out because the "judges" could not agree among themselves—"dogmatic unclarity"—and church-political questions were dominant after Occam's flight.

Grane and Oberman are correct in stating that the theses Luther objected to were at least semipelagian. Now if the Lortz thesis that the Catholic position was deficient is denied, then "Catholic" is equated with "semipelagian."

The Lortz thesis includes the interpretation that Luther's critique of the church "therefore resulted because a number of very important, indeed essential elements of the Catholic profession of faith either were apparently displaced or really could no longer be ascertained in the phenotype of the Catholic confession and life."[4]

2. Hence, in a positive sense, if Luther properly describes the content of his fundamental reformatory knowledge as a new understanding of the *iustitia dei* as passive righteousness, then he newly discovered something fundamentally Catholic, then that which is "reforming" need not be church-dividing.

This position that Luther newly discovered in the "reforming element" something Catholic is not, however, to say that he forced an open door. He turned against the religious praxis and theology of his day with good reason for it was an inadequate presentation of the Catholic faith.

3. Lortz did not speak of the "Catholic Luther" as did Karl August Meissinger in the title of the first volume of his trilogy. What is meant here is Luther up to 1518 and everything traditional in him, that Luther except for the Catholic residue—in opposition to his innovative disposition—was not cast off. Lortz said: "I should like only to note here that I in no way so understand the thesis of the Catholic Luther that Luther became continually

less Catholic with the passing of his life and with the growing animosity against the pope."[5]

If "Catholic" is understood not as a party designation, and it is taken seriously that Luther desired the reform of the church, then I do not understand how Peter Manns and, in another way, Otto Hermann Pesch are able to say that this disposition toward the Catholic Luther suffers from "a manifestly insidious apologetic." "Everything which is valid in the reforming disposition is claimed for 'Catholic truth' and in this way Luther is expropriated; the genuinely 'reforming' however is in this view inevitably dismissed as 'uncatholic' and 'heretical.' "[6]

4. Lortz maintained his assertion that "Luther was subjectively invested from the beginning,"[7] although this thesis "ran into the most criticism."[8] Of course subjectivism in Luther is not to be understood in the modern sense as emancipation from every norm. Luther felt himself bound, in a most marvelous way bound, to the Holy Scriptures, to the Scriptures as an accepted, objective Word of God. However he claimed to interpret the Bible independently of every authority. Here his gospel is at stake. In "The Babylonian Captivity" he wrote: "Neither pope nor bishop nor any other man has the right to impose a single syllable of law upon a Christian man without his consent; if he does, it is done in the spirit of tyranny."[9]

Lortz points out that Luther lays claim to the freedom for himself to decide what is the teaching of Holy Scripture but does not concede this to his opponents in the Reformed camp—Karlstadt, Müntzer and Zwingli—and that therefore he became for these men also a "monastic idol" and a form of papistic tyranny.

In 1965 Lortz responded to the criticism of his thesis. "The expression 'subjectivism' may be unsympathetic; it can be replaced or softened by speaking of a 'subjective disposition' or 'individualism' or 'personalism.' But in terms of the basic issue I believe now as before that I must retain the point; I do not see how one can avoid it."[10]

5. What is to be done in relation to Luther and the Reformation? Pesch is wont to play the tasks of the historian and the systematician against each other, whereby he accuses the "Lortz school" of being stuck in the historical. I think we should have to do both and may not separate one from the other. If I ask: What did Luther consider to be the reformatory element? or, How did he interpret the relationship of grace and gift in the event of justification?— then I must proceed by historical method and ask: What do the sources say and in terms of which temporal horizon, that is, in connection with which mentality, are they to be understood? But if I ascertain that Luther, for example, characterized the sacrifice of the mass as idolatry, an idolatry which has had no worse expression among Jews and heathen, and that he saw no possibility that this church-dividing dissent will ever be overcome; if I must further add that this grave reproach was raised from his central religious

concern for the uniqueness and all-sufficiency of the one sacrifice of Christ on the cross, then I can as historian still maintain that Luther has found no satisfying answer from the side of the theologians of the ancient church. To develop this is the concern of the systematician. If he succeeds in this then what is true today was not false yesterday, nor is the Council of Trent disavowed, but rather the dissent is transcended in the more deeply recognized and better lived truth.

In the example raised by Pesch and Manns of the *simul iustus et peccator*, the issue is more simple and only a *quaestio facti:* Trent did not condemn this formula (DS 1528), and it is intended differently by Luther than it appears in the literature.

NOTES

1. *RD* 1: 176. The addition "full" is in Lortz, *Die Reformation als religiöses Anliegen heute. Vier Vorträge im Dienste der Una Sancta* (Trier: Paulinus, 1948), 136.
2. *LW* 25:261; *WA* 56:274.
3. L. Grane, *Contra Gabrielem. Luthers Auseinandersetzung mit Gabriel Biel in der Disputatio Contra Scholasticam Theologiam 1517*, (Aarhus, 1962), 29.
4. J. Lortz, *Die Reformation. Thesen als Handreichung bei ökumenischen Gesprächen* (Meitingen, n.d.), 21f.
5. J. Lortz, "Martin Luther. Grundzüge seiner geistigen Struktur," in *RR* 1:219.
6. P. Manns, "Lortz, Luther und der Papst," Afterword in *RD*, 6th ed. (1982), 2:383.
7. *RD* 1:176; J. Lortz, *Die Reformation als religiösen Anliegen*, 134.
8. J. Lortz, "Martin Luther," 234.
9. *LW* 36:70; *WA* 6:536.
10. J. Lortz, "Martin Luther," 235.

An Evangelical Expression Regarding Catholic Luther Research

GOTTFRIED MARON

With regard to Martin Luther our century could be called nothing short of a "century of discovery." After the rediscovery of the theological Luther in Protestantism since the Luther anniversary of 1917, which became visible above all in the so-called "Luther Renaissance" of the twenties and thirties, and the Catholic discovery of Luther which likewise was initiated in 1917 but had its first real breakthrough two decades later, there has occurred with and since the Luther anniversary of 1967 (G. Schäbitz) a surprising discovery by East German Marxist historical research of Luther in terms of great revolu-

Translated by Carter Lindberg

tionary consciousness, a discovery whose ideological and political fruits are now certainly becoming visible prior to the approaching Luther anniversary of 1983.

The more recent Catholic Luther research, the origins of which are tied to the name of Franz Xaver Kiefl (1869–1928), reached its breakthrough within only a few years. The decisive representatives of this movement were Joseph Lortz (1887–1975) with his epochal book *Die Reformation in Deutschland* (1939/40), Adolf Herte (1887–1970) with his work *Das katholische Lutherbild im Banne der Lutherkommentare des Cochläus* (1943), and Johannes Hessen (1889–1971) with his study *Luther in katholischer Sicht* (1947). These names characterize three different levels and represent the following: a new disposition in the biographical understanding of Luther as a *homo religiosus* and the recognition of his historical greatness (Lortz); a profound self-critique of the Catholic understanding of Luther with relation to Catholic Luther research (Herte); the first attempt at an integration of Luther into the cosmos of the Catholic Church (Hessen).

Contemporary Catholic Luther research is, so to speak, borne by the "second generation"—all more or less influenced in various ways by Joseph Lortz and therefore in continuous dialogue among one another on this orientation. Historically, the Second Vatican Council signifies a certain turning point; substantively this research is characterized by an astonishing and highly significant rapprochement to Luther which can be described as the discovery of the "Catholic Luther." Three positions appear to me to be particularly worthy of note:

1. Martin Luther as a Catholic possibility. This phrase may be used to paraphrase the position of Otto Hermann Pesch (b. 1932). It is basically presented in his large study *Die Theologie der Rechtfertigung bei Martin Luther und Thomas von Aquin* (1967) and further elaborated in numerous writings and articles. Pesch's positions are constituted by the following: Luther is "fundamentally a Catholic possibility," if Luther's *Gestalt* is not absolutely set from the beginning. Luther is discovered above all as the epochal theologian. His "existential" theology "is legitimately Christian but not the only legitimate Christian theology." Thus as theologian, Luther is placed *next* to Thomas Aquinas and his "sapiential" theology. The consequence of Vatican II that Thomas is no longer seen as the *unicus magister* is also drawn with respect to Martin Luther.

2. Martin Luther as a Catholic necessity summarizes the interpretation of Albert Brandenburg (1908–1978) as represented in his last writings (*Martin Luther gegenwärtig*, 1969, and *Die Zukunft des Martin Luther*, 1977). Brandenburg advances from the discovery of a surprising "presence of Luther" in the contemporary Catholic Church to an intensive and pressing concern for Luther's Catholic "future." Indeed, Luther already in many respects has "found his Council" in Vatican II, therefore the present church

historical and ecumenical movement is to acquaint the whole Catholic Church with Martin Luther. Luther must be effectually received in the Catholic Church as the preacher of repentance, cross, and grace; Luther and the Catholic Church are "related to each other." "The point is that the Catholic Church receive the message from Luther;" "the Church must carry out this reception" if it desires to survive and fulfill its "catholicity in becoming."

3. Luther as a Catholic reality or a very obviously Catholic possibility may be the description of the position of Peter Manns (b. 1923), in whom the impulse of Joseph Lortz continues to work most directly and intensively. This is said in light of the numerous themes elaborated by Manns: Luther's doctrine of justification, his understanding of love and hope, his conception of the saints, and so forth. Manns attempts thereby to inquire behind the polemical Luther and free him from controversial situations in order to clarify his point that Luther's sharp criticism is not "criticism of the Church" but rather was directed at the flagrant errors of the late Middle Ages. From this position Manns is plainly Luther's advocate against the uncatholic deviations of the church of his time, against Melanchthon, and also against contemporary Catholic attacks and false interpretations (R. Bäumer), and generally against an "ecumenism at the expense of Luther" which would be, so to speak, a cheap ecumenism. Manns professes, "I am a student of father Luther" whereby Luther is understood (next to Abraham and Paul) as a "father in faith." It is rewarding "to discover Martin Luther as the 'father in faith' for all of Christendom."

It would be strange if such far-reaching theses did not evoke a reaction within the Roman Catholic Church. The most well-known examples of such a reaction are Paul Hacker (1913–1979) with his book *Das Ich im Glauben bei Martin Luther* (1966) and Theobald Beer (b. 1902) with his new, greatly revised work *Der fröhliche Wechsel und Streit. Grundzüge der Theologie Martin Luthers* (1980). The former characterizes Luther as religiously egocentric and the father of Cartesianism, the latter dismisses him as a biblical theologian for his alleged dependence on Pseudo-Hermes-Trismegistos. What is notable about all these critiques is that the authors do not present them from the position of being themselves Luther scholars but rather as self-educated outsiders who have produced their theses outside the context of the specialized literature. They represent an inflexible one-sidedness but enjoy however the strong support by influential Catholics (Joseph Ratzinger, Hans Urs von Balthasar). Nevertheless, the energetic repudiation of their positions by notable Catholic Luther scholars is particularly noteworthy; it is a sharp inner Catholic critique (in particular of Beer by Manns, E. Iserloh, and J. Wicks, the latter in *Catholica*, 1982, and *Theologische Revue*, 1982).

In many respects the regressive tendencies of specialists, themselves of the Lortz school, are more important. Above all, Remigius Bäumer (b. 1918) who created a sensation with his sketch of Reformation history prepared for the 1980 papal visit to Germany. According to him Luther is to be seen, against the background of a new assessment of Cochläus, as the destroyer of the church. In general there is a revaluation of sixteenth-century Catholic controversial theology. Thus Erwin Iserloh (b. 1915), in the foreword to a work on Johannes Eck (1981), declares his new discovery of the "old truths" in church history. His later, not easily interpreted statements on Luther reply in any case to the question of what is church-dividing in Luther from the point of view of strong, repeatedly affirmed, "Catholic" criteria (in relation to Luther's understanding of the church, ministry, sacraments, and so forth) even if confined to the early (?) polemical phases of the Reformer. Iserloh certainly tends toward a higher valuation of the Lutheran confessional writings, especially the Augsburg Confession, over against the, in many respects, unbalanced and confusing statements of Martin Luther.

More significantly, a continual Catholic reservation against Luther must be stated. This may be summarized in two points. The reproach of Luther's "hatred" extends from Döllinger through Lortz to today. "Luther's hatred toward the papal church is one of the great historical proofs of the destructive power of hatred" (Lortz). Pesch more or less puts the problem to one side in his more systematic approach; Manns attempts to de-polemicize Luther; and Brandenburg is offended by it. However it is certainly only a superficial human characteristic (coarseness) to which he responds when Brandenburg speaks for instance of Luther's "tendency to rancor, to uncontrolled rage and vulgar name-calling, his raving essence."

Nevertheless behind this there stands the issue of Luther's criticism of the church. Most of the substantive reservations about Luther may be traced back to views of his rebellion against the church, and his lack of a sufficient understanding of the "Church." The following exemplify this: the thesis of Luther's "subjectivity" (Lortz); the accusation of his destruction of the church (Bäumer); the apparent deficiency of Luther in relation to the sacraments, teaching office, priestly authority, succession, and so forth (Brandenburg), as well as the church-dividing reservations concerning the ecclesiological realm—especially Luther's understanding of ministry and sacraments (Iserloh).

Finally there is the question of Luther's ultimate theological and ecclesial quality. What is and what is not seen and recognized of Luther by Catholics today? Martin Luther is recognized as a *homo religiosus* (Lortz), a great theologian (Pesch), indeed as a "teacher to us all" (Cardinal Willebrands), and even as a "father in the faith" (Manns). Nevertheless the Roman Catholic church hardly takes up with any seriousness the decisive category of champion of God and prophet (Joh. Hessen in the wake of Fr. Heiler). Presently this is taken up only by D. Olivier who speaks of the battle of the prophets with the priest as the true conception of Christendom; for this he has received considerable criticism.

What should be investigated in this context is not only the role and meaning of "polemic" in church history wherein is encountered very quickly the forms with which Luther identified (Paul, Augustine, Bernhard of Clairvaux), but above all the phenomenon of Luther's "rage" (so Luther himself called it) in its quantity and quality. Of course there is in this powerful man also the phenomenon of personal prejudice and personal rancor (for instance, against Karlstadt). Nevertheless there is testimony that his "wrath" was to a large extent a function, so to speak, of his "office" and not "private" rage (Erasmus Alber: "No rage is noticeable in him except when he takes the field against the papists and the enthusiasts"). Erasmus of Rotterdam grasped well the essential point when he once said: "Perhaps our circumstances have deserved such a radical doctor who must heal by cutting out and cauterizing the sickness." Indeed Luther's *Gestalt* cannot be comprehended otherwise than as the person who sought at the risk of his entire existence to restrain the church of his time from going in the direction which he interpreted in comparison with the message of Jesus and the origins of the Christian faith as a monstrously false development.

Two Questions on Luther's Doctrine of the Justification of the Sinner

PETER BLÄSER

I should like to examine the doctrine of justification in light of the following questions:
1. How does the Lutheran doctrine of justification relate to the thesis of the exclusive efficacy of God?
2. How is justification related to baptism?

Question 1

It is not necessary to prove that for a long time Lutheran theology understood justification as a pure forensic act by which God forgives or does not hold sin against the sinner, and imparts the righteousness of Christ to the sinner. In the last half-century there has been an essential change in evangelical theology. Evangelical theology, building on the work of Reinhold Seeberg in his *History of Dogma* (vol. 4), has more and more emphasized that justification can never be understood as a pure forensic act but rather means an *action* of God that grasps the person in his or her own personal core and also changes the person. It would indeed be substantively correct to

Translated by Carter Lindberg

maintain the formal-forensic character of justification but with the forensic elements bound directly to the real-effective element. Particularly significant in this development, admitted even then, was the new discovery above all by New Testament Theology, although already asserted by Luther, that the Word of God not only has a declaratory but a transforming function. Through the Word of God something occurs; what is expressed in the Word happens. This position which has increasingly prevailed in the last half-century of New Testament theology understands the concept of God's righteousness not only as a forensic judgment but also as a salvation-creating activity by which something happens in the person, and not only in the person but in the world.

Nevertheless this raises the question how this sovereign activity of God is united or is to be united to human self-responsibility. Catholic theology, even Trent, gave no clarification for the relationship of the divine deed and human act, but rather only maintains both of these at the same time. The decisive question here is: Can the acts of the justified person really be understood as his or her acts, or is the weight of God's activity so heavy that there no longer is any room for the free responsible actions of persons? As already mentioned, Catholic theology also has still not found any answer which is able to rationally clarify the relationship of divine activity and human acts. Apparently this is fundamentally impossible for it concerns a genuine mystery that never can be clarified. For to rationally clarify such activity would mean nothing less than clarifying God himself. In any case it would be an absolute misunderstanding if the relationship between God and persons was understood as that between two somehow equally-ranked partners. In my opinion, a large part of the misunderstanding would be removed if we used the biblical concept of the righteousness of God, especially that of the Epistle to the Romans. Here the righteousness of God, understood as the activity of God, means not only the beginning of salvation but also of life in salvation, that is, the ethical life of the justified. Terminologically, even in particular places in Paul, it is difficult or hardly possible to decide what exactly is meant. It is clear concerning this terminological complexity that it is a reasonable concept that the entire life of the justified belongs to the fundamental saving activity of God and that between the saving activity of God and the acts of the justified there cannot be terminological distinctions. Therefore every concept of human independence constructed by individual deeds and a disposability to the grace of God is excluded from the beginning.

If the righteousness of God is understood as the salvation-creating activity of God, then the inner connection between justification and ethics would also become visible. Certainly it was a fundamental misunderstanding when the Lutheran doctrine of justification was deprived of every connection to ethics, and there was even seen in it a warrant for ethical license. But such misunderstandings perhaps resulted because an inner connection between justification and ethics was not exactly the strength of this doctrine, and because the ethics of the justified was understood mainly as an ethics of gratitude. Here in recent years a fundamental change has occurred insofar as the inner relationship between justification and ethics is emphasized (Bernhard Lohse). This relationship would be given without further ado if in the dominant concept of the righteousness of God, the activity of God and the ethical activity of persons given in this activity of God were seen as a unity. On this basis the much discussed question of the sense and range of the *simul justus et peccator* would also receive a new character; it would then be the question of the possibilities and limits of the divine activity in relation to the person who is justified. In the present discussion you can hardly help feeling that consciously or not the concrete experience of the justified is the starting point for all statements about the ethical possibilities of the person. However, if justification is understood essentially as the activity of God toward the person, then just this activity of God would become the starting point of all statements about the ethical possibilities of the justified person. Only thereby would the doctrine of justification become essentially theological speech, that is, be theology. It would speak primarily of God's activity and would also bear an essential characteristic of Reformation theology which is above all "to glorify" the activity of God.

Question 2

No exhaustive argument is needed for the thesis that for a long time in Reformation theology justification was understood predominantly as an individual action. The concern was the personal salvation of the individual, and the *articulus stantis et cadentis ecclesiae* itself had no inner connection to the reality of the church. Already the question, "How do I get a gracious God?" to which the doctrine of justification would be the answer, appears to force an individualistic and spiritualistic interpretation of justification.

A fundamental change was also indicated by the Fourth Assembly of the Lutheran World Federation in Helsinki (1963). The Theological Department's study document describes justification as a once and for all event bound to baptism. This expressly says: "Justification is identified with becoming a believer and occurs through the incorporation into the new community of saints, the church, in baptism." This position won far-ranging recognition throughout ecumenical theology. It is a much stronger recognition than before of what significance baptism has not only for the personal salvation of the individual but as the foundation for the whole ecclesial community, or, as the study document calls it, as the place and center of the incorporation into the communion of saints.

If justification shall retain its central place in the doctrine of salvation, then certainly it must be understood in this way or, if necessary, be completed. Of course even in the New Testament justification and baptism are not formally bound together, but justification and the birth of faith and thereby faith and baptism belong together. For in the New Testament, in any case with Paul, baptism encompasses the birth of faith; and in this respect so also justification, which is promised to faith, is also bound to baptism. Trent in its description of baptism as *sacramentum fidei* certainly has not given any theological clarification to the relationship of faith and baptism, but the affiliation of faith to baptism has been brought to expression. Therefore justification is also bound in some way or another with baptism. Therefore an important and fruitful task of ecumenical theology would be to determine more closely this relationship.

Summary

HARDING MEYER

Incorporating what was said in the two position papers (P. Manns and O. H. Pesch) and the individual panel presentations, the colloquy developed into essentially three major points:
1. The meaning, limits, and possibilities of the Lortzian orientation.
2. The question of the "Catholic" and "uncatholic" or the "heretical" in Luther as the question of the "essence" of the truth.
3. The search for a biblical-theological "category" by which Luther's ecumenical significance can be most adequately characterized and "disclosed."

The meaning, limits, and possibilities of the Lortzian orientation

The conviction was confirmed that the work of J. Lortz, including the later minor writings which ought not be overlooked, continues to be important. This may be maintained first of all with regard to the historical achievement as such, and then with regard to the corresponding position drawn from it which presumably may be that which the Catholic-hierarchical side could be able most easily to receive. Finally this may be maintained also with regard to his contested thesis of the "Catholic Luther," by which Lortz ultimately intends "Catholic" in an ecumenical sense even if on the basis of a "confessional" coloration; "Catholic" as "*Roman* Catholic" does not yet completely preclude this ecumenical sense. In any case the Lortzian orientation is open for an ecumenical awakening, as was shown increasingly by the later Lortz himself. This was described by Manns in his lecture; he noticed a self-critical deepening of the original orientation in Lortz.

Certainly it was also seen and recognized that the Lortzian Luther interpretation possesses a strong biographical stamp and due to this has a certain one-sidedness which, in the opinion of some, allows the question of Luther's "central concern" to be neglected; although on the other hand it is argued that without biographical facts a thorough study of Luther's theology is not possible. From the evangelical side the Lortzian thesis of Luther's "subjectivism," which Lortz held throughout his life, was criticized above all as improper. Luther understood himself expressly as an *exegete of Scripture;* to

Translated by Carter Lindberg

be sure his scriptural exegesis may contain a certain element of experience and is anything but the exegesis of a "cold exegete."

In general there appeared to be progress beyond the method tied to biography and personality which according to some of the participants is largely characteristic of Catholic Luther research in general. This is seen to be one of the most important challenges to Catholic Luther research, especially where it is concerned to deepen or extend with Lortz the Lortzian orientation.

The special question whether Lortz's theme that Luther represents throughout an "exclusive efficacy" of God with its resulting consequences may block a deepening and extension of the Lortzian orientation and may obstruct the way to a further disclosure of Luther's ecumenical significance, or whether it may be given up, was repeatedly addressed. Some held the surrender of this theme to be both necessary and possible; for some Catholics however this continues to be an unresolved problem (P. Bläser).

A particularly important point of the discussion developed the Lortzian distinction between the "Catholic" and the "heretical" (or "uncatholic" or "not fully Catholic") in Luther. The question of the valuation of Nominalism which forms the historical-theological background for this Lortzian distinction was indeed addressed but was not taken up and developed in detail. It was emphasized from the Lutheran side that Luther himself understood his reformatory struggle as a struggle for the "Catholic" and against an "uncatholic" Christendom, and as a struggle within the one, undivided church.

But now how is the Lortzian distinction of "Catholic" and "heretical" (or "uncatholic" or "not completely Catholic") in Luther to be understood? Is it a division of Luther which permits only that in Luther which is acceptable to Catholics to be recognized and taken seriously, but which evades decision on the genuinely and specifically "reformatory"? Is there a concern here for a basically "apologetic" attitude in Lortz which in his case was situationally but not fundamentally determined?

It was emphasized from the position of the Lortz school (Manns) that this distinction by Lortz is not a "division" but rather a dialectically united statement. Lortz's criticism of the heretical Luther does not cancel what Lortz exposes in the criticism of his own Church. It also does not cancel what Lortz adjudges in more positive and more theological valuation to be the essential concerns of Luther. This Lortzian orientation is in light of the question of truth undoubtedly paradoxical. By separating his major theses from their context they can be misinterpreted and lead to misunderstandings. However in the context of the total orientation they are self-correcting. The combination of heretic and reformer is not a contradiction anymore than, analogously, the *simul justus et peccator* is a contradiction.

Another interpretation or mastering of the problem of the "Catholic" and "heretical" (or "uncatholic" or "not fully Catholic") in Luther leads directly to the second major point of the discussion.

The question of the "Catholic" and "uncatholic" or the "heretical" in Luther as the question of the "essence" of the truth

Here lies, as indeed it was rightly said, the *punctum saliens* in the distinction between, on the one hand, Lortz and his school and, on the other hand, the developing Catholic Luther research which is no longer directly following the path indicated by Lortz and which in distinction from the "historical" Luther research of Lortz and his school has been characterized as "systematic" Luther research.

The distinction of "Catholic" and "heretical" (or "uncatholic" or "not fully Catholic") which is complicating the disclosure of Luther's ecumenical significance is approached in the last-named direction of Catholic Luther research by an understanding of truth wherein the "truth" may be encountered only *in* history and *under* its changes. Thus truth is understood basically not as a superhistorically formulatable "constant" which can be held as the standard "next" to the variables of historical expressions (Pesch).

On the basis of this understanding of truth, then, it is obvious that in the course of more recent historical knowledge what was once seen as "uncatholic" and "heretical" will be re-examined and recognized as in reality Catholic or at least as a Catholic possibility. Historical knowledge and the view of *contemporary* Catholic consciousness of faith thus are receiving eminent hermeneutical significance for the interpretation of the past.

As an example, Pesch pointed to the *simul iustus et peccator* which according to him appears to have been condemned at the Council of Trent but *today* can be thoroughly considered as a possible Catholic conception since there is doubt whether the fathers at Trent really understood correctly Luther's thesis.

Such a "change" is, in the context of a "historical" understanding of the truth, also fundamentally conceivable with regard to other controversial theological questions so that the possibilities of ecumenical dialogue and the disclosure of Luther's ecumenical significance basically encounter no limits but may be extended.

A protest was raised to some extent against this conception in the name of a stronger emphasis upon continuity and the constancy of statements oriented to an understanding of the truth ("The truth is always true"—Manns) or by reference to the church's teaching office which says what is "Catholic" without of course being ready at all times with an exhaustive and guiding answer.

Other reports sought to deal with the question of the "heretical" in Luther without entering into the question of the "essence" of the truth and the possibility of "change" from "uncatholic" to "Catholic," attempting in this way to defuse the issue or bring it nearer to a solution. They referred to:

—the distinction between "relative" heresy (the concept of a secondary heresy), such as may exist between confessional churches, and "absolute" heresy in the sense of the denial of the foundation of the faith.

—the fact that, for example, Trent and all the more so the condemnations in the Bull of Excommunication missed Luther, and Trent did not strictly exclude Luther's basic concern.

—All in all, the discussion reflected how, even in the area of Catholic-Lutheran agreement and in the concern for disclosing Luther's ecumenical significance, the question of historically meeting the truth not only is still incomplete but perhaps is not even yet recognized and acknowledged as a possible point of departure and task.

The search for a biblical-theological "category"
by which Luther's ecumenical significance can be
most adequately characterized and "disclosed"

Is there such a category? The following were suggested: "saint," "reformer," "prophet," "teacher of the church." Some (G. Maron, M. Lienhard, D. Olivier) appeared to favor the category of "prophet" insofar as it expresses an important aspect of the activity and work of Luther in and for the entire church. It throws into sharp relief his concern for the divinity of God ("Let God be God!"). Of course it was also questioned (E. Iserloh) whether the "carnal" (*triebhafte*) language of Luther and its de facto disastrous effects could be harmonized with the message of the prophets.

Manns presented the category of "father in the faith" (1 Cor. 4:15) as decisive for the disclosure of Luther's ecumenical significance. He saw in it on the one hand the fulfillment but on the other hand also the continuation and deepening of the Lortzian orientation. It goes beyond Lortz above all in the ecumenical orientation of the interpretation of Luther. Proceeding from the Agape motif as the essential moving force in his theology it may allow the search for the "reformatory" to appear superfluous and at the same time may disclose Luther as an "ecumenical authority." It remains true to the Lortzian orientation in the question of the truth.

LUTHER'S THEOLOGY AND THE FORMATION OF REFORMATION CONFESSIONS

The Importance of Luther's Writings in the Formation of Protestant Confessions of Faith in the Sixteenth Century

GOTTFRIED SEEBASS

In order to study the importance of Luther's theology—even if we consider only its basic tenets—in the formation of Reformation confessions of faith, there is an urgent need for clear delimitations in order to avoid clichés and generalities, at least in an historical approach. In the formation of Reformation confessions of faith we should consider not only the Lutheran confessions, but the totality of the confessions of the Reformation, including those of the English Reformation. Such an investigation would deal with Luther's relationship, both direct and indirect, to the whole confessional tradition of the Protestant Church, and therefore be beyond our scope, yet it would also far exceed the strength of the individual. For the Lutheran aspect to which I will limit myself, there is still a further limitation. Because of the different local church ordinances and Corpora doctrinae, the most widely divergent creeds were in use in the Lutheran camp and neither the Formula of Concord nor the Book of Concord succeeded in uniting the entire Lutheran Church. I will limit myself to the Book of Concord because this work comes commonly to mind when Lutheran Confessions of faith are mentioned.

Our approach to the problem cannot even deal with the Book of Concord in a truly comprehensive manner. To do this we would have to explain the significance of individual creeds in Luther's body of confessions and how they relate to his theology as known from his other writings. In addition we could also ask how other confessions that we know are not from Luther relate to him. To my knowledge this situation does not arise in the Augsburg Confession, only once in the Apology, but more often and more fully in the Formula of Concord. Finally we would have to elucidate in what measure those confessions not written by Luther were influenced directly or indirectly by him. Such an investigation would necessarily end in a global interpretation of the confessional literature from this viewpoint. Wilhelm Maurer undertook the study of the Augsburg Confession using this approach and was soon

Translated by Georges Herzog

confronted with the not totally unjustified criticism that this interpretation through Luther's theology was one-sided and did not do justice to the text. Above all, such an undertaking would soon come to grips with the fundamental difficulty, which is that all that is identified as originating from or influenced by Luther—be it appropriate, vague, interpreted, or divergent—would have to be defined as a possibly problematic choice, or as a different interpretation of his theology. This last consideration makes it wise, for the little time at our disposition, to undertake only a general review of the origin of the Book of Concord.

To begin with, we must say a few words about the three creeds of the ancient church. Otto Ritschl has proposed that their inclusion in Lutheran Church discipline and Corpora doctrinae can be traced in great part to Melanchthonian Traditionalism and permeates this body of doctrines influenced by him. Concurrently, the rigidly applied principle of Scripture is the result of the Gnesio-Lutheran tradition. I am, however, dubious that these observations, in theory quite correct, are practically justified, and I fear that they attribute to Melanchthon what could convincingly be attributed to Luther himself. In this conjuncture we have to point out that there is no mention of any tradition to justify the acceptance of these three creeds of the ancient church, but we observe that they were used in the church services and were a living presence: the Apostles' Creed mainly in baptism, the Nicene Creed in the service, and in many regions, the Athanasian Creed on Sundays. Above all I find it significant that Luther always started from church tradition when he consciously wanted to express his faith in a festive manner. He would then not start from the heart of his own reforming point of departure, through which he can find himself in the anthropological and systematic scheme of faith (concerning the Word in the Law and the gospel) and love (manifested in caring for one's neighbors and patience in carrying the cross). This attitude is attested in his Confession of 1528 as well as in the Schmalkald Articles in which he actually referred directly to the Athanasian Creed. This use of the ancient creeds is comparable to his instinctive use, in his catechisms, of the catechetical tradition of the Western church which he then composed and structured around God's trinitarian process of salvation. Indeed it must be said that Luther was not interested in having his own creed, but in accepting faithfully the confession of the whole church. This comprehensive character of his acceptance is in my opinion still expressed clearly even in the stereotyped *credimus, docemus et confitemur* of the Formula of Concord. This problem will have to be dealt with at a later place. Suffice it now to conclude that the presence of the ancient creeds in the Formula of Concord is perfectly justified and logical. Above all Luther's characteristic approach to the creeds of the early church reflects his attitude to them. Indeed the Formula of Concord professed to belong "to the three universal creeds, . . . as well as to the small, Christian confessions of faith founded on the Word of God." People, and among them Luther, were convinced that these creeds of the early church could pass "the only, unique and true rule and judgment" of the Holy Scripture's Old and New Testaments. In avoiding the debate of Traditionalism and Antitraditionalism we realize that the acceptance by Luther of these three early creeds adequately conforms to his theology.

After our brief observations on the early church creeds we can turn to the Augsburg Confession. Luther's critical comments on this work are well known and do not need to be repeated here in detail. Luther's recognition of its "pussy-footing" character is first a criticism of himself and is not totally negative. Luther regretted above all the absence of any clear rejection of the received teaching of purgatory, of the cult of the Saints and felt the lack of a description of the antichristian character of the papacy. He was not ready to take into consideration whether one could go beyond the Augsburg Confession to counter the adversaries belonging to the old faith. It is hardly necessary to demonstrate that he did not try to distance himself in these epistolary comments, and even B. Lohse's judgment that there is "a certain ambivalence in Luther's position toward the Augsburg Confession" appears to me now as too extreme. We should not overlook the fact that the Augsburg Confession grew rapidly to become one of the fundamental confessional writings, and this with Luther's knowledge. This is also true for the political significance that was attached to this confession soon after the Diet of Augsburg. Luther, who had already set unanimity on confession of faith as a condition of an alliance among Protestants, allowed the Augsburg Confession to become the foundation of the Schmalkald League. The same is also true for the ecclesial significance that was given to the confession in the following years. Because of Ritschl's critical doubts we cannot resolve whether it was still during Luther's life that the Wittenberg doctoral oath was instituted. Through it, the new doctors had to swear allegiance to the teachings contained in the symbols of the ancient church and the Augsburg Confession. There is no doubt that Luther could not have ignored that since the mid-thirties the Confession was taken in a series of church ordinances as a guide in ecclesial teaching and even sometimes as their norm. Nor did Luther protest when the Augsburg Confession was taken, in a version admittedly directed against the partisans of the old faith, as the basis for religious debates. From all this we can draw the conclusion that Luther considered the Augsburg Confession as a valuable synthesis of religious teachings. This confirms indirectly what Luther wrote about the Augsburg Confession in his letter of July 6, 1530 in reference to Ps. 119:46 and Matt. 10:32.

This can only be understood with due consideration of the preparatory stages to the confession. We must here draw attention to the fact that we know much less about these stages than the more recent histories let us suppose. This is particularly the case when we come to investigate Luther's participation in the Augsburg Confession. Little has been said about it in conjunction with the fact that Luther had no direct influence over the formulation of the Confession during the Diet. In reality we cannot find the desired clarity of Luther's participation in the preparatory stages. This is true for the Torgau Articles that are the basis for the second part of the Confessio Augustana. It is still unclear today what was Luther's influence in the preparation of an Apology for the Diet of Augsburg. We are not better informed about the formation of the Schwabach Articles that in essence are the source for the first part of the Confession. Even if they were arranged and put on paper by Melanchthon, they clearly have their source in Luther's 1528 Confesssion of Faith. They are dependent, because of this, on Luther's first complete anti-anabaptist confession. It must be said that Maurer's precise analysis of the Schwabach Articles came to the certainly correct conclusion that they are, to some extent, "a compromise between Luther and Melanchthon." Yet Luther had recognized them and used them as a foundation of the Marburg articles which were in turn used again by Melanchthon for the first part of the Confession of Augsburg.

In these circumstances I am entitled to ask if we can justify historically or factually the exposition and interpretation of the Augsburg Confession in such a manner as to make it seem a witness of Melanchthon's own theology as opposed by Luther. There is no doubt that it can and must be so read in order to notice the possible origin of faulty developments in the realm of Protestant theology. The understanding of the Confession is facilitated when in its first article dealing with the *decretum* of the Council of Nicea, we find a position that is possibly slightly different from Luther's own. We have to realize that Melanchthon has broken up Luther's trinitarian concentration of the confession by presenting his statement on the Creation and Fall more strongly in terms of God's reaching to the sinner through Christ. As a result he no longer develops the idea of God from the Father first, nor the depth of the misery of sin from the redemption in Christ. We shall not overlook the fact that Melanchthon, by placing Luther's view on praising God in the independent articles, introduced an anthropologically oriented scheme of justification and renewal that, because man is implanted in Christ, no longer unites in the same manner as in Luther Christ *pro nobis* with Christ *in nobis*. The result is a slightly one-sided coloration of the concept of faith and a corresponding accentuation of the resulting good works, by which both fail to appear clearly, as in Luther, as works of the Holy Spirit. It cannot be overlooked that Luther—particularly in his Catechism—proceeds clearly from the indivisible unity of the inner and outer, while Melanchthon prefers to describe in the Schwabach Articles and the Augsburg Confession a juxtaposition of visible acts and the hearing Word. Thereby Melanchthon allows for a spiritualization that cannot fully integrate a positive earthly element.

It remains to discover which conclusion to draw, not only because of the following process of equalization, but mainly because of the later increasingly Melanchthonian reception and understanding of the Augsburg Confession. In any case, the Augsburg Confession did not intend to express Melanchthon's theology, but the unity of the churches in the regions of the signatories. Melanchthon's influence is attested to by history because there was later a Lutheran movement to oppose the increasingly Melanchthonian interpretation of the Augsburg Confession by preferring the Invariata and adding to it the works of Luther as the source of their interpretation. According to the Formula of Concord, it is Luther who exposed again the truth of God's Word. And "this same teaching" was "drawn from and conformed to the Word of God, is summarized in the articles and chapters of the Augsburg Confession against the aberrations of the papacy and of other sects."[1] Luther appears as the one "who understood the true and real meaning of the Augsburg Confession better than anyone else, remained by it steadfastly and defended it constantly until he died."[2] Therefore we cannot better perceive "the true meaning and understanding of the Augsburg Confession from any other source than from Doctor Luther's doctrinal and polemical writings."[3]

Even if the Augsburg Confession was conceived as a justificatory document for the new ecclesial orders already in place and as a proof of the consensus on true Christian doctrine in preparation for a possible confrontation on the question of religion, we have to recognize that its first part was clearly dependent on Luther's 1528 Confession of Faith, a polemical writing against his theological adversaries. We find the same motif in the Schmalkald Articles that Luther wrote to answer the pope's announcement of a council. They originated from a request of the Elector of Saxony to know which teaching about the last judgment Luther would defend, what could be conceded to the adversaries, and who wished to see an elaboration of the Augsburg Confession in regard to the papacy. This idea of a completion of the Augsburg Confession is already expressed at the beginning of the Schmalkald Articles. The preceding history explains the festive testamentarian character of the later preface as well as the order of the articles. Quite characteristically, Luther started again—and he referred directly to the 1528 Confession of Faith—with the trinitarian recognition of the "high articles in the divine majesty" but developed the second and the third articles only in subsequent parts. In the center we find the second part that deals with the mission and work of Christ, with our salvation, and expresses forcefully the concepts of *solus Christus* and *sola fide*. Even more clearly than in the second part of the Augsburg Confession, Luther linked to these a strong attack on all the elements of the traditional church that seemed to contradict or darken them: the Mass with its dragontail of purgatory, vigils, pilgrimages, fraternities, cult of relics, and indulgences. Luther also included here the rejection of monastic orders and the papacy. It is only with the third part that we witness the actual development of Reformation teachings, with explanations about grace and the church. Luther was ready to "discuss" the subjects with "learned and reasonable people" as well as with members of his own camp. But, as the conclusion of the Schmalkald Articles shows clearly, Luther did not have in mind a negotiable compromise. Luther had created a precisely defined confession. The extent of the change in his attitude can be seen in the later preface where he said that "we do not ask for a council for our own sake."[4] Yet it would be wrong to conclude that Luther wanted to destroy any attempt to have a council. He did not agree with the rejection of a council adopted by the Schmalkald League and declined his support to the anti-council proposed by John Frederick. He wanted to have a clear confession of faith only because of the coming of Christ. Originally, John Frederick wanted the Schmalkald Articles, already the statement of faith of the Saxon clergy, to be accepted by all and become also the confession of all Protestants. He even thought of having the articles be the basis for an anti-council. What made him change his mind is no longer clear. It seems, however, that Melanchthon stalled an official recognition of the Articles out of concern for the Concordat of Wittenberg he had just signed with the south Germans. As a result the majority of the attending theologians signed only for themselves. Yet John Frederick insisted later that the Articles had been accepted officially by the theologians and the princes of the Schmalkald League. The extent of his admiration for them can be deduced from his order that every minister accept them at the time of his ordination, and from his exhortation in his will that his sons remain faithful to the Augsburg Confession and the Articles. They only gained broader meaning in the post-Lutheran conflicts. In spite of John Frederick's belief that the conflict could not have happened if all had adhered to the Schmalkald Articles, these articles were not only used against any compromise in the question of the Interim and the Adiaphora, but also against the Philippists. The Formula of Concord integrated the tradition of the Central- and North-German Lutheran Corpora doctrinae when it interpreted the Schmalkald Articles as a broader repetition of the Augsburg Confession and "in addition the grounds and reasons are set forth at necessary length for renouncing the papistic errors and idolatries, for having no communion with the papists."[5] Taken in this sense, the articles were not contested by the Philippists.

Luther's greatest contribution to the formation of Protestant confessions of faith and to the Book of Concord is undoubtedly to be found in his catechisms. In this catechetical emphasis we grasp Luther's basic motive in the formation of confessions. In order to expose in a catechetical manner the facts that are necessary to the life and death of the Christian, Luther had striven since 1516 to give in his sermons short expositions that were first published together in 1520 as the "Short Form." In our context, it is impossible to mention the richness of Albrecht Peters's discoveries in his penetrating study of Luther's catechisms. The core of the western tradition of catechisms already leads Luther back to the trinitarian God: the commandments are dependent on the Father, prayer (and later the sacraments) on the Son, but confession of faith on the Spirit who guides the church. The content of the different parts has a trinitarian emphasis when he combines the first article to the Decalogue as the development of the received goodness of the creator with the thankful obedience of the children of God. The second article develops as the center and then in the third article, the sacraments and the Lord's Prayer are taken together as the work of God's Spirit. Only in Christ do we recognize God's heart, only the Spirit unites us with the Son and gives access to the Father. Accordingly, the Decalogue shows what humankind should do or avoid, the confession of faith where humankind can seek and find it, prayer how to seek and get it. We come to faith through the Holy Spirit we invoke, and the law is transformed into a helpful commandment. Peters perceived the contribution of the catechisms to the Lutheran confessions as threefold: the development of the story of the Creation, a story absent in other creeds, guards it as a whole from a narrowing to the soteriological perspective. The inclusion of prayer in the confession demonstrates that the truth of the creed can only be preserved through prayer, through which one participates in God's battle against the devil, the world, and one's flesh. In orthodoxy and orthopraxy, the confessions comprise what is salutary for life and death.

The catechisms, and particularly the Small Catechism, prevailed in the churches of the Lutheran reformation and formed a basic consensus extending far beyond the limits of the territorial churches, long before they were included in the Corpora doctrinae and finally in the Formula of Concord. From then on it was natural that the catechisms appeared everywhere where the Corpora doctrinae indicates a Lutheran reception of the Augsburg Confession and of other works by Melanchthon. The catechism is present in the Formula of Concord in a manner quite different from the other confessions. Luther had already called it a "lay bible." The Formula of Concord brought this idea a step further: "They formulated Christian doctrine on the basis of God's Word for ordinary laymen in a most correct and simple, yet sufficiently explicit, form" in the catechisms. Therefore they can and should help the lay people to differentiate "between true and false doctrine."[6] In opposition to all other creeds, there are in the catechisms elementary and fundamental tenets of faith for everyone. The confession of faith achieves in the catechisms its broadest function when it is used as Luther advocates in his "Introduction to Prayer" for Master Peter the barber; it should be an introduction to learning, thanking, confessing, and praying. Because of this, the catechisms deserve a special place among the confessions of faith.

In this last segment we will try to demonstrate that there was in the Formula of Concord a conscious effort to have a global interpretation of the Confession of Augsburg that would both relate it to Luther and make him be accepted through it. This happened in two ways:

First, all of Melanchthon's confessional writings (the Augsburg Confession and its Apology—the tractatus was already integrated strongly to the Schmalkald Articles as an appendix) were integrated to Luther's confessional works. In doing this the Formula of Concord followed the example of those North- and Central-German theologies that had tried to stop the Melanchthonization of the confessional tradition. The choice of the Lutheran writings was justified with the argument that they all dated from before the controversies that the Formula of Concord tried to resolve and that they were recognized by all sides.[7] But we have to recognize that those writings were selected in which Luther reinterpreted the confessional and catechetic tradition of the church. The choice thus decided was not only historic but was, in a deeper sense, also substantively motivated. It is fully justified from Luther's point of view that the content of these writings is, for the Formula of Concord, "as the sum and the pattern of the doctrine which Doctor Luther of blessed memory clearly set forth in his writings on the basis of God's Word and conclusively established against the papacy and other sects."[8]

But here we touch already on the second element. The Formula of Concord did not draw only from this ensemble of Luther's writings, but referred also to these "more explicit explanations contained in his doctrinal and polemic writings." The Formula of Concord makes ample use of these writings. Although the favorite references are to the Small and Large Catechisms as well as to the Schmalkald Articles, many other works are cited, and in particular one of 1528: "Confession Concerning Christ's Supper." The references to these works are quite general, as is the one in the third article to "the beautiful and splendid exposition of Doctor Luther on St. Paul's Epistle to the Galatians," and in the seventh article different anti-Anabaptist writings are proposed for further investigation by their titles only, "for the sake of desirable brevity."[9]

The question of Luther's inclusion in the Formula of Concord has been answered differently whenever and wherever it was raised. To this end we can prevent examples of the preceding century (I will mention only Heppe and Albrecht Ritschl) as well as from our times. Minute analysis of the individual articles (Lohse, Haegglund) have lately again shown that, from Luther's point of view, "abridgement" and "biases" cannot be avoided. No one can deny that Luther had treated the problems found in the Formula of

Concord with more ideas and depth than its authors. Despite such judgment, consideration of the differences between the time and conditions of Luther and the Formula of Concord leads to the question whether Luther's intentions were not consistently and correctly preserved, so that one could speak of a consensus on the fundamental points (Baur, Lohff). Such an opinion only becomes possible if we follow a prudent interpretation of the articles that also integrates the goals of the Formula of Concord and proceeds through its definitions to the central points. We cannot undertake such an investigation here. However we can indicate the directions of such an interpretation. The intention to praise God and to underline the good works of the Lord Christ pervades the Formula of Concord like a *cantus firmus*. God's glory must be to Christ's benefit. Christ's good works shall not be obscured.[10]

We should not overlook the constant pastoral concern found in the articles of the Formula of Concord. Free will should not be taught in such a manner that the people become lazy nor that they are led to questions and doubts. Consolation should be brought to tormented and troubled souls, reliance and confidence in one's good works should be opposed. The teaching of predestination should not further a sense of security or of unnecessariness of repentance, nor should it provoke pettiness and depression.[11] Let us not forget that the Formula of Concord wanted to divert the attention of people from themselves and their particular theological developments to the preached Gospel. Its goal is to expose the absolute and undoubted reliability and validity of the means of grace, and to make it clear that its effect is not dependent on any condition. Finally, we have to observe that the Holy Scripture is continually referred to as the revelation of the truth in which we believe, and that its Word is placed before and above any theological reflection. The article on the Lord's Supper would demonstrate this point particularly well.

This brings us to the last point still to be dealt with. It could seem that the Formula of Concord had elevated Luther and his writings to the canon of the confessions of faith. This, however, did not happen. The formula intended to accept Luther only "in wisdom and measure, as Doctor Luther . . . expressly asserts by way of distinction that the Word of God is and remains the sole rule and norm of all doctrine, and that no one's writings dare to be put on a par with it, but that everything must be subjected to it."[12] Luther's writings are indirectly subordinated to confessional writings, and these themselves are considered the key to Scripture and the guide to its use.

NOTES

1. *BC* 504; *BSLK* 834f.
2. *BC* 575; *BSLK* 982.
3. *BC* 576; *BSLK* 984.

4. *BC* 209; *BSLK* 411.
5. *BC* 505; *BSLK* 836.
6. Ibid.
7. *BC* 506; *BSLK* 838f.
8. *BC* 505; *BSLK* 836f.
9. *BC* 551, 586; *BSLK* 936, 1005.
10. *BC* 509, 544, 563, 631; *BSLK* 846, 924, 961, 1088.
11. *BC* 530, 554f., 613, 617f., 631f.; *BSLK* 890, 945, 1059, 1066, 1089.
12. *BC* 505; *BSLK* 837.

Luther's Theology in Its Significance for Church Confession

WENZEL LOHFF

The question of the significance of Luther's theology for church confession is first of all an historical one: the question of the significance of an historically powerful teacher of theology for the historical explanation of normative church doctrine. The first points of reference are those of Luther's writings which have been included in the collection of Lutheran confessional writings (the Schmalkald Articles and catechisms), and also the reference that these confessions make to Luther. However that is the theme of the first lecture in this subject area. The answer to the general question of Luther's significance for church confession would indeed require a complete interpretation of the history of dogma. Our aim must be more modest. Within the perspective of "Lutheran theology" we shall raise the question of the significance of Luther's basic theological decisions for the form and binding nature of normative Christian proclamation of faith. Thus there are three areas:

1. The question of how Luther himself made doctrinal decisions and how he therefore participated in the formation of normative, dogmatic tradition.

2. This leads immediately to the question of the significance in general of the dogmatic tradition of the church for Luther's theology.

3. The unique significance of Luther's writings for the evangelical church continually raises the questions: How does Luther's theology relate to the church confession of the Reformation? What is the significance of both of these for evangelical proclamation of faith?

HOW DOES LUTHER HIMSELF PROCLAIM DOCTRINE?

Luther's theological work signifies the beginning of a new, creative period in the formation of normative tradition, which in extent and variety can at least be compared to the formation of dogma in the ancient church. This is not just a question of the explanation of existing classical doctrine, but of a return to the rudiments of Christian proclamation, of a concentration and creative reformulation. In this connection the term "confession" gains a particular stress. The concept of *confessio* contains not only the explanation of correct theological decisions of doctrine but also the living relation of clear

Translated by Patricia M. Williams

witness for the salvation-event and devotion of faith even as far as martyrdom. The whole being of the believer is "confession"[1] (*tota nostra operacio confessio*).

1. Thus a link is made with the vitality and diversity of early Christian formation of confession. If Luther's dogmatic teaching often takes the form of a polemical dispute, the testimony to elementary certainty of faith came first. Thus the doxological motif of the formation of confession is evident in many places, above all in the great hymns ("Nun freut euch lieben Christengemein") and also in the catechisms (especially in the second part), and even in the polemical confession of doctrine there are echoes of this (the Schmalkald Articles, the end of the Preface).

2. The realization of the Reformation in the congregations necessitates then a simplification of the fundamental certainty of faith so as "to condense the meaning of Scripture, comprised of so many passages, into a short and comprehensive word."[2] It actualizes the basic catechetical motif of the confession. Above all, Luther's Small Catechism has been received for centuries as the authoritative crystalization of the certainty of faith.

3. The acquired and acknowledged certainty of faith experiences insurmountable barriers to its reception and indeed, in the destruction of the basic normative tradition of faith by the Enthusiastic movements, subsequently calls forth priority to the polemical and anti-heretical motif of confession and leads to the fact that in the variety of fundamental utterances the main accent is on decisive and distinguishing doctrine. The great summary of confession which Luther presents in the third part of his work "Confession Concerning Christ's Supper"[3] is significant for this and also the fact that he refers back to it in the Schmalkald Articles.[4]

Luther experiences the situation where confession is demanded, as a struggle of certainty of faith against unbelief and heresy, seen again in the apocalyptical perspective of the confrontation with Satan. He must confess his faith because he sees "that schisms and errors are increasing proportionately with the passage of time and there is no end to the rage and fury of Satan" and wants to prevent "any persons during my lifetime or after my death [to] appeal to me or misuse my writings to confirm their error."[5] Confession as defense against heresy has an eschatological dimension. Although its first aim is to witness to the clear certainty of faith against all falsification, at the same time it keeps God's last judgment in view. "I am determined to abide by it until my death and (so help me God!) in this faith to depart from this world and to appear before the judgment seat of our Lord Jesus Christ."[6] These statements gain weight from the central content of the confession of faith: the certainty of salvation arising from justification for Christ's sake through faith. The decisive section of the Schmalkald Articles deals "with the articles concerning the ministry and work of Jesus Christ and our redemption," and brings together fundamental scriptural statements thus: "Inasmuch as this must be believed and cannot be obtained or apprehended by any work, law or merit, it is clear and certain that such faith alone justifies us."[7] Here the center and origin of correct doctrine lie before us. At the same time the motif of Lutheran insistence on "correct doctrine" becomes clear. This is only conceivable in the inseparable relation of justifying faith with normative doctrine which protects its foundation and expression.

4. The central significance of justification as the "means and limit of reformation theology" (E. Wolf) based in Luther's reformatory insight renders possible a graduated importance of normative doctrine, which remains of continuing importance for the formation of consensus in confession. In order to understand this it is necessary to look away from the concrete circumstances which shaped the Schmalkald Articles, as well as from the fact that the concept of normative teaching having degrees of weight was without prospect even within the realm of Lutheranism during the era of growing confessionalism.

In the three sections of the Schmalkald Articles, which are indeed each of greatly differing importance, Luther distinguishes between three different kinds of articles of faith. First come the "high articles of divine majesty," that is, the essence of the ancient church dogmas of the trinity and of christology. The fact that they are "in no quarrel or dispute" is not only a statement based on fact but also the unconditional prerequisite for all further doctrine. For they form at the same time the basis of justifying faith—they constitute correct faith and confession as is shown in the formulation "for both parties (believe in and) confess them."[8] Out of mistrust of the opponents, "belief" was deleted from the original version.

These articles are of course only correctly used in justifying faith. The second section deals with the presentation of the faith which justifies and its use in the service of God and in the structure of the church. An interpretation of the polemic which follows this would of course have to keep to the hermeneutical principle formulated by Luther himself: "This means that the Word of God shall establish articles of faith and no one else, not even an angel."[9]

The rest of the articles in which normative doctrine is discussed form the "third section." Of these Luther says: "The following articles treat matters which we may discuss with learned and sensible men, or even among ourselves,"[10] thus they are open to discussion, subject to the given criteria of reason enlightened by faith. This immediately brings up the question of how, on the basis of a foregoing agreement on fundamental issues, controversial questions of normative church doctrine can be dealt with in the future. That Luther did not only hypothetically accept this possibility is seen in his Preface to the account of faith by the Czechoslovakian brothers.[11] The reception of the dogmatic tradition of the church was also possible within this framework and occurred in new dogmatic summaries of orthodoxy, even if interconfessional discourse within the scope of the legal significance of the territorial state of confession was effectively brought to a standstill.

In the text of confessions, agreed upon in such a manner, the original, reformational conception of confession was maintained—somewhat classical in the exposition of the Apology concerning the significance of confession for the life of faith in the world: "Because of faith they are nevertheless holy and divine works, sacrifices, and the reign of Christ, whereby he shows his rule before the world. For in these works he sanctifies hearts and suppresses the devil. And in order to keep the Gospel among men, he visibly pits the confession of the saints against the rule of the devil; in our weakness he displays his strength."[12]

THE SIGNIFICANCE OF DOGMATIC TRADITION FOR LUTHER'S THEOLOGY

The significance of dogmatic church tradition for Luther's theology has already fundamentally been shown above.

1. First, for Luther it is a matter of a clearly formulated witness of faith. In spite of the fundamental significance of personal certainty for justifying faith, such faith can only be based in that which has preceded it: Christ's gospel. It is an all-encompassing power which grants certainty. It was thus that Luther spoke out above all against the historical scepticism of Erasmus. A Christian must be able to make certain statements about faith or he is no Christian. "For it is not the mark of a Christian mind to take no delight in assertions, on the contrary, a man must delight in assertions or he will be no Christian."[13]

2. This certainty, however, is gained from Holy Scripture, which in its external clarity (in service of the Word) is able to establish inner clarity (in acknowledgment of the heart)[14] in that it witnesses to God as the Trinity and to Christ as the one who suffers and rules for us. The immediate power of the truth of the gospel declares itself in the presence of the Spirit: *Spiritus Sanctus non est scepticus!* Thus faith can rejoice in assertions and, in contrast to Erasmus, can freely be about Christ and his dogmas.[15] Correspondingly in his "confession" in the treatise on the Lord's Supper in 1528 Luther wants "to confess [his] faith before God and all the world, point by point" as "taught us in the Scripture," beginning with the high articles of divine majesty concerning christology and the doctrine of justification through to the doctrine of the church.[16]

3. Thus the reference to the Gospel and Scripture provides a material principle for the establishment and examination of the doctrine of faith. This is necessary because of the obvious possibility of false doctrine, even within the Reformation itself: "By the grace of God I have learned to know a great deal about Satan. If he can twist and pervert the Word of God and the

Scriptures, what will he not be able to do with my or someone else's words?"[17] Thus even church doctrine is subject to the criterion that it be adequate testimony to the fundamental proclamation of the gospel. Luther's well-known criticism—above all in the doctrine concerning the church and the sacraments, which is then accepted into the Lutheran confessional writings—has its starting point here.

Dogmatic teaching is thus to a certain extent relativized through reference to the gospel of the Scripture: its value is a function of its relationship to proclamation according to Scripture. However dogma is also stabilized through this procedure. Luther leaves no doubt as to the certainty of dogmatic teaching acquired in this way. The fact that the examination of doctrine through Scripture is transferred to the insight of the interpretation and the fact that a Christian community has the right to judge doctrine[18] do not cause Luther any uncertainty; on the contrary, the trust in the power of the truth of the gospel is expressed here with an overwhelming certainty, in a trust in the cleansing power of the fundamental proclamation against all falsification. If the discovery of truth becomes thus an open process of interpretation, then the certainty gained will remain powerful in the future and will not be forfeited to historical relativity. "Hence, if any one shall say after my death 'If Luther were living now, he would teach and hold this or that article differently, for he did not consider it sufficiently' etc., let me say once and for all that by the grace of God I have most diligently traced all these articles through the Scriptures, have examined them again and again in the light thereof, and have wanted to defend all of them as certainly as I have now defended the sacrament of the altar. I am not drunk or irresponsible. I know what I am saying and well realize what this will mean for me before the Last Judgment at the coming of the Lord Jesus Christ."[19] The certainty of correct doctrine is valid for all ages to come, as was later stated in the Confessions. Again, this permanent validity is not withdrawn from history as it were, but rather the explanation of the articles of faith makes the development of a dogma completely possible, even necessary when a clarification and decision are required concerning questions of faith. Thus Luther himself in his writings on the Lord's Supper further developed the christology of the old church (the doctrine of the *communicatio idiomatum*) in the interest of the true presence of Christ in the Lord's Supper, and this was then accepted into the Formula of Concord in a modified form.[20]

4. From this it is possible to understand Luther's differentiated attitude to the proclamation of doctrine by the councils. When it is a question of preservation of the gospel, a council can not just autonomously, on the strength of some strange authority, establish a doctrine of faith in the way the "world" thinks: "What a council decides is an article of faith."[21] Doctrinal decisions serve as defence against aberrations of the Gospel. Thus councils may not proclaim new articles of faith, their articles serve much rather for

confirmation of "ancient" doctrine and Luther criticizes the doctrine of the councils where he sees that this criterion has not been observed. "All the other councils too must be viewed in this way; be they large or small. Even though there were many thousands of them, they do not introduce anything new either in matters of faith or good works; but they defend, as the highest judges and greatest bishops under Christ, the ancient faith and the ancient good works in conformity with Scripture."[22] In this sense the doctrinal proclamations of the first four councils of the ancient church (Nicea and Constantinople, Ephesus and Chalcedon) are understood as the "main councils."

Where it is a question of the preservation of the gospel, on the other hand, the council may go beyond the language of Scripture; it does not have to interpret the Scripture in a biblicist way: "But that one should not use more or other words than those contained in Scripture—this cannot be adhered to, especially in controversy and when heretics want to falsify things with trickery and distort the words of Scripture. It thus becomes necessary to condense the meaning of Scripture, comprised of so many passages, in a short and comprehensive word, and to ask whether they regarded Christ as *homoousios*, which was the meaning of all the words of Scripture.[23] The authority of such decisions is based on trust in the power of the Holy Spirit, which embraces and carries the development of doctrine from Scripture. "Thus the Council of Nicaea (as was said) did not invent this doctrine or establish it as something new, namely, that Christ is God; rather it was done by the Holy Spirit, who came openly from heaven to the Apostles on the day of Pentecost and through Scripture, glorified God, as he had promised the apostles."[24] Thus Orthodoxy also develops its conviction as to the inspiration of the confessions in this direction.[25]

5. The gospel itself establishes continuity and development of church doctrine. Affirmation and critical examination of council decisions in this way contain the beginnings of an hermeneutic of dogma which allows as interpretation, even without the means of historical criticism, the preservation of the original truth of faith in the face of the challenge of new situations. As a criterion of correct doctrine this has entered into the confessional books themselves in the "Epitome" of the Formula of Concord. Accordingly, Scripture alone contains the "authority of a judge"; the "symbols and related writings are not a judge as is the Holy Scripture, but are only a witness and explanation of faith setting forth how at various times the Holy Scriptures were understood in the church of God by contemporaries with reference to controverted articles."[26] In this perspective confession appears as the agreement on correct doctrine, based in the defence against heresy. Analogously the Augsburg Confession is then *nostri temporis symbolum*.[27] The additional reference to Luther's writings,[28] however, makes it clear that the explanation of church doctrine beyond the symbolic forms occurs with graduated author-

ity. The era of Orthodoxy, for reasons of the confessional situation already mentioned, already leveled out these differentiations. Yet the awareness of this gradation remained in the effort (though in the end futile) to maintain the distinction between fundamental and non-fundamental articles of faith. The development of comprehensive scriptural proof for dogmatic decisions of the ancient church also belongs to the original achievements of the theological Summae of Orthodoxy (above all that of Johann Gerhard).

THE RELATION OF LUTHER'S THEOLOGY TO CHURCH CONFESSION

The third question of our theme refers once again to the particular significance of Luther's writings for the doctrinal tradition of the evangelical church. This tradition also establishes a special position for Luther's theology vis-à-vis the confessions of the ancient church and of the Reformation period. This is seen not so much in the content of the traditions as in a specific treatment of authoritative church doctrines, or more closely, in a specific freedom of treatment of them, which is established through the unique authority of the gospel which awakens faith. Globally one can say: pre-Reformation theology is carried out by trust in the authority of ecclesial proclamation of doctrine insofar as this is exercised by those of the magisterium who stand in apostolic succession. Integration and incorporation into this tradition establish certainty, which is understood as the certainty of guidance by the Spirit in historical continuity.

Luther himself started from this interpretation. Indeed, the reactions called forth by his theological questioning, the hardening of positions, and the conflict in which the Reformation finally became established made questionable for him and for Reformation doctrine whether the church could guarantee correct proclamation of doctrine in its ministries and councils under all circumstances. In this sense the Reformation signified above all a fundamental crisis of trust with regard to ecclesial proclamation of doctrine and at the same time a different evaluation of the confessions. Over against this the gospel of Scripture is now the example against which all church doctrine is to be measured and oriented and which is set above all proclamation of doctrine. The particular Lutheran duality of "Scripture and confession" as *norma normans* and *norma normata* has its origin here. Reformation proclamation of doctrine is carried in the trust in the direct power of the truth of the gospel, which is repeatedly heard in church proclamation. This trust is won through a new interpretation of Scripture in which one is certain of understanding the gospel clearly. Luther is the great, authoritative interpreter of Scripture, through whom this certainty is made accessible and proves itself. Luther did not understand himself as a reformer or claim the authority of a church teacher. Rather he wanted to be heard as a doctor of the Holy Scripture, as an interpreter of the gospel. Formulated confessions wish to maintain the insight of the gospel only in the face of specific situations and challenges, therefore vis-à-vis the gospel they have a subordinate, preserving function, and therefore the interpreter of the Scripture vis-à-vis them is of course not independent but in a certain sense free. For he is responsible to the whole, positive fullness of the gospel which the confessions want only to protect defensively and only in certain controversies. Thus Luther attempted to make this clear with the example of Augustine: "Perhaps you might say here 'What do you finally want to make of the councils if you clip them so close? At any rate a pastor, indeed a schoolteacher (to say nothing of parents), would have greater power over his pupils than a council has over the church.' I answer; Do you think then that the offices of the pastor and the school teacher are so low that they cannot be compared with the councils? . . . For I can easily prove that the poor insignificant pastor at Hippo, St. Augustine, taught more than all the councils. . . ."[29] The existential fullness of faith surpasses the proclamation of doctrine which draws boundaries.

What does this new assessment of Luther's evaluation as regards church confession signify? Basically it is possible for the free interpretation of the gospel of Scripture and the limiting protection against doctrinal error to stand together in a fruitful relation. This of course requires that the tension between both, between openness and delimitation, should be endured. If this is not the case, however, this can lead to polar positions being taken. This was in fact the case in the history of Protestantism.

Luther and confession in conjunction: The confessional era

The doctrinal controversies of the developing confessional era called forth, religiously and politically, the need for a confessional stance which was as clearly fixed as possible. The function of confessional doctrine was thus fundamentally changed. The confessions are brought together in the Corpora doctrinae, the most important of which has become the Book of Concord. They aim to present, as comprehensively as possible, the "valid" doctrine—and where symbolic doctrinal tradition is not enough, dogmatic theologians step in as interpreters and commentators on the authoritative state of doctrine. Thus Hutter's *Compendium locorum theologicorum* of 1624, one of the most important texts of dogma of the seventeenth century, is first of all a systematic presentation of doctrinal statements of the confessional writings, supplemented by other authorities. In this context Luther himself now becomes a church doctor (even to the extent of speaking about the "prophetic ministry of Doctor Martin Luther"). Indeed the basic insights of his theology have been maintained in confession and dogma: the significance of the gospel for doctrine, the significance of justification for the foundation and form of Christian life. But they are gathered from the existential dialectic of hearing, believing, and confessing (which is echoed in FC XI). They become authoritative church doctrines, which the believer can in principle check against the Scripture, but which in reality is not allowed. They can thus no longer be transmitted beyond the limits of the confessional period. And that a conflict between Luther and the revived doctrinal traditions of the church (to be sure, of a particular church)—for example, in the view of predestination—should be noticed is not conceivable. Luther's significance for the church's confession is that, as the authoritative doctor of the church, he has restored the truth of the gospel against all falsification, so that the evangelical particular church now presents itself as the one that holds the place of the true church.

Luther and confession in disjunction: Neo-protestantism

The Enlightenment and Neo-protestantism have in many ways criticized the reconstruction of the leadership of authority in the confessional era and have thus understood Luther as the pioneering, if not consistent, representative of the spirit of the new era which was critical of authority. A new and still today influential definition of the relation between Luther and church confession came about under the impact of historical-critical research into church history. Thus the difference between Luther's theology and the appropriation of Luther into the confessions and confessionally oriented orthodox dogma came into the light again. In a characteristic way, A. Ritschl already understood this difference—following the Kantian distinction of theoretical and practical reason—as the difference between religion and metaphysics, of direct religious experience and academic-theoretical (and therefore inadequate) theological shaping of this experience. It was Melanchthon who introduced this idea of the church as a school.[30] This conception found classical formulation in Harnack's famous "Wesen des Christentums" (1900). For him the Reformation signifies: "Religion was here brought back to itself, insofar as the gospel and the corresponding religious experience were the central point and are freed from alien additions." Authoritative church doctrine can, according to Luther, only be an addition which makes religious life unclear. "Protestantism counts on the gospel as being something so simple, so divine, and therefore so truly human, that it can most surely be recognized when it is left entirely free and also that it will produce essentially the same experiences and convictions in individual souls."[31] The formulation of such criteria must of course not only distinguish between Luther and the confession, but also between Luther and Luther himself, between the young and the old Luther (or between the medieval and the modern Luther). "Luther would admit nothing but the gospel, nothing but what frees and binds the consciences of men, what everyone, down to the man-servant and the maid-servant can understand. But then he not only took the old dogmas of the trinity and the two natures as the gospel—he was not in a position to examine them historically—he even created new ones."[32]

This statement is therefore significant because it has become a model for a whole series of interpretations of Luther as the father for a free Christianity, unbound by institutions. Of course the obligatory nature of the gospel as the basis of faith is accepted here. Yet this is found apart from dogmatic tradition (as seen already in Ritschl) in a theory of religious subjectivity. And this changes—perhaps a history of Luther interpretation, similar to the history of A. Schweitzer's research into the life of Jesus, could be written as a mirror of the spiritual ideas reigning at that time. The merit of such an interpretation of Luther would perhaps lie in the new exposition of the existential significance of faith, as presented in Luther's theology, vis-à-vis his purely dogmatic evaluation. And the use of categories of contemporary understanding of the world is of course appropriate when an attempt is being made to make Luther's theology fruitful for contemporary faith. But only with this appropriation of Luther—a confessionally based tendency toward the establishment of exclusive oppositions—is the danger avoided of abandoning Luther's theological significance and the understanding of faith gained through him in a series of sometimes new and unconnected interpretations. Only if Luther's theology is understood in all the freedom and depth of his thought, in its fundamental relation to the proclamation of doctrine by the church, which he himself affirmed, can its significance for church confession in its entirety, also from the ecumenical point of view, be understood. To summarize, we can characterize this relation of Luther's theology to church confession as having a variable influence.

Luther's theology, through its conflict-conditioned criticism of authority, posed with new sharpness the question of the authority of church doctrine from the standpoint of the gospel. He emphasized the significance of the existential movement of faith as opposed to identification with previous doctrinal traditions in a unique way, and established, at least incipiently, a new kind of hermeneutic of dogma.

In his struggle with the reconstruction of faith Luther experienced the human situation in a depth and radicalness which surpasses modern thought in many ways and is valid for today. This reconstruction of faith could not be captured by the insertion of Reformation insights into the traditional doctrine as happened in the confessional books. With Luther we experience a new, free, and plural testimony of the assaults on faith, and the certainty of faith which goes beyond anything which his students could say. Thus it makes good sense if Luther's theology has gained normative significance, alongside the confession, as a school for proclamation of faith valid until the present time, as was desired in the Formula of Concord.[33]

Basically however Luther understood his theology not as an expression of subjective certainty but as service in the proclamation of the church, the correct teaching of which passionately concerned him. Just as the sovereign "freedom of a Christian" finds its fulfillment in the fact that the Christian should be "ready to serve" everyone for the sake of love,[34] so the desire for true community of faith is the fundamental expression of the certainty of this faith. Herein lies the positive reference to the Councils and the confessions. This however calls for a judgment of Luther's own theology from the view point of its "ecclesial communicability," as intended in the confessions of the Reformation. This applies particularly to the hardness and the polemics of many passages arising from the conflict-ridden situation. Luther's reference to church confession requires an assessment of his intentions in the light of the confession, and in this the church's confessional tradition also has a regulating significance for the evaluation of the authority of Luther's theology.

What Luther himself says about the necessity of the old symbols with regard to Scripture, that it was necessary for the meaning of Scripture "comprised of so many passages, [to be stated] in a short and comprehensive word," is valid in a modified way for his own theology, for whose "oceanic nature" opens it to arbitrary interpretation by the selection of certain passages, as the history of Luther interpretation shows.[35] Over against the abundance of often accidental statements, the confessions have the significance of showing ecclesial consensus and of giving prominence to that which is fundamental for the knowledge of faith. Thus Luther himself can say of the Apostles' Creed that in it God "revealed himself and opened to us the deepest abyss of his fatherly heart and of his pure, ineffable love in all three articles."[36] The simplified statement of faith has fundamental and formative significance for the abundance of possible (also authoritative) theological doctrine. This is also true for the confession. Therein lies the significance of the catechisms. "There is more in the faith of children than in all the councils. The Lord's prayer and the Ten Commandments also teach more than all the councils."[37] What is valid for the council, is all the more valid for every theology. All theological efforts can only be worth that which is fundamentally intended in church confession: to clear the way for God's gospel so that it awakens faith.

NOTES

1. *LW* 29:143; *WA* 57(3):137,5; Cf. *Theologisches Realenzyklopädie* V: 494.
2. *LW* 41:83; *WA* 50: 527,26.
3. *LW* 37:360f.; *WA* 26:499f.
4. *BC* 287ff.; *BSLK* 409,21.
5. *LW* 37:360; *WA* 26:499.
6. Ibid.
7. *BC* 292; *BSLK* 415,14.
8. Ibid.
9. *BC* 295; *BSLK* 421.
10. *BC* 302; *BSLK* 433.

11. WA 38:78ff. Cf. Jörg Baur, *Luther und die Bekenntnisschriften* (Ratzeburg: Luther-Akademie, 1981), 138ff.
12. *BC* 133,189; *BSLK* 197,53f.
13. *LW* 33:19f.; *WA* 18:603.
14. *LW* 33:26f.; *WA* 18:609.
15. *LW* 33:21ff.; *WA* 18:604ff.
16. *LW* 37:360, 372; *WA* 26:499,509.
17. *LW* 37:361; *WA* 26:500.
18. *WA* 11:409f.
19. *LW* 37:360; *WA* 26:499.
20. *BC* 591ff.; *BSLK* 1017ff.
21. *LW* 41:123; *WA* 50:606,37.
22. *Ibid.*
23. *LW* 41:83; *WA* 50:572,23.
24. *LW* 41:58; *WA* 50:551,32.
25. Cf. David Hollazius, *Examen theologicum,* Prol. 2: q. 27 (1707; reprint, 1981), 1:79.
26. *BC* 465,7f.; *BSLK* 769,30.
27. *BC* 465,4; *BSLK* 768,30.
28. *BC* 505,8; *BSLK* 836,39ff.
29. *LW* 41:131f.; *WA* 50:614,28.
30. Albrecht Ritschl, *Die christliche Lehre von Rechtfertigung und Versöhnung,* 1:260.
31. Adolf Harnack, *What is Christianity?* trans. T. B. Saunders (New York: Harper & Row, 1957), 269,275.
32. *Ibid.,* 291.
33. *BC* 505,8; *BSLK* 836,39ff.
34. *WA* 7:21.
35. *LW* 41:83; *WA* 50:572. Cf. Baur, *Luther.*
36. *BC* 419,64; *BSLK* 660,29f.
37. *LW* 41:41; W%&F
37. *LW* 41:41; *WA* 50:615,3.

Responses

The Final Cause of Justification:
A Marginal Note on Luther and
the Confession of the Church

BRIAN GERRISH

The significance of Luther's gospel for the church, and not for his communion alone, has been more widely acknowledged in our time than ever before. It is entirely right that during our celebration of his birth the emphasis should fall on this momentous new fact. But it may not be out of place to ask, at least in a marginal note, whether Luther's historical limitations, too, have not left their mark on the confession of the church—or on the confessions of the Reformation churches. The criticism often leveled against him in the older literature, that he imposed his subjectivity on the faith of the church, does not seem to me to have been entirely mistaken; rather, it needs to be reformulated more exactly, and without any trace of *odium theologicum*, simply as the recognition of his limits and not as an indictment of his supposed failures or mistakes.

The primary Lutheran confession was not, of course, Luther's document. Some things were omitted from the Augsburg Confession not because of him but despite him. Anyone who thinks Luther's work can be summed up in the three so-called "Reformation principles"—*sola scriptura, sola fide*, and the priesthood of all believers—must be dismayed to find that Melanchthon included only one of them. It is also remarkable that Luther's necessitarianism, for which he had fought so vehemently in the debate with Erasmus, has no place in the confession. Even if these omissions were to be considered limitations, they could not be laid at Luther's door.

But one limitation of the Augsburg Confession—and it is fundamental—can, in a sense, be traced to Luther: namely, the fact that it is *his* religious experience that the confession in effect canonizes. Quite rightly, Melanchthon formulates the claim to catholicity negatively: the Lutheran churches *do not dissent from* the Catholic Church in any article of faith. This is not to claim that the confession is a comprehensive and balanced statement of the Catholic faith; on the contrary, its paramount concern is for one theme, which is singled out as the chief article and is used (in the second part of the confession) as the norm for exposing abuses in the church. There is more than one way in which this chief article is formulated, but essentially it is justification by faith (*tantum fide*); and Melanchthon rightly points out that the Lutheran teaching about it must be referred to the struggle of the terrified conscience, apart from which it cannot be understood.[1] Hence in symbolic type the Augsburg Confession approaches a "declaration": that is, an affirmation and elucidation of a particular item in the Catholic faith against a specific threat to its integrity.

Naturally, this is unexceptionable; in some measure *every* confession has the character of a declaration (in this sense). But difficulties arise when a fundamental part of the church's confession usurps the status of a larger whole. Does this not happen when agonies of conscience are taken to be the invariable matrix of faith, and not rather the problem that required this particular formulation of the faith in the Reformation era? Preoccupation with the terrified conscience runs throughout the Augsburg Confession; but it becomes most visibly problematic when Melanchthon says in the *Apology*, apparently as a universal judgment, that the faith of which he speaks is conceived in terrors of conscience.[2] That it *can be* is certainly an insight for which we thank Luther; but that it *must be* would be very hard indeed to establish from the Scriptures.

In another day, when the Christian proclamation does not *find* a terrified conscience, it may even be supposed that the preacher's task is to *create* one. The risk is then that, instead of taking me out of myself, he may foster in me an egocentric piety in which my sin as *amor sui* (narcissism) is not overcome but actually extended; and this in turn will foster Cyprian's unfortunate image of the church as the Noah's ark to which I must flee to escape the rain of God's wrath. By and large, the confessions of the Reformation churches provide little to draw on when the Christian must face the massive challenge of poverty and injustice that threatens to tear apart the global community of nations; they do not even recognize that my guilt may be my complicity in the sin of exploitation, or that social and economic equity is more than good works done to my neighbor.

It would be absurd to blame Luther or Melanchthon for addressing their problem, not ours. Nor can it be said that their problem is simply antiquated; the point is that, in its sixteenth-century form, it is no longer at the center. And it may well be asked whether there are perhaps other resources to draw from in Luther than those that found their way into the Augsburg Confession. We might, for example, affirm the past confession of the church, even while we recognize the necessity to go beyond it, if we took up the crucial point Luther makes in one of his table talks: that justifying faith is not properly an end in itself. Despite his well-known antipathy toward the "pagan beast" Aristotle, he liked definitions by means of the four causes because even schoolboys and peasants can understand them. In the table talk I have in mind, he defines "faith" by this method and concludes that the final cause of faith is not simply our righteousness but also the glory of God.[3]

The confession of the church today, it seems to me, while it cannot set aside justification by faith, must shift the emphasis of this doctrine from the consolation of terrified consciences to the glorifying of God the Justifier. The problem is not to comfort the conscience of the sinner so much as to quicken the conscience of the justified, to direct his or her gratitude toward the actual needs of the world. For as Luther shows in his superb little 1519 treatise (only two pages long!)[4] on praying the Lord's Prayer forwards and backwards, the glory of God is not simply that he justifies me freely; he receives his glory when I put his kingdom first, not desiring it for the sake of my own blessedness but finding my blessedness precisely in my commitment to his kingdom. The point is not made so forcefully in Luther's catechisms. In short, my justification by faith is not a complete end in itself but demands the question: What is the final cause also of faith? What is my justification good for?

You may detect the accent of a Reformed theologian in these remarks.[5] I have taken it for granted that to speak with this accent was expected, even required, of me. But I wanted to avoid any hint of a Reformed critique of Luther and the Lutheran confession, for the very good reason that the Reformed confessions, too, aside from the catechisms, have surprisingly little to say about the final cause of justification by faith. Despite the famous opening questions of Calvin's Geneva Catechism (1541/45) and the later Westminster Catechisms (1647), the Reformed standards generally represent the church as the society of the saved and not as the agent of God's glory in the world. Some of the Reformed churches have indeed tried to meet the kinds of concern I have raised, notably the United Presbyterian Church in the U.S.A. with its Confession of 1967. But the real confessional landmark in the twentieth century (so far!) was surely the image of the servant church in the pronouncements of the Second Vatican Council (1963–65), from which all of us still have a great deal to learn.

NOTES

1. *BC* 43,17.
2. *BC* 126,142.
3. *WA TR* no. 2191; cf. Melanchthon, *BC* 135,204.
4. *WA* 6:21–22.
5. Cf. Calvin, *Inst*. 3.13.1–2, 14.17, 14.21!

Response to the Theme "Luther's Theology and the Formation of Reformation Confessions"

HANS-JÖRG URBAN

The following reflections refer to the exposition of W. Lohff on the significance of Luther's theology for ecclesial confession. I desire to pose still more pointedly the question of the relationship of Scripture and confession.

Lohff rightly emphasizes the contextuality of Luther's personal confessing and also, logically, his new theological view of doctrine and confession. Luther is challenged to confession in acute confrontation. According to Lohff, Luther experienced the situation in which confession is demanded "as the struggle of the certainty of faith with unbelief and false doctrine."

The steps which Luther takes in this situation are obvious and sufficiently well-known: in the confrontation he relativizes the dogmatic tradition as well as the teaching office and sustains his total certainty by the Holy Scriptures, that is, by the legitimate proclamation of the pure Word of God. The literature presents the question of confession in Luther,[1] turn the problem as you will, so that it is always established that Luther as exegete of Scripture moved against the teaching office, that he primarily places the Scripture against the tradition.

The following attempt to briefly present how Luther carried this out in particular certainly tends to relativize the absoluteness of this opposition of Scripture and teaching office or dogmatic tradition, an absoluteness so frequently vindicated in history and even in the present. This is admitted at the outset.

The first step is that Luther emphasizes the unlimited authority of Christ and his Word in the Scripture. Already in the Ninety-five Theses, God is the *legislator divinus*[2] who demands obedience to his Word. In the controversy with Erasmus, Luther affirms that the entire sense of the confession lies in emphasizing "what God has delivered to us in the Holy Scripture."[3] In particular, there where Luther speaks about heretics and heresy in the early church, it is clear that they are characterized as heretics who teach against the Scripture and persist in this teaching.[4]

The fact that for Luther the Scripture is the unlimited authority even over the confessions can be illuminated from still many other perspectives. I should like only to refer to his statement that the Apostles' Creed is not an independent doctrinal norm but rather is "from the beloved books of the prophets and apostles, that is, from the entire Holy Scripture; and is an excellent short summary for children and simple Christians."[5]

Translated by Carter Lindberg

The second step then is certainly that Luther emphasizes in the controversy, and indeed with growing certainty, that the Scriptures are on his side. With nearly prophetic self-consciousness he says: "Even if I am not a prophet, as far as I am concerned I am sure that the Word of God is with me and not with them, for I have the Scriptures on my side and they have only their own doctrine."[6] At the conclusion of his 1528 "Confession Concerning Christ's Supper," Luther says with all clarity that his own confession is that of all true Christians, and he equates it with the teaching of the Scriptures.[7] Indeed, the further the controversy proceeds the more certain it appears to Luther that he has the Scriptures on his side. In 1531 he writes: "For we, too, err daily in our life and conduct; so do all the saints, as they earnestly confess in the Lord's Prayer and the Creed. But by the grace of God our doctrine is pure; we have all the articles of faith solidly established in Sacred Scripture."[8] He is continually more certain that his doctrine can be refuted by no one by Scripture. His self-consciousness is confirmed in the experience of opposition.

I am thoroughly conscious that still a few motives must be further considered which lead Luther to the *sola scriptura*, but in essentials the above two steps form the concrete and direct context in which Luther held the Scriptures, that is, his confession of the Scriptures, against the teaching office. If this is correct then it must be admitted that what Luther later termed the "Scriptural principle" is logically explained from this connection, and indeed as an *emergency solution* in the sense of the gospel against the suppression of the gospel. Luther's new creation is therefore not the gospel instead of the teaching office, but rather he is interested in the gospel, and therefore he polemicizes against the teaching office in all its appearances up to dogmas and confessions because they in the concrete historical situation of that time subjugate just this gospel and do not allow it freedom. In this extraordinary emergency situation Luther appeals to the power of Scripture itself in non-ideological exegesis and assails at the same time the system of the Roman Church while he exposes its weakness in history and the present in order that the gospel again be set free. He finds himself suddenly in something like a *status confessionis* and pulls the emergency brake. He desires to eliminate a superstructure which has become rotten in order to save the essential and allow it to work out of its own power without alien help. He acts according to the motto: it is better to overcome a crisis with the essential alone and give up at least temporarily other important things which appear in the moment to be non-essential.

Thus I see here an emergency solution in relation to the situation, that is, the crisis, similar to the question of the office of ministry. But does Luther desire to set up a "principle," a new system for the church of the future, from this emergency solution? Does he desire to perpetuate his *status confessionis* as a normal status of the church? Can the church in a normal situation win security from the Scripture alone which he reached in the resistance dependent on a *status confessionis*?

Some things speak against this. First of all is the fact that Luther does not understand the church, even the hidden church, as a platonic image. He states this expressly in his third writing against Emser.[9] Then there is Luther's repeated assertion that he is willing to let the pope and bishops be what they are if they only allow the gospel to be preached freely and purely.[10] Then also Luther's entire theology (not the polemical explosions), seen as a whole, is more stablizing; the *norma normata* indeed taking the right place, being conserved not abolished. This is especially clear in his lasting recourse to the ecumenical creeds, the first four councils as well as the fathers, which he invokes as testimony to his doctrine.[11]

In connection to Luther's statements in "On the Councils and the Church," J. Baur writes:

> For Luther the medieval and modern conviction that the vague and self-contradictory Scriptures must be aided by clear directions proceeding from dogma is intolerable. Nevertheless he does not make this "no" into a principle of fundamental anti-traditionalism. The *scriptura solitaria* of the bourgeois exegetes is not from the *sola scriptura*. "But that one should not use more or other words than those contained in Scripture—this cannot be adhered to, especially in a controversy and when heretics want to falsify things with trickery and distort the words of Scripture. It thus became necessary to condense the meaning of Scripture, comprised of so many passages, into a short and comprehensive word, and to ask whether they regarded Christ as *homousius*, which was the meaning of all the words of Scripture...."[12] Nevertheless no principle of tradition is established. The intentions are very much more radical. Not only should the self-completion of itself by its traditions alone be rejected as supporting the institution, so also should the claim of a spiritualistic immediacy of the person to the Scriptures including the elimination of the preceding testimony of the Church of the Fathers. In the dogmatic decisions of the councils the truth of the gospel proceeding from the light of the Scripture deals with the opposition of human perversion of the gospel. "This explains why the council met and what they had to do, namely, to preserve this ancient article of faith that Christ is true God against the new cleverness of Arius, who, on the basis of reason, wanted to falsify this article, indeed to change it and condemn it."[13]

Therefore I sharpen Lohff's question and state that the actual question today is whether the Reformation tradition has created a new status for Luther's "emergency solution" (the scriptural principle against the teaching office and the authority of confession); whether justice is done to Luther's intention or on the contrary this intention is missed. This is a particularly valid question against the background of the changing history of his scriptural principle. It is well-known how quickly this principle was formalized, a process leading to biblicism, in order to legitimate truth-claims, supported also certainly by historical arguments of continuity with the ancient church. With the changes in relationship to the "letter of Scripture," at the latest in the Enlightenment, up to the modern exegesis, however, this Scripture principle crumbled in the process of a self-supplied critique and can only still be held with crutches, that is, by individual particular ecclesial working with the tradition of Luther's theology. This is legitimate. The question is only whether Luther's intention was treated correctly for he had claimed the entire Christian tradition as support of the scriptural principle.

NOTES

1. Cf. F. W. Kantzenbach, "Aspekte zum Bekenntnisproblem in der Theologie M. Luthers," *Luther Jahrbuch 1963;* K. G. Steck, "Lehre und Kirche bei Luther," in *Forschungen zur Geschichte und Lehre des Protestantismus,* vol. 27 (Munich, 1963); J. Baur, "Luther und die Bekenntnisschriften," in *Luther und die Bekenntnisschriften* (Ratzeburg: Veröffentlichungen der Luther-Akademie, 1981), vol. 2, Erlangen.
2. *LW* 33:88; *WA* 1:533, 527.
3. *LW* 33:20; *WA* 18:603.
4. Cf. *WA* 46:20.
5. *WA* 41:275.
6. *LW* 32:9; *WA* 7:313.
7. *LW* 37:372; *WA* 26:509.
8. *LW* 27:41f.; *WA* 40 2:53.
9. *WA* 7:683.
10. *WA* 30 2:342; 38:379.
11. Cf. *WA* 50:509–653; *LW* 41:3–178.
12. *LW* 41:83; *WA* 50:572, 23–29.
13. *LW* 41:57f.; *WA* 50:531,11–15; cf. Baur, *Luther,* 140f.

The Significance of Luther for Anglican Confessional Documents

STEPHEN W. SYKES

The significance of Luther for Anglican confessional documents is a topic of very considerable complexity, and all that can be achieved in the space available is a certain orientation on the subject. The principal difficulty is the fact that what counts as "Anglican confessional documents" are not confessional documents in the same sense as those of Lutheranism, nor is there any exact Anglican counterpart to the theology of the confessional documents characteristic of the Lutheran tradition. Nonetheless I hold it to be misleading to say (as is sometimes maintained) that Anglicanism is not a confessional church; the truth is rather that the Anglican communion has a confessional basis (as every church must have), but that it is a basis of a somewhat different kind from that found in other Christian churches. The chief difference, I shall argue, is that Anglicans do not attach as high a significance to precise doctrinal formulations in the confession of the Catholic faith as to the offering of common worship. This stance entails not merely a reception of Luther's viewpoint, but also a modification of it. I shall argue that both reception and modification are of ecumenical significance.

First we must clarify the question, what constitutes the confessional document of Anglicanism? Here we must distinguish between the situation in the Church of England and that in the autonomous and self-governing provinces of the Anglican communion. For the *Church of England* the confessional stance is defined by Canon A5, which states:

> The doctrine of the Church of England is grounded in the holy Scriptures, and in such teachings of the ancient Fathers and Councils of the Church as are agreeable to the said Scriptures. In particular such doctrine is to be found in the Thirty-Nine Articles of Religion, the Book of Common Prayer, and the Ordinal.

It should be noted that the 1662 Book of Common Prayer contains a short Catechism to be learned by all before confirmation by the Bishop;[1] and also that the Thirty-Nine Articles refer to two books of homilies (or sermons) as containing "a godly and wholesome Doctrine, and necessary for these times."[2] In the churches of *the Anglican Communion*, on the other hand, there are a variety of statements about faith and order, many of which do not refer to the Thirty-Nine Articles. Moreover all the provinces now have revised their Prayer Books, though most claim that these revisions are based upon the "principles of worship" established by the Book of Common Prayer.

The implications of this distinction between the confessional bases of the Church of England and the Churches of the Anglican Communion are considerable. First, it cannot be said that the Thirty-Nine Articles contribute directly to the confessional basis of the whole Anglican communion. The most that can be said is that they occupy an indirect significance inasmuch as communion with the see of Canterbury (whose confessional stance is governed by Canon A5) is one of the characteristic sources of unity in the Anglican communion. However, even this indirect influence must be qualified by a declaration of the 1968 Lambeth Conference, explicitly relativizing the Thirty-nine Articles to their total historical context.[3] Secondly, in view of the above all the more weight has to be placed on the liturgies of the Book of Common Prayer and of the Ordinal; Anglican liturgical texts are confessional documents, albeit of a particular kind. And thirdly, communion between the autonomous churches of the Anglican communion does not depend on a single liturgical text, but on the use of a family of texts, bearing a family resemblance. The Anglican experience suggests that the family resemblance of liturgical texts can be a sufficient basis for Christian unity.

The contrast between this position and that of Luther, who attaches prime significance to doctrinal agreement, is clear enough, but can be exaggerated. Both directly and indirectly the doctrinal initiative of Luther has set its mark upon the Anglican confessional stance. Thus the Thirty-nine Articles contain borrowings from two Lutheran sources, the Augsburg Confession itself, as mediated by the Thirteen Articles of 1538, which were the outcome of direct consultations between Luther and English theologians, and the Württemberg Confession of 1551, which influenced the revision of the Articles undertaken in 1561 by Archbishop Parker.[4] The doctrinal character of the Book of Common Prayer is determined by explicit belief in the sufficient and perfect efficacy of Christ's sacrificial death, whose benefits are available to all who "truly repent and unfeignedly believe his holy Gospel."[5] This gospel is *heard* in the public reading of Scripture in the language of the people, "the minister that readeth the lesson, standing and turning himself so as he may best be heard of all such as be present";[6] it is *interpreted* by the other elements of the liturgy (the canticles, the creeds, and the prayers); and it is *applied* to the present in the sermon or homily. All that is said or done is subject to the material norm of Scripture, the sole basis of the church's confession. It is the Scriptures which at once relativize and establish the three principal catholic creeds.[7]

In the crucial area of eucharistic theology, the Prayer Book and Articles tend somewhat to the Reformed side of the Reformed-Lutheran divisions;[8] but it should be noted that at the revision in 1564 Elizabeth I consciously omitted an anti-Lutheran formulation of eucharistic doctrine, and in 1571 Convocation likewise removed a statement that a Christian ought not "to believe, or openly to confess the real, and bodily presence" of Christ's flesh and blood in the sacrament.[9]

In the Ordinal and in Articles 23 and 36 the Church of England endorsed the threefold order of bishops, priests, and deacons as the church's tradition "from the apostles' time." However, since Article 34 states that it is not necessary for churches in different countries to have identical traditions and ceremonies, it was also possible for Anglicans to recognize a true apostolic ministry in other countries.[10] Originally, as the content of the ordination services makes explicit, it is fidelity in word and deed to the content of the Holy Scriptures which constitutes ministry in apostolic succession. The subsequent declaration ascribing a quasi-independent validity to any episcopal consecration, understandable enough in the circumstances of 1661, marks a new departure in Anglican self-understanding, scarcely assimilable to its original basis.[11]

In two important respects, however, the Anglican reformation departed from Luther. In the first place, Anglicans employed with increasing insistence the distinction, derived from Melanchthon, between *fundamental and non-fundamental articles*. One of Henry VIII's court chaplains, Thomas

Starkey, already deployed this device in order to legitimate Henry VIII's claim that obedience to the pope belonged to the *adiaphora*, that is, that it was not a fundamental article of Christian belief.[12] Subsequently throughout the sixteenth and sevententh centuries, Anglican apologists asserted, on the basis of appeals to Justin Martyr, Tertullian, and Irenaeus, that Anglicans had restored in all its purity the doctrine of the apostles.[13] This particular insistence on fundamentals has given to Anglicanism a highly static character and inhibited any adequate response to the hermeneutics of doctrinal development. Here, it seems to me, Luther's more subtle combination of a basic faith designed for easy communication, together with an historical-experiential element constantly in theological dialogue with a particular situation, is an important corrective.[14] It should be noted, however, that the demand for the open formulation of "fundamentals" is still apparent on all sides. It has yet to be seen whether the Christian churches are willing to attempt a new formulation of the faith, and in what relation such a formulation will stand to the Apostles' Creed.

A second, markedly non-Lutheran feature of Anglicanism is the enforcement in 1662 of a uniform liturgy, the legally established settlement of the authorized text for public worship. Whereas the Thirty-nine Articles were intended to build only the public teaching of ordained ministers (and certain lay legal officers) of the Church of England, the liturgy was turned into an instrument to achieve uniformity of, at least, outward observance in the whole population of England. In fact it created the reverse, a vigorous independency and the dialectic between conformity and non-conformity characteristic of English culture as a whole. Nonetheless, liturgical control achieved several objectives simultaneously: it afforded a common hermeueutic for the reception of the Scriptures; it promoted public participation in prayer; it protected the laity from the whims of individual ministers; and it provided a bishop with an openly acknowledged basis for disciplining the clergy. In contrast to the seventeenth century attempt to achieve uniformity, modern Anglican developments have tended to confirm Luther's original insight that, while there must be public forms of liturgy, these need not be identical. If they are all to be Christian worship, however, they must have common characteristics.[15] Thus the idea of a common *family of liturgies*, so characteristic of the basis of Anglican fellowship, is of great potential ecumenical significance.

If we turn to the *modern implications* of Luther for the ecumenical confession of a common faith, one principal thought suggests itself; that is, that Christian faith imposes an irresolvable dialectic between *external propositions* and *internal intentions*. External propositions are necessary for the public life of the church; but Christian commitment, trust, and certitude go beyond the external realm into the interior intentions of human existence. The tragedy of this dialectic is that no single set of propositions in the history of Christian faith has ever adequately expressed the depth of interior conversion required of every Christian person.

The Reformation era produced a multiplicity of confessional documents, none of which achieved universal recognition. The modern churches of Christendom have, therefore, to ask themselves whether any new confessional document will achieve what earlier centuries failed to achieve, bearing in mind the still greater pluralism of cultures, tradition, and not least of biblical origins, of which we are now conscious. The necessary dialectic of external proposition and internal intention places a premium upon symbols which the churches already have in common, especially the Nicaean-Constantinopolitan Creed.

Moreover, the rediscovery of the doxological character of the creeds, and the convergence brought about by the liturgical movement, brings into new prominence the fact that *the church's worship is itself a confession,* liturgy in word and deed alike acknowledging the Lordship of Christ. For unlike a discursive (and argumentative!) confessional document, a liturgical text actually incorporates the necessary interplay between external proposition and internal intention. Liturgies imply doctrines (and these doctrines may be true or false), but they are not merely doctrines expressed as prayers, any more than poems are merely ideas expressed in verse and meter. Liturgies occupy a vital position in the dialectic between propositions and intentions because they require the orientation of the believer's intention. Liturgies manifestly need doctrinal criticism, and the abiding significance of Luther for Anglicanism, as for most of the churches of Christendom, is his recall of the church to the love of God expressed in his gracious offer of forgiveness in Jesus Christ, openly declared in the language of the people. But the future ecumenical significance of Luther may lie chiefly in the incorporation of this insight into the converging family of Christian liturgies specifically carrying out Christ's instruction to remember the sacrifice of the cross, in such a way "that we offer with Christ, that is, that we cast ourselves upon Christ with unwavering faith in his testament."[16]

NOTES

1. The 1662 catechism follows Luther's model of using the Decalogue, the Creed, the Lord's Prayer, and the Sacraments as the four topics of catechism. Cranmer's Catechism of 1549 had, uniquely among the manuals of the period, contained no reference to the Sacraments.

2. Article 35, "Of the Homilies," Article 11, "Of the Justification of Man," also refers particularly to the Homily of Justification (by which is evidently meant Cranmer's homily "Of salvation." We should note the phrase "necessary for these times," which includes the possibility of reformulation at a later time.

3. Resolution 43c of this conference contains the suggestion that "when subscription is required to the Articles of other elements in the Anglican tradition, it should

be required, and given, only in the context of a statement which gives the full range of our inheritance of faith and sets the Articles in their historical context." *The Lambeth Conference, 1968* (London, 1968), 41.

4. See further, C. Hardwick, *A History of the Articles of Religion* (Cambridge, 1876); and W. P. Haugaard, *Elizabeth and the English Reformation* (Cambridge, 1970), 249.

5. From the Prayer of Absolution in Morning and Evening Prayer, 1552.

6. The rubric relating to the reading of the Lessons at Morning Prayer, 1549.

7. Cf., Article 8, "Of the Three Creeds": "The Three Creeds, Nicene Creed, Athanasian Creed, and that which is commonly called the Apostles' Creed, ought thoroughly to be received and believed; for they may be proved by most certain warrants of Holy Scripture."

8. Haugaard, *English Reformation*, 266.

9. Ibid., 254, 267. The texts of Article 29 of the Forty-two Articles (1553) should be compared with that of Article 28 of the Thirty-nine Articles.

10. The evidence of Anglican writers of the sixteenth, seventeenth, and eighteenth centuries who were ready to accept non-episcopal churches as genuinely apostolic is given in G.K.A. Bell, *Christian Unity: The Anglican Position* (London, 1948).

11. On this development, see S. W. Sykes "Das Augsburgische Bekenntnis in Anglicanischer Sicht," in H. Meyer, ed., *Augsburgisches Bekenntnis im Ökumenischen Kontext* (Stuttgart, 1980), 48ff.

12. W. G. Zeeveld, *Foundations of Tudor Policy* (Cambridge, 1948), 154ff.

13. Cf. the statement adopted by the House of Bishops in Chicago, 1886, which declared the Nicene Creed to be "the sufficient statement of the Christian Faith" and one of the four essentials for the restoration of unity. After a somewhat complex process of modification this statement became part of what is now known as the Chicago-Lambeth Quadrilateral.

14. See below the argument of D.J. Hall in this volume.

15. Compare the acceptance of liturgical diversity, with a "greater *agreement in certain basic patterns*," spoken of in Articles 75 and 76 of the Lutheran/Roman Catholic Joint Commission statement, *Das Herrenmahl* (Paderborn, 1978).

16. Cited from Martin Luther's *Treatise on the New Testament* 1520, *LW* 35:99; *WA* 6:369, 5–9; in *Das Herrenmahl*, 59.

Summary

HEINZ SCHÜTTE

THE IMPORTANCE OF TRADITION IN LUTHER'S THEOLOGY

Luther started from the tradition of the church whenever he consciously wanted to celebrate his faith through confessions of faith.

—This is true of his 1528 *professio fidei*, the "Confession Concerning Christ's Supper"[1] that was of the greatest importance for later confessions of faith and became, through the Schwabach and Marburg Articles, the foundation of the Augsburg Confession.

—This is equally true for Luther's use of church tradition in the Schmalkald Articles of 1537.

—Both of Luther's catechisms continue the catechetical tradition of the church, and are constructed from the center of the trinitarian process of salvation.

Luther was concerned that his own confession of faith be spiritually in tune with the confession of faith of the entire church.

The integration of the three symbols of the ancient church in the Formula of Concord conforms to Luther's views. He was convinced that the creeds and the dogmas of the ancient church were in total agreement with Scripture. The symbols still had a place in the church services. As for "disclosing Luther's ecumenical significance," we find that Luther's basic theological concepts dealing with the high articles of divine majesty were in continuity with the faith of the old church and the Roman Church. It was his express intention that it be so.

Further, it is important from an ecumenical point of view that although Luther took Scripture as the point of reference, he was not an antitraditionalist. Rather he accepted consciously the ancient tradition of the church, provided it accorded with Scripture. Luther particularly approved of the teaching of the first four councils of Nicea, Constantinople, Ephesus, and Chalcedon. He called them major councils. The authoritative character of the decisions of the councils was for Luther rooted in the confidence of the power of the Holy Spirit.

Translated by Georges Herzog

THE HOLY SCRIPTURE AS *NORMA NORMANS*—
THE CONFESSION OF FAITH
AS *NORMA NORMATA*

Luther accepted the tradition of the church, yet he questioned its legitimacy. He was forced to it because of his extremely precarious situation: he considered his own end and the last judgment as imminently close. He found himself in a polemical and antiheretical confrontation and had a crisis of confidence toward the teachings of the church.

The gospel and Scripture (which attested to God as the trinity and Christ as the one suffering for us) were for Luther the material principle *(norma normans)* for the justification and the examination of the teaching of the faith as transmitted by tradition.

The confessions of faith, that is, the teachings of the church, were for Luther *norma normata*. This resulted in their relativization, but provided they conformed to Scripture, they were at the same time stabilized and gained a convincing quality of certainty.

As for "disclosing Luther's ecumenical significance," we can say that his understanding of Scripture as *norma normans* has been accepted positively in the ecumenical dialogue. According to the Lutheran-Catholic document "The Gospel and the Church," Scripture cannot be "opposed exclusively to tradition, because the New Testament itself is the fruit of the tradition of the primitive church. Scripture has nevertheless a normative function for the entire later tradition because it is a witness of the emerging tradition."

From an ecumenical point of view it is furthermore important to note that Luther has called expressly on the major councils and never advocated any absolute principle of Scripture or any biblicism. He noted expressly: "When it is necessary to preserve the purity of Scripture, a council has the authority to go beyond the mere words of Scripture."[2]

LUTHER AND THE
AUGSBURG CONFESSION

In 1980 the Augsburg Confession could finally be called the "confession of the one faith" as a result of an international investigation that assembled Lutherans and Catholics.[*] More precisely, a "consensus on the main beliefs" had been recognized and the hope was expressed that the still pending points of contention could be resolved (Pope John Paul II expressed in the same words the view of the German Catholic bishops).

Luther's theology was considered and taken as a source in this interpreta-

---

*Editor's note: Harding Meyer und Heinz Schütte, eds., *Confessio Augustana. Bekenntnis des einen Glaubens: Gemeinsame Untersuchung Lutherischer und Katholischer Theologen* (Paderborn Bonifacius; Frankfurt a.M.: Lembeck, 1980); English: George W. Forell and James F. McCue, eds., *Confessing One Faith* (Minneapolis: Augsburg, 1982).

tion of the Augsburg Confession. On the question of Luther's relationship to the Augsburg Confession we arrived, through presentations and discussions, at the following points:

—Luther criticized the Augsburg Confession because he could not find in it the condemnation of some teachings such as those on the papacy or purgatory.

—Luther's denunciation of the "pussy-footing" of the Augsburg Confession was meant also to be a criticism of himself.

—Not only did Luther permit the Augsburg Confession to become the cornerstone of the Schmalkald League, but he let it also become important in the church, let it grow to the rank of a fundamental confession of faith, and accepted it as the starting point of the religious dialogue.

—Luther saw the Augsburg Confession as a valid résumé of ecclesiastical doctrine.

The Augsburg Confession must therefore be understood and evaluated in the context of Luther's theology. (P. Manns has argued for this point particularly strongly.)

While "disclosing Luther's ecumenical significance" we came to conclude that the basic consensus between Lutherans and Catholics, achieved with the help of the Augsburg Confession, did not contradict Luther or his beliefs. Insofar as there is a consensus between Luther's beliefs and the beliefs of the Lutheran Church, we can conclude that the consensus on fundamental dogmas achieved through the Augsburg Confession shows indirectly a consensus between Luther's beliefs and the beliefs of the Catholic Church.

LUTHER AND THE BOOK OF CONCORD, OR RATHER, THE BOOK OF CONCORD AND LUTHER

Is Luther's theology expressed correctly and completely in the Book of Concord?

The Book of Concord used those writings of Luther in which he accepted, in a reforming manner, the traditions of the confessions of faith and of the catechisms and which Luther himself considered the Summa of doctrine.

The Formula of Concord relied also for further explanations on Luther's doctrinal and polemical writings, such as the "Confession Concerning Christ's Supper," and drew generously from them. Furthermore, the Formula of Concord refers generally to Luther's writings.

Luther's fundamental aspiration seemed to have been well preserved in the Formula of Concord according to such scholars as J. Baur, W. Lohff, and G. Seebass, but B. Lohse and B. Haegglund disagree on this point.

Not all of Luther's writings should be seen as normative teachings. Particularly important are all those writings that were intended to be authoritative expositions of the confessions of the church.

In "disclosing Luther's ecumenical significance," we have, however, to take into consideration the totality of his work.

LUTHER'S INFLUENCE ON THE CONFESSIONS OF FAITH OF OTHER CHURCHES

Luther's basic theological views were influential to the Anglican "Book of Common Prayer." The experience of the Anglican community has shown that the unity of the church can be preserved with the help of similar liturgies. The symbols of these liturgies attest to the importance of Christ's sacrifice for all believers. The ensuing vernacular readings announce the Word of God. Anglican theologians believe that there is here a link to Luther's reforming impetus (S. W. Sykes).

The Reformed Churches too have become aware of Luther's ecumenical importance. Placing the kingdom and the glory of God above all other things may be learned from him; yet it has been objected that this idea is not as easily found in the confessions of faith (including the Reformed ones) as in the other writings of Luther.

OPEN QUESTIONS

It is still unclear whether Luther wanted to set Scripture as touchstone of doctrine in principle or only because he thought in the extreme situation of that time the gospel was oppressed by the teaching office. Similarily there are many unresolved questions about which instance might be appropriate in case of disagreement.

Although there should be great caution in assuming the role of preserver of the faith and although any condemnation should be given only in last resort, the situation may arise when it must be said clearly: "This is contrary to what can be taught in the church."

CONCLUSION

Martin Luther's express intention to agree with the church should be considered hermeneutically in the interpretation of his writings, at least when there is any doubt. This could lead to a consolidation of the consensus already achieved and to a resolution of the still pending differences.

NOTES

1. *LW* 37:151ff.
2. *LW* 41:83; *WA* 50:572,23.

THE "ONE HOLY CHRISTENDOM": LUTHER'S DOUBLE-FACETED CONCEPT OF THE CHURCH

The Church as Spiritual-Sacramental Communio with Christ and His Saints in the Theology of Luther

VILMOS VAJTA

COMMUNIO SPIRITUALIS ET CORPORALIS

In his *Sermo de virtute excommunicationis* (1518), Luther begins with the concept of fellowship[1] and describes it as follows: "Fellowship among the faithful is of two kinds: one is inward and spiritual; the other is outward and physical. The spiritual is that of faith, hope, and charity in God. The physical is participation in the sacrament with others; it is the sign of faith, hope, and charity which outwardly extends to fellowship in things, personal relationships, living in community, conversations, and other such kinds of physical association."[2] He repeats this distinction in "A Sermon on the Ban" (1520) with essential amplification of the problem of the authority to exercise the ban. "Fellowship is of two kinds. . . . The first kind of fellowship is inward, spiritual, and invisible for it is in the heart. It means that through faith, hope, and love a person is incorporated into the fellowship of Christ and all the saints. . . ."[3] This is a clear parallel even if in a different formulation; for this is not merely a translation.

The communio spiritualis can be given only by God (*nisi deus solus*), hence a person can exclude him/herself only by his/her sin (*nisi solus ipse homo per peccatum proprium*).[4] The ecclesial authority of excommunication is consequently limited only to the taking away of outward fellowship.[5] However, this exclusion itself thereby remains qualified by whether the person has separated him/herself from spiritual fellowship. The church's ban cannot affect him/her in the spiritual fellowship. The excommunication can be wrong and the person still continue to live in spiritual fellowship with God.[6] On the other hand, there can be persons who are not under excommunication by the church but who are actually outside the spiritual fellowship.[7] In all these cases the limits of excommunication reside with the church; a point we shall pursue later. But the person under the ban is not excluded from the prayer and proclamation of the church.[8] "Justice and truth, together

Translated by Carter Lindberg

with the inward fellowship of the church, must not be omitted for the sake of the outward excommunication."[9] The person who has been unjustly excommunicated can even "go spiritually to the sacrament,"[10] that is, have the benefit in faith of spiritual fellowship "with Christ and his saints."

This distinction in the concept of fellowship stands behind the observation of a kind of "double-facetedness" in Luther's concept of the church.[11] In order to recognize the theological foundation of this distinction it is first of all helpful to call attention to the stated motive for fellowship. Two observations are important here.

Luther concludes his Latin *Sermo* with the warning that the censure of the ban, in opposition to customary usage, should be employed only very rarely. The reason is that the "censure (of the ban) is a kind of law but every law is a power and occasion for sin and without the grace of God the law cannot be fulfilled; and furthermore, the grace of God, that is, the fulfillment of the law itself, cannot be given by them [the popes and their ministers]" and thus the ban essentially gives the opportunity for sin.[12] Similar reasoning is also found in the German sermon where the Reformer argues that such sins "make God angry, although the ban was instituted to appease him." The authority of the ban is given not to destroy "but rather to build up."[13]

These thoughts show that the ban (*excommunicatio*) can be considered under two different viewpoints, namely that of the law (*lex*) and that of the gospel (*gratia,* reconciliation). Thus seen, the ban is closely connected to the "double-facetedness" of fellowship for the ban imposed by the officeholder has to do first of all with outward fellowship. As such however it must be related to spiritual fellowship, that is, to serve the fellowship in which the person is placed under God's grace and is reconciled with God. The ban can never appear to claim that it is a judgment upon the person in relation to spiritual fellowship. This is God's judgment alone.

Thus the theological distinction between communio corporalis and communio spiritualis is at the same time the distinction between law and gospel. The use of the ban can therefore be placed in service of the law (destruction) or the gospel (reconciliation). Between fellowship and excommunication there is a tension corresponding to that of the salvation and destruction of the person. In excommunication itself the question concerns the existing and future fellowship. The distinction between spiritual and physical fellowship reflects this tension. In this perspective we are able to speak of the *ambiguity* (*Zweideutigkeit*) of the church. We must now examine more closely what consequences this has for the concept of the church.

The second observation is connected to Luther's reference that the "two kinds of fellowship" are to be understood "just as there are two things, namely, sign and significance, in the sacrament, as I said in the sermon."[14] Here Luther is referring to his sermon "The Blessed Sacrament of the Holy and True Body of Christ . . ." (1519) and its description of the structure of the sacrament.[15] There the sacrament is seen in three parts: "The first is the sacrament or sign. The second is the significance of this sacrament. The third is the faith required with each of the first two. These three parts must be found in every sacrament."[16]

The sequence plays a subordinate role here. Even the concepts are somewhat dubious. In this early period Luther still has a narrow concept of "sacrament," namely synonymous with the sacramental/external signs. The "significance" can in other respects be exchanged with "Word" (in the sense of the words of institution). Faith ties the two parts, significance/Word and sign/sacrament, to one another.[17] In and of itself it is not surprising that Luther employs this sacramental structure for the "double-faceted" concept of fellowship, for he sees in the sacrament of the altar the primary significance of fellowship, or better: in the reception the fellowship (communicare).[18] Beginning with the distinction of spiritual and physical fellowship we have seen this in close connection with excommunication. Thus the fundamental fellowship-concept of the concept of the church receives a spiritual-sacramental character. The distinction which appears in the concept of fellowship is then finally only the sacramental structure as defined by Luther. On the other hand what Luther says about the spiritual fellowship is of fundamental significance for the understanding of the sacrament. Faith, hope, and love, as we have heard, are given by God alone. Therefore it is logical that the outward, bodily, symbolic action of the sacrament without God's gift of grace (faith) does not effect salvation but only physical fellowship. The outward "sacramental" signs must be received in faith through the work of the Spirit.

Thus the theological contents in the distinction of spiritual and physical fellowship are co-determined: the tension-filled relationship between law and gospel on the one hand and the new sacramental structure as Luther represents it on the other hand. The significance of this analysis for the "double-facetedness" and "ambiguity" of the concept of the church shall now be set forth.

"A SPIRITUALLY INWARD AND A PHYSICALLY OUTWARD CHRISTENDOM"

Luther's tract "On the Papacy in Rome . . ." (1520) is directed against the Leipzig Franciscan, Alfeld, who dealt with the primacy of the Roman papacy in his writing against Luther. In his answer Luther comes to a few fundamental ecclesiological statements among which is found the famous position of the "two churches . . . by two distinct names."[19] For now we may put to one side his statements with regard to the head of the church and concentrate on his concept of the church (Luther prefers "Christendom").[20] "Scripture speaks about Christendom very simply and in only one way," namely "that

Christendom means an assembly of all people on earth who believe in Christ, as we pray in the Creed, 'I believe in the Holy Spirit, the communion of saints.' This communion or assembly means all those who live in true faith, hope, and love."[21] With reference to Eph. 4:5 this is defined not as "a physical assembly, but an assembly of hearts," "in the Spirit," of a "spiritual unity." Luther introduces in this definition of the spiritual reality of the church "the physical community" as "a model of the spiritual community"[22] which is essentially the simple speech of the Scripture. But he excludes another manner of speaking about the church, namely, as "an assembly in a house, or in a parish, a bishopric, an archbishopric, or a papacy. To this assembly belong external forms such as singing, reading, and the vestments of the mass."[23] In addition the entire clerical estate belongs to this second characteristic. A third manner of speaking of the church in which the word "spiritual" is falsely used touches upon the buildings and the various goods administered by the church and its legal determinations. This third type is rejected by Luther because it has nothing to do with essential Christendom. The two others remain "facets," the relationship of which is now to be considered.

We should like first to refer to a certain vagueness of Luther. With regard to "the other manner of speaking of Christendom," Luther speaks somewhat briefly about the outward assembly by which nevertheless he means the worshiping assembly in all places. In a later connection he first refers to what are for him the obvious "signs by which one can note where the church itself is in the world," and calls these the sacraments and the gospel.[24] These "signs" must be incorporated in the other, external-bodily Christendom. Only then can the relationship of the two ways of speaking about Christendom be determined.

We cite now the famous passage where Luther carries out this distinction:

> Therefore, for the sake of better understanding and brevity, we shall call the two churches by two distinct names. The first, which is natural, basic, essential, and true, we shall call "spiritual, internal Christendom." The second, which is man-made and external, we shall call "physical, external Christendom." Not that we want to separate them from each other; rather, it is just as if I were talking about a person and called him "spiritual" according to his soul, and "physical" according to his body, or as the Apostle is accustomed, to speak of an "internal" and "external" person. So, too, the Christian assembly is a community united in one faith according to the soul, although according to the body, it cannot be assembled in one place since every group of people is assembled in its own place.[25]

Already at first glance one can find the same thought structure in this exposition that we found before in the concept of the spiritual and physical fellowship. Therefore our line of reasoning can be applied to the concept of the church itself. This brings us to two important hermeneutical keys which are able to disclose Luther's concept of the church.

1. To begin with, the fundamental spiritual-sacramental structure of the church can be set forth. Therein is grounded the *unity* of both facets. For Luther the concept of the church is determined, just as that of the concept of the sacraments, by three elements: the (spiritual) meaning, the (sacramental) sign and the (Spirit-worked) faith which binds the first two together. This parallelism of thought structure is completely unequivocal but also surprising. For in spite of this theological identity of thought structure Luther never designated Christendom/church as a sacrament. If however this thought structure is recognized as hermeneutically valid, it resolves the problems which certainly have beset Protestant and Catholic theologians, and in the light of this structural analysis should disappear from the debate as false problems:

a) The "two churches" is a question of a theological distinction but in no way that of two different churches. Just as a sacrament can be subdivided by theological analysis into certain constituent parts but may be understood only as a *unity*, so also the concept of the church. The different constituent parts do not aim at division but rather serve clarity of analysis. The church cannot be torn apart into spiritual and physical parts without itself being dissolved. Luther may be criticized for misunderstandable terminology ("two churches") and creating the appearance that it is only a question of an only practical inseparability. But the sacramental structure offsets all such misunderstandings because this expression bestows exactly the integration of outward/physical to spiritual/inward reality.

b) It is in accordance with the church's being-in-the-world that it can be perceived only by outward-physical signs which however are bound essentially with the spiritual reality. It is a question therefore of the hiddenness with Christ in God (Luther cites Col.3:3), a concept which only later characterizes the two facets in the concept of the church as an indissoluble unity.

Thus it is impossible to introduce a value distinction between the spiritual and physical church for these form a single unity by the Holy Spirit. There is no spiritual Christendom without physical Christendom (the signs of the sacraments) being recognized as effective means of the Spirit. But here too Luther's hazardous terminology ("made and outward") caused by polemics must be taken into account. Nevertheless the unity is strongly set forth by the anthropological analogy (body-soul are indivisible just as are the outer and inner person according to Paul).

2. Our analysis of the fellowship concept referred furthermore to the relationship between law and gospel. In relation to the above quotation the application of these theologoumena can solve certain further problems. As Luther speaks of the "other manner" of Christendom/church he pronounces judgment on it and writes, "There is not a single letter in Holy Scripture saying that such a church, where it is by itself, is instituted by God."[26] We have already pointed out that in his polemic Luther left out of account the

"external" signs of the church. Thus it would at first be intelligible that where the signs instituted by God are not present, the church is not to be found. However Luther places the accent presumably elsewhere, namely upon the words "where it is by itself." This would show that the bracketing of the spiritual assembly of Christendom and the one-sided emphasis, indeed the sole determination of Christendom by its physical-outward form, is to be seen as contrary to Scripture. But then the objection is judged clearly as a determination of the church by the law, that is, the outward as the essence of Christendom. Then the outer gestures, the hierarchical ("clerical") estate, and the exercise of external piety which is tied up with it will pretend to be the "spiritual Christendom." "Although the little words 'spiritual' or 'church' are violated here when they are applied to such externals, since they refer only to the faith which makes true priests and Christians in the soul, this manner of speech has spread everywhere—to the not unimportant seduction and error of many souls who think such external glitter is the spiritual and true estate of Christendom or of the church."[27] Luther certainly knows that canon law and human laws do characterize the church in this way but that this is not the point in the present discussion.[28] Thereby there is agreement with the earlier reference and Luther's rejection of the third way of speaking of the "church."

Consequently, Luther can only accept the physical, outward Christendom provided that this is seen together with the spiritual-inward Christendom. Then he can still criticize the abuses of this outwardness but not miss the signs of the church instituted by Christ. Thus what is of decisive significance for him is "where it is by itself." Where the spiritual-inward Christendom is interpreted by the outward-physical, then the church considered primarily as the creation of the Holy Spirit by the gift of faith, hope, and love disappears. It is in this connection that the "two churches by two distinct names" are critically justified for thereby the essential and true church as God's creation (and not "made" by persons) is recognized. The concern here is no longer with a simple "*double-facetedness*" of the church but rather with its possible misinterpretation. Then the church could stand as law alone and the trust of faith in God's hidden activity *in* the outward and physical is transferred *to* these themselves. But this means to lose the church as gospel. Therefore the concern is with the "*ambiguity*" of the church. This follows from the analysis of the given possibilities of meaning by the structure. The alternative is in an isolated legalistic understanding or an interpretation which resolutely adheres to the relation between the "good law" (physical-outward) and the spiritual-inward work of God (gospel). Although Christendom can be recognized in the physical-outward reality, that is, as the communio corporalis, it is however itself, through the physical-outward elements, a spiritual fellowship "which may be numbered with the worldly community."[29] Put otherwise: the church may indeed be accessible as a social phenomenon in human society for sociological investigation but its *essence* cannot be grasped by these means. Only theology can disclose the true church according to its spiritual-sacramental reality.[30]

"THE FELLOWSHIP OF CHRIST AND ALL THE SAINTS"

In "A Sermon on the Blessed Sacrament of the Holy and True Body of Christ, and the Brotherhoods" (1519), Luther developed the above-cited thought structure of a spiritual-sacramental fellowship of the church. We take this writing as an exemplary presentation of Luther's articulation of his doctrine of the church and its decisive marks.

To begin with, Luther envisions the fellowship as the "significance," that is, the spiritual reality, which is given through the "signs" of the bread and wine.[31] At the end of the writing he summarizes the double movement of fellowship and ties this together with love and unity as the essential contents of this fellowship in the following manner: "This fellowship is twofold: on the one hand we partake of Christ and all saints; on the other hand we permit all Christians to be partakers of us, in whatever way they and we are able. Thus by means of this sacrament, all self-seeking love is rooted out and gives place to that which seeks the common good of all; and through the change wrought by love there is one bread, one drink, one body, one community. This is the true unity of Christian brethren."[32]

In this summary two things are first of all conspicuous: on the one hand Luther unites the fellowship of Christ and all *saints,* on the other hand he speaks of the *"we"* of all Christians. Thus it appears in the first case he means the blessed departed (dead) saints and in the second case the still-living Christians. The connection "Christ and all saints" is a continually used expression in the sermon and in most cases characterizes the saints in heaven *and* on earth in the sense of the Creed (communio sanctorum). Christ and the saints form a "spiritual body." On this basis we are able to read the sermon so that "the fellowship of Christ and all (his) saints" refers equally to the militant *and* triumphant church. "To receive this sacrament in bread and wine, then, is nothing else than to receive a sure sign of this fellowship and incorporation with Christ and all saints."[33]

In this fellowship, so understood, there is a double movement, namely from the Head of the Body, Christ, to all saints and, as the fruit of this movement of love, a movement of love among the saints themselves. In the sacrament Christ's righteousness is distributed and received, a righteousness in which the saints have a part. The fact must be emphasized that the saints receive as community the righteousness of Christ and by faith have obtained a "gracious exchange."[34] "This fellowship consists in this, that all the spiritual possessions of Christ and his saints are shared with and become the property of him who receives this sacrament."[35] Thus the spiritual-sacramental reality of the fellowship exists therein that Christ through his love gives all saints participation in his gift of salvation, uniting himself with the saints, and entering into their battle against sin, death, flesh, and the world.[36]

Luther turns to two Bible passages in particular in order to describe the fellowship among the saints. 1 Cor. 12:25f. is a clarification for him of the sacrament, that is, how the spiritual gifts work in the physical fellowship: "The members have [the same] care for one another; if one member suffers, all suffer together; if one member is honored, all rejoice together."[37] In the same way he exegetes Gal. 6:2 ("Bear one another's burdens, and so fulfil the law of Christ."). Only here it is emphasized that Christ as the Head is the first "bearer" of suffering and thereby makes possible the bearing of one another's burdens.[38] In any case it is to be noted that even if here Christ is the example of the relationship of the members of his body, the saints are at the same time those who "bear the misfortune of *Christ and his* saints."[39] The union of Christ with his saints through love concerns the Head himself. Therefore he bears the holy fellowship and he is himself borne by them, while the members of his body exercise their service of love to one another. Christ identifies himself with the suffering and needy.

The fellowship of Christ and all saints which finds its realization through the distribution and reception of the sacraments has various forms of expression. According to the extent that everything is in common the fellowship can share need and joy for and with one another in all cases. As the life of the Christian remains a battle against sin and the anxiety of death he can count on the help of the fellowship which intercedes for him. Thus the struggle between the anxious sinner and the enemy of life is not led in isolation but rather all the members of the fellowship are on his side. This is all the more promised and signified by the sacramental signs "that this sin is assailing not only you but also my Son, Christ, and all his saints in heaven and on earth."[40] The sinner is borne and protected by the intercessions of the fellowship.

The fellowship exists for one another also in bodily need. Luther refers to ancient Christendom where the celebration of the sacrament was connected with the collection of material gifts to be distributed to the needy. Thus he explains the designation "collect" and complains that this action has gotten lost. But he concentrates everything upon the celebration of the mass without which there are not the necessary fruits.[41] He brings up this example often in later writings where he polemicizes against the sacrifice of the mass in order to restore the genuine offering of the fellowship.

However, Luther knows that the celebration of the sacrament does not awake movement to the neighbor in everyone who receives its gifts. For the fellowship is to be a transformation of persons through love. Just as Christ and his saints have received us, as Christ has humbled himself in order to bear the sins and needs of humanity, so "through this same love we are to be changed and to make the infirmities of all other Christians our own."[42] This means "we are changed into one another and are made into a community of love." What this means is, on the one hand, becoming one inwardly with Christ and his saints, and on the other hand conformity with Christ.[43] For Luther this transformation of the person as the spiritual-sacramental meaning of the fellowship takes the place of the theory of the transubstantiation of the bread and wine. This latter is of subordinate significance. For where the person himself is not changed but only the gifts received and their fruits taken, the fruit of the sacrament disappears. He who does not desire to take upon himself the risk of fellowship with Christ and all saints does not receive from the "sacrament of love" what it can give. For one is transformed by love and taken into the spiritual body. He who despises this "cannot but receive death in the sacrament" (1 Cor. 11:29).[44] He who desires to belong to the "natural body of Christ" without the "spiritual" is not helped at all for "a change must occur [in the communicant] and be exercised through love."[45]

Luther saw in the brotherhoods of his time an expression of self-serving love which isolates persons from each other. Under the appearance of "fellowship" the opposite of Christian love was exercised. "For in them men learn to seek their own good, to love themselves.... And so perishes the communion of saints, Christian love, and the true brotherhood which is established in the holy sacrament, while selfish love grows in them."[46] This critique is against every type of misuse of "fellowship" and retains its sharpness against similar phenomena in church history.

Luther believes that these brotherhoods would be able to serve the neighbor only when they give and distribute all their collected material to the needy. Then they could exercise "works of true brotherhood; they would make God and his saints look with favor upon the brotherhoods."[47] True fellowship could take the place of the "biased brotherhoods." "Then the spiritual and material works of the brotherhoods would be done in their proper order."[48]

This overview of the content of the sermon shows in a concentrated way the development of Luther's foundation of the spiritual-sacramental communion with Christ and his saints. Herein is created the theological basis of Luther's ecclesiology for his later theology which develops and deepens this ecclesiological foundation and concretizes the communio-ecclesiology in particular contexts.[49]

NOTES

1. The concept of communio first appears in this period to move into the foreground of Luther's concept of the church. There are particular studies of his earlier writings, especially his lectures on the Psalms. After Karl Holl ("Die Entstehung von Luthers Kirchenbegriff," in *Gesammelte Aufsätze* (Tübingen, 1948)

LUTHER'S DOUBLE-FACETED CONCEPT OF THE CHURCH

1:288–325, and Holsten Fagerberg ("Die Kirche in Luthers Psalmenvorlesungen 1513–1515," in *Gedenkschrift für Werner Elert* (Berlin, 1955), 109–118) there are two important monographs: Joseph Vercruysse, *Fidelis Populus* (Wiesbaden, 1968), and Scott Hendrix, *Ecclesia in Via* (Leiden, 1974). The relationship of these early phases to the later development is a complicated problem which cannot be dealt with here.

2. WA 1:639,2.
3. LW 39:7; WA 6:64,1.
4. LW 39:7; WA 6:64,1,6.
5. WA 1:639,19.
6. WA 1:642,29.
7. WA 6:65,26.
8. WA 1:639,34.
9. WA 1:643,3.
10. LW 39:22; WA 6:75,37.
11. Ferdinand Kattenbusch speaks of the "Doppelschichtigkeit in Luthers Kirchenbegriff" in *Theol. Studien und Kritiken,* 100/1 (1927):197–347. He sees correctly that Luther always speaks only of *one* church even when he makes distinctions concerning it. He formulates his comprehensive thesis, with which we fully agree, as follows: "In his decisive, inwardly guiding view Luther hardly comes to terms with any other concept with such quiet certainty than that of the church. It is simply and only to him the communio sanctorum" (342). But Kattenbusch uses the concept of "double-facetedness" in a broader understanding than we shall in the following. Although he correctly interprets the "double-facetedness" in regard to "spiritual-bodily" and "inner-outer" in discussion with other theologians, he broadens the concept to the relationship between church and state (242ff.) and to the "religious" and "ethical," whereby the unity of both marks are maintained (266ff.). Finally, he offers a "clarification of Luther's concept of the 'double-facetedness' of the concept of the church on the basis of the three hierarchies" (314ff.).
12. WA 1:643,18.
13. LW 39:21; WA 6:75,2.
14. LW 39:7; WA 6:64,1.
15. It should be pointed out that the other sermon on baptism and penance from the same year presents exactly the same sacramental structure.
16. LW 35:49; WA 2:742,7.
17. Further details in Vilmos Vajta, *Evangile et sacrement* (Paris, 1973), 122–144.
18. LW 35:50; WA 2:743,7.
19. LW 39:70; WA 6:296,38.
20. Cf. Johannes Heckel, "'Die zwo Kirchen'—Eine juristische Betrachtung über Luthers Schrift 'Von dem Papsttum zu Rom'" in *Das blinde, undeutliche Wort "Kirche,"* ed. S. Grundmann (Köln-Graz, 1964), 111–131.
21. LW 39:65; WA 6:292f.
22. LW 39:68; WA 6:295,26.
23. LW 39:69; WA 6:296,30.
24. LW 39:75; WA 6:301,3.
25. LW 39:70; WA 6:296f.

26. *LW* 39:70; *WA* 6:296,30.
27. *LW* 39:69f.; *WA* 6:296,24.
28. *LW* 39:70; *WA* 6:296,35.
29. *LW* 39:68; *WA* 6:295,23.
30. Cf. Herbert Olsson, "Kyrkans synlighet och fördoldhet enligt Luther" in *En Bok om Kyrkan av Svenska teologer* (Stockholm, 1942), 306–326; German: "Sichtbarkeit und Verborgenheit der Kirche nach Luther," in *Ein Buch von der Kirche* (Göttingen, 1951), 338–360.
31. *LW* 35:50; *WA* 2:743,7.
32. *LW* 35:67; *WA* 2:754,10.
33. *LW* 35:51; *WA* 2:743,20.
34. *LW* 35:60; *WA* 2:749,32.
35. *LW* 35:51; *WA* 2:743,27.
36. "Christ with all saints, by his love, takes upon himself our form (Phil. 2:7), fights with us against sin, death, and all evil. This enkindles in us such love that we take on his form, rely upon his righteousness, life, and blessedness. And through the interchange of his blessings and our misfortunes, we become one loaf, one bread, one body, one drink, and have all things in common. O this is a great sacrament, says St. Paul" (Eph. 5:32; *LW* 35:58; *WA* 2:748; 750).
37. *LW* 35:52; *WA* 2:743,39.
38. *LW* 35:54f.; *WA* 2:745,31.
39. Ibid.
40. *LW* 35:53; *WA* 2:744,28.
41. *LW* 35:57; *WA* 2:747,26.
42. *LW* 35:58f.; *WA* 2:748,20.
43. *LW* 35:59; *WA* 2:748,30.
44. *LW* 35:62; *WA* 2:747,29; 750,30f.
45. *LW* 35:62; *WA* 2:751,16.
46. *LW* 35:69; *WA* 2:755,30.
47. *LW* 35:69; *WA* 2:755,14.
48. *LW* 35:71; *WA* 2:757,6.
49. Yngve Brilioth, *Nattvarden i evangeliskt gudstjänstliv* (Uppsala, 1926); English: *Eucharistic Faith and Life* (London, 1930), believes that "the sacramental mystery of community perhaps has never found such a brilliant expression as in this small writing" (163. Cf. 165 where Luther's greatest achievement is seen as the rediscovery of the motif of community). Paul Althaus, *Communio Sanctorum. Die Gemeinde im lutherischen Kirchengedanken* (Munich, 1929), 75 n.95, however, thinks, "The sources for the understanding of the Lord's Supper as sacrament of communio extend from 1519 to 1524." In the second part of our study, which was presented at the Consultation but cannot be printed for reasons of space, it is shown that the time span extends into the theology of the "old" Luther. However Althaus is right when he says, "Luther's concept of the church as fellowship did not remain living in Lutheranism and did not enter into its doctrinal development" (23). Cf. also P. Althaus, *Die Theologie Martin Luthers* (Gütersloh, 1962), 254–278; English: *The Theology of Martin Luther* (Philadelphia, 1966), 294–322.

"A People of Grace":
Ecclesiological Implications of
Luther's Sacrament-Related Sermons
of 1519

HANS-WERNER SCHEELE

Life is richer than our ability to comprehend and describe it conceptually. In particular, the *life of faith* surpasses everything that can be grasped in reflection and articulated in words. Connected with this there is the fact that the Christian witness is capable of proclaiming more than he himself realizes and in particular more than his statement formulates directly.

In view of these realities, in the following pages *ecclesiological questions* will be posed with regard to texts of Luther which were in no way conceived as contributions to ecclesiology. We are dealing here with a few relatively brief pastoral writings which were composed in a very limited period of time.

Luther brought together[1] first of all three sermons which appeared one after another and dedicated[2] them to the widowed Duchess Margaret of Braunschweig-Lüneburg. Impressed by her "devotion to Holy Scripture," he sent her, in the middle of October 1519, "several sermons . . . on the holy, highly esteemed and comforting sacrament of Penance, of Baptism and of the holy Body."[3] In view of misunderstanding and misuse they should all help believers to "seek peace in God's grace through the Holy Sacraments."[4] The titles are: "A Sermon on the Sacrament of Penance,"[5] "A Sermon on the Holy and Blessed Sacrament of Baptism,"[6] and "A Sermon on the Blessed Sacrament of the Holy and True Body of Christ and the Brotherhoods."[7]

A further "A Sermon on Preparation for Death"[8] will also be taken into consideration here. This sermon arose from the request of one of the advisors of Frederick the Wise by the name of Marx, or Markus Schart—that Luther write instructions for him for the correct preparation for death. The request, transmitted via Spalatin, could not be fulfilled straightaway due to various other demands—not least of all the Leipzig Disputation.[9] The first copies were finally sent out on November 1, 1519.[10] There was soon a great demand for copies, so much so that by the end of 1525, twenty-one reprints were necessary.[11]

To sum up, the four sermons named above are characterized as *relating to*

Translated by Patricia M. Williams and Harry McSorley

the sacraments. This is what specifically distinguishes them from the other sermons[12] published in 1519. The words "sacrament related" can also point to a basic intention which influenced Luther at that time. For Luther it is essentially a question, confronted with the ultimate seriousness which is presented in the face of death, that "we must earnestly, diligently, and highly esteem the holy sacraments, hold them in honor, freely and cheerfully rely on them, and so balance them against sin, death, and hell that they will outweigh these by far. We must occupy ourselves much more with the sacraments and their virtues than with our sins."[13] Christian life and death is on the whole essentially related to sacrament. Thus must it also be for theology in general and ecclesiology in particular. Luther goes so far as to formulate even the decisive answer of faith in relation to the sacraments: "I can say with Mary in firm faith, 'Let it be to me according to your words and signs.' "[14]

What consequences does this have for the view of the "congregation of believers"? What truth does the sure sign *(wartzeichen)*[15] show to *the whole church*, the *"sign"* Sacrament? In face of the difficulties which the attempt of the Second Vatican Council provides for many who respond to this formulation of the question, it is worth taking up the elements of the answer Luther offers us in 1519. Perhaps one can find some help for advancing the Catholic/ Lutheran dialogue on word and sacrament and the related question of ministry. At the same time there is a need to resist as much as possible the temptation of a sacramentalistic narrowness. If a reduction should result from the concentration, then Luther would be misunderstood just as much as the sacramental reality. Thus the aim and limits of our task are laid down. Accordingly we ask what the above-named sermons have to tell us about 1) the development and 2) the nature of the Church.

ON THE DEVELOPMENT OF THE CHURCH

The question as to the development of the church can be put in two ways: on the one hand as an inquiry into its first chronological origins, and on the other hand as a direct question as to what constitutes the Church now and always. Without doubt the latter has priority for Luther. Information about the past moves him less than the confrontation with what is given and demanded at present. Correspondingly, it is a question of 1) what happens with God ever anew so that the church can be realized, and 2) what should happen, respectively, with the people in the church.

From the Side of God

Every Christian begins with the event of baptism, which is a life-long process so that "this life is nothing else than a spiritual baptism which does not cease till death."[16] The church is subject to the same law of life: it constantly needs the grace of its origin, without "an unceasing spiritual baptism" it is condemned to death. Only if it *becomes* or develops is it church. The trinitarian God must each time say anew: "Let it become!"; he must create always anew the wonder of pardon, the mediation, and the transformation. There is only a church if he constantly gives it.

Our world is incessantly threatened by *sin, death, and hell*. The uncanny thing about these dangers is that they do not come from outside but that they exert their harmful power within the very inner depths of people. This makes it difficult to recognize them realistically and it makes it impossible to resist them. A person cannot deal with these threats by his own strength. He exists in the spell of sin whose earthly fruit is death and whose lasting outcome is known as hell. Luther's sermon on the call to death sketches our situation with hard, pregnant strokes. Only those who become aware of this situation are able to appreciate what *God's grace* signifies. Luther summarizes this impressively at the end of his sermon. He reassures the one who lacks assurance: that God "In Christ he offers you the image of life, of grace, and of salvation so that you may not be horrified by the images of sin, death, and hell. Furthermore, he lays your sin, your death, and your hell on his dearest Son, vanquishes them, and renders them harmless for you. . . . And to relieve you of all doubt, he grants you a sure sign, namely, the holy sacraments."[17] God saves from sin, death, and hell, in that he takes them upon himself. According to the will of the Father, the Son suffers them for us and thus imparts life, mercy, and blessedness. God's Word bears witness that God's sacrament works in his "sign . . . and promise."[18]

This all says something fundamental about the church. Only through God's grace is the church possible in a world of sin, death, and hell. The church, in regard to its creation and re-creation, is through and through "a people of grace."[19] If the church turns to the image of this grace then it has the image of its basis for existence before it. Luther portrays this in a shocking way. He states categorically: "The picture of grace is nothing else but that of Christ on the cross and of all his dear saints."[20] How is the "and" to be understood? Does it not of necessity impair the unique dignity of God's son, who became human, and his sacrificial death? Does it not cancel out the first assertion "no other but Christ"? Does it not contradict both the *solus Christus* and the *sola gratia*? We cannot evade these questions by thinking that the problematic formulations were a slip of the tongue that we can forgive and forget. Nor is it merely a question of quickly supposing Luther is speaking improperly. Luther really intends exactly that image of grace given us when he speaks of Christ *and* all his saints. This becomes abundantly clear when he expressly emphasizes that precisely this in its entirety is the *effective image* of grace. The "saints" are not placed so close to Christ that a fleeting glimpse does not allow us sufficiently to distinguish them from Christ. They are in fact included in his acts of salvation. A thought that one can often find in Luther is: "Grace and mercy are there where Christ on the cross takes your sin from you, bears it for you, and destroys it." So far so good. But Luther continues—practically in the same breath: "Likewise, all the saints who suffer and die in Christ also bear your sins and suffer and labor for you, as we find it written, 'Bear one another's burdens and thus fulfil the command of Christ.' "[21] The conviction stated here of the salvific significance of the saints and their involvement comes under discussion again when Luther advises: "Thus when you look at Christ and all his saints and delight in the grace of God, who elected them, and continue steadfastly in this joy, then you too are already elected."[22] One of the most impressive statements on the meaning and blessing of the veneration of saints points in the same direction: "Similarly, death, sin, and hell will flee with all their might if in the night we but keep our eyes on the glowing picture of Christ and his saints and abide in the faith. . . ."[23] All three of these statements, each worth considering, contain a catchword which is indispensable for our comprehension: Christ; mercy; faith. When the saints act like Christ and act with Christ so that their engagement in the work of salvation becomes fruitful, then that happens through Christ. From him they receive salvation and the gift as a task to serve him. That "God's grace" can be observed in the saints is a fruit of *grace* and not its root. The involvement of the saints is not a factor which is independently effective alongside the act of grace, but a direct effect of the one grace of God. From man, what is required is not partly faith and partly autonomous activity. The enlightening image of "Christ and his saints" carries out its salvific function only when it is grasped in *faith*. Of course something more is involved than merely taking cognizance of the image; an "exercise," a "study," and a "putting into practice" of this image is necessary.

In all this it can be seen that concrete means of mediation also always belong to God's act of grace. These are not acts which are thought of and organized by man; they belong to God's acts. To the pardoning of the sinner, which frees from guilt, and which is at the same time a blessing, to the granting of life and salvation, belongs the transmission of the liberating message and the sign which guarantee and symbolize these. In my opinion: the development of the church proceeds always anew from God's *Word and Sacrament*. They are unmerited and unmeritable gifts of grace: "God gives you nothing because of your worthiness, nor does he build his Word and sacraments on your worthiness, but out of sheer grace he establishes you, unworthy one, on the foundation of his Word and signs. Hold fast to that and say, 'He who gives and has given me his signs and his Word, which assure me that Christ's life, grace, and heaven have kept my sin, death, and hell from harming me, is truly God, who will surely preserve these things for me. . . .' "[24] It is not so that God's actions build up some assets that we are able to produce. He lays the foundation, he builds us up. Everything is a gift from him. It is also not so that he lets the Word and the Sacrament pass from his hands into human hands. He himself directs the human hand so to speak, he himself speaks through the human mouth: "In the sacraments your God, Christ himself, deals, speaks, and works with you through the priest. His are not the works and words of man. In the sacraments God himself grants you all the blessings we just mentioned in connection with Christ."[25] The one message that is transmitted in word and sacrament says to each individual: "Christ's life has taken your death, his obedience your sin, his love your hell, upon himself and overcome them."[26] Immediately after this Luther speaks again of the communion of saints as well as of its inclusion in the salvation event. At the same time the social or ecclesial components of the sacrament are impressively brought under discussion. Luther explains: "Moreover, through the same sacraments you are included and made one with all the saints. You thereby enter into the true communion of saints so that they die with you in Christ, bear sin, and vanquish hell."[27] Correspondingly Luther says of the sacrament of the altar that it "is a sign and promise of the communion of all angels and saints that they love me, provide and pray for me, suffer and die with me, bear my sin and overcome hell."[28]

If one takes seriously the already-mentioned inclusion of the believer in the communion of saints, then one finds oneself in face of a miracle of *change*. It does not only concern each redeemed person; it belongs essentially to the development of the church. In the sermon on the "True Body of Christ," Luther deduces it from the mystery of the eucharistic change: "For just as the bread is changed into his true natural body and the wine into his natural true blood, so truly are we also drawn and changed into the spiritual body, that is, into the fellowship of Christ and all saints and by this sacrament put into possession of all the virtues and mercies of Christ and his saints."[29]

Whoever is incorporated into the body of Christ is required to contribute what is his to this process. God does not treat humans like stones which can be added to a building by means of external intervention; he wants to include them as creatures of his love into the pardon, transmission and change.

From the Human Side

When we ask about the human contribution to the existence of the church, we do not turn away from the divine action in order to deal with a further factor. It is much more a question of ascertaining how God concretely includes humans into his actions. The key word for this incomprehensible mystery is *faith*. Pardon, transmission, and change are directed toward the faith which God wants to give and which a person must accept and live, "practice and strengthen."[30]

In faith human beings entrust themselves unconditionally to God. He is not satisfied with the acknowledgement of grace; he stretches out towards it, he takes refuge in it: "For it is not enough to know what the sacrament is and signifies. It is not enough that you know it is a fellowship and a gracious exchange or blending of our sin and suffering with the righteousness of

Christ and his saints. You must also desire it and firmly believe that you have received it."[31] The believer knows of his helplessness, of his dependence on saving grace; he allows himself by virtue of grace to be grasped and formed by grace; he opens himself to it and allows himself to be penetrated by it: "This faith is of all things the most necessary, for it is the ground of all comfort. He who does not possess such faith must despair of his sins."[32] With regard to the sacrament of penance Luther formulates this pointedly: "This sacrament does not depend on the priest, nor on your own actions, but entirely on your faith; you have as much as you believe. Without this faith you could have all the contrition in the world, but it would still be only the remorse of Judas that angers rather than reconciles God. For nothing reconciles God better than when one does him the honor [of acknowledging that] he is truthful and gracious; and no one does this except the one who believes his words."[33]

God's *Word and Sacrament* are an unrenounceable help in order to come to faith. They bear witness to God's gracious act on which faith rests. They are there precisely to provoke, challenge, and evoke faith. The sacraments are nothing other than "signs which help and incite us to faith. . . . Without this faith they serve no purpose."[34]

The covenant sign of baptism demands the *covenant acceptance* of faith which belongs to the development of the covenant people's church. If God "allies himself with you and becomes one with you in a gracious covenant of comfort," then there is a double consequence: "In the first place you give yourself up to the sacrament of baptism and to what it signifies. That is, you desire to die, together with your sins, and to be made new at the Last Day. . . . In the second place you pledge yourself to continue in this desire, and to slay your sin more and more as long as you live, even until your dying day."[35] When Luther in another place speaks of the *vow* of baptism, this is to be understood as a variation on the theme of faith: "to believe" (*glauben*) is "to vow" (*geloben*).[36] Since Christ's whole life is nothing else than "a spiritual baptism without interruption until death,"[37] then faith "without interruption" is demanded. Where this is realized, the church lives and grows.

Faith and the church: both are an impenetrable *mystery*. This mystery lies in God's sovereign action which cannot be explained or replaced or completed by us. Now however that which is impossible for us is undertaken by God: God wants to draw humans into his activity. Luther refers to this mystery when he says of baptismal faith: "In baptism we all make one and the same vow: to slay sin and to become holy through the work and grace of God, to whom we yield and offer ourselves, as clay to the potter."[38]

God wants everything: his decision for us and our decision for him, his action and grace and our efforts against sin and for holiness. If we say and live our agreement in the right way for God's will and action, then we are not stealing anything for ourselves which does not belong to us; rather we are giving God what belongs to him; we are giving ourselves like clay in the potter's hands.

Naturally everything which determines the development of the church is of importance for its nature. Thus, with what we have already discovered before we can now deal with the express question of the nature of the church.

THE NATURE OF THE CHURCH

The fact that the Second Vatican Council in all its endeavours toward understanding and renewing the church avoided presenting a definition of the church has been welcomed. Instead of this the Council took from the Bible the statements about the nature of the church and developed them in their peculiarity and in their relatedness. Luther proceeds in the same way. He does not produce any *definition* of the church; he himself speaks of the Church by means of basic ecclesial terms that are inspired by Holy Scripture. The most important of these are: 1) the people of God; 2) communion; 3) brotherhood; 4) the body of Christ. The basic law which determines the understanding of these words and which is essential for the realization of the Church is known as 5) solidarity. If we turn to the individual concepts, we should not disregard the fact that essentially they belong together. They point from different sides to a reality which calls not only for a many-sided but also, if possible, an approach from all sides.

God's People

The church is "a people of grace"[39] not only because it is called into life through God's *grace*. The beginning, middle, and consummation of the church stand as a sign of divine grace. This grace constantly provides it vital energy and its essential form. Its members are "children of mercy" and "people of God's good will."[40] What God began in them with baptism, so he continues throughout their life, towards the goal of completing his work in glory: "through baptism they have begun to become pure; by God's mercy with respect to the sins that still remain they are not condemned; until, finally, through death and at the Last Day, they become wholly pure. . . ."[41]

The abiding *bond* between God and his people is expressed especially through the idea of the *covenant*. That God "allies himself with you and becomes one with you in a gracious covenant of comfort"[42] is not only assured for each Christian; it is valid *a fortiori* for all of God's people. By the power of grace the people are called and obliged to wage a life and death battle; the always-necessary fight against sin. We should be recognized as "a people of Christ, our Leader, under whose banner of the holy cross we continually fight against sin."[43] Because of this constantly necessary insertion into the sign of the cross, God's people as a whole is really a *community of the cross*.

The call to belong to God's people is issued equally to everyone, just as the answer of faith is expected from everyone. We all receive the one baptism:

"We all make one and the same vow . . . no one is any better than another."[44] This baptismal vow can be discharged in various ways. From its roots, for example, can come the vow of the spiritual state in general and the ministry of bishop or pastor in particular. No special community next to that of all the baptized is being established here and certainly no special world next to baptism; here the vow of baptism can find an especially intense fulfilment "for the spiritual estate, if it is as it ought to be, should be full of torment and suffering in order that he who belongs to it may have more exercise in the work of his baptism than the man who is in the estate of matrimony."[45] Similarly bishops and pastors "should be well practiced in sufferings and works, and at every hour be ready for death—to die not only for their own sake, but also for the sake of those who are their subjects."[46] This reverence for the priestly service allows Luther to say: since God himself "speaks and acts through the priest, we would do him in his Word and work no greater dishonor than to doubt whether it is true."[47] With regard to the sacrament of penance Luther gives the cogent advice: "You must trust in the priest's absolution as firmly as though God had sent a special angel or apostle to you, yes, as though Christ himself were absolving you."[48]

It should not be overlooked that alongside these and similar statements in our sermons a *counter movement* is announced. Among other things this emerges in the way Luther allows the minister of the sacrament of repentance to fade into the background in favor of the almost isolated *word and faith event*.[49] So it would appear logical when finally also the possibility of lay-absolution is presented and explained, that: "Indeed where there is no priest, each individual Christian—even a woman or child—does as much. For any Christian can say to you, 'God forgives you your sins, in the name,' etc., and if you can accept that word with a confident faith, as though God were saying it to you, then in that same faith you are surely absolved."[50]

Communion

What it means that the church is communion is disclosed less by means of a study of the concept than through concentration on the center of ecclesial life, the *Eucharist*. This sacrament "signifies the complete union and the undivided fellowship of the saints."[51] While many Christians even now think of the word communion exclusively as the individual encounter with Christ, which is imparted to the individual communicant, Luther establishes that it really involves much more: "Christ with all the saints"[52] and the Christian with all the saints. Exactly this is the "significance or effect of this sacrament," its real sense and aim; therefore, "to go to the sacrament" means "to take part in this fellowship."[53] These are embodied in the body of Christ with all his members: "to receive this sacrament in bread and wine, then, is nothing else than to receive a sure sign of this fellowship and incorporation with Christ and all saints. It is as if a citizen were given a sign, a document, or some other token to assure him that he is a citizen of the city, a member of that particular community."[54]

Who are these "saints"? First of all, all our contemporaries on this earth who live in grace. In addition, the unequally large multitude of those who have been called home by the Lord and who now live with him in indestructible, although not quite perfect, communion.[55] Finally, Luther also counts God's angels among this number. So he says to those who are approaching death: " 'The priest has given me the holy body of Christ, which is a sign and promise of the communion of all angels and saints that they love me, provide and pray for me, suffer and die with me, bear my sin and overcome hell.' "[56]

The horizon and area of influence of the church thus reach far beyond the boundaries of our earth. Through Christ, with him and in him the communion is boundless and the *interchange of life* inexhaustible. That all of this does not correspond to the emanation of an abstract, quasi-cosmic set of laws, but is of a thoroughly personal nature, can be made clear by a further basic concept that expresses an essential characteristic of the church.

Brotherhood

Luther's eucharistic sermon from 1519 concludes with a moving reference to the *fruit* of the sacrament of the altar, "to communion and love." More precisely, a double communion is given: "On the one hand we partake of Christ and all saints; on the other hand we permit all Christians to be partakers of us, in whatever way they and we are able."[57] By means of the transformation of such love, "one bread, one drink, one body, one community" are realized. When Luther adds "this is the true unity of Christian brethren,"[58] then he makes accessible to us what brotherhood means in connection with the church. It is a question of a bond that reaches into the depths, that gives to and demands ultimate things from all those who are the children of the one Father and the *brothers and sisters of Christ*. The church is not an anonymous mammoth society; it is a community with a face and a heart.

The "one, inner, spiritual, essential brotherhood common to all saints"[59] distinguishes itself essentially from the "natural" brotherhood which exists in a family and from the "partisan" brotherhood which is established and organized by human beings. In both of these the bond is limited in various ways. The brotherhood in Christ is "the divine, the heavenly, the noblest, which surpasses all others as gold surpasses copper or lead."[60] It is "so closely united that a closer relationship cannot be conceived. For here we have one baptism, one Christ, one sacrament, one food, one gospel, one faith, one Spirit, one spiritual body, and each person is a member of the other."[61]

A further basic biblical concept is mentioned in these last words which states something essential about the church.

LUTHER'S DOUBLE-FACETED CONCEPT OF THE CHURCH

The Body of Christ

Even the analogy of the family of flesh and blood is not sufficient to express realistically the inner bond within the church. The *organic unity* of flesh and blood, the unity of the body, takes us further. God's word encourages us to risk this bold comparison. Indeed Christians in the church find themselves not only like the members of a community, they are called to live as the members of a body. Through the sacraments they are literally "incorporated."[62]

Luther adds two observations to elucidate the *intensity of the "incorporation"*: he recalls the change of the bread and wine as well as the new unity which grows out of eating and drinking. As "out of the bodies of many grains there comes the body of one bread, in which each grain loses its form and body and takes upon itself the common body of the bread," as the grapes "in losing their own form, become the body of one common wine and drink,"[63] so out of many "through the interchange of his blessings and our misfortunes, we become one loaf, one bread, one body, one drink, and have all things in common."[64] Different from a union through "nails, glue, cords, and the like," eating and drinking leads to a new, organic unity; "one divisible substance" results "of objects joined together": "Thus in the sacrament we too become united with Christ, and are made one body with all the saints."[65] Luther skillfully links the motive of the one body with that of the gracious exchange between Christ and the believers: Christ accepts us to such an extent in his body that he acts for us, as if he were what we are. In turn it is up to us to accept him as if we were what he is so that we in turn become like him.[66]

From this come concrete demands for our life. Luther formulates this arrestingly: "See to it also that you give yourself to everyone in fellowship and by no means exclude anyone in hatred or anger. For this sacrament of fellowship, love, and unity cannot tolerate discord and disunity."[67]

Solidary Community

It would seem justified immediately to provide the word solidarity with regard to the church with an exclamation mark and to understand it as an imperative. Nevertheless in this very context it is first of all an indicative. It refers to something *"given"* in the deepest and most beautiful sense: solidarity of the first order. Solidary action of the best quality stands on the threshold, in the center and at the summit of the church. The church lives *from* solidary action and *through* it, before being able to adopt it completely and to begin to live *in* it.

The maxim of solidarity, "one for all and all for one," has found unique realization in Jesus Christ. He lived radically and totally for all and gave himself for everyone. All are called to decide for him, to accept his action and thus himself, and to entrust their actions and thus themselves to him. If we follow this call then he will take over our sins and we will receive his love, then he will suffer our death and we will rejoice in his life, then he will suffer hell for us and we will share his heavenly glory. The church lives from and for the realization of this solidary exchange. The church is the place of solidarity granted by God for the price of his solidarity in a basically unsolidary world.

To the concrete form of the solidary exchange there belongs, according to Luther's declared conviction of 1519, that the *"one for all"* of Christ is co-completed by his saints. After they, as all people, were directed to his redeeming action and while this is continually the case, they stand as redeemed by his side. "Christ's sufferings and life" "together with the lives and sufferings of all the saints" are for the good of the believer and should "be his own."[68] Luther assures the person who devoutly receives the Lord: "Christ and all his saints are coming to you with all their virtues, sufferings, and mercies, to live, work, suffer, and die with you, and that they desire to be wholly yours, having all things in common with you."[69] The communion of the church exists in the fact that "all the spiritual possessions of Christ and his saints are shared . . . and become the common property" and "again all sufferings and sins also become common property; and thus love engenders love in return and [mutual love] unites."[70] "Christ with all saints, by his love, takes upon himself our form, fights with us against sin, death, and all evil. This enkindles in us such love that we take his form, rely upon his righteousness, life and blessedness . . . and have all things in common."[71]

Neither the Reformation discovery of justification solely by grace nor the knowledge of the distressing false forms of the veneration of saints keeps Luther in 1519 from outlining the place of saints in the salvation event and from demanding the corresponding consequences from the believers. He assures the individual Christian who is approaching death that "the saints and all Christians" turn to him. "There is no doubt . . . that all of these in a body run to him as one of their own, help him overcome sin, death, and hell, and bear all things with him."[72] Correspondingly Luther joins with the demand to believe in God and to honor him, the appeal to call on the "angels . . . the Mother of God, and all the apostles and saints," without doubting that they would be heard.[73] Such prayer is necessary, not because without it the saints would not help, but "to make our faith and trust in them, and through them in God, stronger and bolder."[74]

Just as solidarity is not allowed to stop at the limits of the world, so also it has to go beyond the limits of the church. The love received is to be passed on in every direction; it should show itself everywhere as "a love . . . which seeks the common good of all."[75] "You must take to heart the infirmities and needs of others, as if they were your own. Then offer to others your strength, as if it were their own. . . ."[76] This means, then, not only to give to individuals individual acts of love: "This is what it means to be changed into one another through love, . . . to lose one's own form and take on that which is common to all."77

NOTES

1. See Luther's letter to Georg Spalatin of Dec. 18, 1519 (WA Br. 1:594f., 19–25).
2. Details in H.-U. Delius, ed., *Martin Luther Studienausgabe* (Berlin, 1979), 1:244f.
3. WA 2:713.
4. WA 2:713.
5. *LW* 35:9–22; WA 2:714–723.
6. *LW* 35:29–43; WA 2:727–737.
7. *LW* 35:49–75; WA 2:742–758.
8. *LW* 42:99–115; WA 2:685–697.
9. See *WA Br* 1:381, 17f., and 508, 12f.
10. See *WA Br* 1:584.
11. For details see Delius, *Martin Luther Studienausgabe*.
12. "Sermo von der Betrachtung des heiligen Leidens Christi" (WA 2:136–142); "Sermo de duplici iustitia" (WA 2:145–152); "Sermo vom ehelichen Stand" (WA 9:213–220 or 2:166–171); "Sermo vom Gebet und von der Prozession in der Kreuzwoche" (WA 2:175–179); and "Sermo vom Wucher" (WA 6:3–8).
13. *LW* 42:100; WA 2:686.
14. *LW* 42:101; WA 2:686.
15. *LW* 42:114; WA 2:697.
16. *LW* 35:30; WA 2:728.
17. *LW* 42:114; WA 2:697.
18. *LW* 42:110; WA 2:694.
19. *LW* 35:36; WA 2:732.
20. *LW* 42:104; WA 2:689.
21. Ibid.
22. *LW* 42:106; WA 2:690.
23. Ibid.
24. *LW* 42:110; WA 2:694.
25. *LW* 42:108; WA 2:692.
26. Ibid.
27. Ibid.
28. *LW* 42:111; WA 2:694; cf. also *LW* 42:112; WA 2:695.
29. *LW* 35:59; WA 2:749.
30. *LW* 35:61; WA 2:750.
31. *LW* 35:60; WA 2:749.
32. *LW* 35:36; WA 2:732.
33. *LW* 35:16; WA 2:719.
34. *LW* 42:100; WA 2:686.
35. *LW* 35:33; WA 2:730.
36. *LW* 35:40; WA 2:735.
37. *LW* 35:30; WA 2:728.

38. *LW* 35:41; *WA* 2:735.
39. *LW* 35:36; *WA* 2:732.
40. Ibid.
41. Ibid.
42. *LW* 35:33; *WA* 2:730.
43. *LW* 35:29; *WA* 2:727.
44. *LW* 35:41; *WA* 2:735.
45. *LW* 35:41; *WA* 2:736.
46. Ibid.
47. *LW* 42:101; *WA* 2:686.
48. *LW* 42:110; *WA* 2:694.
49. Cf. *WA* 2:715–717 and 720f.
50. *LW* 35:12; *WA* 2:716.
51. *LW* 35:50; *WA* 2:742f.
52. *LW* 35:51; *WA* 2:743.
53. Ibid.
54. Ibid.
55. See *LW* 42:104–105; *WA* 2:689.
56. *LW* 42:111; *WA* 2:694; see also *LW* 42:112–113; *WA* 2:695f.
57. "In conclusion," *LW* 35:67; *WA* 2:754.
58. Ibid.
59. *LW* 35:70; *WA* 2:755.
60. *LW* 35:70; *WA* 2:756.
61. Ibid.
62. *WA* 2:692; cf. *LW* 42:108; see also *LW* 35:55; *WA* 2:746, 14.
63. *LW* 35:58; *WA* 2:748.
64. Ibid.
65. *LW* 35:59; *WA* 2:748.
66. *LW* 35:59f.; *WA* 2:748f.
67. *LW* 35:61; *WA* 2:750.
68. *LW* 35:52; *WA* 2:744.
69. *LW* 35:61; *WA* 2:750.
70. *LW* 35:51–52; *WA* 2:743.
71. *LW* 35:58; *WA* 2:748.
72. *LW* 42:112; *WA* 2:695.
73. *LW* 42:113; *WA* 2:696.
74. Ibid.
75. "In conclusion," *LW* 35:67; *WA* 2:754.
76. *LW* 35:61–62; *WA* 2:750.
77. Ibid.

Responses

Some Comments on Professor Vilmos Vajta's Lecture
METROPOLITAN JOHN OF HELSINKI

When Vilmos Vajta deals with his theme "The Church as the Spiritual-Sacramental Communio with Christ and His Saints" in such an extensive and deep way, it seems almost improper to offer only short comments on his paper. However, I shall respond to certain points of his long and learned treatise in all modesty and simplicity.

To begin with, I face the perennial difficulty of a non-Lutheran reader commenting on a Lutheran theological paper on Luther: first, one presupposes that there is and must be something wrong in Luther's own reasoning, and, second, that the Lutheran writer tries to understand and explain everything as if there were nothing wrong. This dilemma is in the background because it is difficult to get away from the idea, that whenever a phenomenon leads to division and disunity in the church, it cannot be entirely in harmony with the Orthodox tradition.

The paper begins with a very basic problem which seems to need further clarification. When dealing with Luther's view of the character and meaning of excommunication, Vajta makes it quite clear that the authority of the church pertains only to the so-called communio corporalis. This raises the question, at least from the point of view of the Orthodox tradition, of how this can be understood in the light of the Gospel teaching on the power of the keys: "I will give you the keys of the kingdom of heaven, and whatever you bind on earth shall be bound in heaven, and whatever you loose on earth shall be loosed in heaven" (Matt. 16:19). And, "If you forgive the sins of any, they are forgiven; if you retain the sins of any, they are retained" (John 20:23). The latter passage is traditionally interpreted in light of the former one. Both passages represent quite clearly the idea that, from the point of view of the church's power of the keys, there is no such distinction between the communio spiritualis and the communio corporalis as that of Luther according to the interpretation of Vajta. The solution of this problem is of vital significance for the whole structure of Luther's reasoning and teaching on these central matters concerning the nature of the church and the power of the keys.

The ancient church does not have such a distinction. This can be seen from various canons pertaining to excommunication and penance. This may likewise be seen in the liturgical prayers connected to the mystery of repentance (confession). Against this background we have to ask: How can Luther's teaching be understood? Other questions are related to this. How should we understand the statement that the unjustly excommunicated can "go spiritually to the sacrament" and enjoy the *communio spiritualis* with Christ and His Saints? To say that faith binds together the two aspects or kinds of communio is not an answer to our question. Our question is also related to the character and role of divine grace and thus to the character of the Eucharist. When it is asserted that the external sacrament without faith is without grace and does not bring about anything but the communio corporalis, there seems to be reason to ask whether the reality of sacramental grace has its basis decisively in persons and not in the ordinance of God.

Luther's use of the words *Kirche* and *Christenheit* is of interest in this connection. Is the former often rejected because it may seem to point to a role of the power of the keys (and the hierarchy) which Luther does not accept? Does not the very word "Christenheit" represent a different type of ecclesiology, where the main emphasis is put on the believers in a one-sided way at the cost of the constituting role of the priesthood for the entire *esse* of the church?

It is of positive interest, particularly from the Orthodox point of view, that Luther sometimes sees the worshiping congregation, in all places, as the external expression of "Christenheit" or, in other words, of the Church of Christ. This seems to offer a point of connection to that ancient Orthodox ecclesiology, taught by many fathers, according to which the Church of Christ is basically, concretely and visibly in all places where the local congregation is gathered around its bishop for the celebration of the Eucharist. To what extent does Luther make use of this traditional interpretation? Or, what factors prevent a more consistent following of this approach? It would be interesting here to have this question elucidated more extensively. Is it a negative factor for Luther that the role of the priesthood here, too, in a natural way receives an emphasis which he does not find acceptable?

How should we understand Luther's interpretation of the communio with Christ and his saints as the "spiritual reality" given through the *signum* of bread and wine? For the ancient fathers bread and wine are not merely a *signum* of something; they are changed, they become and they are the body and blood of Christ, that is, Christ really and truly is present, although the Mystery remains a mystery and the church does not try to explain how the change takes place. How are we to understand the character of the real presence of Christ and the unique role of this in view of the interpretation that the communio implies that we enjoy (receive) Christ *and* his saints?

It may be possible to interpret this to mean that the former (Christ) is the basis and the presupposition of the latter, although the two are connected by the word "and," which does not seem to allow such an understanding, at least not immediately. If this interpretation is possible, it would enable us to find with Luther a view which comes near to the Orthodox understanding of the communio with Christ, the partaking of Christ and divine grace, as a factor which unites us with each other and brings about love and unity. Regardless of this question, which as such is of great significance, we have every reason to state that the remarkable and obvious emphasis which Luther puts on love, unity, and fellowship in connection with Holy Communion is essential and positive from the Orthodox point of view. There seem to be various expressions here which factually point to the same direction as the traditional, and now rediscovered and restrengthened, idea of "liturgy after the Liturgy," that is, first participation in the Holy Things and then concrete service in life.

It is not possible to discuss the many other points of interest in Vajta's paper. I can only briefly indicate some of them here: the role of Christ as the only head of the church and his relation to the body of the church; the distinction between Christ's function as head and as Lord; the relation of these problems to the ancient teaching on sanctification and deification *(theosis);* the distinction between "sacrament" and "sacramental sign"; the idea of imitation as regards the lives of the saints; the veneration of the saints; the salvation of the whole world, again in light of the *theosis;* etc. These are highly problematic and hard to understand. There are also other points which seem to have their parallels in a far more fruitful and positive way in the Orthodox tradition. Most of the problems are, directly or indirectly, related to ecclesiology in its various aspects, not least as regards the authority of the church and the distinction between the communio corporalis and the communio spiritualis.

Ecclesiological Tendencies in Luther and Wesley

GEOFFREY WAINWRIGHT

Methodists and Lutherans have no particular fondness for each other. Perhaps the Moravians of Herrnhut may take the blame for that. On his unhappy journey to America John Wesley had made contact with the Moravians, and these links were maintained after his return to London and played an important part in his so-called "evangelical conversion" of 24 May 1738. That experience of Wesley's not only set him off on a fifty-year career of tireless evangelism, it also became a prototype of spirituality for the Methodists who owed their (new) life to the preaching of Wesley and his helpers: the rather "pietistic" character of Methodism is therefore understandable.[1] So such a "true" Lutheran as Dietrich Bonhoeffer could consider "Methodism" the religious analogue to the pernicious existentialist philosophers and the psychotherapists.[2]

On the other hand, Wesley's conversion occurred, it is true, while a text from Luther's own hand was being read, namely his *Preface to the Romans*, which describes faith and the works of love which flow from it in exactly the same way as Wesley also would preach them to the end of his life. But the Luther, whom Wesley got to know during and after his visit to Germany from June to September 1738, was the Luther of the Moravians. A practical separation was to take place between Wesley and the Moravians on account of the doctrine of mystical "stillness" or "quiet," which came to rule in the Moravian congregation in London with the arrival of Philip Molther and was then defended against Wesley's criticism by Zinzendorf himself.[3] Meanwhile Wesley came across Luther's large commentary on Galatians (1531–35), which he rejected after too quick a reading during a coach ride. "With some justification he recognized in Luther," says Martin Schmidt, "the source of the mystical indifference of the Herrnhuters which caused him so much concern."[4] With some justification? It would doubtless be unfair to accuse the Reformer of underestimating the instituted means of grace and the good works of the justified; but we shall have to take note of the passivity in the Lutheran understanding of salvation. Evidently this tendency did not please the more actively minded Wesley.[5]

It may be that the Moravian intermediaries are in part responsible for mutual misunderstandings between Lutherans and Methodists. Two British Methodists, E. G. Rupp and P. S. Watson, now figure among the most respected Luther scholars in the English-speaking world; both have interpreted the Reformer sympathetically, without giving up their love for Wesley.[6] In the other direction, Franz Hildebrandt—a Lutheran convert to Methodism in the chance circumstances of the Second World War—has interpreted John Wesley in a very Lutheran and "unpietistic" way.[7] Nevertheless the bilateral conversations between the Lutheran World Federation and the World Methodist Council have had to recognize "important divergences" in matters of salvation.[8] Questions of salvation are of their very nature questions of ecclesiology.

Let us begin phenomenologically. The German Reformer sought the renewal of the (western) church. Such a renewal was to be achieved only through a theologically radical critique of existing church practice, since the practical life of the church was but the outcrop of false views of God, human beings, and salvation. Reactions to Luther's program of reformation varied with geography and led to church separations. Where the program was carried through with the cooperation of godly princes, Lutheranism took over the role of the *corpus christianum*. Two hundred years later, Wesley sought the renewal of an evangelical Church of England with which, on the surface at least, he had no theological quarrel: he appeals to its confessional writings from the Reformation period (Thirty-nine Articles, Book of Common Prayer, Homilies, Catechism) and tries to prevent his Methodist societies from thinking or behaving in a separatist way (for example, they are not allowed to hold "competitive" meetings at the hours of parish worship).[9] After the separation of the English Methodists from the Anglican Church—which had not been wished by Wesley and which took place only after his death, and then only gradually—Methodists were probably nowhere in danger of becoming a state church or even a folk church.[10] The end of the eighteenth century was no doubt too late for that, purely on grounds of secular history.[11] Although there is no proof of direct links with the left wing of the Reformation, Howard A. Snyder has recently shown how problematic the "Constantinian turn" was for the "radical Wesley": Wesley spoke several times of "that evil hour, when Constantine the Great called himself a Christian."[12] For Wesley it was not only a matter of the authority of "established" bishops who hindered his work of evangelism; it was much more (though the two are connected) a matter of the great gap, in both quantity and quality, between the officially Christian population of England and "the congregation of English believers."[13] With the ambiguous and controversial notion of "nominal Christians" (*Taufchristen*) we now come directly to theology.

So let us begin theologically with baptism. Luther preserved from medieval Christendom the generalized practice of infant baptism. Social and political considerations contributed to its maintenance.[14] But the relationship between infant baptism and justification through faith was not without its problems. The various and fluctuating arguments with which Luther over the years defends infant baptism impress one less as an *embarras de richesses* than as a *testimonium paupertatis*.[15] In Wesley there is a tension between infant baptism, which he kept in practice, and the deliberate emphasis on a personally experienced faith.[16] This tension is scarcely tackled by Wesley in a theological way; but neither does he establish a positive relation between its two poles. To the end of his life, Wesley looked on infant baptism as a sacramental regeneration;[17] but he also held that by the age of nine or ten one had "sinned away" one's baptism and needed a (new) new birth for salvation. He preached: "Lean no more on the staff of that broken reed, that ye *were* born again in baptism."[18] How that offends Lutheran ears accustomed to the *baptizatus sum!* Luther was thinking of the believer faced by temptation, Wesley was exhorting the unbeliever or the no longer believing: is the difference in context sufficient to allow a reconciliation between Luther and Wesley?

When modern Methodists expound infant baptism, they think first of "prevenient grace," for which infant baptism is said to be an effective, or at least a useful, sign.[19] Wesley taught the universal occurrence of prevenient grace on account of the world-redeeming Cross of Christ; such grace enables the positive acceptance of the gospel in response to preaching. Correspondingly, Methodists have a more active conception of faith than is usual among Lutherans. Thus Edmund Schlink, for example, defends infant baptism in terms of the "pure passivity" of faith.[20] Although the Methodist Churches practice infant baptism, and although their theologians stress prevenient grace in the Wesleyan sense, yet Methodist talk of faith probably sounds Pelagian in Lutheran ears: there is an excess of human activity.[21] For my part as a Methodist, I would say that it is a permanent part of the Lutheran ecumenical task to warn others against exaggerating that grain of truth which the great Tradition at least secretly allows to Pelagianism, namely a certain "synergism" which raises human beings without diminishing God.

The question of baptism is itself the question of church membership. As a definition of the church Wesley several times quotes Anglican Article 19, which is strongly reminiscent of the Augsburg Confession, 7: "The visible Church of Christ is a congregation of faithful men, in which the pure Word of God is preached, and the sacraments be duly administered." Wesley emphasized the *coetus credentium*.[22] He wanted to bring English people back to a "living faith." Where Methodist preachers worked, Methodists did not only gather among themselves but also went to the parish church, to hear where possible the Word of God and, since Wesley harbored no Donatist scruples about evil-living Anglican parsons as ministers of grace (cf. Augsburg Confession, 8), to receive the sacraments. But faith works by love (Gal. 5:6 was a favorite text of Wesley); and those who did not produce fruits of the Spirit but fell back into the works of the flesh were then no longer admitted into Methodist societies (the penitent were naturally welcomed back with joy).[23] In all of this Wesley was saying nothing one way or the other about people's official membership in the Church of England. But at the very point where he is at his most ecumenical (say in the "Letter to a Roman Catholic"), he denies the name of Christian to those whom the apostle also excommunicates, such as whoremongers, blasphemers, drunkards, cheats (cf. 1 Cor. 5:11).[24] Faced with such passages, even such an admirer of Wesley as A. C. Outler speaks of "Montanism."[25] Lutherans often suspect Methodists of "moralism." For all the dangers of hypocrisy I would rather interpret the phenomenon as "ethical seriousness." Wesley saw it to be Methodism's providential call to "spread scriptural holiness through the land."

Willy-nilly, the Methodist societies and the Wesleyan "Connexion" of the eighteenth century turned into a "Church," in the fragmentary sense which that word bears when it stands for a "denomination." Membership discipline gradually relaxed, yet without ever disappearing altogether. A persistent trace of our societary origin is found in the distinction we make between (simple) members (by baptism children are recognized as belonging to "Christ's flock") and "full members," that is, those who have publicly professed their faith and take part in the Lord's Supper.[26] Lutherans see such a terminology as derogatory to baptism.

Baptism, church membership: the ecclesiological question can also be put from the closely related viewpoint of justification. In Lutheran eyes, the proper doctrine of justification is the *articulus stantis et cadentis ecclesiae*. Following Luther and the Anglican confessional writings Wesley considered justification through faith as the distinguishing mark of the gospel over against the Roman Church.[27] Between Luther and Wesley, between Lutheranism and Methodism, the accents are, however, unmistakably different. That is connected with our respective beginnings as a folk church and as a society or free church. On both sides we have to examine ourselves in the light of the gospel. Therein lies the importance of the correction brought from within Paul's writings themselves by the German Methodist exegete Walter Klaiber to the one-sided emphasis which his Lutheran teacher Ernst Käsemann places on the justification of the *godless*. Klaiber closes his "study of Paul's understanding of the Church" with these words: "That justification of the godless is justification of the believer and *vice versa* marks the poles of the tension in which the Church must take shape. This must prevent the folk church from appealing to the *justificatio impii* in order to justify a 'religion without decision'; it must also warn the free church against allowing the congregation of believers to become an 'association of the religiously qualified.' "[28]

The best possibility for Lutherans and Methodists to reach ecclesiological agreement is probably offered by the eucharist. Wesley esteemed the sacrament as highly as Luther did. For Wesley as for Luther, "the worship of the congregation gathered in the name of Jesus," to use Peter Brunner's expression, was the concrete form of the church.[29] An eschatologically oriented Lord's Supper was for Wesley the privileged place of a doxological communion of the saints on earth as in heaven:[30]

> Happy the souls to Jesus joined,
> And saved by grace alone;
> Walking in all Thy ways we find
> Our heaven on earth begun.
>
> The church triumphant in Thy love,
> Their mighty joys we know;
> They sing the Lamb in hymns above,
> And we in hymns below.
>
> Thee in Thy glorious realm they praise,
> And bow before Thy throne;
> We in the kingdom of Thy grace,
> The kingdoms are but one.
>
> The holy to the holiest leads,

> From hence our spirits rise,
> And he that in Thy statutes treads
> Shall meet Thee in the skies.

The rediscovery in the seventeenth and eighteenth centuries of old liturgical texts from the Eastern church allowed Wesley to reach conceptions of presence and sacrifice, anamnesis and epiclesis, which anticipate the Lima text of Faith and Order.[31] In our century, the liturgical and ecumenical movements have helped both Lutherans and Methodists towards a renewal of eucharistic forms and sacramental practice.[32]

From a Methodist viewpoint, eucharistic unity demands corresponding churchly structures at all geographical levels, in order that "all in each place," in "churches which are themselves truly united," may be "united with the whole Christian fellowship in all places and all ages."[33] Methodists, particularly of British origin, retain from their origins an ecclesiologically significant sense of the "provisional" character of their own existence.[34] For that reason, Methodists of the British kind (though unfortunately not the American, who took for themselves an ecclesial autonomy from Anglicanism at a very early stage) have almost always been willing to enter into organic unions with other churches.[35] As a concrete movement for reformation, Luther and the first Lutherans were in principle "provisional," too. Yet because in the sixteenth century nothing less than the truth was at stake, they quickly acquired a marked "confessional" identity, which characterizes Lutheranism to this day. If now an ecumenical consensus in faith, in all *quod ad unitatem requiritur et sufficit,* is coming within reach, then Lutherans too should be prepared, in the service of a *unitas fratrum* to be realized at local and universal levels, to surrender their purely "denominational" structures.[36]

NOTES

1. The relative importance of 24 May 1738 in Wesley's biography has been variously evaluated; see J. Ernest Rattenbury, *The Conversion of the Wesleys* (London: Epworth Press, 1938). In *John Wesley in the Evolution of Protestantism* (London: Sheed & Ward, 1937), the Belgian Catholic Maximin Piette puts more weight on the resolve to a regular and holy life which Wesley made in 1725 under the influence of readings in Thomas à Kempis and Jeremy Taylor, soon to be followed by William Law. Apart from the entry in his *Journal* (intended for publication), the later Wesley rarely speaks of the experience of May 1738. The external occasion for him to take up field-preaching, with lasting success, was supplied by George Whitefield's invitation to collaboration in March–April 1739. Certain remains the fact that Wesley's evangelistic career would be unthinkable without its basis in "the religion of the heart" personally discovered on 24 May 1738.

2. D. Bonhoeffer, *Letters and Papers from Prison*, ed. E. Bethge (New York: Macmillan Co., 1967), letter of 8 June 1944.

3. Documentation in A. C. Outler, *John Wesley* (New York: Oxford University Press, 1964), 353–376.

4. M. Schmidt, *John Wesley—A Theological Biography,* vol. 2, part 1 (Nashville: Abingdon Press, 1972), 56.

5. For references to Luther in Wesley's writings, see H. Carter, *The Methodist Heritage* (London: Epworth Press, 1951), 221–231.

6. See E. G. Rupp, *Luther's Progress to the Diet of Worms* (London: SCM Press, 1951) and *The Righteousness of God* (London: Hodder & Stoughton, 1953); P. S. Watson, *Let God be God* (London: Epworth Press, 1947) and *The Message of the Wesleys* (New York: Macmillan Co., 1964).

7. F. Hildebrandt, *From Luther to Wesley* (London: Lutterworth Press, 1951) and *Christianity according to the Wesleys* (London: Epworth Press, 1956). Schmidt, the author of a two-volume theological biography (see note 4), was a Lutheran.

8. Report on the Bristol meeting of May 1980:

> (14) In both Methodism and Lutheranism the spiritual experience of the founder has entered into doctrinal formulations. The personality differences between Luther and Wesley along with the changed socio-cultural-historical-ecclesiastical contexts contributed to different expressions of Christian experience. So Methodists understand it as personal appropriation of the Gospel, as constant interplay between God and persons, and as being receptive to God's action. There is in this tradition an affirmation of God's complete redemption in Christ. Lutherans, on the other hand, look at Christian experience as dialectical. The Christian is always, at the same time, both saint and sinner (*simul justus et peccator*), living every moment dependent on God's grace. Justification covers the entirety of Christian living. . . .

> (19) Furthermore, we agree that, on the basis of Scripture, the person who is justified always lives by God's grace as that is received through faith; here the concept of faith also includes obedience. But it is also at this point that important divergences occur. Lutherans understand faith as building upon the righteousness of Christ alone, then expressing this new relationship in Christian obedience which is a continual struggle against the fallen nature. Such a struggle may produce self-condemnation and despair as one stands accused by the law. The awareness of this condemnation leads back to a trust in Christ's righteousness as the only ground of salvation.

> (20) Methodists question this understanding of Christian experience as it is set against a scriptural background. They do not see Paul and the other New Testament writers as viewing the Christian life as remaining permanently under the accusation of the law. Transformed by Christ, the life of faith is set free to conform to the will of God so that Christians may live as redeemed persons through the power of God. . . .

> (22) Both justification and sanctification are built upon the essential foundation of the gracious initiative of God. This initiative implies the election of persons by God, although Methodists emphasize free grace for all while

traditional Lutheran teaching uses the language of predestination as better suited to its model for understanding how God in Christ invites all persons into new relationship with him.

9. Right until his death in 1791 Wesley continued his strong opposition to a separation with the Church of England: separation would be a sin against love and would be a counter-witness to non-believers (see, e.g., his sermons of 1786 "Of the Church" and "On Schism" and his 1789 sermon on "The Ministerial Office"); but he had for several years taken practical and legal steps which ensured Methodism at least a semi-autonomous existence. Wesley was likened to a rower who "looked one way, while every stroke of his oar took him in the opposite direction." The most detailed study is Frank Baker, *John Wesley and the Church of England* (London: Epworth Press, 1970).

10. Methodism spread to every part of England and in some counties for a while almost took on the appearance of a folk church; but becoming a state church was naturally out of the question. After Wesley had in September 1784 "set apart" two "Superintendents" for North America, the Methodists in the United States by Christmas of the same year constituted themselves "The Methodist Episcopal Church." Negotiations with American "Anglicans," who had meanwhile acquired bishops by way of Scotland, led to no result. Since independence, the Constitution of the U.S.A. has favored religious "pluralism."

11. A small and partial exception is Tonga, where the royal family became Methodist.

12. Howard A. Snyder, *The Radical Wesley and Patterns for Church Renewal* (Downers Grove, Ill.: Inter Varsity Press, 1980), especially 9, 80–82, 93–96.

13. The latter expression is found, for example, in the Minutes of the 1744 Conference as a definition of "the Church, in the proper sense."

14. It was precisely such factors which won Zwingli back to infant baptism. Karl Barth linked infant baptism with the desire, even in our own times, to preserve Constantinian Christendom (see *Church Dogmatics* IV/4 [Edinburgh: T. & T. Clark, 1969], 168).

15. Some texts in J. D. C. Fisher, *Christian Initiation—The Reformation Period* (London: SPCK., 1970), 3ff.

16. R. E. Cushman, "Baptism and the Family of God," in D. Kirkpatrick, ed., *The Doctrine of the Church* (Nashville: Abingdon Press, 1964), 79–102.

17. This is confirmed in detail by B. G. Holland, *Baptism in Early Methodism* (London: Epworth Press, 1970).

18. For example, the sermon of 1748 on "The Marks of the New Birth" reads: "The question is not, what you was made in baptism (do not evade); but, what are you now? Is the Spirit of adoption now in your heart? To your own heart let the appeal be made. I ask not, whether you *was* born of water and of the Spirit; but are you *now* the temple of the Holy Ghost which dwelleth in you? . . . Say not in your heart, 'I *was once* baptized, therefore I *am now* a child of God.' Alas, that consequence will by no means hold. How many are the baptized gluttons and drunkards, the baptized liars and common swearers, the baptized railers and evil-speakers, the baptized whoremongers, thieves, extortioners? What think you? Are these now the children of God? . . . Lean no more on the staff of that broken reed, that ye *were* born again in

baptism. Who denies that ye were then made children of God, and heirs of the kingdom of heaven? But, notwithstanding this, ye are now children of the devil. Therefore, ye must be born again. And let not Satan put it into your heart to cavil at a word, when the thing is clear. Ye have heard what are the marks of the children of God: all ye who have them not on your souls, baptized or unbaptized, must needs receive them, or without doubt ye will perish everlastingly."

19. The "Statement on Holy Baptism" of the 1952 British Methodist Conference was strongly influenced by the widely read work of W. F. Flemington, *The New Testament Doctrine of Baptism* (London: SPCK, 1948), particularly 130–147 ("The New Testament Baptismal Teaching in its Relation to the Baptism of Infants").

20. E. Schlink, *The Doctrine of Baptism* (St. Louis: Concordia, 1972).

21. His fellow Lutherans will find very provocative Eilert Herms' recent description of faith as "a human deed and good work"; he sharply distinguishes faith from revelation, which is God's act and gift and necessarily conditions faith. See *Theorie für die Praxis–Beiträge zur Theologie* (Munich: Chr. Kaiser, 1982), 26f.

22. Wesley's language is inconsistent when he draws distinctions between the "visibility" and the "invisibility" of the church. These terms may serve to designate the church in its "gathered" or in its "scattered" existence respectively; but elsewhere Wesley thinks rather of the "inwardness" of "true faith" in contrast to merely "outward" membership of the Church. In the sense of the first distinction we read: "What do you mean by the Church? A visible church (as our Article defines it) is a 'company of faithful (or believing) people: *coetus credentium*.' This is the essence of a church, and the properties thereof are (as they are described in the words that follow) 'among whom the pure Word of God is preached, and the sacraments duly administered.' Now, then (according to this authentic account), what is the Church of England? What is it, indeed, but the 'faithful people, the true believers of England'? It is true, if these are scattered abroad, they come under another consideration. But when they are visibly joined by assembling together to hear 'the pure Word of God preached' and to eat of one bread and drink of one cup, they are then properly the visible Church of England. . . . A provincial or national church, according to our Article, is the true believers of that province or nation. If they are dispersed up and down, they are only a part of the invisible Church of Christ. But if they are visibly joined by assembling together to hear his Word and partake of his Supper, they are then a visible church, such as the Church of England, of France, or any other. . . . The Article mentions three things as essential to a visible church: first, living faith, without which, indeed, there can be no church at all, neither visible nor invisible; secondly, preaching (and consequently hearing) the pure Word of God, else that faith would languish and die; and, thirdly, a due administration of the sacraments, the ordinary means whereby God increaseth faith" ("An Earnest Appeal to Men of Reason and Religion," 1743, §§ 76–78). But in his controversy with Calvinists Wesley adopts the distinction in the sense of "the outward, visible church" and "the invisible church, which consists of holy believers" ("Predestination Calmly Considered," 1752, § 71). Between the two passages not only linguistic differences may exist, but practical tensions may also emerge. On the level of fact, Wesley can and must admit the presence also of unbelievers in the visible church, even in the assembled congregation (cf. Augsburg Confession, 8); yet theologically, he does not react in any

way "spiritualistically," as though even "the true church" could somehow exist in the air, that is, without Word, sacraments, and works of love. Here Wesley remains true to the classical Reformation.

23. The "Rules of the United Societies" applied already to the "awakened," that is; those who had "a desire to flee from the wrath to come, to be saved from their sins," and *a fortiori* to those who had reached the "fulness of faith" and meet weekly in the "bands."

24. "This leads me to show you, in few and plain words, what the practice of a true Protestant is. I say 'a true Protestant,' for I disclaim all common swearers, Sabbath-breakers, drunkards, all whoremongers, liars, cheats, extortioners—in a word, all that live in open sin. These are no Protestants; they are no Christians at all. Give them their own name: they are open heathens. They are the curse of the nation, the bane of society, the shame of mankind, the scum of the earth" ("Letter to a Roman Catholic," 1749, § 12; cf. the sermon "Of the Church" § 28).

25. Outler, *John Wesley*, 316.

26. So, for example, *The Methodist Service Book* (London: Methodist Publishing House, 1975).

27. So, for example, "An Earnest Appeal to Men of Reason and Religion," §§ 57–60. Wesley can also write in an oversimplifying way: "Who has wrote more ably than Martin Luther on justification by faith alone? And who was more ignorant of the doctrine of sanctification, or more confused in his conceptions of it? . . . On the other hand, how many writers of the Roman Church . . . have wrote strongly and scripturally on sanctification, who, nevertheless, were entirely unacquainted with the nature of justification!" (Sermon of 1788 "On God's Vineyard").

28. W. Klaiber, *Rechtfertigung und Gemeinde: Eine Untersuchung zum paulinischen Kirchenverständnis* (Göttingen: Vandenhoeck & Ruprecht, 1982), 265.

29. P. Brunner, *Worship in the Name of Jesus* (St. Louis: Concordia, 1968). For Wesley, see above, note 22.

30. *Hymns on the Lord's Supper* (1745), no. 96. The third part of this collection (hymns 93–115) bears the title "The Sacrament a Pledge of Heaven." Cf. J. E. Rattenbury, *The Eucharistic Hymns of John and Charles Wesley* (London: Epworth Press, 1948); A. R. George, "The Lord's Supper" in *The Doctrine of the Church* (as in note 16), pp. 140–160.

31. *Baptism, Eucharist and Ministry* (Geneva: W.C.C., 1982).

32. Wesley celebrated the Lord's Supper and received communion with a frequency quite exceptional in the Church of England of the eighteenth century (he received communion on average once every five days throughout his ministry). Cf. J. C. Bowmer, *The Lord's Supper in Early Methodism* (London: Dacre Press, 1951). In the nineteenth century Methodists forgot Wesley's exhortations to "constant communion"; cf. J. C. Bowmer, *The Lord's Supper in Methodism 1791–1960* (London: Epworth Press, 1961).

33. These formulations come from the World Council of Churches Assemblies in New Delhi (1961) and Nairobi (1975); cf. G. Wainwright, "Conciliarity and Eucharist," *Midstream* 17 (1978): 135–153. In reply to the *Caveat against Methodists* of the Roman Catholic bishop Richard Challoner, Wesley defines the true "catholic" church thus: "Such is the Catholic Church, that is, the whole body of men, endued with faith

working by love, dispersed over the whole earth, in Europe, Asia, Africa, and America. And this Church is 'ever one' [the quotations are from Challoner]; in all ages and nations it is the one body of Christ. It is 'ever holy'; for no unholy man can possibly be a member of it. It is 'ever orthodox'; so is every holy man, in all things necessary to salvation; 'secured against error,' in things essential, 'by the perpetual presence of Christ and ever directed by the Spirit of Truth,' in the truth that is after godliness. This Church has 'a perpetual succession' of pastors and teachers. And there have never been wanting in the reformed [= *reformatorisch*] Churches, such a succession of pastors and teachers; men both divinely appointed and divinely assisted; for they convert sinners to God—a work none can do unless God himself doth appoint them thereto, and assist them therein; therefore every part of this character is applicable to them. Their teachers are the proper successors of those who have delivered to them, down through all generations, the faith once delivered to the saints; and their members have true spiritual communion with the 'one holy' society of true believers. Consequently, although they are not the whole 'people of God,' yet are they an undeniable part of his people" (*Journal*, 19 February 1761). In the ecumenical twentieth century we have come to see more clearly that the unity and the holiness of the Una Sancta are inseparable both inwardly *and outwardly*. That is the motive for the eschatological search within history not only for the concrete holiness of the Church but also for its structural unity.

34. A. C. Outler, "Do Methodists have a Doctrine of the Church?" in Kirkpatrick, ed., *The Doctrine of the Church*, 11–28; G. Wainwright, "Methodism's Ecclesial Location and Ecumenical Vocation," *One in Christ* 19 (1983). The diachronic sense of our own provisionality is accompanied by our synchronic sense that the particular calling to spread holiness demands a "catholic" context in the true meaning of the term. C. W. Williams describes Methodism as "a society in search of the Church": *John Wesley's Theology Today* (Nashville: Abingdon Press, 1960), 216.

35. Methodists of the British type have joined in church unions with Christians of other traditions in South India, North India, Papua-New Guinea, Australia, France, Italy, Zambia, and so on. The same is true of Methodists of the American type in Belgium and Pakistan, and of Methodists of both British and American origins in Canada. In 1969 and 1972 the Church of England twice refused reunion with the British Methodist Church; and in 1982 the English Anglicans again declined to enter a "Covenant" with the Methodists, the United Reformed, and the Moravians.

36. The "unity in reconciled diversity" favored by the Lutheran World Federation leaves the problem of doctrinal and pastoral authority intact; cf. Harding Meyer, "'Einheit in versöhnter Verschiedenheit'–'konziliare Gemeinschaft'–'organische Union'; Gemeinsamkeit und Differenz gegenwärtig diskutierter Einheitskonzeptionen," *Oekumenische Rundschau* 27 (1978): 377–400.

Response to Vilmos Vajta

TUOMO MANNERMAA

The paper by Vilmos Vajta is so impressive that it is difficult to add much or to suggest new accents. On the other hand, it seems worthwhile to choose another viewpoint from which the subject may be seen in another light. Some cautious questions on certain of Vajta's formulations may then follow from the changed perspective.

I belong to those theologians who think that Luther's entire theology can and must be seen in analogy to the patristic doctrine of deification. In itself such a procedure is indeed not an immediate necessity for Luther research, but with regard to the contemporary state of research and in an ecumenical perspective, especially with reference to the Lutheran-Orthodox discussion, a change of viewpoint indeed appears permitted and necessary. At least the old problems can be discussed in a new and interesting way: the colors of the kaleidoscope will form new configurations when it is turned. Naturally, this can only be indicated here but in no way fully carried out. In the theological discussion there are many references, for example, G. Kretschmar, that the doctrine of justification and the patristic-Orthodox doctrine of theopoiesis have the same intention. Regin Prenter, for example, to refer to a Scandinavian theologian, says: "This doctrine (the theopoiesis of the person) which from the Protestant side has so often been questionable, expresses the same intention as the evangelical doctrine of justification by faith alone: only by God himself, that is, by the Holy Spirit, is the person able to have faith in God and to love God and thereby be righteous. God in Christ is himself the righteousness of the person. But this includes the point that the person who is righteous in faith is taken into the being of God."[1] Naturally, for me the inner multi-facetedness of the doctrine of deification on the one hand and the doctrine of justification on the other hand is familiar. However, to me what matters is that even in the doctrine of justification, to continue speaking with Prenter, the person is taken into the *being of God*.

This insight, on the contrary, has been in no way self-evident in Protestant Luther interpretation. As is well-known, there has been, at least since the time of Albrecht Ritschl, a persistent and frequently unexpressed philosophical-theological tradition of prejudice which continually distrusts and disavows faith as fellowship of being with God. In this tradition reality is conceived two-dimensionally: on the one hand from the mechanistic causal nexus determining nature; on the other hand from the human *person*. Persons are constituted by their will and thereby are raised over nature. Religion is then only fellowship of will with God, and its place is the relationship between the person and nature. Thus religion is no fellowship of

Translated by Carter Lindberg

being. Being is expressly a determination of mechanistic nature. For that reason the concept of being violates the essential personal reality of persons. Because metaphysics and mysticism interpret religion as fellowship of being, they are condemned by the standard of the Ritschlian tradition. Metaphysics and mysticism make God a thing and therefore an idol. Mystical religion as fellowship of being is pagan, whether it be Roman Catholic or Orthodox. Mysticism and metaphysics on the one side and Protestant faith as a relationship of will to God on the other side are as mutually exclusive as fire and water. Ethical transcendence is the only thing possible.

This "ontology of will" is the secret that is also behind K. Holl's Luther interpretation. Everything, even the smallest difficulty, receives its clarification in Holl's conception from the ontology of will. The much-discussed relational ontology of existential Luther interpretation is actually an unconscious reflex to this alleged tradition. Even the ontology of the Word as event in the Barthian school appears to be a heritage of just this conception (e.g., in H. J. Iwand).

The impressive lecture by Vajta appears in certain formulations, but not in substance, to render tribute to this problematic tradition. Vajta says: "For the metaphor of the bride and the bridegroom cannot mean 'mystical union' or a merging of the soul in the divine self. This is blocked in the early as well as the late theology of Luther by his theology of the cross."* I agree, of course, that Luther does not know a "merging of the soul." But why not "mystical union"? If the essential thing in mysticism is the relationship of *being* with God, and this is what those who dispute Luther's mysticism have always meant, then the Christian's union of faith with God is certainly and univocally a "mystical union" and the real union may be more closely specified. The Luther text to which Vajta refers does not establish the formulation. Luther is speaking here of those "who contrive I know not what with the bridegroom Christ." Luther's *theologia crucis* cannot at all be used against the concept of a real union of the Christian with Christ. Nevertheless, God does the work of his left hand exactly in order to bring to completion the work of his right hand, that is, in order to bring the person to real fellowship with Christ. Luther himself in the above-cited text places the Word as such against false mystical experiences. But the Word creates exactly a fellowship of being with God in Christ: "There his Word is so identical to him that the divinity is totally within it, and he who has the Word has the whole divinity."[2]

If now Luther's theology shall be sketched from the perspective of the doctrine of divinization, one can proceed from the pair of concepts, faith and love, as Vajta has correctly presented them: "Therefore all Christian doc-

---

*Editors' note: This statement is in the second part of Dr. Vajta's paper, which is not printed in this volume for reasons of space.

trine, work, and life is briefly, clearly, and abundantly grasped in the two parts, FAITH AND LOVE. . . ."[3] But in his discussion of these concepts Luther's expression nearly always echoes the doctrine of theopoiesis. In faith the person becomes like a god and participates in the divine nature; in love the person becomes a servant and distributes the divine gifts to his/her neighbor. Here a representative text from Luther shall speak for itself:

> That is, as I have often said, faith makes us lords and love makes us servants. Indeed by faith we become gods and participate in the divine nature and name, as Psalm 81 says: "I say, you are gods, sons of the Most High." But by love we become equal to all. According to faith we need nothing and have completely enough. According to love we serve everyone. By faith we receive good things from above from God. By love we let them go out to the neighbor. Just like Christ who according to his divinity needed nothing but according to his humanity served everyone who was in need.

Then follows the important passage where the divinity of Christ and faith are described analogously:

> We have often said enough about this, that we too by faith must be born as God's children and gods, lords, and kings just as Christ in eternity was born of the Father a true God. And again by love to help the neighbor just as Christ became man to help us all. And just as Christ did not merit that he is God by his works or by becoming man but rather had this by his birth without all works before he became man. Thus we also have the childhood of God, that our sins are forgiven, death and hell do not harm us; all this is not merited by works or love but is received without works and love by faith in the gospel by grace. And as Christ first and foremost after he is the eternal God, became man to serve us, so we also do good and serve the neighbor when we are already through faith are without sin, living, holy, and children of God."[4]

The idea of theosis is expressed in the text above all in that Christ and the Christian are described with parallel qualities (*Eigenschaften*) and with the same constitution. Faith and love are conceived in real analogy to the Incarnation. From this point on all the central concepts of Luther's theology of faith and love are described with the nomenclature of the theosis doctrine. One may think as Luther of the communicatio idiomatum between the Christian and Christ from the perspective of the theosis doctrine. Luther says:

> And we are all filled with every kind of God's abundance. This is expressed a great deal in the Hebrew manner of speech that we are filled in every way and we become full of God, showered with all grace and the gifts of his Spirit who has made us courageous, illumined us with his light, and is living his life in us, making us holy by his holiness, awakening love in us by his love. In short, that everything, that he is capable of, is fully in us and works powerfully so that we are entirely deified, having not a particle or a few pieces of God, but rather all his

fullness. Much has been written about how the person shall be deified; there they have made ladders to mount up to heaven and many such things. But that is vain piecework. But here the right and nearest way is indicated, how to come up to be filled of God; that you lack nothing but rather have everything in a heap; that everything which you say, think, do, in sum, your entire life is entirely godly.[5]

Many of the important ecclesiological concepts which Vajta used, as for example, "sacramental," "conformitas," "spiritual communion," "distance between head and body," "participation of spiritual goods," and so forth, still need what is not possible here: a closer examination from this perspective. Then it would probably still more clearly show that Vajta's explanations, if they may be understood under the signs of real fellowship (theosis), present an essential contribution to Lutheran ecclesiology.

NOTES

1. Regin Prenter, *Theologie und Gottesdienst. Gesammelte Aufsätze* (Århus and Göttingen, 1977), 289 n. 10.
2. *EA* 2, 10, 178.
3. *WA* 10.1:1, 100, 8–10.
4. *WA* 17 2:74, 25–75, 11.
5. *WA* 17 1:438, 14–28.

Summary

GEORG KRETSCHMAR

In recent years ecclesiology has come to have a continually greater significance in the ecumenical dialogue. Today the decisive differences between the church of the Augsburg Confession and the Orthodox as well as the Roman Catholic Churches is placed or sought above all in how the churches are living and understood. In another way this is also a controversial theme between Lutherans and churches deriving from holiness movements, such as the Methodists.

Against this background the disclosure of Luther's ecumenical significance means first of all to raise and introduce into the conversation Luther's own description of the church independently of how much of it has or has not entered into the doctrinal formation of the Lutheran Church. Vajta's investigation has undertaken this, proceeding from the writings of 1519/20.*

The church is, according to its essence, fellowship with Christ and his saints, whereby fellowship with the saints on earth and in heaven grows from participation in Christ. Luther's well-known distinction between the "two churches," the visible and the hidden, corresponds then to the bodily and spiritual fellowship; that is, this distinction means two facets of the one church which are related similarly to each other as the visible sign and the invisible *res* in the sacrament. In spite of all the sharpness of the distinction of the two facets or aspects, they belong fundamentally inseparably together.

In this way the visible church is ambiguous: it can be understood as merely a social assembly or a form of government, or from the perspective of the spiritual church from which it lives. The fact that Luther renders the word ecclesia in German by *Gemeine* or *Christenheit* is related to this ambiguity.

This understanding of the structure of the church in analogy to the sacrament is in accord with the fact that this fellowship, gathered in the Holy Spirit, has its original location in the worshiping assembly. Here, in worship, it is most immediately clear that the fellowship as spiritual-sacramental

Translated by Carter Lindberg
*Editors' note: Unfortunately the originally planned lecture by Professor H. Jorissen could not be presented due to illness. Therefore many perspectives of Dr. Vajta's lecture which would have been supplemented by the Roman Catholic view were only raised in the discussion, and even there only partially discussed. The expanded response of Bishop Dr. P.-W. Scheele replaces the lecture of Jorissen.

communio embraces not only the present living Christians but extends into heaven, and that worldwide Christendom is bound up in the fullness of the individual worshiping assemblies.

This fellowship of the saints, of Christians united with Christ and with one another, also extends into daily life, right up to the assumption of guilt, and it has significance for the environment of the church above all by prayer. The church on earth struggles and suffers as fellowship with Christ and the saints in the certainty of fulfillment in heavenly glory.

This presentation, taken from the specific statements by Luther which are often in a polemical context, is, as a striking summary, not at variance with the thrust of Luther's ecclesiology. On the one hand, it was only suggested that these sacramental aspects be supplemented by the incarnational aspects; on the other hand, reference was made to the fact that there was not adequate time to discuss to what extent these orientations from 1519 are maintained in the following decades, and how far they are supplemented or overlaid by other perspectives.

Further inquiries, very important in themselves, into particular themes such as Luther's understanding of the doctrine of the sacraments, excommunication, and the limits of the "mystical" could not be pursued. Instead the discussion concerned the understanding of the presented conception of Luther and above all, how far it implies a critical question to the Lutheran Churches.

In spite of the lengthy clarification of how the spiritual relates to the outward side of the church, the theme of the *notae ecclesiae* arose and with it the connection between the classical definition which, proceeding from Article 7 of the Augsburg Confession, understands Word and sacrament as the *notae ecclesiae* and the listing of a much greater number of such signs, especially in the older Luther, where office, prayer, suffering, and other such things are named, by which the true church can be recognized. Both enumerations have their rightful place: Word and sacrament as the "real signs" are but the presupposition that the church is existing in which there is prayer and suffering for Christ's sake. The distinction between facets of the church is necessary because the church can be corrupted in terms of its visible, bodily side.

Further, the attitude in the Lutheran Church toward the saints in heaven was discussed. Here also Vajta's lecture and its propositions were not contradicted. The discrepancy between Luther together with the Augsburg Confession and its Apology, on the one hand, and the praxis existing in the Lutheran Churches today, on the other hand, was not discussed.

Finally, there was concern about how Luther's ecclesiology as described in the lecture in sacramental concepts relates to the statement of Vatican II that the church is as it were a sacrament, that is, sign and instrument for the fellowship between God and humankind and the redemption of the world

(Lumen Gentium 1). First of all both are different series of statements and therefore the question of how far that statement of Vatican II can be recognized by Lutheran theology is not prejudiced by Luther's ecclesiology. There was not a real discussion of this question. Nevertheless from the Lutheran side concerns were expressed against the use of sacramental terminology for the church.

Luther's ecclesiology is indisputedly connected to the doctrine of justification. Therefore the thesis of a certain correspondence between the Orthodox doctrine of theosis and the Lutheran doctrine of justification (T. Mannermaa) was an important contribution to the disclosure of Luther's ecumenical significance, as was also the comparison between Methodist and Lutheran ecclesiology (G. Wainwright). The difference existing between the Methodists and Luther in the understanding of baptism needs further clarification. Finally there was the concern about what it means to say that Christians are saints. There was unanimity that to this holiness as the gift of baptism there belongs, for Luther, not only holiness as a life-long struggle with sin but also the remaining danger of backsliding.

This ecclesiology of the Wittenberg Reformer offers possibilities of agreement in the ecumenical dialogue. From the Orthodox side reference was made to the rooting of the church in worship, which invites comparison to the contemporary Orthodox eucharistic ecclesiology, and to the emanation of worshiping fellowship into daily life (Metropolitan John); from the Catholic side the sacramental structure of the church was raised up which was developed in Luther's 1519 sermons on the sacraments (Bishop Scheele).

The relationship between the insights from this fellowship-ecclesiology and the otherwise most-discussed themes in the area of the doctrine of the church was not clarified or not discussed. If the visible side of the church is the sign for its hidden essence, then there are, in spite of all ambiguity, nevertheless valid structures of the historical church. Certainly the proclamation and the sacraments after all belong to this, but then, coordinated to them, are mandated the office of preaching and the administration of the sacraments. What this means and how far this line of reasoning may be drawn out could not be further discussed any more than what it means if the Reformation Church Orders are characterized as emergency measures. Finally, Luther's position on the papacy was touched on without being essentially thematized. Also undiscussed was to what extent modern concepts as "institution" are suited for interpreting Luther's distinction between the outer and the spiritual church. Certainly the question of the connection between the church and holiness also needs further work.

The lecture was a very helpful report on Luther's ecclesiology which covered the familiar patterns. Precisely because of this the discussion could only address a few questions and aspects from the area of Luther's ecclesiology in the ecumenical context. It would be desirable in the future if the rootedness of this ecclesiology in the Holy Scriptures and in the thinking of the church fathers was also incorporated.

4

LUTHER'S MOTIF
SIMUL IUSTUS ET PECCATOR
AS AN APPROACH TO THE
NOVUS HOMO AND TO THE
NOVA CREATURA

Justice and Injustice in Luther's Judgment of "Holiness Movements"

CARTER LINDBERG

"It is," said Luther, "a fictitious expression to speak of a 'holy man,' just as it is a fictitious expression to speak of God's falling into sin; for by the nature of things, this cannot be."[1] In Luther's judgment "holiness movements" may be more or less creative depending upon their leaders but, creative or not, they are nevertheless fiction. It is no wonder that his judgment elicited equally strong replies. Contemporaries railed against Luther for placing doctrine over life, neglecting self-mortification and conformity to Christ;[2] for perverting the gospel into a spurious, fictitious faith alone which displaced discipleship of the cross by the cheap grace of a "honey-sweet Christ."[3] Later generations concerned with the development of Christian holiness may be less polemical but they are no less pointed in judging Luther. Pietism acknowledged that although Luther had laid the groundwork he had not proceeded to emphasize the ethical verification of faith in the new life.[4] Sharply put: "Justification is fiction, rebirth is fact."[5] The founder of Methodism and "father" of contemporary holiness movements stated: "Who has wrote more ably than Martin Luther on justification by faith alone? And who was more ignorant of the doctrine of sanctification, or more confused in his conception of it?"[6] And in our own time one of the more vehement Lutheran charismatic leaders claims that Lutherans have too often missed the message of the regenerating power of the Holy Spirit by reading the Bible through "Lutheran eyeglasses."[7]

Even this cursory review of judgment and counterjudgment reveals the potential for the *ad hominem* attacks so well known with regard to Luther's relationship to the persons he polemically labelled *Schwärmer*.[8] This is an important element of the Reformation controversies which unfortunately continues to color the present. Our concern, however, is with Luther's *theological* judgment and therefore we shall bracket psychological judgments. This means we are immediately confronted by a problem of terminology. It does not require a great deal of insight to recognize that addressing others as "fanatics" or "enthusiasts" is less than constructive for historical-theological research, not to mention ecumenical dialogue. No term is problem-free, but to designate the *Schwärmer* and consequent holiness movements as renewal movements has the following advantages: it is the contemporary self-designation of Neo-pentecostal and charismatic movements; it has not yet accumulated negative connotations; and it provides an umbrella large enough to cover the diverse concerns for personal and ecclesial holiness which run through these movements from Luther to the present.

We shall begin with a brief description of Luther's understanding of the *novus homo, nova creatura,* in light of his motif *simul iustus et peccator.* Luther's initial colleague, Karlstadt, was an important influence in the development of Luther's judgment of renewal movements. Therefore we shall sketch Karlstadt's theology of renewal and Luther's judgment of it. The validity of relating Luther's judgment to post-Reformation renewal movements depends upon both the validity of Luther's judgment with regard to his contemporaries and the extent to which later renewal movements incorporate and continue the concerns of the sixteenth century renewal. Space precludes more than an overview.

Theologically, Luther's judgment was that holiness, like justification, is always alien; it is extrinsic not intrinsic to the person; it is *extra nos*. "Once a Christian is righteous by faith and has accepted the forgiveness of sins, he should not be so smug, as though he were pure of all sins. . . . He is righteous and holy by an alien or foreign holiness. . . ." Sin is forgiven but it still remains.[9] The Christian, that is, the forgiven sinner, is therefore simultaneously righteous and sinner. This motif is the key to Luther's judgment of all renewal movements.

Simul iustus et peccator *and the* novus homo, nova creatura

Over half a century ago Rudolf Hermann argued that Luther's whole theology is comprised in the formula "righteous and sinner at the same time." The concept expressed by this formula is so central to Luther's thinking that none of his theological statements can be understood without reference to it. A number of recent studies also stress this as the characteristic signature of Luther's thought.[10] Luther's radical understanding of justification and the *novus homo coram Deo* as *simul iustus et peccator* may be sharply distinguished from both the medieval tradition and the Reformation renewal movements by a simplified diagrammatic formulation. To the questions of where and how fellowship with God may occur both answered that fellowship with God occurred on God's level and that the sinner must somehow ascend to God. The operative principle is that like is known by like. Therefore regardless of its theological orientation—scholastic *facere quod in se est* or mystic *Gelassenheit*—Luther's theological context emphasized a process in the Christian designed to diminish sinfulness and increase righteousness in the pilgrimage toward fellowship with God. The Augustinian motif, that the Christian is "partly righteous, partly sinner" while striving for inner renewal and obedience to the Christ *in me*, was rejected by

Luther as a process—no matter how grace assisted—which was oriented to achieving holiness and fellowship with God.

Luther's breakthrough to a new understanding of the righteousness of God is well known and need not be reviewed here. The discovery that God's righteousness is a gift, not a demand, displaces the principle of likeness by that of unlikeness as the basis for fellowship with God. The sinner does not ascend to God; rather, God descends to the sinner.[11] The emphasis upon God's descent to and acceptance of the sinner by grace alone is vividly expressed by Luther's images of the marriage between Christ and the sinner and his emphasis upon God's testament rather than covenant. Unlike the medieval use of the bride-bridegroom imagery wherein the bride (the sinner) is purified for this union, Luther depicts the bride as a "poor, wicked harlot."[12] The unilateral giving action of God is clearly evident in his testament. "A testament, as everyone knows, is a promise made by one about to die, in which he designates his bequest and appoints his heirs. . . . [I]f you have a letter and seal, and believe, desire, and seek it [your inheritance], it must be given to you, even though you were scaly, scabby, stinking, and most filthy."[13] These images illustrate Luther's radical understanding of God's justification of the sinner. There is nothing which the sinner can bring to God in order to attain forgiveness—except his or her sin! It is only the ungodly, only the sinner, who is acceptable to God. Paradoxically, to acknowledge sin is to justify God and thereby oneself. "Real sin," not likeness to God, is the presupposition for justification.[14] "Beware of aspiring to such purity that you will not wish to be looked upon as a sinner or to be one. For Christ dwells only in sinners. . . ." "If you are a preacher of grace, then preach a true and not a fictitious grace; if grace is true, you must bear a true and not fictitious sin. God does not save people who are only fictitious sinners. Be a sinner and sin boldly, but believe and rejoice in Christ even more boldly, for he is victorious over sin, death, and the world."[15]

Luther's radical understanding of justification leads to a radical understanding of the person before God. Justification *extra nos* means that fellowship with God is not the raising of like to like by love but rather the acceptance by faith of God's judgment upon the unlike. There is therefore no avenue of access to God other than faith. There is no special human faculty, however defined, which, sufficiently "like" God, will enable the person to ascend to fellowship with God.

For Luther the person is always the whole person. His use of the terms "flesh" and "spirit" does not reflect anthropological dualism but the biblical-theological distinction of the person's relationship to God. Both terms refer to the whole person as he or she relates to God. "The cause of their error is that . . . they make a metaphysical distinction between flesh and spirit as though these were two substances; however, it is the total man that is flesh and spirit, spirit insofar as he loves the law of God and flesh insofar as he hates the law of God."[16]

There is therefore no "higher power" or intrinsic capacity of the person which can warrant God's relationship. Indeed, humanity is characterized by the ability to "misuse the best in the worst manner."[17] The whole person is a sinner not just some "lower" portion of him. "We are nothing but sin. . . ."[18] Sin is being curved in upon the self; it is the desire to be God and the concommitant refusal to let God be God.[19] Sin, therefore, is so radical that only God's gracious imputation of Christ's righteousness can overcome it.[20] The sinner's acceptance of God's judgment enables him or her to live as righteous in spite of sin.

By "letting God be God" the sinner is allowed to be what he or she was intended to be—human.[21] The sinner is not called to deny his or her humanity and seek "likeness" (*similitudo*) with God. Rather, the forgiveness of sins occurs in the midst of human life. The Christian before God "is at the same time both a sinner and a righteous man; a sinner in fact, but a righteous man by the sure imputation and promise of God that He will continue to deliver him from sin until He has completely cured him. And thus he is entirely healthy in hope, but in fact he is still a sinner. . . ."[22]

The significance of the *simul* motif for Luther's judgment of renewal movements is that it precludes a progressive sanctification which attributes growth in righteousness *coram Deo* to the Christian. This may be spelled out by an examination of the following aspects of the motif: 1) it is a confession of faith, not a universal philosophical truth; 2) it is a living dialectic, not a doctrinal abstraction; 3) it was developed prior to Luther's conflicts with the *Schwärmer* and thus was not a reaction to them; 4) it remained a consistent theme throughout Luther's career; 5) it presents an understanding of sanctification in temporal-qualitative rather than quantitative terms.

1. *Simul iustus et peccator* is a confession of faith in which the believer expresses his or her situation before God and humankind.[23] Luther praises God's great mercy that he makes holy not fictitious sinners but real true sinners.[24] This is not a metaphysical, psychological, or ethical statement; it is rather spiritual and theological.[25] The point for Luther is not whether God accepts or rejects our works but that he forgives.[26] It is through forgiveness that the person receives new life—the new life which in accepting God's judgment accepts forgiveness. Already in the *Dictata* and then in his *Lectures on Romans*, Luther linked the new life with confession and the *simul* motif.[27]

2. Luther's *simul* motif is a living dialectic, not a lifeless doctrinal abstraction. Luther's faith was anything but a comfortable and placid piety. The heights and depths of this faith were not merely sequential but also simultaneous. The obvious difficulty in giving this experience linguistic formulation drove Luther to paradoxical expressions: "No Christian has sin and every

Christian has sin."[28] "The saints are always sinners in their own sight, and therefore always justified outwardly. But the hypocrites are always righteous in their own sight, and thus are always sinners outwardly."[29] The believer is his/her own accuser and, paradoxically, it is in agreement with God's judgment that the accused is defended.[30] Sharply put: the goal of Luther is to become a sinner, whereas the goal of the pious is to overcome sin and become holy.[31]

Luther's emphasis upon the *simul* is not some sort of timeless dialectic of reconciling opposites but rather a temporal history of salvation process between God and persons. The *simul* formula "cannot be relieved of its tension into a via media, but rather the simul indicates a coincidentia oppositorum."[32]

3. We have sketched Luther's *simul* formula on the basis of his early writings, especially the *Lectures on Romans* (1515–16) to show that this central theological orientation is present prior to his criticism, beginning in the 1520s, of contemporary efforts to achieve holiness or perfection as expressed in monasticism and the renewal movement he labelled *Schwärmerei*.

4. At the same time we wish to point out that this motif is not limited to the young Luther but remains a central concern throughout his career.[33]

5. The final point is that, from the standpoint of the *simul*, sanctification is to be understood in temporal-qualitative rather than quantitative terms.[34] Here the complex issues of our subject come to the fore: the Christian as *novus homo, nova creatura*, growth and progress in sanctification and holiness. The new life of the baptized is a life of struggle and advance under the eschatological viewpoint of the new time of the coming of Christ rather than the anthropological viewpoint of measurable steps toward fulfillment of the Law.[35]

The holiness of *novus homo* is, like justification, an alien holiness.[36] This does not preclude growth and progress but views it as the gift of God rather than the achievement of the person. It is, in short, always progress under the sign of the *simul*. Just as justified sinners are real, not fictitious, sinners, so the *novus homo* is a real, not fictitious, *nova creatura*. The progress of the *novus homo*, however, is not measurable by growth in holiness but as life in repentance. It is a life lived between the times, between the now and the not yet. The new life is in progress because it is life under the time of the coming Christ, but like justification it is passive because the person is "being acted upon."[37]

This life of penitence is the life of faith. "Faith, however, is a divine work in us which changes us and makes us to be born anew of God, John 1 [:12f.]. It kills the old Adam and makes us altogether different men, in heart and spirit and mind and powers; and it brings with it the Holy Spirit."[38] The God-initiated and sustained process of becoming the new person begins with baptism and continues through to death and resurrection.[39] This is God's work for Christians sin daily. Accordingly the Christian remains simultaneously sinner and righteous throughout life.[40] *Coram Deo* the *novus homo* possesses no intrinsic holiness which can be measured, but rather his holiness is extrinsic as he approaches in time the holiness to be given in death and resurrection at the Last Day.[41]

SIXTEENTH-CENTURY RENEWAL MOVEMENTS AND LUTHER'S JUDGMENT OF THEM

The relationship of salvation and sanctification was central to the conflict between Luther and contemporary renewal movements. This is a broad, complex issue for it involves ethical and social as well as theological issues.[42] Since we cannot here pursue all of these, we shall concentrate on the renewal theology of Karlstadt. To a great extent, Karlstadt provided both the stimulus and substance for Luther's judgment of renewal movements. Clearly there were other persons, for example, Müntzer, who were important in influencing Luther's judgment, but the central role of Karlstadt makes him paradigmatic.

Karlstadt urged a process of mortification of the outer person for the sake of inner regeneration. On the basis of Jesus' words on cross-bearing for discipleship, "Karlstadt declared that a surrender of self and a circumcision of delight in creatures must precede regeneration or love of God. . . ." In his emphasis upon the necessity of the circumcision of the heart, he sometimes stated this was beyond human ability and solely the activity of God; at other times that love and righteousness are contingent upon the extent that the person's heart is circumcised.[43] The point, however, is that a new life of obedient conformity to Christ is to follow spiritual rebirth. This emphasis, plus the fact that the new life of the regenerate Christian is shaped by the Law, led Karlstadt's major sympathetic biographer to subtitle the second volume of his Karlstadt study, "Karlstadt as the Pioneer of Lay Christian Puritanism."[44] "Karlstadt thought the proper understanding of Christian freedom pertained not primarily to the Christian's freedom apropos laws, but rather to the regenerated man's ability to obey them."[45]

One becomes a member of the church through the inner experience of regeneration, an experience which is recognized by the person's life. The new community is also to manifest such fruit. "God has given a general law to which the whole believing people, and each congregation and each person should hold and conform. . . . That God's covenant concerns every individual community and in addition each household . . . is shown so often in Deuteronomy alone that I think it unnecessary to adduce evidence."[46]

This covenant ecclesiology does not eliminate the role of the minister. Public preachers are necessary and should evidence divine, regenerating grace as well as have an inner call. The minister must be holy to proclaim

God's holy word. "For the proclamation is a speech of faith which proceeds from the heart through the mouth. Therefore the outward confession or preaching of the death of Christ is a sign or fruit of the inner righteousness...."[47] "He who wants to handle pure and holy things blamelessly should be as pure and holy as the things which he grasps and handles."[48] Karlstadt's emphasis here calls to mind the Donatist position, but it is not clear whether Karlstadt wishes to go that far.

What is clear, however, is that the fundamental question for Karlstadt was not "How do I find a gracious God?" but rather "How can man fulfill the Law of God?"[49] This is a basic orientation for later renewal movements as well. From Pietism through to the present charismatic renewal, the central concern is not the unconditional forgiveness of sins but the quest for the power to fulfill the will of God.[50] Karlstadt's early expression of this is expressed in his "151 Theses" (1517), where instead of Luther's *theological simul* he presents a *moral simul*: "The righteous man, therefore, is simultaneously good and evil...." Thus "the outer man is able to become a temple of God."[51] The true sense of the law is first understood by the spiritually reborn whose freed spirit now understands the spirit of the law. The gospel is understood in the sense of a new law (*nova lex*), a law of the spirit and life (*lex spiritus et vitae*) mediated by Christ. The Christian is thus given the power to do good works. These works are the presupposition for a second justification, a justification by the law which is an advancing sanctification through fulfillment of the law.[52]

We have focused on Karlstadt because it was Karlstadt who basically formed Luther's opinion of the renewal movements of his day. What Luther attacked in Karlstadt he continued to see in other "Karlstadtians"—a mixture of law and spirit which subverted the good news of God's forgiveness into the bad news of human legalism. Thus in response to the Christians in Strasbourg, Luther wrote:

> Ask your evangelists ... to turn you away from Luther and Karlstadt and direct you always to Christ, but not as Karlstadt does, only to the work of Christ, wherein Christ is held up as an example, which is the least important aspect of Christ.... But turn to Christ as to a gift of God.... For such matters these prophets have little sympathy, taste or understanding. Instead they juggle with their "living voice from heaven," their "laying off the material," "sprinkling," "mortification," and similar high-sounding words.... They make for confused, disturbed, anxious consciences ... meanwhile Christ is forgotten.[53]

Numerous essays by historians and theologians, some of whom are heirs to the movements Luther attacked, confirm the formal validity of Luther's extrapolation from Karlstadt to other holiness leaders and groups.[54] Luther's response to their orientation is to ask, "What makes a person a Christian?"[55] Luther's own answer is a resounding rejection of *anything* done by a person to ground salvation in him or herself.[56] Not even faith makes a person a Christian! "Always something is lacking in faith. However long our life, always there is enough to learn in regard to faith."[57] Luther criticized Karlstadt, Müntzer, and the *Schwärmer* in general for submerging the gospel in the externals of a quest for sanctification, while they in turn accused Luther of relying upon faith alone.

Faith in God is worked by the Holy Spirit "when and where he wills," "by hearing." The Word is a living word of address; it comes from outside the person and proclaims what Christ has done for us. Luther's critique of the renewal is that they invert this order. "Dr. Karlstadt and his spirits replace the highest with the lowest, the best with the least, the first with the last. Yet he would be considered the greatest spirit of all, he who has devoured the Holy Spirit feathers and all."[58]

Luther is certainly not rejecting religious experience and works; rather he is rejecting the order of salvation of the renewal. They invert reality, making the Word of God dependent upon faith, and consequently choose their own means of ascent to God rather than receive God's descent to them. In every area of Christian life they change gospel into law and thereby put the burden of proof for salvation back upon the Christian. But faith wants certainty.[59]

The great danger Luther saw in the renewal movements is that they would either continue papist works-righteousness, albeit of their own type, or dissolve the certainty of salvation into the even more terrifying psychological works-righteousness of introspection and interiorization. Without awareness of the *simul* aspect of the Christian faith and life there is the perennial danger of grounding faith in oneself. The Christian is *simul iustus et peccator* in faith as well as works, therefore he/she is to look to Christ for certainty. In self-reflection the Christian confronts him/herself not as a believer but as a non-believer, or in any case as one who does not know whether he/she believes. In this existential situation Luther's position is "I do not know whether I believe; but I do know in whom I believe."[60] Faith is certainly necessary but the Christian is to rely upon God's grace, not his/her own faith.[61] Luther saw in the renewal the same elements he had struggled with in the monastery. It is not surprising, then, that he viewed Karlstadt and the others in terms of a relapse into a monastic works-righteousness.[62]

With regard to the Donatist tendencies in the renewal, Luther states that to rest the promise of God upon our faith or works is to be "like butter in sunshine."[63] "It is not a fruit of the Spirit to criticize a doctrine by the imperfect life of the teacher."[64] On the other hand, Luther himself did not take a Donatist position against his opponents.[65]

Luther saw, behind the orientation to the inner Word and the consequent emphasis upon sanctification, a dualism with severe consequences for theological anthropology. Such a dualism cannot cope with the ambiguity of life because it fails to grasp the dialectical tension of a theology of law and gospel where the Spirit is mediated by external means to the Christian who is simultaneously sinner and righteous. To the favorite passage of Karlstadt and others, "It is the spirit that gives life, the flesh is of no avail" (John 6:63), Luther opposed his holistic theological anthropology. "Thus you should learn to call him 'fleshly' too who thinks, teaches, and talks a great deal about lofty spiritual matters, yet does so without grace. . . . On the contrary, you should call him 'spiritual' who is occupied with the most external kinds of works. . . ."[66] Luther defines living according to the flesh as unbelief, a condition which continues to plague the Christian. Only a godly Christian can make such a confession. "Now it is a marvelous thing that he who is righteous before God and has the Holy Spirit says that he is a sinner. It is right, however; he confesses what he has been and still is."[67] "Thus a Christian is righteous and sinner at the same time, holy and profane, an enemy of God and a child of God. None of the sophists will admit this paradox because they do not understand the true meaning of justification. This was why they forced men to go on doing good works until they would not feel any sin at all."[68]

In summary we may say that Luther opposed all orders of salvation which confused justification and sanctification. Any faith "that attributes more to love than to faith . . . (imagines) that God regards and accepts us on account of the love with which we love God and our neighbour after we have already been reconciled. If this is true, then we have no need whatever of Christ." Because Christians do not have perfect fear, love, and trust toward God, they are condemned by the law no matter what program of regeneration and sanctification they are involved in fulfilling. "For the true God does not regard or accept us on account of our love, virtue, or newness of life (Rom. 6:4); He does so on account of Christ."[69]

Therefore the church is not a community of the recognizable elect but an institution with earthly means of communicating the gospel. The church, therefore, is recognized not by its holiness of life but by the "possession of the holy word of God." "Now, wherever you hear or see this word, preached, believed, professed, and lived, do not doubt that the true *ecclesia sancta catholica*, 'a Christian holy people' must be there, even though their number is very small. . . . And even if there were no other sign that this alone, it would suffice to prove that a Christian, holy people must exist there, for God's word cannot be without God's people, and conversely, God's people cannot be without God's word."[70]

In our earlier discussion of Luther's theology we proposed the heuristic device of asking where and how fellowship with God occurs. The answers derived from Luther's theological motifs stressed that fellowship with God occurs not in heaven but here on earth through God's gracious acceptance of the sinner. Thus righteousness *coram Deo* is not an intrinsic capacity or possession of the Christian but a continuous gift. All efforts to usher in the

Kingdom of God both politically and spiritually are therefore repudiated as theologies of glory. Christ's kingdom cannot be visibly identified with either remade social order or "reborn" persons but only with God's Word. The certainty (*certitudo*) of the presence of God is always and only his Word, not human works, lifestyles, feelings, or even faith. Thus Luther continually repudiated all attempts by his opponents to create security (*securitas*), whether it be by spiritually authenticated leadership, lifestyle, or exegesis.

Luther's first encounters with what we call renewal movements were through Karlstadt and Müntzer. On the basis of this Luther created a stereotype which he then found confirmed by later events. Unfortunately, Luther all too frequently extrapolated these initial experiences and judgments onto others who seemed to him to share one or another characteristic with Karlstadt and Müntzer. Thus Luther has been criticized for his rush to judgment against the renewal movements of his day which precluded brotherly if not ecumenical dialogue. Recently there have been scholarly attempts to minimize the theological differences between Luther and Karlstadt. Three studies in particular reduce Luther's judgment to the level of tactics and strategy for maintaining leadership and promoting reform, a form of "sibling rivalry," and biographical factors. Both Ronald Sider and James Preus[71] argue that the main issue was the strategy and timing of the reform. Karlstadt's leadership in Wittenberg during Luther's stay in the Wartburg alarmed Luther and impelled him to return to Wittenberg in order to "recapture" his leadership role and eventually to rationalize his position by analogies to the biblical prophets and apostles. Except for Karlstadt's views on images and the Lord's Supper, it is claimed that his theological differences from Luther were not fundamental. Their different accents are seen in terms of their different biographies. Karlstadt emphasized fulfilling the divine law but that does not mean that Luther's accusation of works-righteousness is correct, for Karlstadt always speaks of fulfilling the law by the reborn. Luther's monastic experience of anxiety before the judgment of God made him hypersensitive regarding any emphasis upon sanctification. On the other hand Karlstadt's experience of renewal and change in his life was related to his earlier experience of striving for success in life and career.[72]

I have no quarrel with the understanding that theology and biography are intimately related.[73] But it is unacceptable to reduce one to the other. There is no doubt that Luther had a personal stake in the progress of the Reform movement, as did every other reformer. But to say that the simplest explanation for Luther's displacement of Karlstadt in the Wittenberg Movement is Luther's motivation "to reclaim personal leadership of a movement he felt was more his own than anyone else's"[74] fails to see that both Luther and Karlstadt were living out of their respective understandings of the truth of the gospel. The personal involvements and tactics of both reformers were informed and shaped by their theologies.[75] For Luther the priority of the

Word alone precludes evangelical compulsion, whereas for Karlstadt personal inability to root out superstition necessitates evangelical compulsion.[76] Nevertheless, we need to be sensitive to the fact that Luther's theological critique of his contemporaries is colored with harsh invective and *ad hominem* arguments which serve no useful purpose in today's ecumenical dialogues.

A constructive contribution to the present ecumenical dialogue is Luther's dialectical relating of doctrine and life which understands doctrine not merely in terms of content but in terms of its function: "Doctrine directs us and shows the way to heaven. . . . We can be saved without love . . . but not without pure doctrine and faith." Doctrine and life are incomparable, not at all on the same level; and therefore the devil's argument about "not offending against love and the harmony among the churches" is specious.[77] The function of doctrine is the proclaiming the forgiveness of sins as unconditional promise. That is why the church stands or falls on the basis of its relation to the doctrine of justification by grace alone through faith alone. Thus Luther's relationship to the renewal movements of his time is not an incidental chapter in church history but related to the fundamental apprehension and sense of the Reformation.[78]

POST-REFORMATION RENEWAL MOVEMENTS

The implicit contemporary relevance of Luther's judgment of the renewal movements of his day may be drawn out by its application to selected post-Reformation renewal movements. We shall restrict ourselves to commenting on aspects of seventeenth- and eighteenth-century Pietism and contemporary charismatic renewal.[79]

The central motif for Pietism is rebirth. Martin Schmidt argues that the Pietist motif of rebirth replaced that of justification and stems from both pre-Reformation spiritualism and Reformation renewal figures such as Karlstadt and Müntzer.[80] Even when Pietism made an appeal to justification it converted it to its own use so that justification became a moment in the all-encompassing motif of rebirth.[81] The significance of Spener's *Pia Desideria* is not so much its particular proposals for reform but its orientation to theological thinking: "Our entire Christianity exists in the inner or new man. . . ."[82] This is the locus for Spener's fundamental opposition between old and new birth, the world and God. The essential task of the Christian is to preserve himself unstained by the world.[83] The "world" has to do with the concrete temptations and errors of daily life—ambition, desire for fame, pride, greed, and so forth. "The opposition between the world and salvation is so deep that it must be overcome by an event sui generis—an event that only knows *one* analogy, birth. This event can have only *one* creator, God himself. . . ."[84]

In developing these perspectives, Spener reintroduced into theology the medieval use of the principle that like can only be known by like.[85] Thus the characteristic of Spener's view of rebirth is its teleological orientation toward the new man and his growth. Consequently he polemicized against the opinion that faith could be the embodiment of the relationship to God and Christian conduct. Faith is not able to carry the entire content of the new being, it requires completion through its fruit, love, or at least by the decisive modifier "living."[86] This emphasis upon the new person is the point of departure for perfectionism, a hope to be realized in history. This reduces both ecclesiology and theology to a form of Christian ethics.[87]

Pietism overcomes radical doubt not by hearing the Word of God as an address of promise but by experientially verified faith. Thus Pietism introduces the usage of modifiers for the term faith: weak faith, living faith, powerful faith, and so forth. Luther's straightforward position—that faith simply takes God's promise as true and honors it in that it does not take God to be a liar[88]—is displaced by discussions about the quality of faith and its accomplishments.

This orientation allows the development of a hermeneutic of the Bible as the pattern for life. In the final analysis Pietists viewed Scripture as the confirmation and legitimation of their own experience.[89] The idea of an order of God, the goal of which is personal renewal, displaced justification as the mid-point of Pietist theology. This is a shift away from Luther's *pro nobis* emphasis and his dialectic of *simul iustus et peccator*. Pietism emphasized the visible formation of the renewed person verified by the ethical fruits of faith. Rebirth signifies a higher nature and quality of being. Luther, on the other hand, remains with an ongoing battle between the old and new person which is never transformed into a visible victory on earth. Victory always remains the judgment of God not the possibility of the Christian. The dynamic of Pietism was not Luther's dialectic of law and gospel, sin and grace, damnation and faith, but rather the development of the power of faith in renewal and good works.[90]

Pietism's displacement of justification by rebirth denotes a shift from Luther's theocentric orientation to an anthropocentric orientation. This comes into sharper focus when we recall our earlier diagrammatic mode of expressing Luther's theology in terms of God's *descent* to the sinner as opposed to the motif of the sinner's *ascent* to God. To Luther the gospel is radical good news because it is the proclamation of salvation not a program for salvation. God promises to accept the *sinner*. God descends to the person who is unlike himself. The Aristotelian theorem is turned inside out—unlike is known by unlike. We have already referred to Spener's discussion of rebirth in just the opposite terms. God loves the sinner but because only like may be known by like it is necessary for the sinner to be reborn.[91] As harsh as it sounds, this seems to be a classic case of what is thrown out the front door (by Luther) returning through the back door (by Pietism).

This motif of ascent toward God through rebirth and renewal explains the synergistic expressions within Pietism. Persons cooperate in the process of salvation. This is not merely a modification of Luther's central position but a reversal of it. The person is thrown back upon him/herself and his/her experience of faith for the certainty of salvation. Whenever, no matter to what extent, the burden of proof for salvation rests upon the believer, the only options are pride or the despair of uncertainty for the person is really being asked to overcome him/herself. It is of interest that Schmidt sees a line of development here from Francke to Nietzsche. Unlike Luther, who guides sinful believers toward the unconditional truth of God's Word and the invariability of God's promise, Francke refers them back to their faith. From a modern perspective the catechetical sermons of the great Halle pietists appear related to contemporary existential theology.[92] The question of the modernity of Pietism echoes Troeltsch's evaluation of the continuity of Reformation Spiritualism and Anabaptism with the modern spirit, and more recent studies linking charismatic renewal with medieval asceticism and Reformation Anabaptism. This common link of medieval and modern was already intimated by Luther when he equated the papacy with the enthusiasts in the Schmalkald Articles.[93]

Pietism departs from Luther in its understanding of the relationship of faith and works. Spener and Francke among others tended to regard works as the verification of faith or at least a sign of faith. The ethical fruits of faith thus become indications of a person's degree of growth in faith and the quality of his existence in grace. Luther is not concerned for such goal-determined inferences. Although Luther can express the view that works are signs of faith, his major perspective is that our standing in justification cannot be determined by the form of our sanctification.[94] This is also applicable to the church. While for Luther the true church remains hidden from the eyes of persons, Pietism's "kernel-community," while remaining within the church, may be distinguished from other Christians by perceptible, examinable signs of piety. Thus in this way the concept of the church approaches that of an ideal, independent community of saints.

Contemporary renewal movements not only are analogous to the renewals of the Reformation and Pietism but also have ties to Pietism through the Wesleyan movement. "Seen historically, the (charismatic) movement belongs to those movements which have grown out of the soil of classical German Pietism. Thus it is characteristic for the charismatic movement that it has returned in a changed form with its impulse of this tradition as it has become effective in the Methodism of England and North America, in the holiness movements and in the Pentecostal movement."[95]

The charismatic renewal expresses its concern for regeneration and the *novus homo* through its emphasis upon baptism in the Holy Spirit with the attendant signs of edification and sanctification, the charismata. Throughout the charismatic renewal the emphasis is upon receiving the power of the

Holy Spirit to become and be a new person. The gospel is expressed in terms of "a quality and style of life." The fullness of the Holy Spirit is sought with the view "to receiving power to live the Christian life more effectively and fruitfully."[96] There is an overriding concern among Lutheran charismatics for sanctification which dissolves the dialectical tension of such classic Lutheran motifs as the *simul*.

Charismatic theology is oriented toward a covenant-type theology in distinction from Luther's emphasis upon testament. While not explicitly spelled out, this orientation is expressed through emphasis upon baptism with (or in) the Holy Spirit with a consequent growth in sanctification. A primary means to personal sanctification is speaking in tongues. The results range from assurance of salvation to cessation of smoking.[97] The new life of sanctification is a life patterned upon Jesus, which not only gives guidance in the details of life but also separates one from the world. Separation from the world is the recognition both of the impending destruction of the world and that discipleship to Jesus means commitment to spiritual warfare. The Christian therefore should pray for the charismatic gifts and cooperate in the Spirit-wrought manifestation of sanctification in his life. Mortal sins, that is, sins over which we have control by God's Spirit, cannot co-exist with manifestations of the Holy Spirit. It is in this perspective that the third use of the law is advocated.[98]

The primary concern for charismatic theology does not seem to be that of the forgiveness of sins but rather that of power to lead a new life. Certainly these questions are not mutually exclusive but there is a marked difference in accent. The primary understanding of justification here is that of liberation and empowerment. This charismatic orientation toward power and the presence of God leads to a striving for more experiences and more faith. Baptism in the Spirit gives "more of Jesus." In a manner reminiscent of Pietism there is the penchant to qualify faith, baptism, and the Christian life by adjectives such as "living," "spirit-filled," and so forth. In theological terms we would say charismatics are more interested in sanctification than justification. Furthermore, this interest is colored by the concern to achieve security in faith by a *praxis pietatis*.

The fundamental problematic is that salvation is understood in terms of the expression of a particular spiritual praxis. And this praxis is not sufficiently distinguished from that salvation which issues from God. The eschatological reservation—that we live by faith, not by sight—is forgotten. The charismatic movement is permanently in danger of foreclosing the ultimate by its desire to realize it in the penultimate.

This critique is confirmed by an American theologian with charismatic experience, Richard Jensen. He argues that the renewal is sometimes characterized by striving for *more* than is required. "By doing the *more* that is required, we can move from the realm of Christ to the realm of the Spirit.

... from sin to holiness ... from justification to sanctification, from first faith to total faith, from water baptism to Spirit baptism.... Speaking in tongues in this system almost becomes a sign that we have moved beyond Christ and his grace for sinners to a higher and more advanced state."[99] This means that the emphasis upon holiness and sanctification as experientially legitimated by baptism in the Spirit and tongues shifts the burden of proof from God to the person. "Then we are caught up in the endless cycle of *more*. To become holy always requires more of us: more faith, more good works, more obedience, more everything. Until we receive the initial evidence of our holiness, speaking in tongues, we must live under a cloud of guilt over our lack of spiritual achievement. When we do receive the evidence of our holiness we are tempted to be proud of our achievement."[100]

The emphasis upon sanctification in terms of self-development is evident in the works of two authors of particular influence in charismatic renewal, Morton Kelsey and Watchman Nee. In terms of theological anthropology the issue, as presented by Kelsey and Nee, is a dualism which spiritualizes the person in a legalistic direction.[101] Kelsey provides "twelve rules" and Nee lists "seven steps" for training our souls to be open to our inner spiritual world. "But as soon as one adds twelve rules or seven steps to our relationship to God and his Spirit it becomes quite clear that grace is not *alone*. Both Kelsey and Nee are really talking about grace *plus*. It is grace *plus* human openness. It is grace *plus* obedience to the rules and steps. It is grace *plus* man's plunge within and into himself."[102] The characteristic emphasis throughout charismatic literature on the person being open to the Holy Spirit and living in expectation of the Spirit's free gifts is a mark of charismatic anthropology rather than pneumatology. From the perspective of the Reformation, persons are not "open" by themselves, but are rather sinners whose openness to God is blocked by sin and evil. If the human problem is being closed in upon the self then exhortation to be open can at best only create sufficient guilt to which the gospel of forgiveness may be addressed. At worst this exhortation and application of the law creates either pride or despair. Again we are reminded that the charismatic emphasis is not so much on the forgiveness of sins as it is on empowerment.

But it is precisely *within* him/herself that the person is a sinner. The spirit/flesh opposition is not a dualistic anthropology but two different ways of life. The biblical view of the person sees him or her in totality and uses the terms spirit and flesh to designate personal orientation. Dualistic anthropologies oppose spirit and flesh as references to the inner and outer person, and thereby lead to a separation of justification and sanctification. "As we follow the rules and get in touch with our spiritual 'within,' spiritual experiences result. Such experiences, speaking in tongues for example, are then interpreted as qualitative signs of a deep walk with the inner spirit. Spiritual experiences are easily identified as the signs of *our* (note the 'our') sanctification, growth and maturity." The results are pride and divisiveness.[103]

The charismatic may respond that the call to openness comes not from within the person but rather from the Holy Spirit, and therefore one may expect such a stance to be fulfilled. The theological consequence of this, however, continues to be a conception of the person as a being who is open toward God, as one whose essence is disposable toward God. The tension between the person as *imago Dei* and sinner thus collapses. In Luther's terminology this is the collapse of the person as *simul iustus et peccator* into the person as *partim iustus, partim peccator*, for whom sin is being displaced by righteousness. This is a theology of progressive sanctification which introduces a third use of the law in place of the dialectic of law and gospel, and emphasizes the growth of the individual over the community.

If, as some Mennonite scholars claim, the charismatic movement is heir to concerns of Reformation renewal movements, then there is an "old-new" wine implicit in charismatic theology which may burst the traditional Lutheran wineskins. For Luther, grace was unconditional. And justification by this grace alone through faith throws the shadow of works-righteousness over personal efforts at holiness. This grace, this forgiveness of sin, mediated by Word and sacraments, was Luther's answer to his quest for a gracious God. The charismatic quest is for a gracious community and a holy life. Again, these are not exclusive concerns but the accent is sufficiently different to create two different theologies and life-styles. The renewals' search for a biblically paradigmatic community of faith and a life-style of obedience led to an emphasis upon an ontological change in the life of the believer as opposed to the *simul* anthropology of Luther. For the renewal movements: "Revelation is indeed received in the midst of disobedience, but for the purpose of repentance and growth in holiness. It is conditional."[104]

We need to remember that the theme of sanctification was no less emphasized by Luther than by his contemporary "charismatic" opponents. The difference as Luther saw it was that his opponents inverted the order of God's relationship to persons. For Luther only the external proclamation of the gospel and the material reception of the sacraments may call a person out of self-work and self-reflection. It is self-help and self-sanctification which is put to an end by God's promise: "I am here for you." Luther saw in Karlstadt the subtle return of justification by the good works of mortification and discipleship which displaced the "external" work of God, who comes to us in Word and sacrament.

The renewals' emphasis upon the *novus homo* as the point of departure for perfectionism, a hope to be realized in history, has the following ecclesiological and theological consequences: Applied to the pastorate it has the ring of Donatism, for only the pastor who is a true Christian is able to lead others carefully on the way of the Lord. Applied to theology it leads to a devaluation of doctrine and an emphasis upon the life of the individual and the life of the church. Applied to ecclesiology it reduces the church to an *ecclesiola* of the like-minded, like-experienced and like-disciplined, based on conceptions of the primitive church. Applied to ecumenics it results in a transconfessionalism dependent not upon doctrinal agreement but upon a particular Christian life-style. Finally, and perhaps the most serious consequence, applied to the Christian life it leads to an anxious and insecure conscience.

Thus Luther proclaims: "Let us thank God, therefore, that we have been delivered from this monster of uncertainty and that now we can believe for a certainty that the Holy Spirit is crying and issuing that sigh too deep for words in our hearts. And this is our foundation: the gospel commands us to look, not at our own good deeds or perfection but God himself as he promises, and at Christ himself, the Mediator. . . . And this is the reason why our theology is certain: it snatches us away from ourselves and places us outside ourselves, so that we do not depend on our own strength, conscience, experience, person, or works but depend on that which is outside ourselves, that is, on the promise and truth of God which cannot deceive."[105]

Ever since Luther's attack on Karlstadt there has been a strong Lutheran anxiety that all types of renewal orientations endanger justification by grace alone. Luther sharply attacked his opponents on the basis of his stereotype of them. Their own sharp responses only served to confirm what Luther's stereotype led him to expect. Successful dialogue with contemporary renewals will be related to maintaining the validity of Luther's insight into justification and sanctification in terms of the new person being simultaneously righteous and sinner while remaining sensitive to the dangers to understanding caused by stereotyping.

NOTES

1. *LW* 12:325; *WA* 40 2:347,29–31.

2. Hertzsch, 2:93,36–94,2; 98,33–99,2. On Francke cf. Heinold Fast, ed., *Der Linke Flügel der Reformation* (Bremen: Schünemann, 1962), 246ff.

3. Franz, 321–343; Hans Hillerbrand, "Thomas Muentzer's Last Tract Against Martin Luther," *MQR* 38 (1964):20–36. Franz, 228,9; 234f.; 222ff.; 318,22ff.

4. Philipp Spener, *Pia Desideria*, ed. Kurt Aland (Berlin, 1955), 42,8–13; 79,35f. Johann Arndt, *Sechs Bücher vom Wahren Christentum* (Stuttgart: Steinkopf, n.d.), 791.

5. *WNM* 51–90, 91–111, 129–168; 162ff. M. Schmidt, *Pietismus* (Stuttgart: Kohlhammer, 1972), 14.

6. John Wesley, *The Works of John Wesley* (London, 1872), 7:204. Cf. also George Marsden, *Fundamentalism and American Culture* (New York and London: Oxford University Press, 1980), 73.

7. Hans Frøen in Norris Wagen, ed., *Jesus Where Are You Taking Us?* (Carol Stream, IL: Creation House, 1973), 113–134, 205–222.

8. Cf. Mark Edwards, *Luther and the False Brethren* (Stanford, Calif.: Stanford University Press, 1975), 201f.

9. *LW* 12:328; *WA* 40 2:352,33f. Cf. *LW* 12,367; *WA* 40 2:407,30–408,23.

10. Rudolf Hermann, *Luthers These "Gerecht und Sünder zugleich"* (Darmstadt, 1960) (1930), 7. Cf. Wilhelm Link, *Das Ringen Luthers um die Freiheit der Theologie von der Philosophie* (Munich, 1955), 77–85; Steven Ozment, *Homo Spiritualis: A Comparative Study of the Anthropology of Johannes Tauler, Jean Gerson and Martin Luther (1509–16) in the Context of their Theological Thought* (Leiden: E. J. Brill, 1969), 131–185; Heiko A. Oberman, "Simul Gemitus et Raptus: Luther und die Mystik," in I. Asheim, *Kirche, Mystik, Heiligung und das Natürliche bei Luther* (Göttingen: Vandenhoeck & Ruprecht, 1967), 20–59, 59; Gerhard Ebeling, *Luther: Einführung in sein Denken*, (Tübingen: J. C. B. Mohr, 1964), 15; Michael Baylor, *Action and Person, Conscience in Late Scholasticism and the Young Luther* (Leiden: E. J. Brill, 1977), 228ff.

11. *WA* 5:128,36–129,1.

12. *LW* 31:351; *WA* 7:55,26; 1ff.; 25,34.

13. *LW* 35:88; *WA* 6:361,3–7. Cf. also *LW* 27:268; *WA* 2:518–521; and Kenneth Hagen, *A Theology of Testament in the Young Luther. The Lectures on Hebrews* (Leiden: E. J. Brill, 1974); and "The Testament of a Worm: Luther on Testament and Covenant," *Consensus* 8 (1982):12–20, 16: "Research on Luther's use of testament, covenant, and cognates to 1525 shows that, except where Luther sees covenant as a synonym for the testament of Christ, he uses *Pactum* and *Bund* pejoratively and in negative contexts."

14. *WA* 3:298,6ff.; 291,26–28; 55 2:24,6–12; 33,1–4; *LW* 10:240–243. Cf. David Steinmetz, *Luther and Staupitz: An Essay in the Intellectual Origins of the Protestant Reformation* (Durham, N.C. Duke University Press, 1980), 140, 130, 134, 139; Ozment, *Homo Spiritualis*, 182.

15. *LW* 48:12f.; *WA Br* 1:35,24ff.; *LW* 48:281f.; *WA Br* 2:370–372.

16. *WA* 2:415,6–10.

17. *LW* 31:41; *WA* 1:354 (thesis 24).

18. *LW* 12:307; *WA* 40 2:322,6–11.

19. *LW* 25:291; *WA* 56:304,25ff.; *LW* 31:9ff.; *WA* 1,225 (thesis 17).

20. *LW* 24:347; *WA* 46:44,34–38.

21. *LW* 12:343; *WA* 40 2:373,25–35.

22. *LW* 25:260; *WA* 56:272,16–20; Cf. also *WA* 57:165,12–13; 2,497,13.

23. Link, *Das Ringen Luthers*, 77.

24. *LW* 31:63; *WA* 1:370,9ff.

25. *LW* 25:322; *WA* 56:334,3f.

26. *LW* 31:64; *WA* 1:370,26f.

27. Cf. Marilyn Harran, "The Concept of Conversio in the Early Exegetical Writings of Martin Luther," *ARG* 72 (1981):13–33, 26–27.

28. *LW* 12:328; *WA* 40 2:352,24f.

29. *LW* 25:257; *WA* 56:268,27–30.

30. *LW* 25:188; *WA* 56:204,24f.

31. *LW* 25:217–218; *WA* 56:232,34ff.; *LW* 25:215; *WA* 56:231,6ff. Baylor, *Action and Person*, 223: "Luther drew an important distinction between 'becoming' a sinner

and 'being' one. By 'becoming' a sinner he meant coming to the condemnation of the whole self which he equated with humility; 'being' a sinner meant for Luther remaining in the prideful, natural condition that is confident of the person's ability to fulfill divine law." Cf. *LW* 12:304,310f.

32. Oberman, "Simul Gemitus et Raptus," 59; Hermann, *Luthers*, 21.
33. *LW* 26:232ff.; *WA* 40:368,26ff.
34. Hermann, *Luthers*, 234ff.; R. Hermann, *Luthers Theologie*, ed. by Horst Beintker (Göttingen: Vandenhoeck & Ruprecht, 1967), 111f. For a critique, cf. Axel Gyllenkrok, *Rechtfertigung und Heiligung in der frühen evangelischen Theologie Luthers* (Uppsala, 1952), 112ff.
35. *LW* 26:342; *WA* 40:526,2–527,9.
36. *LW* 35:411; *WA DB* 7:421,6–15.
37. *LW* 25:433–434; *WA* 56:441,14–442,22; *LW* 11:496; *WA* 4:364,9–25; Gyllenkrok, *Rechtfertigung und Heiligung*, 79–98, 102ff.
38. *LW* 35:370; *WA DB* 7:11,6–9.
39. *BC* 445; *LW* 35:36; *WA* 2:732,25–33.
40. *BC* 432. Cf. Paul Althaus, *Paulus und Luther über den Menschen*, (Gütersloh: Mohn), 1963⁴, 74–77.
41. *LW* 35:32f.; *WA* 2:729,19ff.
42. Cf. George Williams, "Sanctification in the Testimony of Several So-Called Schwärmer," in Asheim, ed., *Kirche, Mystik, Heiligung*, 194–211, 195.
43. Ronald J. Sider, *Andreas Bodenstein von Karlstadt. The Development of His Thought 1517–1525* (Leiden: E. J. Brill, 1974), 216, 220ff.
44. Barge. Sider, *Karlstadt*, 280.
45. Sider, *Karlstadt*, 282. Cf. also R. J. Sider, "Karlstadt's Orlamünde Theology," *MQR* 45 (1971):191–218; 352–376; Karlstadt, "Von Abtuhung der Bylder," ed. by H. Lietzmann, (Bonn, 1911), 44; Ulrich Bubenheimer, *Consonantia Theologia et Jurisprudentiae: Andreas Bodenstein von Karlstadt als Theologe und Jurist zwischen Scholastik und Reformation*, (Tübingen: J. C. B. Mohr, 1977), 244.
46. R. J. Sider, *Karlstadt's Battle with Luther* (Philadelphia: Fortress Press, 1978), 56f.
47. C. Lindberg, "Karlstadt's 'Dialogue' on the Lord's Supper," *MQR* 53 (1979):35–77, 58f.
48. Hertzsch I, 15.
49. Kähler, 37*; Bubenheimer, *Consonantia Theologia*, 285.
50. Cf. the introduction in Kilian McDonnell, *Presence, Power, Praise: Documents on the Charismatic Renewal*, 3 vols., (Collegeville: Liturgical Press, 1980). Cf. Marsden, *Fundamentalism*, 79f., 84. On male authority, cf. Larry Christenson, *Die christliche Familie* (Marburg/Lahn: Edel, 1975).
51. Kähler, 8*–37*.
52. Bubenheimer, *Consonantia Theologia*, 275f., 286.
53. *LW* 40:70; *WA* 15:396,16–26; *LW* 40:134; *WA* 18:116,13–18.
54. *LW* 26:396; *WA* 40:603,25ff. Cf. James Stayer and Werner Packull, eds., *The Anabaptists and Thomas Müntzer* (Dubuque & Toronto: Kendall Hunt, 1980).
55. *LW* 40:67; *WA* 15:394,1–5.
56. *LW* 31:344f.; *WA* 7:50,15f.

57. *LW* 40:253; *WA* 26:166,2f.
58. *LW* 40:83; *WA* 18:66,17–20.
59. *WA* 10 3:15,6–12; *LW* 40:260f.; *WA* 26:172,17ff.; *LW* 40:83; *WA* 18:66,12f.; *LW* 35:164,170ff.; *WA* 16:371,14ff.; 384,19ff.
60. Otto Hof, "Luthers Unterscheidung zwischen dem Glauben und der Reflexion auf den Glauben," *KuD* 18 (1972):294–324, 323f., also 294ff.
61. *LW* 40:252; *WA* 26:164,39ff.
62. *LW* 40:222f.; *WA* 18:213,29ff.
63. *LW* 40:252; *WA* 26:164,23.
64. *LW* 40:57; *WA* 15:218,5f. Cf. *LW* 41:151f.; *WA* 50:630,34–631,5.
65. *LW* 40:251; *WA* 26:164,5–11.
66. *LW* 35:371f.; *WA DB* 7:13,5ff.
67. *LW* 36:355; *WA* 19:515,19–21.
68. *LW* 26:232f.; *WA* 40:368,26–29.
70. *LW* 41:150; *WA* 50:629,28–35.
71. Sider, *Karlstadt*, 104–147, 197ff., and *Karlstadt's Battle*, 4; James Preus, *Carlstadt's "Ordinaciones" and Luther's Liberty: A Study of the Wittenberg Movement, 1521–1522* (Cambridge, Mass.: Harvard University Press, 1974), 2.
72. U. Bubenheimer, "Andreas Rudolff Bodenstein von Karlstadt," in Wolfgang Merklein, ed., *Andreas Bodenstein von Karlstadt. 500–Jahre–Feier* (Karlstadt, 1980), 5–58, 37,52,38,40.
73. Gordon Rupp, *Patterns of Reformation* (Philadelphia: Fortress Press, 1969), 120; Willis Stoesz, "The New Creature: Menno Simon's Understanding of the Christian Faith," *MQR* 39 (1965):5–24, 17 n. 82.
74. Preus, *Wittenberg Movement*, 51. Cf. my review of Preus in *MQR* 52 (1978):273–275.
75. Cf. C. Lindberg, "Theory and Practice: Reformation Models of Ministry," *Lutheran Quarterly* 27 (1975):27–35, and "Conflicting Models of Ministry—Luther, Karlstadt and Muentzer," *Concordia Theological Quarterly* 41 (1977):35–50.
76. Lietzmann, "Von Abtuhung der Bylder," 19. Cornelius Dyck, "The Life of the Spirit in Anabaptism," *MQR* 47 (1973):309–326, 319: "There is a dimension of Luther's *simul iustus et peccator* here which the Anabaptists vigorously rejected, in principle, as being at the heart of the ethical failure of the Reformation."
77. *LW* 27:41f.; *WA* 40 2:51,13ff.
78. Karl Steck, *Luther und die Schwärmer* (Zurich: Zollikon, 1955), 5.
79. For a comprehensive treatment of what follows, cf. my study: *The Third Reformation? Charismatic Renewal and Lutheran Tradition*, (Macon, Ga.: Mercer University Press, 1983).
80. Cf. Martin Schmidt, "Epochen der Pietismusforschung," in Berg and Dooren, eds., *Pietism und Reveil* (Leiden: E. J. Brill, 1978), 22–79; *WNM* 331f.; 9–23; Bubenheimer, *Karlstadt*, 40; Kenneth Davis, *Anabaptism and Ascetisism* (Scottdale, Pa.: Herald Press, 1974).
81. *WNM* 171f., 173 n. 14.
82. *WNM* 130, 170ff.; Spener, *Pia Desideria*, 79, 35f.
83. Spener, *Pia Desideria*, 39, 19.
84. *WNM* 136.

85. *WNM* 271.
86. Spener, *Pia Desideria*, 17,21; 35,9; 61,14; 66,33; 79,1,36; 18,1; 29,9; 61,11; 28,21.
87. *WNM* 168.
88. *WA* 4:287,5; 360,8; *LW* 21:347; *WA* 7:593,26.
89. M. Schmidt, "Der Pietismus und das moderne Denken," in K. Aland, ed, *Pietismus und Moderne Welt* (Witten: Luther, 1974), 9–74, 40.
90. *WNM* 327ff., 159, 173, 238ff.; Eberhard Peschke, *Bekehrung und Reform. Ansatz und Wurzeln der Theologie August Hermann Franckes*, (Bielefeld: Luther, 1977), 142f.
91. *WNM* 186, 271.
92. *WNM* 233f., 237.
93. K. Davis, "Anabaptism as a Charismatic Movement," *MQR* 53 (1979), 219–234; *BC* 312,4.
94. Peschke, 143. Cf. W. Joest, *Gesetz und Freiheit. Das Problem des tertius usus legis bei Luther und die neutestamentliche Parainese* (1961), 213 n. 244.
95. Christof Ziemer, "In und neben der Kirche. Charismatische Bewegungen der DDR," *Die Zeichen der Zeit* 6 (1979):218–226, 224, 221. Cf. McDonnell, 1:lvi, Martin Schmidt, *John Wesley*, 2 vols. (Zurich: Gotthelf, 1953–1966), 1:271–273; 2:59–60, 255–259, 273f., 407; Arnold Bittlinger, *Papst und Pfingstler*, (Frankfurt a. M.: Land, 1978), 173ff.; Marsden, *Fundamentalism*, 72–101.
96. Larry Christenson, *Social Action Jesus Style* (Minneapolis: Dimension Books, 1976), 96; *The Charismatic Renewal Among Lutherans* (Minneapolis: Bethany Fellowship, 1976), 48.
97. Larry Christenson, *Speaking in Tongues* (Minneapolis: Dimension Books, 1975), 78f.
98. Cf. Theodore Jungkuntz, "Ethics in a Relativising Society," and "Response to Dr. Lazareth," *The Cresset*, Occasional Paper 3 (1978), 13, 15, 57–59.
99. Richard Jensen, *Touched by the Spirit* (Minneapolis: Augsburg, 1975), 115.
100. *Ibid.*, 118.
101. *Ibid.*, 101. Cf. Morton Kelsey, *Encounter with God* (Minneapolis: Bethany Fellowship, 1972); Watchman Nee, *The Normal Christian Life* (Ft. Washington, PA: Christian Literature Crusade, 1957).
102. Jensen, *Touched by the Spirit*, 99.
103. *Ibid.*, 102f., 98. Cf. Carl Maxcy, "Catholic Spirituality, Catholic Ethics and Martin Luther," *Ecumenical Trends* 10/4 (1981): 55–57, 57: "In my opinion, the twisted spirituality which has plagued Roman Catholics in the twentieth century is also partially the result of the post-Freudian obsession with self-analysis. The tendency is quite 'ecumenical,' because it afflicts Christians of every denomination. Our culture has told us that introspection is the proper *modus operandi* in life. As a result contemporary spirituality has turned increasingly to naval-gazing and has made us unable to get outside ourselves. . . . A healthy person is one who looks outside for truth and meaning. . . ."
104. C. J. Dyck, "Hermeneutics and Discipleship," in J. B. Horst, et al., *De Geest in het geding opstellen Aangeboden aan J. A. Oosterbaan*, (Willink, 1978), 57–72, 72.
105. *LW* 26:387; *WA* 40 1:589, 15–19, 25–28.

Luther's Significance for Contemporary Theological Anthropology

MARTIN SEILS

It is probably not difficult to defend the proposition that Luther has little or no significance for contemporary theological anthropology. In a certainly correct provisional sense this proposition could be substantiated by the fact that Luther is only seldomly referred to in the considerations and statements of contemporary theological anthropology.[1] In a somewhat more exact sense it could be said that "theological anthropology" has only in the last decades become a more developed and defined area of theological thought and expression. It is a matter of allowing theological speech "to be verifiable in the horizon of the analysis of human existence,"[2] which did not take place, at least programmatically, in Luther's anthropology. In one of the deeper dimensions of the first sense, it must finally be pointed out that between Luther's thoughts on the person and those of contemporary theological anthropology there lies that change which Freud refers to as the three "humiliations" of humankind in the development of the modern period: cosmologically he/she is displaced along with the earth from the center of the world by Copernicus; biologically he/she is declared to be the result of mutation and selection by Darwin; and psychologically he/she is interpreted by Freud himself as only painfully able to maintain the self between the powers of the id and superego.[3]

In fact, considering such givens it seems presumptuous to wish to speak of "Luther's significance for contemporary theological anthropology." However, one should pause for a moment before declaring our theme irrelevant. There is after all the noteworthy fact that precisely today attention to Luther's understanding of the person is intensifying considerably. It may not be entirely accidental that there is no theme so frequently requested in connection with the 1983 Luther anniversary where I come from than that of Luther's understanding of the person. It is certainly of greater significance that it is exactly this theme of Luther's anthropology that has been treated in recent years in major monographs in Luther research. This is evident from Wilfried Joest's *Ontologie der Person bei Luther,*[4] Gerhard Ebeling's exegesis

Translated by Patricia M. Williams

of Luther's disputation "De homine,"[5] and the presentation of Luther's anthropology by Albrecht Peters in the handbook volume "Der Mensch."[6] But the fact which undoubtedly has greater meaning is that, in connection with reflections on contemporary theological anthropology, the idea is continually pushed, even if often only tangentially but nevertheless with a certain inquiring interest, that there could exist a closer relationship to Luther's anthropological statements and reflections than is presupposed considering the distance in time. Doubtless there exists a hardly explicit feeling of a certain closeness and correspondence, and not only in the case of the relation between philosophical and theological anthropology but also in reference to the "existential" depth dimensions of the understanding of humankind and also, finally, in the direction of the understanding of the coordinate relationships of humanity and the world, even that—in a certain dynamic interpretation of this coordinate relationship—anticipation of Luther is supposed. All of this is hardly verifiable. But it intrudes upon one. We have hardly more than to pursue this impression for the moment if we want to try to follow up the theme "Luther's significance for contemporary theological anthropology." Whether this will allow us to speak really in a decisive sense of a "significance" of Luther for the theological anthropology of the present may still remain open. Perhaps the conversation will be more about the significance which Luther could have. What we wish to do is to attempt to pose the question of Luther's relevance to contemporary theological anthropology in general and discursively rather than apostrophically.[7]

We are not able to proceed methodologically by presenting the main features of Luther's anthropology, followed by the presentation of the fundamental thrust of contemporary theological anthropology, and then under the question of Luther's relevance seek to place both areas in relationship, although this would certainly be the more clear and thorough way. But this is already precluded by reason of space. Instead it will only be possible to take up and discuss a few areas of the theme of which it is supposed or can be supposed that something in them of Luther's "significance" for contemporary theological anthropology becomes apparent. This is, so it seems, first of all the area of the relationship and difference between a "natural," philosophical theological anthropology and one which stems from revelation and the Scriptures. The next area is that which concerns the question of the "eccentricity" or "relationality" of Luther's understanding of the person and its reception or rejection in contemporary theological anthropology. Third, there is the not-unrelated problematic of the understanding of "image of God" in persons with regard to Luther and present theological anthropology, which in any case must be expressed. Fourth, it should certainly be concerned with what, according to Luther, is termed the "total determination" of the person, thus the *simul* of being spirit and flesh, righteous and sinner. Fifth, the relationship of humankind to the world should be investigated in

Luther and in contemporary theology, even if here a "significance" of Luther perhaps at least can be spoken of considering the difference of the times.

THE RELATIONSHIP OF PHILOSOPHICAL AND THEOLOGICAL ANTHROPOLOGY

Contemporary theological anthropology is, to a large exent, conscious that it has been influenced and is still being influenced in its own particular and delimited areas of subject and work by the developments of philosophical anthropology. The external proof which is continually used for this is that the catch phrase "theological anthropology" does not appear in volume one of the handbook *Die Religion in Geschichte und Gegenwart* until the third edition in 1957.[8] Of course there have always been anthropological trains of thought in theology and of course there has been what could be called a "Christian view of humankind" for a long time, even if the particulars and sometimes even the basic views are plural. But that empirical view gained during the 19th century, in which the person is determined by his/her becoming visible and questionable to him/herself in the course of the development of the modern period, has made possible anthropological concentrations in philosophical models. Karl Rahner, who on the Catholic side has decisive interest in such models, might be right when, under the catch word "theological anthropology" in the lexicon *Sacramentum Mundi*, he speaks of anthropology as the "still unfulfilled task of theology" and in the sense that "Catholic theology has not yet developed a systematic anthropology which corresponds to the knowledge the person has attained of him/herself as a 'subject.' "[9] Evangelical theology has perhaps worked more fully on the anthropological thematic from the point of view of models of theological anthropology.[10] Basically, however, what Rahner says of Catholic theology holds for these models.

The general situation is that all contemporary models of theological anthropology take up the basic thrusts of philosophical anthropology and by the relationship to them seek to secure and prove the relevance of theological statements. Hermann Fischer says, "The growing independence of theological anthropology and the related reception of the concepts of anthropology common to the other sciences is thus significant for the development of a new type of theology. It receives the challenge of modern thinking and seeks the specifically Christian theme and concerns in the mode of dialogue, to bring to expression the cooperation and critique with and in the other sciences."[11] And thereby it expresses what most of these models in fact bear and determine. Fundamentally, this was already so, as in the case of Bultmann and Rahner referring to Heidegger's fundamental ontology of being (Dasein), even if the problematic of the philosophical legitimizing of theological statements here at times has been subjected to a very reflexive and nowise neglecting consideration of its own theological reference of determination. The things move somewhat closer together as Wolfhart Pannenberg first of all starts from the human "openness to the world"[12] and later wants to orient it to the "experience of bestowed freedom in connection to the experience of the world."[13] Or as Jürgen Moltmann, defining it somewhat less from the problematic of subjectivity and somewhat more from the problematic of responsibility for the world, says, the "being human of persons" comes "to reality in the human kingdom of the Son of Man."[14] Also Eberhard Jüngel, although starting with Karl Barth from the proposition that "the person of Jesus Christ . . ." means "a decision over the being human of all humans,"[15] basically shares the opinion that theological speech concerning human beings must "be verifiable in the horizon of human analysis of being."[16] It may be seen that Rahner's opinion that human being is "to be referred to the absolute mystery"[17] participates thoroughly in the general intention of verification of contemporary theological anthropology.

There is of course in contemporary theological anthropology, as for instance in Jüngel, the decisive applying of models of the "new person" and then, in the case of Christ as the "God-corresponding person,"[18] which (although belatedly) poses the general problematic of verification. Of course there is, moreover, above all the proper theological contribution of Christology, justification and the problematic of freedom to the proposed anthropology. The main feature, however, is rather that which, expressed with all caution, enlarges or excessively raises connections to general anthropological reasoning which is then also drawn into empirical legitimation of theological anthropology.

In this connection now it seems Luther's advance in his "Disputation Concerning Man" (1536), his only comprehensive basic outline of anthropology, is being examined and noted with growing interest. Luther starts in his theses from the—at that time—current Aristotelian-scholastic definition of the person as "animal rationale."[19] He then narrows his view somewhat to human ratio, saying of it that it is "something divine."[20] Then he emphasizes, however, arguing throughout, that a comparison of philosophical and theological knowledge about the person shows that philosophically we "know almost nothing about man."[21] And he places into the middle here in connection with the thesis formulated on Rom. 3:28 that the definition of the person as "whole and perfect" is gained essentially from theology by the "fulness of its wisdom,"[22] "that the person is justified by faith."[23] He proves this by an account of the loss and recovery of the human "image of God" in the history of salvation the crucial point of which is the thesis that the person as the fallen creation of God is "freed and given eternal life only through the Son of God, Jesus Christ."[24]

Jüngel, in his model of a theological anthropology which appears as a theological report in a series on anthropology, referred to Luther's advance in the disputation "De Homine."[25] He says that it belongs to the incontestable insight of theology on anthropology "that the person, in evil as well as good, is hidden from him/herself."[26] "The whole person" is "as such only experienceable where the totality of the person is already transcended."[27] If "the person" would "experience himself as *totus homo*," he must "experience more than himself."[28] "Because the person can experience more than himself and insofar as himself as total person, there is generally theological anthropology, there is thus something like a definition of the person."[29] Jüngel then gives attention to Luther's "De Homine" with regard to this definition. It is not totally clear whether Jüngel wanted to recapitulate Luther's thought process in his prior train of thought. Certain echoes let this be supposed. Then the being-in-exile *(Verwiesensein)* of the person in which he eludes in himself the totality appears to be the data to which Jüngel connects his anthropology and also sees Luther tied. This easily reminds one of Rahner's "human exile *[Verwiesenheit]* in mystery."[30] If Jüngel speaks of the "wholeness of man" transcending the experience of the "whole man," where Rahner continually brings to expression the "mystery," might he at least terminologically, but even probably in substance, be determined by Luther's "De Homine"?[31]

The question whether Luther means the same thing or whether here there is, certainly then a very productive, misunderstanding poses itself when one sees the certain kind of perplexity which Peters is plunged into in attempting to appraise Luther's advance in "De homine" on the basis of a thoroughly exhaustive and illuminating analysis of the total reasoning of the disputation.[32] On the one hand, there was the possibility from Luther's theses and under the evidence of their intention to open "the world-oriented philosophical view to the narrative of salvation history."[33] "On the other hand the short formula *Homo theologicus* stretches a radical dividing line between this-worldly and theological anthropology."[34] Peters sees a "tension which is not completely to be resolved"[35] and pleads for a third possibility, which in his opinion accords with Luther: "An anthropology in the view of salvation of one for whom Christ's salvation is already a secretly completed creation."[36]

But Ebeling, who sees Luther's method as more unified and coherent, brings philosophical and theological anthropology into relationship differently. In his certainly not yet finished analysis of Luther's "De homine,"[37] he thinks Luther has already followed "a theological-critical intention" in his conception and presentation of the philosophical definition of human being. "Here the specifically theological statements are, as far as possible, for the time being left out of consideration in order to set in motion an imminent critique of the philosophical definition."[38] He subjects the philosophical definition of human being to the question, "Which cognito hominis does it express?"[39] Although according to Luther the philosophical definition contains some accurate things about the human relationship to the world, it is still lacking in reference to human self-knowledge. "The experience of powerlessness in the human relationship to the self is therefore the major scope of Luther's critique of the philosophical definition of the human being."[40] But this critique *is* already thoroughly directed by the conviction that "the whole and perfect person" must be theologically defined with Paul to the effect "that the person is justified by faith."[41]

If Ebeling is correct, the contact between the philosophical and theological definition of being human is going on in Luther not so very much logically and on a high level as rather in contrast, and it must indeed be said, in an undermining manner. Luther in no way denies or avoids the dialogue. But he "inquires behind it," and indeed does so from the outset from a theological perspective. His intentions for verification are highly existential. He asks whether the philosophical statements in their provisionalness and limitedness, yes inadequacy, already present everything about the person; whether in this manner of definition it must not also be recognized that this is not the totality already experienced or to be experienced, but rather could be experienced under the encouragement of the Word of God. The certain ontological nexus of contact, so Jüngel formulated it, certainly in Luther's sense, as the principle of theological anthropology in dialogue with philosophical anthropology means that "the person can experience more than himself and only in this way can experience himself as the whole person."[42]

THE "BEING-PLACED-OUTSIDE-ONESELF" OF THE BEING HUMAN

Jüngel has emphasized something in connection with the anthropological statements and analyses raised by us that we have up to now left out of consideration. Where he says that "the whole person as such" is "only experienceable where the totality of the person is already transcended,"[43] he adds: "This means that the person becomes a whole person not from within, not out of himself, but rather only from outside himself. To the truth of the *totus homo*, of the whole person, belongs the structure of the *nos extra nos esse*, the being-outside-ourself. If the person wants to experience himself as the *totus homo*, he must experience more than himself."[44]

It is not only the "more." It is what Jüngel really knows; it is being drawn out of oneself in such a way that one's fundamental being is dependent upon something outside oneself. Jüngel has not expressly indicated that he is referring here to Luther. But nowadays nearly everyone knows that this dimension, which Joest has termed the "eccentric character of being a person" in Luther,[45] is a deeply rooted and inseparable structural element of Lutheran anthropology. It is already present in Luther's commentary on the Magnificat: "Hence she does not glory in her worthiness nor yet in her unworthiness, but solely in the divine regard, which is so exceedingly good and gracious that He deigned to look upon such a lowly maiden, and to look upon her in so glorious and honorable a fashion."[46] It finds its most pregnant expression in the Galatians commentary (1531): "And this is the reason why our theology is certain: it snatches us away from ourselves and places us outside ourselves, so that we do not depend on our own strength, conscience, experience, person or works but depend on that which outside ourselves, that is, on the promise and truth of God, which cannot deceive."[47]

In certain areas which developed in contemporary evangelical theology, anthropology has expanded this concept of Luther, which he tied to a sharp polemic against the substance concept in theological anthropology, to a comprehensive relational ontology which determines theological statements not only in anthropology but in all areas.[48] Jüngel's theme of the "God-corresponding person" is thus in the same way as Ebeling's emphasis on the *coram*-relationship, constitutive of the being human of the person: *coram Deo, coram mundo,* and *coram meipso*.[49] Such relational thinking may be noted also in Catholic theological anthropology. It does not seem to come directly from Luther but from the Ebner-Buber I-thou- philosophy. Thus the author of "Mensch als Person" in the dogmatic compendium *Mysterium Salutis,* after raising the problems of substance-ontological thinking, states: "We are thus in our deepest personal being not something for ourselves but we are essentially the response which always knows itself upheld by the call of God."[50]

It is this, but not everywhere so. It is to say nothing of the anthropology which maintains the Christ-event has its anthropological scope in the enablement and qualification for human self-realization. Here in any case there is no sense in which the significance of Luther can be spoken of. Otherwise it relates to the anthropology of "freedom" and "liberation," if one may use these cliche-ridden catchwords. Pannenberg's respectable attempt in approaching the "problematic of the self-understanding of the person" to gain a "corroboration of the reality of God,"[51] indicates an extrinsity of the person above all there where he/she seeks to gain the experience of the reality of God from the "experience of bestowed freedom."[52] Pannenberg can expressly say: "The reality of God, on which the person is dependent in the structure of his subjectivity, is encountered only where, in the context of his world, he receives himself as a gift in the experience of freedom."[53] But this bestowal is always received in mediation; it "is encountered as a reality only in the context of the experience of the world. The way it is encountered is that in the context of the historical world of any person, freedom is something which actually comes about in a particular way on some occasion. Thus the divine reality, on which man finds himself to be dependent in the structure of his subjectivity, reveals itself in the actual coming about of freedom as a power over the world in which he finds himself, and therefore as a reality."[54] The "extra," which Luther means, was clearly not only the transcending disclosure of a universal historical-teleological connection of dependence in place of a freedom dependent on subjectivity. It was, however, the person being torn out of him/herself. Only in this way can the person come to him/herself in the confession of sin and the consolation of grace. "Therefore, man in this life is the simple material of God for the form of his future life."[55] Between Pannenberg's question of how "God is conceivable as the basis of human freedom"[56] and Luther's statement in the above thesis from "De homine" there is a very distinct material and temporal distance. It is thus completely clear that Pannenberg's question refers in the sharpest way to the problem of the relevance of Luther for contemporary theological anthropology. Where justification must be empowerment to avail oneself of one's freedom, that human depth no longer appears to be visible or responsive which led Luther to let man as "simple material" be dependent upon God's justifying grace. This is said without polemical passion. Pannenberg in fact has raised here one of the most important questions to be addressed if we are to deal with Luther's significance for contemporary theological anthropology.

A question also arises here, of course, in relation to what is held in one way or another in all contemporary Catholic anthropologies: the concept of an anthropological "nature." Every reasonable person knows that this is impossible to discuss adequately here. But it is at this point, and not only in the models of contemporary Catholic anthropology, that there lies perhaps the essential point in the relationship between Luther's anthropology and that of the present. This is enormously complicated. On the one hand, it is necessary to speak at least of the train of thought of a theology oriented to *Heilsgeschichte* and its demands on contemporary anthropology; to speak of openness, dependence, or incorporation of the person in the Christ-"mystery." On the other hand, it demands the axiom of the "unindebtedness" *(Ungeschuldetheit)* of grace identifying a "nature" in the person which does not simply have a claim upon this grace. The then identified "nature," however, brings into anthropological reasoning a historically and dogmatically determined fall of the self which in any case does not allow dependence in the sense of Lutheran extrinsity to be further interpreted. The "supernatural existential" is of service exactly in this connection. But it is explained concretely only with difficulty, not to mention that it designates a natural-supernatural relationship of the person to grace and seeks to retain dogmatic support in exclusion of the Lutheran "extrinsity of grace." The fruitfulness of these tensions and relations for the model of contemporary theological anthropology cannot be overlooked. It is an abstract human being who cannot even be God's "simple material" but who, on the other hand, signifies the limits of the barely possible as "referring" to God. As is well known, on the basis of his theology of the cross, Luther abandoned all historical and dogmatic considerations of a human "nature," in any case in relation to justification. "The love of God does not find, but creates, that which is pleasing to it."[57] His disputation "De homine" shows that he maintained the justification-relation for the fundamental anthropological-relation. For instance, it is not only the sinner but the person of "this life" who is characterized as the "simple material of God for the form of his future life."[58] In any case, Luther's significance for contemporary theological anthropology is not least in that his *extra nos* continually raises and keeps alive the question whether any anthropologically locatable condition of being human permits the fact to be evaded that grace and justification of the person can only simply be given; and that finally this is what the person needs for "this life" and this is what can help him/her.[59]

THE "IMAGE OF GOD" OF THE HUMAN BEING

There seems to be agreement in contemporary theological anthropology that the theme of the image of God is a key theme of theological anthropology. The author of the above-mentioned article in *Mysterium Salutis* writes: "The doctrine of the image of God in the human being is the basic theme of Christian anthropology and includes all its themes in itself so that a systematic doctrine of the person can be developed from it."[60] From the evangelical side, Jüngel introduces his "material foundation of evangelical anthropology" with the proposition: "The God-corresponding person means in the Bible the image of God, imago Dei. The biblical texts will have to be examined for a material foundation of theological anthropology according to the image of God."[61]

Compared with this it is striking that in Luther the image of God does not appear to be any independent or prominent theme of his anthropology. Althaus[62] and Joest[63] manage to devote studies to Luther's anthropology without the image of God being an express concept. Most other presentations of Luther's theology are similar in this.[64] This is because Luther in fact had no interest in anthropological reasoning which reaches beyond the infralapsarian nexus of being a sinner and the justification of the person. However, precisely because his reasoning proceeds from this nexus, his theological grasp of the doctrine of the divine image, when it takes place, is extraordinarily momentous. He knows, of course, the old distinction, following Gen. 1:26, of the *imago* and *similitudo Dei* which, on the one hand, speaks of a relatively indestructible divine image of the human being, and on the other hand, an original righteousness bestowed in addition to it which is lost in the fall, repaired again by Christ and sacramentally infused into the person.[65] However, he does not divide these but joins the divine image and the original righteousness, and sees the image "in relationship to God's Word."[66] Nevertheless, this is a reference to the original person being enabled to live from the gift of God's promise: "Similitude and image of God is true and perfect knowledge of God, loving God above all things, eternal life, eternal joy, eternal security."[67] For Luther this is already a reference to

Christ: "But the image of the invisible God is the Son, through whom all things hold together."[68] However, the next sentence shows that Luther is here thinking not so much of the incarnated Son of God as of the eternal Son of God who participated in the creation of the world and humanity, the Second Person of the Trinity. However, Luther also knows the connection here to the history of salvation: "Again, the heavenly image is Christ, who was a man full of love, mercy and grace, humility, patience, wisdom, light and everything good; also that all his essence was righteous, that he served everyone, and would harm no one. We must also bear this image and be conformed to him. It also belongs to this image how he died and suffered, and everything that was in him: his resurrection, life, grace and virtue, everything there is righteous, so that we also are to put on this same image."[69] What is in outline here is completely determinative in the disputation "De homine." Here the theological definition of the person as a sinner to be justified is embedded in a history of salvation account of the person as originally made in the divine image to which he/she will be eschatologically restored.[70]

We have dwelt at length on Luther's statements here because it could not be presupposed that they are well-known. If we see correctly, contemporary theological anthropology with regard to the image of God in the person has two particularly predominant concerns. One that is particularly apparent in Catholic anthropology is that of an anthropological rootedness of "human relationship to God."[71] This corresponds to the Catholic doctrinal tradition and is manifest today in the following solid and thoughtful definition: "The divine image exists . . . in the essential and abiding reference of the person to God as the foundation and form of his/her being."[72] Here relationality and substantiality are united in a balanced way. On the one hand, in a cautious but perceptible modification of conventional doctrinal tradition, the personal structuredness of the God-person relationship is satisfied. On the other hand, there is mediated with the doctrinal tradition the orderedness-toward-God of the person which is in the human soul: "The human spirit reaches beyond all the things of the world and finds its fulfillment only in the unification with its divine original image."[73] On another hand, there is a christological centering of the concept of the divine image which is expressed by Catholics as well as evangelicals. Here Barth's basic anthropological thesis is followed: "The ontological determination of humanity is grounded in the fact that one man among all others is the man Jesus."[74] This leads, for instance, to Hans Küng's thesis of Jesus as the "definitive standard."[75] Jüngel completes this in his anthropological model by the theology of the Word and Incarnation: "The true being of the person is through the Word of address which enables correspondence to that movement of God in Jesus Christ toward the person. This movement of God toward the person forbids human ascent toward divinity. Just as God was revealed as Lord in his lowliness, so the image of God is only in participation in this lowliness appointed to be the 'glory of the child of God.'"[76]

Both concerns, that of seeing the divine image of the person in an "essential and abiding" relationship to God and that of finding only in Christ the essentially "God-corresponding person," could enrich each other. This is seen where Rahner calls Christology "the radical and unrivaled repetition of anthropology," "so that post-incarnational anthropology must always be read as deficient Christology, and Christology always as the goal and basis of anthropology because it has historically and unsurpassedly come to light in Jesus what and who the person is."[77] But both concerns can also run into very radical conflict with each other. A controversial problem would be the extrinsity of the Lutheran understanding of the person. In the last analysis it excludes mediation. Nevertheless, both concerns have their great significance in the field of contemporary theological anthropology. The one teaches how to see and open the anthropological core as disclosable *coram Deo*, even if in secret. The other shows in the loss of God or in the usurpation of God in existing persons the concrete knowable person of the divine image. Luther's fundamental concept is in contrast to this, so it seems, and only acquires with difficulty a reasonable contemporary relevance. It is the concept of the tension-filled existence of the person in life and human history which has its sense and promise in God placing it in Christ under justifying grace and thereby preserving in a saving way the human image of God. But it can be that this human and life historical view of things, which seeks to grasp it in existential-personal depth and to comprehend its essential finality, nevertheless still retains anthropological significance.

THE PERSON AS THE *SIMUL* OF "FLESH" AND "SPIRIT"

Immediately after Luther speaks in "De homine" of the image of God in persons as that which comprehends in history the life of the person, a life determined by God in Christ, he says: "Meanwhile, man lives in sins and daily is either justified or becomes more polluted."[78] This statement expresses a mature form of his conviction that the person, who must be defined theologically as the sinner being justified, is not removed and cannot emerge from the constituent elements of this definition during earthly life. Thus the person remains sinner and righteous at the same time and also remains, in the sense of Pauline theology, "flesh" and "spirit" at the same time.

The existence of this formula in Luther hardly needs to be substantiated. In the early *Lectures on Romans*: "*Simul iustus et simul peccator*, a sinner in fact but a righteous person by the sure imputation and promise of God."[79] In his "Preface to the Epistle of St. Paul to the Romans" (1522), Luther says: "Thus 'the flesh' is a man who lives and works, inwardly and outwardly, in the service of the flesh's gain and of this temporal life. 'The spirit' is the man who lives and works, inwardly and outwardly, in the service of the Spirit and of the future life."[80] Then: "Whatever, therefore, does not proceed from faith is flesh."[81] Thus, and exactly here, Luther thinks "extrinsically." He can say: "I am a sinner in and by myself apart from Christ. Apart from myself and in Christ I am not a sinner."[82]

The *simul* thus holds *diverso respectu*.[83] I am a sinner "in fact"[84] or "as far as myself and my flesh";[85] I am righteous "because of the mercy of God imputed to me in the promise of Christ, that is, propter Christum."[86] Now this certainly does not mean that my righteousness would not be real in actual life. Luther emphasizes: "For Christ continues to be formed in us, and we are formed to the image of God, this continues throughout the time we are living."[87] The latter certainly holds in the strong sense: "To progress means always to begin anew."[88]

Above all Luther acquired his distinction of "flesh" and "spirit" as exegetical knowledge in Romans through laborious dialogue with the medieval "constitutional trichotomy" of the person. The struggle was in the attempt to apprehend Paul under the terms "flesh" and "spirit," understood as the struggle within the person drawn down by the "body" as "flesh" while related to God by the "spirit." "The soul shall, so to speak, tip the scales, realizing the ascetic turning away from the transitory world and toward the true God; the rebellious body being compelled under the direction of the spirit."[89] Luther grasps that it is not a question of a struggle within the person but rather about the person in which God and Satan, righteousness and sin oppose each other. The person is not uninvolved in the struggle, only the person cannot decide the outcome. The power change *(Machtwechsel)* occurs in Christ, in whom God sets up his grace over humanity. "For his grace is not divided or parceled out, as are the gifts, but takes us completely into favor for the sake of Christ our Intercessor and Mediator. And because of this, the gifts are begun in us."[90]

The Lutheran *simul* is that area of his anthropology which, on the one hand, is most strongly noticed and contested, yet, on the other hand, has been least received in contemporary theological anthropology. There is great fascination here especially concerning the area from the *extra* to the *servum arbitrium*. Luther's concepts in their decisiveness are continually irritating but, exactly for this reason, challenging and innovating. In Luther's view the person is so totally delivered up to the Word of justification, even if affected by it and in the process of becoming, that he can be received and made free in his personal center only by God's grace. Indeed, without this there would be the expectation that the person him/herself could add something to his/her graced self-realization: "The person is prior to works."[91] But the person also at the same time cannot expect during his/her lifetime to be taken out of the process of becoming, to be promoted in justification and faith: "We are not yet what we shall be."[92] Perhaps this fascination is still perceptible when

Rahner strives to go as far as possible into the *sola gratia* and also behind the *simul*. "The doctrine of grace will not say anything at all different than that the person by God's act, by the free, uncompelled act of God, really inwardly and truely becomes a righteous person out of a sinner. He can never judge this righteousness which is continually threatening and hidden in him. He can take no autonomous position over against God."[93] This statement is one of the closest approximations to Luther's *simul* appearing in contemporary Catholic theology. That this is clearly only an approximation and in no case a reception or identification is readily obvious.

In the newer evangelical anthropologies, Luther's *simul* appears, with the exception of anthropologies which have grown directly out of the Lutheran train of throught, to play hardly any role. This may perhaps be due to the exegetical complications which Luther's *simul* raises.[94] But that is not the only factor. Rather it lies, on the one hand, in the anthropological starting point of humanity as a more or less self-realizing subject. From this perspective, reference to the state of sin in the justified person can be, at best, partial but never total, and thus there is no speech of the total *simul*. On the other hand, however, there is also in this a certain conceptually valuable advance of an "inclusive" Christology and soteriology which views the concrete person in Christ as already really reconciled and liberated, and which emphasizes justification and faith as well as their "extra." However, it can view this only as obedient recognition and acceptance of an already-existing state of reconciliation. Luther's *peccator in re* is here deeply and in a way, the justification of which must be thoroughly discussed, put into question. Jüngel's anthropological model, as far as we can see, passes over the *simul* in silence. This is also true when it is held that the "Person Jesus Christ" signifies "a decision over the being human of all persons" and when in establishing this it is said: "In Him the future and also in this respect the entire history of the human race is decided. In Him also the essence of the human being is also ontologically decided."[95] Luther clearly emphasizes the fundamental point that regardless of the specific personal history of unique individuals and how they relate to the Christological turning point, the saving *extra nos* is coming to pass in Christ. He distinguishes this from the ontologically distinguishable significance of the individual which he also grants, not to the extent of a self-controlled subjectivity but nevertheless to an individual life history which, as such, has significance in God's *Heilsgeschichte*. Only where this is held to be significant can Luther's thesis also have significance: "Meanwhile, man lives in sins and daily is either justified or becomes more polluted."[96]

THE PERSON ENGAGED IN RESPONSIBILITY FOR THE WORLD

"The basis of freedom cannot be a being that already exists, but only a reality which reveals to freedom its future, the coming God."[97] This is what

Pannenberg says of the "corroboration of the reality of God," by which he means that it does not lead past "the problems of man's self-understanding" in the modern period.[98] "The humanity of the person comes to its reality in the human kingdom of the Son of Man. In the Kingdom of the Son of Man the divine image of the person is fulfilled."[99] Moltmann applies this to that person who, in his view, corresponds to the "criteria for a theological criticism of man."[100] And Jüngel also emphasizes, at the conclusion of his "Bemerkungen zur Gottebenbildlichkeit des Menschen als Grundfigur theologischer Anthropologie":[101] "The God-corresponding-person is . . . he who remains among persons, by and for them, but in such a way with them the person becomes more human: Homo homini homo, the person who is considered human by others."[102]

What we are hearing here is what we have heard throughout in a variety of expressions but which nevertheless is finally the unitary theme of contemporary theological anthropology which voices the this-worldly finality of the person; just what the essential finality of the person appears to be is sometimes very difficult to make out. What is clear here is, above all, that theological anthropology sees humankind adapted and included in the perspective of the New Testament, but now also with all kinds of motives stemming from the present enriched concept of the Kingdom of God. Its goal is a *vita aeterna* which at least runs throughout the coming future of the biblically proclaimed Kingdom of God but is also often merged into one another. There is a lot standing behind this. First of all, there is the modern historicizing of the world ratified in the reception of the concept of the Kingdom of God, by which there also enters a historicizing of the Christian goal of hope. There is the modern socialization *(Vergesellschaftung)* by which the concept of the Kingdom of God is accommodated and thereby also the finality of the Christian image of being human conforms to a societal understanding of humanity. Further, behind this there is, with more or less closeness to the concept of the Kingdom of God, in the course of the development of the modern period, an even stronger accommodating drive towards human liberation from self-alienation and thereby the desire for a human person and a more human world. Finally, what also stands behind this which fuses the other features into a comprehensive character is the shift in the conception of God from "metaphysical" to historically understandable, complying with persons in history and at the same time innovating and developing the "coming" God. All of this is concentrated in an unavoidable yet at the same time demanded and feasible human responsibility for the world. "The idea of the person as made in the image of God binds freedom over against the world with responsibility for the world before God."[103] The reconciled and liberated person "does not emigrate inward into the purity of the heart. He also no longer loses himself in dreams of a better world. . . . He can therefore give himself up to this unredeemed world with love, humility and patience without having to fear losing himself, and without the compulsion of having to realize himself. He does not need to earn the love and recognition of God but rather can act freely from a recognized and loved existence."[104]

What does Luther's understanding of the person have to do with this? It is completely clear and has been continually written that it is precisely the extrinsity of the person bound up with the Reformation concept of justification which has brought a revolution of human relationships to the self and to the world. No longer was there a world in the person to be lifted up to God, while God at the same time graciously grasped the movement and in the last analysis also enabled it and permitted it to succeed. Rather, the person here stands under that "triune gift" of God which Luther so impressively described in his 1528 "Confession."[105] When the person is incorporated in the giving encounter with the Word, in a "hearing" made responsible by his conscience, this allows him to live from the comforting confidence in God. The world is the field, on the one hand, of a rational perception of mission, and on the other hand, the crucial test of love arising from faith. Thus it is already an area in which the person is living dependently and committedly as human.

Ebeling has shown, in his minute analysis of "De homine," how Luther's formulation of the conventional medieval philosophical opinions received by theology about the person already shows a reorientation. "As so often happens, there is discovered in the Luther texts, under the cover of medieval language and conceptions of life, a deep movement which without already being univocally determinable suggests a change in the foundation."[106] Above all, Ebeling finds in the theses on reason that Luther, by his way of dealing with the traditional definitions, brings "into view the person as homo faber."[107] "Because the person is understood as *animal rationale*, he/she is understood essentially as doer. Strictly speaking, this is unsuitable in reference to that which he/she is, but rather it is in reference to that which he/she has done and can do. . . . The person is therefore defined as a historical essence, and indeed in the sense that he/she makes history."[108]

If Luther's understanding of being human is completely an anticipation of the tendencies which set the tone for the modern era, so it is however in another perspective more restrictive, in any case in a particular manner, to the concepts which are important to contemporary theological anthropology. It is not Luther's ecclesial or social conservatism which is under discussion here. If Luther is being represented, the apparent breakthroughs which are everywhere must also be registered. It is not only his much-criticized "individualism of salvation" which is then the concern, although it may not be overlooked. It is that for Luther the divine finality pervaded everything by the binding of the individual's life history to the cross of Christ; and this really cannot be deleted when it concerns Luther's speaking to the anthropological opinions of contemporary theology. But what is essentially important are Luther's distinctions: the distinctions of law and gospel, person and work, faith and love, and also and above all here, the distinction of the kingdom of the world and the kingdom of Christ. This is not the place to present the particulars of the consequences of these distinctions which are never separations but always differentiations of relationships. Basically it is a matter of two things in all of them. First, it is a matter of distinguishing between the person's being as a demand of God and his/her becoming as a gift of God in Christ, and to bring this distinguishing into a final relationship. Second, it is a matter of so understanding the being of the person as being determined and co-determined that it retains that tension which directs the person to the divine gift, but also from here on allows the person to be dependent on this act. Luther distinguishes finally for the sake of the gospel, thus for the sake of the purity and encouragement of the consolation of grace. He distinguishes because he believes that the cross of Christ is the only fact by which the person is enabled to live liberated, justified, and active in this world.

Luther's distinctions are complicating. They are complicating in particular there where one would like direct transformation, direct engagement, direct realization. They are complicating in themselves and just the same way for contemporary propositions like, "the humanity of the person . . ." comes "to its reality in the human kingdom of the Son of Man."[109] "And as earth and heaven were in the beginning for the form completed after six days, that is, its material, so is man in this life for his future form, when the image of God has been remolded and perfected."[110] Thus says Luther. One may not overlook where the scope of this statement lies. It lies in this respect that all essentially creative acts in the world and in the realization of salvation are ascribed to God as the one who is called the essential former of the world and of persons. In order to be sufficiently precise, one must emphasize that it is ascribed to him alone, the three-in-one God. Exactly this emphasis does not exclude but rather includes the point that Luther teaches: that the person is to be understood as one with God, collaborating and co-forming the world. And indeed this holds true for both realms, the one in which the person is living and acting by his/her reason and conscience for the neighbor; and the other, in which he/she, as justified sinner, may render love flowing from faith to all persons.

The attempt to fathom "Luther's significance for theological anthropology" leads to a highly ambivalent situation. On the one hand, changes and impulses exist in him which clearly help set the tone of the statements of contemporary anthropology. On the other hand, the impression may not be put aside that contemporary theological anthropology, with good reasons, is thinking and formulating among orientations and problems which had not yet been reached by Luther. But a final remark also seems to be allowed. It is the pressing thought that the knowledge potential of the Lutheran anthropology in many, sometimes even very important, respects by no means is exhausted; on the contrary, it is still available for our use.

NOTES

1. It is perhaps not typical but nevertheless noteworthy that in the article on anthropology in the compendium of Catholic dogmatics, *Mysterium Salutis*, Luther is mentioned altogether six times, only two of which, in the area of the doctrine of sin, are expressly concerned with Luther's thought.
2. Eberhard Jüngel, "Der Gott entsprechenden Mensch, Bemerkungen zur Gottebenbildlichkeit des Menschen als Grundfigur theologischer Anthropologie," in his *Entsprechungen: Gott-Wahrheit-Mensch, Theologische Erörterungen* (Munich, 1980), 291.
3. Cf. Albrecht Peters, *Der Mensch* (Gütersloh, 1979), 22.
4. Wilfried Joest, *Ontologie der Person bei Luther* (Göttingen, 1967).
5. Gerhard Ebeling, *Lutherstudien, 2: Disputatio de homine*, 1 & 2 (Tübingen, 1977 and 1982).
6. Peters, *Der Mensch*, 27–59.
7. A delimitation of the concept "contemporary theological anthropology" may be taken up only with difficulty. Hermann Fischer discusses this in his "Tendenzen zur Verselbständigung der theologischen Anthropologie," in H. Fischer, ed., *Anthropologie als Thema der Theologie* (Göttingen 1978), 9–19. In general we have not gone to material prior to 1957, when the catchword "theological anthropology" emerged in the third edition of the *RGG* for the first time. This is an expediency, but it nevertheless has certain reasons.
8. Cf. Fischer, "Theologischen Anthropologie," 12.
9. *SM* 1:181.
10. Fischer, "Theologischen Anthropologie," 11f.; Peters, *Der Mensch*, 214–216.
11. Fischer, "Theologischen Anthropologie," 17.
12. Wolfhart Pannenberg, "Anthropologie und Gottesfrage," in his *Gottesgedanke und menschliche Freiheit*, 2d ed. (Göttingen 1978), 21; English: *The Idea of God and Human Freedom*, trans. R. A. Wilson, (Philadelphia: Westminster Press, 1973), 91: "I have made an attempt in this direction, by taking further, in debate with Arnold Gehlen, the anthropological outline given by Max Scheler, and studying the theological relevance of the phenomenon of man's openness to the world." This occurred above all in his *Was ist der Mensch?* 6th ed. (Göttingen, 1981).
13. Pannenberg, "Anthropologie," 27; *Idea*, 96.
14. Jürgen Moltmann, *Mensch, Christliche Anthropologie in der Konflikten der Gegenwart* (Stuttgart-Berlin, 1971), 161; English: *Man, Christian Anthropology in the Conflicts of the Present*, trans. John Sturdy (Philadelphia: Fortress Press, 1974), 111.
15. Jüngel, *Mensch*, 297.
16. *Ibid.*, 291.
17. Karl Rahner, "Mensch," SM 3:411.
18. Cf. the title of his essay, note 2.

19. *LW* 34:133–144; *WA* 39 2:175–177.
20. *LW* 34:137. Thesis 4.
21. *LW* 34:137. Thesis 11.
22. *LW* 34:138. Thesis 20.
23. *LW* 34:139. Thesis 32.
24. *LW* 34:138. Thesis 23.
25. Jüngel, *Mensch*, 293, cf. also 309.
26. *Ibid.*, 292.
27. *Ibid.*
28. *Ibid.*
29. *Ibid.*, 293.
30. *SM* 3:412.
31. "Wholeness" and "whole man" may come from thesis 20, *LW* 34, 138.
32. Peters, *Der Mensch*, 27–32.
33. *Ibid.*, 32.
34. *Ibid.*
35. *Ibid.*
36. *Ibid.*
37. Cf. above note 5.
38. Ebeling, *Lutherstudien* 2/2:464.
39. *Ibid.*, 465.
40. *Ibid.*
41. *LW* 34:138f. Theses 20, 32.
42. Jüngel, *Mensch*, 293.
43. *Ibid.*, 292.
44. *Ibid.*
45. Joest, *Ontologie*, 233, and the arguments on 233–274. Cf. also Karl-Heinz zur Mühlen, *Nos extra nos, Luthers Theologie zwischen Mystik und Scholastik* (Tübingen, 1972).
46. *LW* 21:314; *WA* 7:561.
47. *LW* 26:387; *WA* 40 1:589.
48. Cf. Joest, *Ontologie*, 238–250.
49. G. Ebeling, *Dogmatik des christlichen Glaubens* (Tübingen, 1979), 1:334–355, especially 353–355.
50. *MS* 2:648.
51. Pannenberg, *Anthropologie*, 26; *Idea*, 96.
52. Pannenberg, *Anthropologie*, 27; *Idea*, 96.
53. Pannenberg, *Anthropologie*, 27; *Idea*, 96.
54. Pannenberg, *Anthropologie*, 26; *Idea*, 95f.
55. *LW* 34:139. Thesis 35.
56. Pannenberg, *Anthropologie*, 23; *Idea*, 93.
57. *LW* 31:41; *WA* 1:354.
58. *LW* 34:139. Thesis 35.
59. *Ibid.*, Thesis 32.
60. *MS* 2:814.
61. Jüngel, *Mensch*, 300.

62. Paul Althaus, *Die Theologie Martin Luthers*, 5th ed. (Gütersloh, 1980).
63. Cf. above note 4.
64. Peters, *Der Mensch*, 43–49.
65. *Ibid.*, 43.
66. *Ibid.*
67. *LW* 1:60; *WA* 42:46.
68. *LW* 1:224; *WA* 42:167.
69. *WA* 24:50.
70. *LW* 34:138. Thesis 21.
71. *MS* 2:815.
72. *Ibid.*, 814.
73. *Ibid.*
74. Karl Barth, *Church Dogmatics* 3/2 (Edinburgh: T & T Clark, 1960), 132. Cf. Jüngel, *Mensch*, 304.
75. Hans Küng, *Christ sein* (Munich-Zurich, 1974), 378.
76. Jüngel, *Mensch*, 316.
77. *MS* 2:417.
78. *LW* 34:140. Thesis 39.
79. *WA* 57:165.
80. *LW* 35:372; *WA DB* 7:12.
81. *LW* 27:250; *WA* 2:509.
82. *LW* 38:158; *WA* 38:205.
83. *WA* 39 1, 492.
84. *WA* 57:165.
85. *WA* 39 1, 552.
86. *WA* 39 1, 492.
87. *WA* 39 1, 204.
88. *LW* 25:478; *WA* 56:486.
89. Peters, *Der Mensch*, 37.
90. *LW* 35:370; *WA DB* 7:8.
91. *WA* 39 1, 69.
92. *LW* 32:24; *WA* 7:336.
93. *MS* 2:349.
94. Cf. Paul Althaus, *Paulus und Luther über den Menschen* (Gütersloh, 1938, 1958[3]).
95. Jüngel, *Mensch*, 297.
96. *LW* 34:140. Thesis 39.
97. Pannenberg, *Anthropologie*, 23; *Idea*, 93.
98. Pannenberg, *Anthropologie*, 26; *Idea*, 96.
99. Moltmann, *Mensch*, 161; *Man*, 111.
100. Moltmann, *Mensch*, 156; *Man*, 108.
101. Cf. above note 2.
102. Jüngel, *Mensch*, 317.
103. Moltmann, *Mensch*, 160; *Man*, 110.
104. Moltmann, *Mensch*, 166; *Man*, 115.
105. *LW* 37:366; *WA* 26:505f.

106. Ebeling, *Lutherstudien*, 2/2:201.
107. *Ibid.*, 202.
108. *Ibid.*
109. Moltmann, *Mensch*, 161; *Man*, 111.
110. *LW* 34:140. Theses 37, 38.

Responses

Luther's Ecumenical Significance: *Simul iustus et peccator* and the *nova creatura*

JAMES F. McCUE

Like good preaching, Luther's theology is powerful but elusive. Its power derives from its fierce concentration on what Luther sees as *the* issue confronting Christians in a given time and place. Its elusiveness derives from the same source. His concern focuses much more on the Christian's *aestimatio sui*, the Christian's self-understanding in his or her situation before God.

The elusiveness arises because Luther often makes use of a kind of hyperbole that in a preacher would not seem extraordinary, and he likewise shares the preacher's freedom not to say everything all at once. His is a kerygmatic theology. The result of this is that it is often difficult to know how he could say what he does on topic B, given what he has said elsewhere on topic A.

For example, we read, in a disputation of 1543: "Charity is the evidence of faith and makes us have confidence and firmly to establish (ourselves) from the mercy of God, and instructs us, to make us steadfast in our vocation through good works. And then it is clear we are to have faith with works following."[1] Similar texts abound.[2] What makes Luther's meaning elusive is that it is not immediately clear how such texts are to be understood, in light of what Luther says elsewhere, in such abundance and with such vigor, against charity as a basis for confidence of salvation or against the possibility of our works being anything other than an expression of our sinfulness. Each set of texts requires us to ask whether we have properly understood the other—whether the prima facie meaning is the correct or adequate one.

Luther was himself aware of significant shifts in emphasis in his writing. In a very interesting passage in the Third Antinomian Disputation, he writes:

> True it is, that at the early stage of this movement we began strenuously to teach the Gospel and made use of these words which the Antinomians now quote. But the circumstances of that time were very different from those of the present day. Then the world was terrorized enough when the Pope or the visage of a single priest shook the whole of Olympus, not to mention earth and hell, over all which that man of sin had usurped the power to himself. To the consciences of men so

oppressed, terrified, miserable, anxious, and afflicted, there was no need to inculcate the Law. The claimant need then was to present the other part of the teaching of Christ in which He commands us to preach the remission of sin in His name, so that those who are already sufficiently terrified might learn not to despair, but to take refuge in the grace and mercy offered in Christ. Now, however, when the times are very dissimilar from those under the Pope, our Antinomians—those suave theologians—retain our words, our doctrine, the joyful tidings concerning Christ, and wish to preach this alone, not observing that men are other than they were under that hangman, the Pope, and have become more secure, forward, wicked violators—yea, Epicureans who neither fear God nor men. Such men they confirm and comfort by their doctrine. In those days we were terrorised so that we trembled even at the fall of a leaf. . . . Now, however, these Antinomians in preaching not repentance, but security, assuredly do not rightly divide the Word of God, but tear and dissipate it, and thereby destroy souls. Our view has hitherto been and ought to be this salutary one—if you see the afflicted and contrite, preach Christ, preach grace as much as you can. But not to the secure, the slothful, the harlots, adulterers, and blasphemers. If you will not do this you will be a party to their iniquities.[3]

And, more hyperbolically, we have the following from the *Table-Talk:* "If I now had to begin the gospel, I would do it in another way. To abandon the people veiled under the papacy and to come secretely to the help of so greatly disparate and anxious consciences. Therefore the preacher should know the world and not be like me who was a monk and thought that the world was so good that it would come running in order to hear the gospel; but the opposite was the case."[4]

Luther conceived of the Christian life as a passage, under the Word of God, from complacency through despair to faith and loving service. He also came to recognize that *complacency and faith can both be nourished by the same theological formulae*. This is the significance of the antinomian text. Within Luther's perspective it is quite possible for his own manner of presenting the gospel to be seriously inadequate and even destructive, given the wrong time, place, and audience.

I stress this because it seems to me essential if we are to deal constructively with the problem of Luther's ecumenical significance. For if we are not very careful we can end up with an understanding of Luther that makes him the antithesis of everything before and almost everything since. Paul did not understand the human situation in *simul iustus et peccator* fashion;[5] neither did Augustine. Indeed, if the Augsburg Confession 20,17 is correct, that the doctrine of justification "is to be referred to that conflict of the terrified conscience, nor can it be understood apart from that conflict," one may wonder whether Paul would have been altogether able to get the point. If we are not careful, and it seems to me that Professor Lindberg's paper is not careful enough, we are left with Luther simply as the great ecumenical naysayer. If, however, we take the same kind of care to relate Luther's theology to non-Lutheran traditions as one must take to relate that theology *to itself*, we may come up with a more satisfactory result: "What was the *Sitz im Leben* of Luther's *simul iustus et peccator*?"[6]

I have argued elsewhere[7] that the situation was fundamentally shaped by the evolution of penance, its practice and theory, since the eleventh century, and by the structure and some of the content of scholastic theologies. There was a twofold result: either a tendency toward complacency, based upon a minimalist interpretation of the law: "I am all right because (by God's grace, if one were an Augustinian) I am fulfilling the law"; or a tendency toward despair: "I can never fulfill—and be sure that I have fulfilled—the conditions necessary for the forgiveness of sins." Luther's theological revolution of 1515–1518 involves the transformation of the Pauline-Augustinian tradition in a way that will address these two different but closely related problems. The *Lectures on Romans* is focused almost exclusively on complacency, but in the years immediately following, ideas already developed in *Romans* are brought to bear as well on the terrified or despairing conscience.

But both these problems presuppose that we are dealing with what I might call "good medieval Catholics"—men and women who have tried to do God's will and fulfill the law. Some have been led to think that they *have* fulfilled the law and therefore have earned[8] salvation, and while they may think of themselves as dependent on God's empowerment they do not think of themselves as standing in need of forgiveness. Others suffer fear of damnation despite their best efforts. Luther takes over in a sometimes underarticulated way certain aspects of the preceding tradition. The Christian life is obedience to God's will, of course. *But* God makes more radical demands on us than is commonly recognized. And we will never reach a point at which we can say that we have done what we should have and that our acts no longer need forgiveness. Hence our justification can never have any basis other than God's forgiveness *propter Christum* of our abiding sinfulness. Under God's forgiveness, and empowered by it, we are gradually being changed into the *novus homo*, the *nova creatura*. The change is real, "substantial." In an interesting criticism of a certain kind of scholastic theology, he writes: "It is an insult to divine grace if it is taught that it has only this imaginary relation; where as the Scripture says, the grace of God renews and changes and transforms (us) into new persons daily. And this is done not with regard to abolishing but by the changing of our substance and life."[9]

But there are two important qualifications. First, in this life, one never *fully* becomes the *nova creatura*—we are on our way but have not yet arrived—so that it is literally true that anyone of our acts if scrutinized to its depths would deserve condemnation. The text just cited continues: "This itself is indeed the grace of the New Testament and the mercy of God, that, since we are born through the Word of truth and reborn through baptism; as if we were the beginning of some creature of his. Meanwhile the favor of God supports and sustains us, not imputing to death what sins are left in us. It allows true sin until we evolve into perfect new creatures. . . ."[10] And secondly, the Christian life must not become *reflexively* a process of building oneself up as the *nova creatura*. The Christian life is not a process of supernatural self-building.

It is because of this concern with the Christian's *aestimatio sui* that the *simul iustus et peccator* stands as a necessary complement to any notion of the *nova creatura*. Luther was coming out of a religious culture in which there was a strong tendency to think of the Christian life as an accumulation of spiritual goods. Luther's response to this is strong and uncompromising. There is growth in the Christian life: the evidence for this in Luther is unmistakable. But it is necessary that growth or progress always be understood as a daily new beginning: "to advance is always a matter of beginning anew."[11] One begins *daily* from one's condition of sinner.

How is this related to the question of Luther's ecumenical significance? Luther's theology grew out of a diagnosis of the major ills of the church of his time, and was capable of considerable flexibility as these needs seemed to change. Accordingly, in order to relate Luther's theology to the various church communities of the present, one must ask carefully and sympathetically whether they are indeed beset by the problems from which Luther's theology would free them. One should not assume that all Christian traditions that focus primarily on the *nova creatura* rather than on the *simul iustus et peccator* are always guilty of Pelagianism, not letting God be God, blasphemy, idolatry, and all the theological crimes which a florid Lutheran rhetoric sometimes ascribes to them. But I think that it is a measure of Luther's abiding ecumenical significance that he forces us to ask the question and to recognize that the answer cannot be given in a once-for-all way by reference only to church documents and an official theology. It must be sought continuously by asking how Christians do stand before God and one another.

Finally, let me suggest that the largely bourgeois churches of the West stand in a situation analogous to that of the church in Luther's time. We either have domesticated the law in the form of a kind of middle class niceness or neighborliness, and on this basis are able to satisfy ourselves that we are good Christians. Or we collapse into guilt and despair over the possibility of ever living as Christians in a world ruled by the modern equivalent of Paul's principalities and powers. Will the dialectic of law and gospel, of the *simul iustus et peccator*, enable the churches to bear the terrible demands being made of them in, for example, Matt. 25:31–46, without putting up qualifying defenses all around it? And will it prove a resource to the churches as we try in our differing ways to be Christs to one another, and especially to the least in a world in which we can never succeed and in which to progress will be indeed to start every day anew from the beginning? Can the *simul iustus et peccator* provide for us an approach to the *nova creatura* in a world in which God demands the impossible for us and asks it in full seriousness? In the answer to these questions lies one answer to the question of Luther's ecumenical significance.

NOTES

1. WA 39 2, 248, 11–14. Translation by editor.
2. Cf. Ole Modalsli, *Das Gericht nach den Werken* (Göttingen, 1963), passim, for texts of this sort.
3. WA 39 1, 571,10–572,15; 574,5–11. English translation from James Mackinnon, *Luther and the Reformation* (New York and London: Longmans, Green & Co., 1930), 4:171f.
4. WA TR 2, 178,4. English translation by editor.
5. Cf. Paul Althaus, *Paulus und Luther über den Menschen* (Gütersloh, 1958) and W. Joest, "Paulus und das Luthersche *simul iustus et peccator*," *KuD* I (1955):269–320.
6. Though I share Professor Lindberg's conviction that theology cannot be reduced to biography, it does seem to me legitimate and even necessary to understand Luther's theology in its relatedness to the history of the church, and in this sense to Luther's biography. And though in a certain sense it is true that "Doctrine and life are incomparable, not at all on the same level" (Lindberg), totally to separate them would be to forfeit one of Luther's more important accomplishments.
7. Cf. J. McCue, "*Simul iustus et peccator* in Augustine, Aquinas, and Luther: Toward Putting the Debate in Context," *Journal of the American Academy of Religion* 48 (1980):81–96; also, J. McCue, "The *Sitz im Leben* of the Doctrine of Justification," *Clergy Review* 67 (1982):269–274; On the role of scholasticism in impeding the articulation of the obvious, see the forthcoming study, "Double Justification at Trent: The Tension Between Piety and Theology in Sixteenth Century Roman Catholicism," in C. Lindberg, ed., *Piety, Politics and Ethics: Studies in Honor of George W. Forell* (Kirksville, MO: Sixteenth Century Journal Publishers), 1983.
8. There are, of course, differences and ambiguities in medieval understandings of merit. It did not seem necessary to catalogue them here, since the nuances which they would introduce would not substantially change what is said in the text.
9. WA 7:109,17–21. Translation by editor.
10. WA 7:109,23–28. Translation by editor.
11. LW 25:478; WA 56:486,7.

Reassessing Luther's View of Karlstadt

CALVIN AUGUSTINE PATER

My recent research has involved the discovery of definite historical links between Andreas Rudolff-Bodenstein von Karlstadt and the Mennonite/

Baptist traditions. I have, therefore, become increasingly concerned that the record be set straight between Luther and Karlstadt. This is no longer purely a matter of fidelity to historical facts (significant as that is), but this should now be seen as a matter of genuine ecumenical importance. Since Luther was often unjust in his characterization of Karlstadt, I am focusing on two basic issues that help to clarify briefly Luther's view of Karlstadt, as expressed in "Against the Heavenly Prophets" (1524–1525).

WAS KARLSTADT VIOLENT?

In Karlstadt's "The Kingdom of God Suffers Violence, and the Violent Seize It" (Matt. 11:12) there is a constant polemic against the "New Pelagians" who claim they must seize the Kingdom of God by boldly laying hold of salvation.[1] Augustine, commenting on Psalm 147, argues that the violent are the oppressed who seize God by binding themselves to him, as Jacob did when he wrestled with the angel. Karlstadt rejects all externally or internally violent interpretations of Matt. 11:12, rejecting the entire exegetical tradition in relation to this passage. The violent are not in any way to be identified with believers. The church is constantly seized by violent physical or spiritual powers; it is called to experience repression and persecution:

> Through suffering and persecution, one comes to the experience of spiritual poverty, of which Christ says: "Blessed are the poor in Spirit, for to them is the Kingdom of Heaven." Suffering, oppression, and anguish are the divine disciplinarians who offer spiritual poverty. Ridicule and exile create understanding. "Lord take not from my mouth your Word of truth, in which you made me hope, and granted comfort in oppression." Now the members of God's Kingdom learn through inner struggle [*anfechtung*] that God's Word is their life, hope, and comfort. Therefore, those who want to destroy God's kingdom with violence, spend themselves in a lost cause. The Word of God is the sword that the persecuted grab; the hammer with which they pound their opponents; the fire with which they burn their enemies.[2]

Karlstadt's church consists of the persecuted and the despised who are oppressed physically by the violent on earth, and assailed spiritually by the devil and his minions. The church resists only with spiritual weapons, for the weapons of its warfare are not carnal.

Now how did Luther manage to conjure Karlstadt, who preaches nonresistance at the personal level, into a "seditious spirit"? In "On the Removal of Images," Karlstadt applauds the decisions of the "Christian Council of Wittenberg" to remove images from the churches. Karlstadt wants the council to establish conditions conducive to the exercise of religion. He regards the Ten Commandments as perpetually binding, without exempting the prohibition of images,[3] for the New Testament does not abrogate the earlier prohibition, and Paul confirms it when he cites as an example of the

Gentiles' ignorance of the glory of God, their construction of "images resembling mortal men, or birds, or animals, or reptiles."[4]

Luther of course opposes Karlstadt's argument. Nevertheless, says he, "I have allowed and not blocked the outward removal of images, as long as this is done by the proper authority and without tumult and riots."[5] Thus as regards the practical implementation of the removal of images, there is no difference between Karlstadt and Luther, for Karlstadt's program of removal is to be put into effect by "the community" (*gemein*), or, as he notes elsewhere, "where Christians rule."[6] But Luther distorts this: "My Karlstadt always very nicely ignores this point, and what Moses commands [to be done through the authorities], he applies to the rabble."[7] Thus Luther creates the transition from the Christian rulers in a community to the rabble who act without authorization.

Having artfully implicated Karlstadt with violence involving images, Luther now needs a transition from images to people. But in the treatise that Luther has before him,[8] Karlstadt specifically restricts the use of the Old Testament, especially passages that preach holy war or other outward violence. Only God's explicit command excuses Old Testament examples of killing.[9]

Karlstadt explains away Jer. 48:10, "Cursed is he who keeps back his sword from bloodshed," by restricting it, "for this is said of the vengeance of God."[10] Earlier, Karlstadt had denounced Jephthah for sacrificing his daughter to fulfill a vow made to God. Jephthah sets up his own law against God's, which declares: "Thou shalt not kill."[11] Despite this type of evidence, Luther now makes the following transition from his earlier insinuation that Karlstadt approves of mob rule:

> This is and is honestly called a riotous and rebellious spirit, who despises government and does as he pleases, as if he were lord in the land and above the law. Where the rabble is allowed to break images without authorization, one must also permit anyone to go ahead and kill adulterers, murderers, the disobedient, and the like. For God commanded the people of Israel to kill them, just as much as he wanted them to remove images. Thus although I said that Karlstadt is not a murderous prophet, he does have a rebellious, murderous, and riotous spirit within him, which, given the opportunity would be revealed.[12]

The correspondence in which Karlstadt spurned Müntzer's overtures was not known to Luther.[13] But Luther knew that Karlstadt had been involved in the drafting of the "Epistle of the People of Alstedt on How to Fight like a Christian."[14] The theme of this letter is pronounced in the beginning:

> We completely avoid all worldly resistance. No one commands it, for Christ told Peter to sheathe his sword, and did not allow him to fight on his behalf, for the hour of his suffering was near. Likewise when we are to suffer for the sake of

God's justice, let us not reach for knives and spears and challenge God's eternal will with our violence, for daily we pray *Thy* will be done.

On August 22, 1524, Karlstadt and Luther argued as follows at the Inn of the Black Bear in Jena:

Karlstadt: To this I add that you treat me violently and injustly when you lump me with the murderous spirit [i.e., Thomas Müntzer]. I have no dealings with the spirit of insurrection. This I protest publicly before these brethren, one and all.
Luther: Dear Lord Doctor, that is unnecessary. I have read the letter that you who are in Orlamünde have written to Thomas, and I certainly learned from it that you reject the insurrection.[15]

Luther, therefore, knew that Karlstadt opposed violence and urged non-resistance, even in the face of tyranny. He also realized that some of his readers knew that Karlstadt preached non-resistance. To this he responded as follows:

"But," you say, "Dr. Karlstadt does not want to murder. That you can see from the letter that those of Orlamünde wrote to those of Alstedt." Answer: "I also believed this, but no longer. Now *I no longer ask what Dr. Karlstadt says or does* [my italics]."[16]

Luther's charge that Karlstadt was violent stems from his basic conviction. Luther preached about the freedom of the Christian, and he argued that since Christ's kingdom is not of this world, the Reformation does not come through the coercion of consciences, but through the preaching of the Word.[17] In practice, however, Luther is intolerant (though less so than most of his contemporaries), and he has his doubts about the efficacy of the Word (which proves that he was human). Thus he coerces the consciences of people like Karlstadt, by charging them with political violence and appealing to the civil authorities for the removal of such dissenters as revolutionaries.

Unless we learn to ignore Luther's caricatures of the proponents of what became the free churches, or of traditional Catholics, or of the Jews, Luther becomes a stumbling-block for ecumenical understanding. Whatever one thinks of the sectarian proclivities or the so-called Donatism of the radicals, such sectarians did not excommunicate Rome or Wittenberg, except as a reflex. It is somewhat difficult to seek fellowship with those who would exile you, imprison you for life (Luther's implied suggestion for dealing with Karlstadt),[18] or torture or murder you in the name of Christ.

KARLSTADT'S *IUSTUS* WHO IS MADE *SANCTUS*

Karlstadt's doctrines of justification and sanctification must be read in conjunction with his doctrine of predestination. This doctrine undergoes considerable modification during Karlstadt's career in Wittenberg. In his *151 Theses* of April 26, 1517, Karlstadt posits a weak doctrine of *conditional* election, combining this with *sola gratia* and effective perseverance. *Sola gratia* is safeguarded by the claim that all good is derived from God, and the existence of evil is Satan's or man's own doing. "The good we wish comes only from God," and "we commit evil and the good comes to us."[19] These two themes of the person's or Satan's total responsibility for evil, and of God as the sole cause and origin of good, remain the two constants in Karlstadt's view of predestination. They determine Karlstadt's consistent rejection of double predestination (for God does *not* cause evil) and Karlstadt's polemic against the *facere quod in se est* of some of the late-medieval scholastics.

Following his *151 Theses,* and in preparation for his battle with Eck, Karlstadt teaches *unconditional* election in 1518, for "humans cannot hold on to the grace, given by God, with their own powers."[20] Doing one's utmost (*facere quod in se est*) is to defy God by relying on one's evil self rather than a good God.[21] Although God elects unconditionally, reprobation is conditional. Karlstadt, imitating his mentor Johann von Staupitz, cites Hos. 13:9 (Vulg.): "Israel, you cause your own misery, for your salvation alone comes from me." Karlstadt concludes: "From us comes perdition, from God assistance and good and salvation."[22]

The final stage of Karlstadt's understanding of predestination is achieved when he realizes that even a doctrine of unconditional election, without parallel reprobation, makes God capricious and partisan. Although God is free, he has bound himself to humans with his promises. Thus God willingly follows definite rules of justice and decency in dealing with human beings; he is not an arbitrary tyrant or a feudal lord. Therefore Karlstadt can even apply *human* rules of decency to God:

> Let it be granted that our [natural] powers do not propose or desire any good before they encounter God, and that the person who is not transformed by God must fall [that is, the status of those who are passed by in a scheme of unconditional election]. Then God is guilty of the Fall. You see, if you do not help me if I should fall, and you could save me, then you are responsible for my fall.[23]

Thus Karlstadt, whose God does not sin by acts of commission or omission, is led to reject any form of predestination.

From Luther's perspective, the stage has now been set for uncertainty and works' righteousness. To the contrary, Karlstadt spurns any positive human contribution to salvation. Now if God does not force himself on the sinner, and the sinner is by nature unable even to reach out to God, how shall the twain become one? Karlstadt had some difficulty extricating himself from this deadlock. But to the rescue came none other than John Chrysostom. As Karlstadt was reading Chrysostom's Homily 41:6 on Matthew, he experienced a Reformatory Breakthrough:

> But if you desire not even to be punished here [on earth], pass judgment on yourself: exact your own penalty. Listen to Paul when he says, "If we would judge ourselves, we shall not be judged" [1 Cor. 11:31]. If you do this, you are advancing to obtain a crown. "But how are we to exact our own penalty?" one may ask. Weep, groan bitterly, humble and chastise yourself, remember your sin specifically. This is no small torture to your soul. Whoever has experienced contrition, knows this is the utmost punishment of the soul. Whoever recalls his sins, knows the anguish thus produced. Therefore God rewards such repentance with righteousness, saying: "First confess your sins, that you may be justified" [Isa. 43:26 LXX].[24]

Or to put it in Karlstadt's own words:

> If someone wishes to perform a God-pleasing service, he—to sum it up—has to sweep himself with his judgment. All of God's absolutions depend and are erected on the condemnation of our transgressions of divine commands. As the apostle says: "If we condemn ourselves, God will not condemn us."[25]

Such "sweeping" Karlstadt also calls *Gelassenheit* (surrender of self to God):

> Then you have surrendered and allow to take place what God does with you in accordance with his will. Therefore, what you claim for your ego, your self, your own, is destroyed, and the blessed ego sprouts forth.[26]

In this manner Karlstadt reconciles Chrysostom and the medieval mystical tradition with *sola gratia* and a modern concept of God as a loving egalitarian. Karlstadt has now overcome the inherent *uncertainty* concerning salvation that must lie at the root of any predestinarian theology that posits a partisan God. Therefore Karlstadt expresses his appreciation for the contribution of the Scholastics and their concept of God, and their staunch unwillingness to make God responsible for evil.[27] How does the contrition mentioned by Chrysostom and Karlstadt come about? One turns to Scripture to learn about salvation through self-condemnation. However, the Scriptures are not universally available, and this acts as a barrier to the universalism of the divine intent regarding predestination. Karlstadt apparently does not solve this problem until later, when he suddenly accepts the idea of a purgatory for those who were sincere pagans or Catholics. They are to be instructed in the city of souls, where they will learn to recognize God in the noonday sun of clarity. At this point they choose for or against their old selves.[28]

Although mere sincerity and a good moral life do not determine salvation, they are clearly important, for example in determining whether one is instructed in the city of souls. Beyond that, Karlstadt insists that the Christian life includes a pattern of moral transformation of the individual and of society. Thus justification is joined to the life of sanctification:

> We contend that we must ascribe to justification: mortification, perdition, de-

struction, descent to hell, and in contrast: vivification, salvation, renewal [and] the return from hell. For the Christian life is fashioned according to the acts of Christ, and whatever Christ did on the cross, [and his] death, burial, resurrection and ascension towards heaven, ought to correspond to the life of the one who has been justified.[29]

In this vein, Karlstadt refers to a life in *gelassenheit*, where one leaves father, mother, brother and sister, and friends (Luke 14: 25–7) to lead a life of self-denial, carrying one's cross to follow Christ (Luke 9:23–6).[30] Karlstadt also uses a legal index for judging believers. Men who go on a pilgrimage, for example, and who do not provide for their families are judged on the basis of 1 Tim. 5:8 to be unbelievers, for according to the fruit, the tree is known.[31] Faith is joined to love and love issues in divine works:

> God's love, together with God's truth, runs through all work that God's living voice places in the hearts. Thus it is impossible that true faith exists without love: just as impossible as the [isolated] existence of God's love without faith and truth.[32]

Faith issues forth in love, also in the life of the community. In the social realm the idea of the *imitatio Christi* is of course impossible to apply. Thus Karlstadt turns to the Old Testament's social legislation. The laws of Moses express divine law, and are not comparable to the merely natural law contained in the *Sachsenspiegel*.[33] Thus Luther is right when he claims Karlstadt is a legalist.

If we use the nature-grace model, we can say that for the Scholastic, grace crowns nature and absorbs it structurally. For Luther, grace represents a vertical relationship, while he accepts the horizontal dimension as a natural given. Karlstadt's model is the overcoming of the human ego, or in the broader sense, nature, by divine grace. Similarly, God's laws are to replace human laws that are nothing but "dung."[34] This requires a radical restructuring of society, which cannot be realized given Karlstadt's aversion to the use of power. At the most only a part of society will voluntarily follow this ideal in the life of the sect.

However, where Karlstadt's concept of grace conquering nature can be realized at large by those who, unlike him, are not averse to seizing power, the inevitable outcome is a movement towards egalitarian Christian revolution. With the creation of the Republic of the United Netherlands and during Cromwell's rule in England, and with the birth of the United States by means of revolution, such ideas came to partial fruition. Where the quietistic form of Christianity prevailed, however, the egalitarian revolution was carried out by the Sons of Nature.

NOTES

The titles of Karlstadt's writings have been abbreviated. For exact identification, they have been supplied in parentheses with the number assigned to them in E. Freys and H. Barge, *Verzeichnis der gedruckten Schriften des Andreas Bodenstein von Karlstadt* (Reprinted Nieuwkoop, 1965). Karlstadt's *Von abtuhung der Bylder* (88) has been reprinted by Leitzmann, *Kleine Texte,* Bd.74. This is cited as KT 74. Several other writings have been reprinted by Erich Hertzsch in *Karlstadts Schriften aus den Jahren 1523–25,* I–II (Reprinted Halle, 1956). Such writings are cited as KS. Original treatises are cited by leaf number (A, A2, usw.); back pages are cited as Av, A2v, usw.

1. *Das reich gotis leydet gewaldt* (63), s. Av, etc.
2. Ibid., ss. [C4], C3v.
3. *Von abtuhung der Bylder* (88), KT 74, 20:19ff., especially 21:30–40.
4. Ibid., KT 74, 22:11–26, cf. Röm 1:23.
5. *LW* 40:85; WA 18, 68, 17–19.
6. *Ob man gemach faren soll* (138), KS I, 80:28–30: "Ein jeglich gemein, sie sey klein oder gross, sol für sich sehen, das sie recht und wohl thu, und auff niemants warten." Ibid., 85:23–25: "Wo wir herschen die gott bekennen, und götzen finden, sollen wir sie weg nemen, und mit ihnen geparen als gott gebotten."
7. *LW* 40:89; WA 18, 72, 6–8.
8. Cf. WA 18, 67nl, 68nl, etc. *Ob man gemach faren soll* (138) = KS I, 73–97.
9. KS I, 86:30—87:14.
10. KS I, 84:8–10.
11. *Von gelubden unterrichtung* (50), E3v.
12. *LW* 40:89; WA 18, 72, 9–18.
13. Cf. *Thomas Müntzer, Schriften und Briefe,* ed. Günther Franz and Paul Kirn, "Quellen und Forschungen zur Reformationsgeschichte," 33, 386–87, 415–16 (July 1524).
14. Ibid., 571–73.
15. WA 15, 336, 11–16.
16. *LW* 40:105; WA 18, 88, 6–9.
17. *LW* 40:84; WA 18, 67, 9–17.
18. H. Barge, *Andreas Bodenstein von Karlstadt* II, s. 391–93 (24 September 1528).
19. E. Kähler, *Karlstadt und Augustin,* s. 16*, Th 22, 26. (26 April 1517). Kähler harmonizes Karlstadt with Augustine; my interpretation challenges this.
20. V. Löscher, *Vollständige Reformationsacta* II, s. 104, Th. 399 (May, 1518).
21. *Corpus Catholicorum* I, s. 61:190.
22. Ibid., 55:159.
23. *Ap Got ein ursach sey des Teuffelischen falhs* (114), B3.
24. J. P. Migne, *Patrologia Graeca* LVII, s. 450. Karlstadt mentions his dependence on Chrysostom in *Ausslegung etzlicher heyligenn geschrifften* (15), [C4], without giving an exact reference: "Wiltu von got ein absolutorien erlangen, so mustu dich bevor vorurteylen . . . als Chrysostomus leert."
25. *Ausslegung etzlicher heyligenn geschrifften* (15), A2.
26. Ibid., Bv.
27. *Ap Got ein ursach sey des Teuffelischen falhs* (114), B3v–[4].
28. *Ein Sermon vom Fegfeür* (95), C, usw.
29. *Epitome De impii iustificatione* (13), A3.
30. *Missive vonn der gelassenheyt* (38), B3-v.

31. *Von gelubden unterrichtung* (50), A3v.
32. *Wie sich der gelaub und unglaub gegen got und dem teufel halten* (139), C3v.
33. *Anzeyg Hauptartickeln Christlicher leere* (145), KS II, 99: 27–30.
34. *Ob man gemach faren soll* (138), KS I, 96:37–38.

Luther and the Anabaptists on *simul iustus et peccator* and the New Creature

JOHN S. OYER

This paper is a response to certain problems which Carter Lindberg raised in his excellent paper. He used Karlstadt as his example of a Luther contemporary who moved toward "holiness" or a "renewal movement." I assume that I was invited to participate in this symposium because of my study of the Anabaptists, so I will address myself to their likely reaction to the *simul* motif.

In an otherwise excellent study, perhaps Lindberg's greatest strength becomes in turn a weakness, probably a minor one. He declares that to Luther *simul iustus et peccator* is a confession of faith rather than a universal philosophical truth.[1] But his subsequent explanation of the theme is so thorough that it convinces at least this reader that Luther in fact believed, not merely that this is the way God has graciously worked in himself only, but that this is the way God works universally with all persons. If this truth about God's work with humans is not philosophically based and defended, at least it seems to be universally, theologically, and anthropologically valid, exclusively so.

LUTHER AS ECUMENICALLY ATTRACTIVE FOR THE SIXTEENTH CENTURY

All Christians would agree that Luther opened up and released the Word in Scripture, and held up the seriousness of sin as absolutely destructive of the God-human relation, with both a penetrating theological insight and also a skill in articulation seldom matched in the sweep of church history. Of course there were other Christian spokespersons, both in his own time and prior to the sixteenth century, who cared intensely about these and other issues of religious importance to Luther. To us late in the twentieth century it seems appropriate to add that long before higher criticism, Luther brought a sedulousness of study to Scripture which helped to release it in its fullest and most enlivening power; and long before Auschwitz and Sartre he recognized the mystery and power of evil. Surely most Christians are grateful to him for these and other contributions.

The *simul* motif itself was ecumenically attractive and theologically viable in the sixteenth century, more particularly to that loose and taxonomically indefinable "reform movement" called the Anabaptists. Some observations:

1. Most Anabaptists believed devoutly that sin continued after conversion, baptism, and incorporation into the church—indeed, that throughout the Christian's entire life the reality of evil in general and personal sin in particular was an inevitable condition of life. There were a few individuals among them who held up the possibility of a sinless existence.[2] But the major leaders whose works have survived in quantity sufficient to make them worth special study make it abundantly clear that the condition of the Christian was always seriously marred by sin. On that point they agreed with Luther; and those who knew Luther from his writings, and they were few in number, probably were grateful. Perhaps the clearest evidence of their belief in sin's endless continuity was the insistence of the "General" Anabaptists[3] on the practice of discipline in the form of excommunication, and even the ban among some of them. Indeed, in at least one instance under Bucer's persuasion some of them agreed to return to the Evangelical Church only if that church added excommunication to its constitution.[4]

(It must be added parenthetically that there was great variety among renewal movements, and therefore much of what Lindberg says about Luther's views of them is justified; many Mennonite scholars have not seen this as clearly as they should have, in large part because an earlier hostile historiography on Anabaptism compelled them to recognize and explain the reality about a type of Anabaptist who was neither spiritualistic nor socially—or even theologically—irresponsible. The religious landscape of Luther's life was peopled with a wide variety of *Schwärmer* of the types who elicited his condemnation; and they included more than a few bona fide Anabaptists by anyone's definition.)

2. But the Anabaptists began to protest the theological extension of Luther's *simul* motif at a crucial point: they insisted that some degree of ontological change took place in the regenerated or sanctified Christian.[5] On this point a more detailed examination of a few representative Anabaptist leaders is necessary.

I choose to examine four Anabaptists: Menno Simons, Balthasar Hubmaier, Michael Sattler, and Melchior Rinck, the first three because their teachings and activities were formative for Anabaptists in crucial areas—the Lowlands, Moravia, and South Germany-Switzerland. Rinck is chosen because his thought and leadership were formative for those Anabaptists who lived in Luther lands; his anti-Reformation objections and his program of Christian and church life are the most self-consciously anti-Lutheran of this quartet. But these four are chosen also because they represent the variety of Anabaptism itself. They differed on even basic "Anabaptist" issues: for example, defenselessness, or degree to which the congregation regulated the lives of its members. This disadvantage, in our having no discrete normative

Anabaptism so that the term Anabaptism is itself a misnomer, always makes it difficult to converse about the Anabaptists' relations with other Reformation-era groups.

Of the four, Menno laid the heaviest emphasis on the new birth itself. That new birth in Christ, the direct result of a repentance wrought in the human by the Holy Spirit, so completely remade the human being that he/she was able to live in obedience to Christ. In the words of one theologian, Menno combined justification and sanctification into a dialectic whereby the human did cooperate with God, at least by implication, in his/her own salvation.[6] Menno's hint of synergism was made strange and infinitely more complex by his docetism. But Menno also repeatedly denied both perfectionism and a justification apart from the grace and work of God.[7]

Hubmaier was probably the most synergistic of these four Anabaptist leaders. He believed that the grace of God in Christ changed all humans so that they could will to repent. He cast in stronger terms than did Menno the fundamental truth that God in his grace granted regeneration, within which lay also the power finally to do good; by this grace the person was enabled to kill daily the sin within him/her to use Hubmaier's term. Sinlessness, to Hubmaier, was not at any stage the human condition. But that grace which enabled one to do good also made the human a partner with God in salvation. Finally, Hubmaier considered the congregation the emissary of Christ, empowered by God's grace to aid each member to live above that sin, which still had to be killed daily.[8]

Of the four, Sattler had the least to say on soteriology, primarily because so little of his total thought either was recorded or has survived. But his most recent interpreter declares that he too believed and taught that the grace of God not only saved the human but also enabled the person to carry out the teachings of Christ and perform good works—the human had experienced in regeneration a metaphysical change on the basis of which he/she could live on a different moral plane. Sattler and Menno were the most vigorous in their teaching on the necessity of discipline, by which the church aided regenerated Christians to repent again and again, to live within repentance and yet still live morally.[9]

Rinck's *ordo salutis* was to "better oneself, abstain from sin, wish to repent, and have faith in the forgiveness of sins," on the surface a piece of rank Pelagianism within a medieval mysticism. But Rinck always vehemently insisted—and he was asked often—that each step in this mystery of the sinner's movement toward God was itself the work of God.[10] Perhaps we could posit for him by way of explanation a power of God which consisted essentially of inviting and attracting the sinner, who moved in turn toward God by God's kindly but imperative beckoning, all entirely within the power of God as against the individual's inclination or disinclination. The result was not an imputed righteousness, but a justification which bore with it, still within the gracious activity and power of God, an ability of the individual to abstain from sin and to live a moral life—not completely, but substantially.

These four Anabaptists, who differed so much in their soteriological formulations from those of Luther, departed from Luther, largely unselfconsciously out of their recent Catholic past. Of the four, only Menno seems to have certainly read Luther on soteriology; and he formulated his views in part in reaction against Luther but especially Lutheran teaching and practice as he encountered them. Rinck, who could have read Luther, seems not to have done so; his encounters with Lutheranism were with a cheap grace version of the earliest Evangelical preaching, in no degree fair to the position of Luther.[11] But all of them espoused views on regeneration in particular which were incompatible with the *simul* motif. And all of them seem to have been closer to any of several strands of late medieval Catholic soteriology than to Luther. Taken as a whole, if Anabaptists were neither Catholic nor Protestant, if they were *sui generis* as several scholars have suggested,[12] they fitted somewhere between Catholicism and Lutheran Protestantism, inclining unselfconsciously significantly more to the Catholic side.

ANABAPTIST ANSWERS TO MORE SPECIFIC CHARGES BY LUTHER ARISING OUT OF THE *SIMUL* MOTIF

Legalism. Does a works-righteousness, within which the human offers his/her own works to God as a means of earning salvation, develop in turn into a set of rules or laws which form a structural framework for good as against evil behavior? If legalism means only that (1) regeneration includes a God-given human capacity to obey God, and (2) the attempt to assemble a church of Christian believers who tried to live morally, then the Anabaptists certainly were legalists.[13] But if legalism means the development of a code of moral laws, obedience or disobedience to which determined one's eternal destiny, then the answer is much less clear. Perhaps the Hutterites in developing their *Ordnungen* became legalistic. Today's Hutterites and Amish are not legalistic in my opinion. I think that most Anabaptists were not.

God's role as sole initiator and dynamic of the process by which the human was restored from sin to fellowship with God.[14] It is obvious that some Anabaptists were synergists. But some and perhaps many insisted that they accepted and taught that salvation and the capacity to obey God were the singular work of God himself. It is also obvious that this problem was not one to which they felt compelled to speak among themselves. They spoke on this topic most generally when they were trying to answer some accusation from Protestant quarters, when they were accused of works-righteousness.[15] Again, there were indeed Anabaptists whose salvationist views included some degree of the individual's works of love playing a role in the restoration of fellowship between the human and God. One or two of them were positively crass in their declarations that works indeed, and even exclusively, saved the human. But the majority of Anabaptists answered negatively.[16]

The Christian life is always one of penance.[17] To this the Anabaptist would have probably agreed, in the sense that the Christian in this life always continued to live in sin and therefore needed continuously to repent. When Luther turned the "always penitent" into a negation of the Christian also—simultaneously—living a moral life in some degree before the great Hereafter, then Anabaptists' cries of antinomianism began to fill the air. Or a corollary of this point: the Anabaptists did indeed believe that the Christian could and ought to make some unmeasurable progress in holy living, in this life. When those in Luther lands spoke to this point, they almost always cast it otherwise: they accused Lutherans of preaching a false faith because it did not issue in moral living.[18]

Failure to accept the truth of the *simul* motif led some to the internalization of religion, perhaps to an excessive mysticism.[19] Some Anabaptists were indeed mystics; one thinks especially of some of the Anabaptist followers of Thomas Müntzer such as Hans Hut. But generally they did not slip into a pervasive mysticism. This is especially noteworthy in the encounter of some of them with Spiritualists such as Schwenckfeld.[20]

SOME CONCLUDING OBSERVATIONS

Within the broad sweep of church history, a strongly deterministic *simul* justificationism lies at one end of a spectrum, at the other end of which would be Pelagianism. In the normal course of human developments one would expect a position somewhere in between to be the point for convergence of interests, by common consent among Christians of many persuasions.

If the *simul* motif can be restricted to mean that the Christian sins daily and therefore needs the grace of God daily, then some consensus could likely appear. But when *simul iustus et peccator* is taken to mean the exclusion of any possibility of moral improvement on the part of regenerated Christians, then agreement seems unlikely. Surely monasticism has been better than Luther made it out to be; why should we accept his extreme reaction against it to be theologically binding on us all?

Indirectly, but never directly, the Anabaptists said to Luther: "In soteriology you are too radical, you change too much the Catholic soteriology, especially on the relation between faith and works, to the detriment of morality." If legalism is a danger at one end of the soteriological spectrum, then surely antinomianism is the danger at the other end.

NOTES

1. Carter Lindberg, "Justice and Injustice in Luther's Judgment of 'Holiness Movements,'" 164 above.

2. For example, implicit in the followers of the unnamed "Prophet," in the ecclesiastical Territory of Fulda-Hersfeld; see Paul Wappler, *Die Täuferbewegung in Thüringen von 1526-1584* (Jean: Fischer, 1913), 81-85.

3. For this paper I have decided to use Heinrich Bullinger's term "General" Anabaptists, despite its lack of clarity, primarily because it represents the opinion of a staunch opponent of the Anabaptists that there was a clustering of less obnoxious Radicals. See Bullinger, *Der Widertöufferen vrsprung/fürgang/Secten/wäsen* ... (Zürich: Froschauer, 1560), esp. folios 17a-19a; see Heinold Fast, *Heinrich Bullinger und die Täufer* (Weierhof: Menn. Geschichtsverein, 1959), 122-27. George H. Williams's "Evangelical Anabaptists," although clearly defined with specific Anabaptists as belonging, has been rejected by too many students of Anabaptism who themselves have not yet bothered to provide a replacement. The need to find a suitable term is obvious. But hereafter in this paper "Anabaptists" will mean Bullinger's *Gemeine Täufer*, or approximately that.

4. "Was der Bucerus mit den widerteufern zu Marpurg disputiert hat," in *Urkundliche Quellen zur hessischen Reformationsgeschichte*, Vol. 4, *Wiedertäuferakten 1527-1626*, Günther Franz et al., eds. (Marburg: Elwert, 1951), 213-37. See Franklin H. Littell, "New Light on Butzer's Significance," in *Reformation Studies. Essays in Honor of Roland H. Bainton*, Franklin H. Littell, ed. (Richmond, Va.: John Knox Press, 1962), 145-67.

5. What word should one use for sanctification, a term which the Anabaptists themselves seldom if ever used? George H. Williams, "Sanctification in the Testimony of Several So-Called *Schwärmer*," in Ivar Asheim, ed., *Kirche, Mystik, Heiligung und das Natürliche bei Luther* (Göttingen: Vandenhoeck & Ruprecht, 1967), 194-95, lists a large number of sixteenth-century and present-day expressions, too long to enumerate here but well illustrating the point that there is no consensus on what term to use.

6. J. A. Oosterbaan, "The Theology of Menno Simons," *MQR* 35 (1961): 194.

7. Ibid., 187-96; Willis M. Stoesz, "The New Creature: Menno Simons' Understanding of the Christian Faith," *MQR*, 39 (1965): 9-14. See also many citations from Menno himself, *The Complete Writings of Menno Simons*, trans. Leonard Verduin, ed. J. C. Wenger (Scottdale, Pa.: Herald Press, 1956), 55-58, 123, 146, 337-39, 439, 569, 947-48.

8. See Balthasar Hubmaier, "Ain Summ ains gantzen Christenlichen lebens," 1525, in Gunnar Westin and Torsten Bergsten, eds., *Balthasar Hubmaier: Schriften, Quellen zur Geschichte der Täufer*, Vol. 4 (Gütersloh: Gerd Mohn, 1962), 160-61; Hubmaier, "Von dem Christenlichen Tauff der gläubigen," 1525, ibid., 111-12. See also Rollin Armour, *Anabaptist Baptism: A Representative Study* (Scottdale, Pa.: Herald Press, 1966), 32-34, 42-43, 56-57.

9. Arnold Snyder, "Sattler's Soteriology," chap. 10 of "Life and Thought of Michael Sattler, Anabaptist" (to be published in 1983 by Herald Press, Scottdale, Pa.).

10. Hearing of Rinck, August 17 and 18, 1528, printed in Franz, *Wiedertäuferakten*, Art. 4:8. See also Williams, 200-202.

11. See John S. Oyer, *Lutheran Reformers Against Anabaptists* (The Hague: Nijhoff, 1964), 222-23, with appropriate citations to primary sources.

12. Robert Friedmann, *The Theology of Anabaptism* (Scottdale, Pa.: Herald Press, 1973), esp. Introduction and Part One. Walter Klaassen, *Anabaptism: Neither Catholic Nor Protestant* (Waterloo, Ont.: Conrad Press, 1973), 77.
13. Lindberg, "Justice and Injustice," 166ff. above.
14. Ibid., 161ff. above.
15. Oyer, *Lutheran Reformers Against Anabaptists*, 219–23.
16. This latter was true of Menno. But some of Rinck's disciples seem also to have learned this from him—Heinz Ot and Adam Angersbach, for instance.
17. Lindberg, "Justice and Injustice," 163f. above.
18. Many illustrations. Testimony of Adam Angersbach, in Wappler, *Thüringen*, 328. Testimony of vax Baumgart, in Franz, *Wiedertäuferakten*, 64–69.
19. Lindberg, "Justice and Injustice," 168 above.
20. See William Klassen, *Covenant and Community: The Life, Writings and Hermeneutics of Pilgram Marpeck* (Grand Rapids: Wm. B. Eerdmans, 1968), passim. Or see William Klassen and Walter Klaassen, trans. and eds., *The Writings of Pilgram Marpeck* (Scottdale, Pa.: Herald Press, 1978), several tracts but especially "The Admonition of 1542."

Simul Iustus et Peccator: A Catholic Position

HANS MARTENSEN

What problems arise from the motif *simul iustus et peccator* for an ecumenical disclosure of Luther's significance? I should like to refer to a few, but by no means all, of the perspectives on this question.

Although personal factors may be uninteresting in this regard, I should like to begin with an entirely personal remark: I have no difficulty but rather to the contrary find it necessary to accept for myself the formula *simul iustus et peccator*. I am myself *totus peccator* in this sense! Not a part of me but rather I, in my total self, am in need of salvation. If Christ were to withdraw his hand from me for only a moment I would be, not partially, but totally, lost and condemned. At the same time I am *totus iustus* by the promise of Christ in the trust that he through the Holy Spirit will lead me to the end of the plan of the Father.

Nevertheless I must grant that to all appearances there is an unreconcilable contradiction between Luther's *simul iustus et peccator* and the statements of the Council of Trent. Although the literal expression *simul iustus et peccator* is not found in the Tridentine texts and thereby is not *expressis verbis* condemned, nevertheless the statement is made in the Tridentine decree on justification which with regard to the issue can hardly be understood other than as a rejection of the *simul iustus et peccator*.

Translated by Carter Lindberg

Already in the introduction to the Decree on Justification, justification is understood as *"passing" from sin to righteousness,* and already this seems to exclude the *simul*.

The question is sharpened in the section on the causes of justification. Here it is said: "The only formal cause is 'the justice of God, not the justice by which he is himself just, but the justice by which he makes us just' (Augustine), namely, the justice which we have as a gift from him and by which we are renewed in the spirit of our mind. And not only are we considered just, *but we are truly said to be just, and we are just, each one of us receiving within himself* his own justice, according to the measure the Holy Spirit imparts to each one as he wishes (1 Cor. 12:11), *and according to the disposition and cooperation of each one*."[1]

Further it is said: "For although no one can be just unless he is granted a share in the merits of the Passion of our Lord Jesus Christ; still, in the justification of the unjustified that is precisely what happens when, by the merit of the same most holy Passion, *the charity of God is poured forth by the Holy Spirit in the hearts (Rom. 5:5) of those who are justified and remains in them....*"[2]

In Canon 11 we read: "If anyone says that men are justified either through the imputation of Christ's justice alone, or through the remission of sins alone, *excluding grace and charity which is poured forth in their hearts by the Holy Spirit and inheres in them* ... let him be anathema."[3]

Justification is described as a radical change of the person and is different in the individual according to degree and kind corresponding to his/her disposition and cooperation. It speaks not only of an "infusing love" but also of an "infusing grace." At this point we only parenthetically refer to the fact that the Decree on Justification speaks in other places also about the advancing sanctification of the justified.

What is its opinion of Luther's doctrine of justification according to which I am a sinner *in re* and only righteous "outside of myself," *in Christo,* according to which we are "not yet" righteous but righteous only "in faith in the promise" (cf. the Luther citations in the lectures of C. Lindberg and M. Seils)? Is an agreement in the doctrine of justification still possible? Is it still possible here to "disclose Luther's ecumenical significance" for Catholics?

Although the sentences of the Tridentum maintain their obligatory character for us Catholics, I nevertheless maintain that such an agreement in the doctrine of justification is possible. I feel completely comfortable with the Tridentine statements. But I also feel comfortable with the *simul iustus et peccator*. Is this reasonably possible? I call to your attention, by way of suggestion, a few viewpoints which may serve to clarify this question.

1. Confessional formulae can never exhaustively and with complete unequivocalness and clarity express God and his truth. Even in the most important and truest statements of Councils and the Holy Scripture itself

there is something included which proceeds beyond the statement itself. The final subject of faith is not the literal formulation but what is meant by this formulation. This does not relativize the statement nor remove its obligatory character. But it means that a statement correct and binding in itself can be supplemented by other statements on the basis of newer circumstances and data. (The Christological statements of Nicea and Chalcedon—one nature or two natures in Christ—are examples of this.)

2. This being the case, does the mystery of faith transcend understanding and logical speech as something like a *complexio oppositorum* or "paradoxes" of faith statements? Is there in the traditional Catholic sense a "dialectical theology"? Put another way: are there not also in Catholic theology, especially but not exclusively with the mystics, statements of faith in the form of apparent contradictions?

3. In this sense, is a pluralism of faith statement possible and, under particular conditions, even necessary? Certainly pluralism in an absolute sense means irrationalism and logical contradiction: a doctrine claiming to exhaust the absolute truth.

But if no dogma is able to exhaustively express God and his truth, then the possibility and perhaps even the necessity of a pluralism results from the humility and confession of our human-spiritual poverty. Thus, for example, the Latin Church says that the Holy Spirit proceeds "from the Father and the Son," while the Orthodox confess the Holy Spirit proceeds exclusively and only "from the Father." Is it possible for both churches to preserve their different formulations of confession of the faith but nevertheless fully recognize each other?

4. It is helpful to distinguish between, on the one hand, faith statements and theology which develops on the basis of faith statements, and, on the other hand, "spirituality" or "piety." "Spirituality" or "piety" as well has to do with faith statements and theology, but it is not, however, identical with them. In the Catholic Church there has always been a plurality of "spiritualities," represented for example in the various communities of orders. There have been similar phenomena in the Lutheran Churches also, even if to a lesser degree; one thinks of holiness movements, Pietism or Rationalism.

For a Catholic the *simul iustus et peccator* could appear as an expression of a "spirituality" which is indeed specifically Lutheran but which nonetheless is lived and experienced by many, not all, Catholics. In the Malta Report the question is posed whether "justification" is absolutely the center of the gospel or whether this same center can be characterized also by other biblical concepts and can find its expression in other biblically based types of piety. Can, for example, the Johannine concept of "life" or "eternal life" have the same position of value as the Pauline concept of "righteousness"?

Still another example is given by recourse to Lindberg's lecture. There he mentions that Luther always used the words *pactum* and *Bund* as synonyms for "testament," although he always polemicized against the concept of covenant. Apart from the question of whether this is or is not a correct interpretation of Luther, a piety is in fact conceivable which is more strongly based upon the concept of "testament" and rather dislikes the concept of "covenant" because "testament" presupposes only God's activity but "covenant" presupposes two acting subjects. But is it not essential that a "spirituality of testament" allow itself to be complemented by a "spirituality of covenant" because the concept of covenant is also grounded in central statements of the New Testament?

In order that such a plurality of faith statements and spiritualities does not lead to onesidedness and narrowness, it is necessary that they be embedded in the greater, universal community of the church which knows itself to be committed as the community of the Holy Scriptures.

5. Thereby a question is posed to the Catholic Church as well as the Lutheran Church:

Can the Catholic Church recognize in Luther's statements on the *simul iustus et peccator*, and on justification in general, a legitimate intention of faith, which the Tridentine concerns do not contradict, even if they pose other accents of piety and may not be harmoniously coordinated into the Tridentine statements?

Can the Lutheran Church so understand the *simul iustus et peccator* and its own "confessional identity" that on this account it does not have to condemn the statements of Trent and their contemporary exegesis in the Catholic Church as anti-evangelical?

6. Such a kind of overcoming of the mutual condemnations and a consequent mutual recognition has its price:

"Reconciled diversity" in the sense that the essential content of the faith is fully recognized in the other, although it there receives in part other forms of expression, will be painful. Are we Catholics ready to pay this price? But even after such a reconciliation Luther will remain a difficult dialogue partner who, in a certain sense, even "gives offense" for the Catholic Church. Indeed, Luther will always disturb the Catholic Church.

But reconciliation also has its price for the Lutheran Church. If it is ready to allow itself to be complemented by the Catholic, this has ecclesiological consequences which may not be realized without contradictions and without challenge. Luther's *theologia crucis* will be experienced in anguish precisely in such a reconciliation because the cross of Christ judges the true and false within Lutheranism as well as the true and false in Roman Catholicism.

NOTES

1. DS 1529; TCT 563 (emphasis added).
2. DS 1530; TCT 564 (emphasis added).
3. DS 1561; TCT 585 (emphasis added).

Summary

JAMES R. CRUMLEY, JR.

Historically, Luther's formulation of *simul iustus et peccator* has attracted considerable attention and raised questions about its compatibility to other teachings about justification and sanctification. Our discussion has indicated that interest in this topic continues, as do serious reflections about the adequacy of this understanding to express the gospel.

There seems to be agreement that Luther developed his motif of *simul iustus et peccator* from the context of the medieval system of penance. For some this would raise the question of whether this motif is adequate for the present day. Others see this medieval context still valid for the present day, although in a different form. The conscience still needs to be terrified. As a result, this motif is acknowledged by many as pastorally and theologically useful.

While consensus appears about the original setting, all agree further work is required. Terms should receive clearer definition; the exploration of the relationship of *simul iustus et peccator* to scholastic theology must be continued. How does Luther's formulation relate both to the Council of Trent and the teachings of the Free churches? All conclude these items merit careful study. For example, one participant suggested that Luther's teaching here is Catholic in character and agrees with the Council of Trent. Another wondered whether Luther's major teaching of *simul iustus et peccator* and a possible minor teaching of *partim iustus, partim peccator* could together provide a bridge for an ecumenical convergence for Catholics and Free church persons with Lutherans.

Contemporary research on the New Testament and historical scholarship offer promise of possibilities of transcending old conflicts. It is now recognized that "gift" involves "task," that there is the proper place for "fruits" in the Christian life, that the Council of Trent did not condemn the formulation *simul iustus et peccator*, and that Luther understands the Christian life as a "process" wherein grace does change a person through faith into a new creation. This recent scholarship discloses that the *simul* motif of Luther has great implications for sanctification. It urges that Luther's view be seen as a whole and cautions against the older study that failed to account for his entire work and thought.

Based on these insights, the discussion relating to the Council of Trent and Luther revealed several possibilities of agreement. Probably this Council and

Luther cannot be fully harmonized. But the Council did not reject Luther's main teaching. It did not condemn Luther or Karlstadt by name. The pastoral character of Trent, as contrasted to a dogmatic character, can be appreciated. Although the Catholic tradition has usually expressed itself in *partim,* the *totus* does appear. This terminology is not completely strange to Catholics. The recognition by Lutherans of the possibility of growth in the justified person has also added to the narrowing of differences.

It was pointed out that the topic of theological anthropology specifically received little discussion in the plenary session. This comment is accurate, disclosing areas for further study and the continuing importance of the two papers.

Another omission in the discussion was any identification of convergence between the Lutheran and Free church traditions. While Lutheran-Roman Catholic dialogue has advanced far, Lutheran dialogue with the Free churches has not. It has been commented that Lutherans need a maturity for Free church dialogue of the same type which Roman Catholics have revealed in their dialogue with Lutherans. The interpretation of Karlstadt is a critical item for this dialogue. Many agree that Luther's views of Karlstadt dominate discussion. Disagreement exists about the accuracy of Luther's perceptions. Was Karlstadt a Donatist or not? Opposing views are evident in regard to the views of doctrine. For Luther, we are saved by doctrine (understood as the gospel or Jesus Christ). It was proposed that what is needed is a *simul* motif in doctrine to remind us that the question is not one of truth or heresy, but rather that we all speak both at the same time. Also positions about the Christian state, or its possibility, call for discussion. All of these items, and more, point out that an important agenda between Lutherans and other Reformation churches remains.

The discussion on this topic was wide-ranging. It offered many provocative conclusions and suggestions which do not lend themselves to a simple summary. Nonetheless some tentative conclusions do seem to be possible. First, Luther's teaching of *simul iustus et peccator* remains a crucial area for uncovering Luther's ecumenical significance for Lutheran relations with the Free church traditions and the Roman Catholic tradition. Second, biblical and historical scholarship conducted across denominational lines, while certainly not solving all questions and problems, has led Lutherans and Roman Catholics to the point where they may state that the motif of *simul iustus et peccator* need no longer be divisive for them. Third, serious discussion of this motif and its ecumenical implications is urgently needed between Free churches and Lutherans, especially since such conversations to date have shown only the enormous task before them. Fourth, granted that theological investigation of *simul iustus et peccator,* involving Free churches, Lutherans, and Roman Catholics, has a certain historical logic, such explorations cannot be done at this moment in ecumenical history without the active participation of Anglican and Orthodox Christians.

AUTHORITY, AUTHENTICITY, AND RELEVANCE OF CHRISTIAN WITNESS IN LIGHT OF LUTHER'S UNDERSTANDING OF SCRIPTURE AND THE WORD

"No Other Gospel": Luther's Concept of the "Middle of Scripture" in Its Significance for Ecumenical Communion and Christian Confession Today

INGE LØNNING

> Paul subordinates himself, an angel from heaven, teachers on earth, and any other masters at all to Sacred Scripture. This queen must rule, and everyone must obey, and be subject to, her. The pope, Luther, Augustine, Paul, an angel from heaven—these should not be masters, judges, or arbiters but only witnesses, disciples, and confessors of Scripture. Nor should any doctrine be taught or heard in the church except the pure Word of God. Otherwise, let the teachers and the hearers be accursed along with their doctrine.
>
> LW 26:57–58

> For doctrine is like a mathematical point. Therefore it cannot be divided; that is, it cannot stand either subtraction or addition.
>
> LW 27:37

> The Lord thereby shows us the right way to interpret Moses and all the prophets and gives us to understand that Moses with all his stories and images point to him and belong to Christ and signify him, namely, that Christ is the point in the circle around which the entire circle is drawn, and looks toward him, and whoever directs himself to him belongs also in the circle. For he is the central point in the circle, and all stories in the Sacred Scripture, if they are correctly read, go towards Christ.
>
> WA 47:66, 18–24

THE END OF THE HISTORY OF DOGMA?

Preliminary remarks on the importance of Luther's understanding of the authority of Scripture

In his classic history of dogma, Adolf Harnack proclaims Luther—or, to be more exact, Luther's Prefaces to the New Testament—as the end of the history of dogma.[1] Indeed the Reformer, in Harnack's judgment, traps himself in a flagrant theological contradiction[2]—he could even defend on very

---

Translated by Patricia M. Williams and Harry McSorley

emphatic dogmatic grounds non-existent words of Scripture, such as the well-known EST in the text of the Last Supper; however there can be no doubt "that the position Luther took concerning the New Testament in his Prefaces is the correct one, i.e. the one which corresponds to his faith."[3] Thus the presentation of the entire history of dogma of the Christian church can only be brought to a close with a reference to the exemplary figure of the true Luther, the one who opens up the future, and who set before the Protestant theology of the nineteenth and twentieth centuries the task of "engaging in criticism with Luther against Luther in the interest of faith."[4]

In 1983, the Luther-year, hardly anyone will talk of such an epochal significance of Luther—at least not in an expressly ecumenical context. On the one hand, the present state of Luther research does not allow us to make such an unproblematic distinction between Luther's two supposedly irreconcilable theological profiles: the "reactionary-medieval" and the "progressive-modern." On the other hand, Harnack's view of the end of the history of dogmatics contains controversial-theological problems, which are perhaps not too warmly welcomed on today's agenda. At least a disclosure of Luther's ecumenical significance could hardly be expected to come directly from Harnack's view. What Harnack found and praised in Luther as the great turning point in the whole history of theological thought has repeatedly been expounded by the Reformer's critics from other confessional traditions as a fatal theological deviation.

Thus, for example, at the beginning of this century it was stated quite clearly by Anglicans that, precisely in his Prefaces to the New Testament, Luther had not only separated himself from the Catholic Church but also dissolved every idea of a true canonicity of Holy Scripture.[5] And twenty years later in his well-known essay on the scriptural principal of the Reformed Church, Karl Barth, praised his own confessional tradition for having "basically not approved Luther's arbitrary way of preparing for himself a kind of selective Bible based on his highly individual dogmatics and we think the Reformed tradition was correct on this point."[6] Essentially the same charge against Luther's supposed subjectivism is made today as it was in the past by Roman Catholic theology.[7]

Harnack's effusive Lutheran judgment of the end of the history of dogma and the unanimous interconfessional condemnations of Luther's subjectivity as erosive of theological substance to a large extent complement and confirm one another. Both estimates of Luther's peculiar stance with regard to understanding the authority of Scripture agree on a decisive point: Luther's view is truly revolutionary. Yet this interpretation of Luther's position is by no means new, nor did it first appear only in the nineteenth century. Rather, the revolutionary assessment by Luther's theological opponents is as old as that position itself. The accusations of Luther critics of later centuries can for the most part already be found in a clearly defined form in 1520 in the work of Ambrosius Catharinus:[8] "Apologia pro veritate catholicae et apostolicae fidei ac doctrinae adversus impia et valde pestifera Martini Lutheri dogmata." Here we find the fixed interpretation schema of opposition between objective truth and subjective feeling.[9] Above all the necessary connection between church authority and the authority of Scripture is clearly emphasized: what is to be learned from Luther's example is the fact that a person who starts to doubt the doctrinal authority of the church will necessarily end up rejecting the authority of the Holy Scripture.[10]

The central question of the understanding of authority is definitely a theme with variations. Thus the first phase of the Catholic critique of Bultmann in the 50s and 60s stretched the historical line of connection to such an extent that it tended to consider the destruction of the authority of the Scriptures "in modern Protestantism"[11] as the mature fruit of that which Luther had sown with his criticism of ecclesial doctrinal authority.[12] If we, in the era of ecumenical endeavours—indeed also within the field of Luther research—have learned to understand the questions of the understanding of authority in a slightly more nuanced way, then it must also be stated that we are still far from having answered the questions to any extent, both with regard to the present problematic of an ecumenical theology, as well as with regard to the task of a correct interpretation of Luther. We are by no means finished with the provocation inherent in Luther's understanding of the authority of Scripture. It might be a fruitful challenge for ecumenical communion and Christian confession today if we attempt to determine a bit more exactly the present theological significance of Luther's understanding of the authority of Scripture by addressing the question of "the theological principle of the Reformation as an ecumenical problem."[13]

THE THEOLOGICAL PRINCIPLE OF THE REFORMATION AS AN ECUMENICAL PROBLEM

In his fine essay "Über die beiden Prinzipien des Protestantismus,"[14] Albrecht Ritschl established that the origin of the common manner of speaking about the formal principle (*sola scriptura*) and the material principle (*sola gratia/sola fide*) of Reformation theology is to be found in the neo-Lutheran dogmatics of the early nineteenth century.[15] The interpretative framework embedded in this mode of expression presupposes a sharp division between the question of authority and the question of content with regard to understanding Scripture. The scriptural principle only delimits the extent of what is normative. The understanding of what is normative, however, requires correct guidance by means of a second principle that involves content. Against this background the *sola scriptura* comes to be seen with a certain inevitability as the structurally parallel alternative to the formula "Scripture and tradition," understood additively, just as the material principle logically appears as the alternative to a dogmatic understanding of Scripture which is expressed in such formulae as "nature and grace" and "faith and works."

To the post-Tridentine controversial theology, such an interpretative scheme had to be obvious, and indeed on both sides of the established confessional fence. It should be obvious that Luther's position on the problem of scriptural authority/scriptural understanding can only with difficulty be made to fit such a scheme. The difficulty can perhaps most easily be seen by looking at the history of the way in which his statements critical of the New Testament canon had been transmitted.[16] From a somewhat hesitant apologetic stance vis-à-vis the harsh accusations of anti-Reformation polemics,[17] the Lutheran tradition moves between the intermediate stage of a well-balanced theory of a two-fold canonicity of the New Testament[18] to a position of almost total forgetfulness of Luther in this respect.[19] A reminiscence, however, remains until today in the confessional doctrinal tradition of Lutheranism in the extraordinary fact from the point of view of theological history, that Lutheranism has not made a dogmatic determination concerning the biblical canon.[20] The silence of the Lutheran confession in this respect is indeed in itself ambiguous. From its Reformation roots, however, this should best be interpreted, perhaps, by means of the common, though somewhat contradictory term of an open canon. To the extent that this expression signifies more than a fundamental revisability of the limits of the canon, it necessarily points to the impossibility of a strict, formally understood scriptural principle.[21]

In the history of development of the Roman Catholic/Lutheran controversial theology, there are unmistakable signs of a real shift of fronts with regard to the problem of the authority of Scripture. The original anti-Reformation position, which, through concentration on the infallibility of the ecclesial magisterium defended intact the formal authority of the Holy Scripture against the supposedly destructive subjectivism of Luther, gradually moves towards the assertion of the material insufficiency of the Scripture and the consequent necessity for an additional, orally transmitted truth of revelation. In the process of this shift of accent there also follows, unavoidably, an interest in pointing out argumentatively the inadequacies of the written and the advantages of the oral transmission of the truth of revelation that has been entrusted to the church.[22] On the Lutheran side, the undefended position of Luther, which has its theological uniqueness above all in the fact that the authority of Scripture is derived from the essentially *oral* nature of the gospel,[23] is replaced by an increasing formalization of the authority of Scripture. The material sufficiency of Scripture, which is challenged more and more fiercely by the opposing side, must be argumentatively defended. The inevitable consequence is the elaboration of the essentially *written* character of divine revelation, which takes away from the opposition between law and gospel its constitutive function for the understanding of the authority of Scripture.[24] In the process of this shift of accent, then, questions about the authority of Scripture and questions concerning the understanding of Scripture fall further and further apart in the confessionally defined universe of Lutheran thought, which becomes clear in the unfortunate fate of the original Reformation thesis of the clarity of Scripture. If authority of Scripture and understanding of Scripture are disjoined, this thesis will either be silently relativized and put aside, or it will be overtaxed in the service of a one-sided intellectualistic concept of revelation and will thus be surrendered as an easy prey to historical criticism.[25]

This controversial-theological development has shown itself to be fateful not only for a correct understanding of Luther's thought, but also for the possibilities of a truly ecumenical theology, that is, one that is represented in open discussion and capable of correction. Indeed theology is always a polemical venture inasmuch as true knowledge and talk of God are critically related to the distorted ideas of God of a fallen world. A theology which is so extensively determined by a supposedly fundamental contrast to another confessional position within the church, that thought and reasoning are shaped by this contrast alone, is inevitably driven into the inflexibility of all purely reactive human endeavours. The already defined statement of the question of the controversy allows no new approach, no new, critical direction of the question. In practice this means: every question which is not incorporated as co-determinative into the agreed upon structure of the confessional controversy will be excluded by both sides. This perhaps also explains the fact that there is an ecumenical reservedness about Luther's theology both within and outside of the confessional tradition of Lutheranism. Within the framework of the opposition between a formalized principle of Scripture and Tradition, there is no room for a correct understanding of Luther's intentions in the matter of the relation of theology to Scripture.

Everything in the universe of Luther's Reformation stands or falls with the thesis of the clarity of Holy Scripture. That Christian theology is substantially bound to the task of interpretation of Scripture, that is, that it grows out of the struggle to resolve this task and leads into the struggle concerning the constantly renewed resolution of this same task,[26] all this can only be understood when the clarity thesis is presupposed. The same is true of the unprecedented theological concentration on the understanding of the central message of Scripture and the remarkable calmness with regard to the question of the limit of the canon of Scripture. The function of the thesis of the clarity of Scripture, however, is only properly recognized when the essential content has been somewhat correctly determined. For Luther it is not a question, as is later the case with Orthodox dogmatists, of the quality of transparency *(perspicuitas)*, which statements of Scripture should in a specific way have. Rather, the expression *claritas scripturae* should be understood quite unambiguously from the contrast between light and darkness and the imagery associated with these two concepts.[27] In the controversy with Erasmus, the alternative is worked out with special sharpness. Either one starts, like Erasmus, from the point that Scripture is dark and must be clarified by means of an authoritative interpretation in order to attain the necessary clearness or, conversely—like Luther—one starts from the illuminating power of the message of Scripture and the necessity of clarifying all human agencies of interpretation. There are, of course, according to Luther's view of Scripture, signs which are obscure. It is decisive, however, that all the key teachings of Scripture *(res scripturae)* lie in bright daylight.[28] This has been so since Christ's resurrection: the incarnation, the doctrine of the Trinity, the atonement, the Lordship of Christ, all these have become accessible through the fact that Holy Scripture henceforth is presented as the pure proclamation of Christ and only as this.[29]

Previously in the fundamental methodical statements in "De servo arbitrio," the thesis of the clarity of Scripture is described as "our first principle"[30] which must form the basis of all theological proof. To want to prove such a basic principle is, in general discussion, an absurd and impossible enterprise. In theology, however, in view of the bad habit which presupposes the obscurity and ambiguity of Scripture, it is unavoidable.[31] That Scripture is to be considered[32] a spiritual light, much brighter than the sun, is based characteristically on the use of a set of central light statements from both Testaments. Thus the function of the external clarity of Scripture *(claritas externae scripturae)* is defined more precisely in that the church openly distinguishes and judges spirits and dogmas and thus makes possible the certainty of faith in Christ.[33]

That the clarity of Scripture is based on its gravitation towards Christ is seen very distinctly in Luther's "Prefaces" to the Bible. The vivid conception of luminosity is also encountered here, and indeed in a central place: the Letter to the Romans is described as a bright light, "almost sufficient to illuminate the whole of Scripture"[34] (the Old Testament). It is not by chance that in the same context the promotion or urging of Christ *(Christus treiben)* is presented purely and simply as the criterion of the New Testament. The context is the passage, much debated, both in the Reformation century as well as in later centuries, from the "Preface to the Epistle of James":

> The office of a true Apostle is that he preaches about the suffering, the resurrection and the office of Christ, and that he lays the same foundation for faith as Christ himself says in John 15: "You will witness concerning me," and all upright sacred books agree on one thing, that they all collectively preach and promote Christ. Likewise, the true criterion for criticizing all books is to see whether they promote Christ or not, since all Scripture manifests Christ, Romans 3, and Paul will know nothing except Christ, 1 Corinthians 2. Whatever does not teach Christ is not Apostolic, even if Peter and Paul should teach it. On the other

hand, whatever preaches Christ is apostolic, even if Judas, Annas, Pilate, and Herod should do it!³⁵

Here it is manifest that the criterion of "promoting Christ" is to be understood as a theological equivalent to the traditional formal criteria of apostolicity and inspiration which criteria thereby receive a material precision and profile. The attribute of apostolicity only becomes understandable in its polemically sharpened form when considered against the background of the Pauline "no other Gospel" (Gal. 1:8), which played a demonstrably decisive role in Luther's theological development.³⁶ The attribute of inspiration is insolubly linked to the attribute of "that which promotes Christ" insofar as the Holy Spirit is the only agent in this world capable of "promoting Christ," that is, of communicating Christ and his consummated salvific work to faith.³⁷

It should of course be noted that the criterion—or *prufesteyn*—in its critical function is nothing other than the opposite side of the first and most fundamental theological statement of Luther's "Prefaces" to the Bible—there is one and only one Gospel.³⁸ On the other hand, a formal idea of the tradition, in this case a concept of literary genre, is filled with content in Luther's thought process. It is not by chance then that this directly brings about a corresponding material interpretation of the concept of the New Testament.³⁹ The reference in "De servo arbitrio"⁴⁰ to Christ's resurrection—more exactly, the breaking of the seal on the tomb—as the all illuminating revelation of Scripture, corresponds exactly in content to the definition of the concept of gospel, which, with an allusion to the David and Goliath story, defines the gospel as the good news of "a true David, who has fought and overcome sin, death and the devil."⁴¹ This definition is then directly extended into the thought of the intrinsic unity of the gospel: "Thus we see now that there is no more than one gospel, just as there is only one Christ, since the gospel is and can be nothing else than a sermon on the Christ of God and the son of David . . ."⁴² From the main ecumenical declaration of the Reformation, Eph. 4:3ff.,⁴³ theological reasoning would need to make more precise that the unity of faith, the unity of baptism, the unity of the church, and the unity of God are insolubly bound to the essential unity of the gospel.

In two respects Luther's scriptural principle—which we, with complete historical reason, feel able to define as *the* theological principle of the Reformation—would require yet another conceptual addition in order to become completely comprehensible. It is a matter of the convergence, or better, the tendential unification of the two questions of the authority and the content of the message of Scripture. Luther quite understandably proceeds from the tradition that the Holy Spirit is the author of Scripture. In place of the interpretative schemes which were based upon the subtle theory of the multiple meanings of Scripture, Luther makes only the simple declaration, that the Holy Spirit is the most simple author in Heaven and on earth, and that his words therefore can only have the simple literary meaning—the one, simple, ordinary, historical sense. If this meaning is nonetheless constantly misunderstood and ruined by false interpretation, this can be explained by the fact that it, precisely in its simplicity, by definition, is sharply opposed to the subtleties of all human doctrine. God's wisdom, revealed to faith in the mysterious majesty of the crucified Christ, and the wisdom of this world mutually exclude each other, and Holy Scripture is to be attributed a special position among books as the unique witness to this wisdom.[44] Christian theology is and will remain possible only as an interpretation of Scripture because Christ, as the wisdom of God, only makes himself heard through this against respective contemporary human doctrine. Thus theology should be understood as consistent exegesis, in service of the correct proclamation of the one gospel.[45] In the preaching of Christ, Scripture, in its overwhelming clearness, attains its goal, in that man, freed from his illusions, is established as conscience and the certainty of a challenged faith is realized.[46]

One comes perhaps closest to a precise determination of the fundamental theological controversy of the Reformation period when one understands it as the opposition of two alternative concepts of unity with regard to Scripture and church, one intensive and the other extensive. From the very beginning in anti-Reformation arguments the extensive conception of unity clearly emerges which considers both the unity of Scripture and the unity of the church as a unity to be understood from and defended to the church's limits. Understood in this way, unity can only be maintained in that an authoritative agency sets and guarantees the limits without error, and every questioning of the limits is taken as implicit questioning of the authority of the guaranteeing agency and, quite logically, as injurious of unity. Reduction through disobedience then is naturally to be considered as the permanent danger of heresy, which threatens the unity that is based on preserving the completeness of revealed truth. For the one who thinks not only of the unity of Scripture but also of the unity of the church as stemming only from a common center and returning to this common center, the danger of heresy will, on the contrary, assume the actual form of extension, an extension which can be seen potentially in the claim for authority of the guaranteeing agency of interpretation. According to this understanding the threat to unity logically comes from the "second" center, from the arbiter of Scripture[47] that stands outside Scripture. For the intensive conception of unity the main concern is to hold on to a consensus in the central things, not as a minimum that is to be extended but as a definitive maximum of ecclesial unity. This can only happen through the distinction of the necessary and the non-necessary through an interpretation of Scripture that is continuously to be undertaken in the context of each situation.[48]

The above by no means exhausts the problematic of center and periphery or middle and limits which is embedded in the theological principle of the Reformation.[49] As a provisional result, however, one should perhaps remember the picture which K. L. Schmidt suggested as a correct understanding of the Canon: "I would not compare a *book canon* which presents itself thus with a *mountain* surrounded by a stone wall, but with an *oasis* which has no walls or hedges around it but which is nevertheless limited. This limit, which is not sharply outlined and thus cannot be grasped in one single view, is set by the spring or the cistern which supports the oasis."[50] From the contrast of both stylized concepts of unity and from the theological principle of the Reformation understood in this way, the present ecumenical problematic of the theme "canon and church" could be examined. Of course one should keep in mind that the ecumenical problem still lies in the threatened unity of the church and not in a unity of the confessions that is somehow to be reestablished.

CANON AND CHURCH— UNITY OF THE SCRIPTURE AND UNITY OF THE CHURCH

Since the beginning of the 1950s this theme has been on the theological agenda. The unleashing factor was Ernst Käsemann's provocative question: Does the New Testament canon form the basis for the unity of the Church or is it rather the basis for the multiplicity of the confessions?[51] The discussion evoked by Käsemann's arguments in favour of the second alternative has been heavily influenced by the Evangelical-Lutheran/Roman Catholic confessional grouping. This also holds true, of course, for the really intensive debate in the 50s on the theme of early Catholicism in the New Testament,[52] and also for the extension of the canon/church discussion in the complex of questions dealing with Scripture and tradition. The latter culminated ecumenically on the one hand in the Faith and Order conference at Montreal (1963),[53] and on the other hand led to significant nuances in the confessional position in the simultaneous and extensive discussions within Catholic theology on the historical and dogmatic interpretation of Trent's doctrine of Scripture and tradition.[54] From here there is a clear line of connection to the bilateral dialogues, especially the Malta Report (1972), which took up and dealt with the particular motifs and questions of the twenty years of discussions and thus provided initiatives for new discussions.[55]

The question, which has remained unanswered in the whole process until now, is the provocative question of the outcome.[56] That it has not been possible to lead the discussion to a satisfactory conclusion is probably due to the somewhat unfortunate formulation of the alternative question. On the one hand, by exclusion of the Old Testament there is already a dangerous simplification of the problem canon/church.[57] On the other hand, it is a symptom of an unclear and therefore a misleading definition of the problem, when the two main realities, "Unity of the Church" and "Multiplicity of Confessions," are presented as completely parallel areas and therefore open to competition. Without doubt it can be argued that the historical form of the New Testament can *explain* the fact of the present multiplicity of confessions. But it can hardly be maintained that the "Unity of the Church" can be shown as a concrete fact in history. There can be meaningful talk of a *foundation* of the non-concrete reality of "Unity of the Church," but on no account of a *foundation* of the multiplicity of confessions in the same sense of the word. Because of this unfortunate alternative, Käsemann's argument was bound to awaken the impression of a hardly recommendable separation of historical and dogmatic questions. Historically it must be ascertained that all present confessions invoke the canon (that is, parts of the canon) with equal right. Then one can seek one's refuge dogmatically in pure decisionism. But the thesis was not meant in this way.[58] That this misunderstanding is likely is connected to the suppression of the theme of the clarity of Scripture which comes to expression in this misleading definition of the problem. In the discussions in the 50s and 60s it was repeatedly declared that radical historical criticism had intensified the problem of unity, which lies in the canon/church theme.[59] This is, of course, so, insofar as the work on the differences and the contradictory theological tendencies within the canon question traditional presuppositions of a historical nature. That talk about *the* Scripture is rendered difficult by the critical, detailed work of historical research, is also indisputable. Whether the theological problems are really qualitatively intensified by this, is an open question. At any rate, until now it has hardly been possible to successfully bring such an intensification of the problems to expression in a corresponding intensification of the formulated statement of the questions. If one were to compare the theological controversies of the Reformation with the same modern problematic one would have to say there has been a blunting of the basic questions. This blunting of questions also explains the inadequacies of the "formulae for unity" which have been suggested, such as the Hans Küng formula "Catholic breadth—Evangelical concentration," which he sharpened into the recommendation "that Catholic theology should try increasingly to take the New Testament seriously in *Evangelical concentration* and that Evangelical theology should try to take the New Testament seriously in *Catholic breadth.*"[60]

What is problematical in such attempts is not only the vagueness of conceptualization but also the presupposed compatibility of both realities. It is of course justified to ground such a compatibility hypothetically. The recommended exchange of both confessional recipes for the study of Scripture seems to presuppose something else, however—namely that an objective balance of both by means of such a rapprochement is to be expected. If this is so, then there is probably no more room to take seriously the problems of the varying theological conceptions of *unity*. The difficult main question of the Reformation—of how the authority of Scripture (and the authority of the church) and the understanding of Scripture relate to one another—could only then with difficulty be given its due. Once again then the theme of *claritas scripturae* is excluded.

"HIERARCHY OF TRUTHS" AND "MIDDLE OF THE GOSPEL"— WAYS TO BASIC CATHOLIC-EVANGELICAL CONSENSUS

In her recently published dissertation "Fundamentalkonsensus i dialogen mellan romersk-katoliker och lutheraner?" Iris Wikström has very conscientiously presented and critically analyzed the discussions which were evoked by the Malta Report.[61] She reaches the conclusion that the extensive agreement on the understanding of justification[62] that is asserted in the report was actually thought of within the framework of the first model of interpretation (hierarchy of truths) and that strictly speaking it can only be justified and defended within this framework of ideas.[63] She thinks she is also able to establish that the expression "middle of the gospel," practically disappears from the ecumenical vocabulary in the post-Malta discussion,[64] which may be connected to criticism of the formula from the Lutheran side.[65] The truth and relevance of the declaration of an extensive dogmatic consensus on the doctrine of justification are not contested by this. What is disputed is that such a consensus is really based on the asserted "convergence"[66] of two different models or methods of thought supposedly specific to each confession.

The thesis of the convergence of both models obviously lies along the line of Küng's formula "Catholic breadth—Evangelical concentration." The thesis is in part more precisely formulated, insofar as the model of the hierarchy of truths is a clarification of the mutual relations of the two main areas within the formula. In relation to the expression "Evangelical concentration," however, the "middle of the gospel" is a step backward rather than forward. Linguistically this expression introduces a pictorial idea (center—periphery) which is difficult to combine with the concept of gospel as used theologically.[67] In addition, there is the fact that this expression has no firm footing[68] in the terminology of the confessional tradition, which makes the comparison with the model of the hierarchy of truths contestable. It is therefore no loss if this expression should really disappear from ecumenical discussion. It remains an interesting question, however, how it can be used with such matter of factness in such a thoroughly thought through text.

If one should respond to this question in light of the Lutheran tradition, the immediate answer which arises is that the "middle of the gospel" has unexpectedly replaced the "middle of Scripture." On the basis of what we sketched in the first part of this presentation, this may seem astounding. The confusion can be explained, however, if one also takes into consideration the role of the interpretation of Scripture in the document. The completely general references to historical-critical research in the area of biblical scholarship have throughout no function in determining the content, but only a relativizing function. By means of this, historical distance is achieved which is able to serve as legitimation for the non-acceptance of certain theological problems as they have been formulated in the tradition.[69] This would all of course be in order if the old problems could really be considered as overtaken by concrete interpretation of Scripture and systematic-theological argumentation and replaced by formulations which better deal with the matter. However, it is rather to be feared that the generalizing references to historical research serve to blunt the formulation of the theological questions.[70] The tendency then goes in the direction of a fascinating version of ecumenical theology which rids the world of all controversies by washing away the contours linguistically, but it is one which hardly points towards a new future. From the perspective of Luther's theological presuppositions it could be asked whether such a theological mode of operation does not implicitly betray as its basic principle (not brought to full consciousness) the thesis of the obscurity of Scripture.

The ecclesial significance of extensive agreement or of a fundamental consensus cannot be decided as long as the question of the *importance* of the doctrine of justification has not been answered.[71] In the Malta Report the non-acceptance of this question in the theologically fundamental section of the report takes its revenge in the short-winded expression of opinion on the question of eucharistic communion by individual members of the dialogue in the understanding of ecclesial ministry implied in this. It is once more confirmed here that the theological problematic of the different conceptions of unity is not to be resolved through the setting forth in formulae of two supposedly equivalent and converging models: "hierarchy of truths" and "middle of the gospel."

AN ECUMENICAL PRINCIPLE OF SCRIPTURE

The history of ecumenical theological endeavours in our century can be understood to a great extent as a history of "cyclical fluctuations" with regard to the questions of authority, use, and understanding of Scripture. This of course is connected with the trivial fact that the Bible plays a central, practical role in all confessions, and above all in the carrying out of divine worship. If one disregards the marginal anomalies with regard to the Old Testament canon, it is a fact that the Bible belongs to those few things that are common to all and which offer the only possible theological basis for discussion on which all could really meet. And precisely in this quality of being a common basis the historical multiplicity and the theological tension of Scripture appear clearly because the actual ecclesial situation is formed by these same traits. That one has always turned with great hopes to a joint study of Scripture as an ecumenical method can therefore cause just as little surprise as the fact that new disappointments always arise from it.

Undoubtedly historical Bible research plays an important role in this picture inasmuch as it has developed practically into the de-confessionalized area of theological activity. On the one hand, this will overcome the oppositions between the established confessional traditions of exegesis through a consensus on what "is there" in the Bible. On the other hand, it can also accentuate the contrasts, precisely because historical-exegetical consensus makes a dogmatic delimitation all the more necessary. By means of an extensively de-confessionalized exegesis of individual scriptural passages, the contrasts with regard to the total picture and the actual, normative use of Scripture will perhaps increase. Here the problems run straight across all the individual confessions to the extent that the connection between historical exegesis and systematic theology is made problematic. It seems doubtful whether interpretation of Scripture still has or can still have any obligatory function at all.

Today the call for an ecumenical disclosure of Luther belongs in this very context, and indeed not as a factor of relativization or dissolution, but more as a claim on the self-image of theology as *theology,* that is, as discourse about God that is determined by the central message of Christ in Scripture. This claim wants to be heard precisely here in the actual area of problems of historical and systematic theology. Everything stands and falls with the relation of theology to Scripture: the necessarily assertive character of God's declarations, from which it follows that the author of Scripture, the Holy Spirit, is no "sceptic,"[72] the unique function of the message of Christ to destroy all human doctrine, and the "first principle," the conviction of the luminosity and the unlimited potential of light in Scripture. Above all it is worth once again taking seriously the simple either-or for all theological activity: one proceeds basically either from the *claritas* or the *obscuritas scripturae.* There is no middle path.

NOTES

1. Adolf Harnack, *History of Dogma,* trans. Neil Buchanan (New York: Dover, 1961), 7:268f.
2. *Ibid.,* 235.
3. *Ibid.,* 224.
4. *Ibid.,* 248.
5. H. H. Howorth, "The Origin and Authority of the Biblical Canon according to the Continental Reformers, 1: Luther and Karlstadt," *Journal of Theological Studies* 8 (1907): 321–365. Cf. above all the following statement "This attitude of Luther meant his adoption of individual private judgement in deciding upon the canonicity of a Bible book. It in fact reduced the whole matter to a mere subjective question of

personal caprice and choice, in which any good Christian might decide the most critical of all questions by internal illumination alone" (334). "Assuredly a more elastic, uncertain and arbitrary rule of canonicity was never invented" (354). "It is perfectly clear from those facts that Luther had not only definitely cut himself off from Church, but had entirely discarded the Church's and everybody else's Canon of the Bible" (365). A similar argument is found in R. E. Davies, *The Problem of Authority in the Continental Reformers*, (1946), 56f.: "It is impossible to assert that a certain source of religious truth is objectively authoritative on the evidence of one person's subjective experience. In fact, instead of an objective religion we find a blank subjectivism. . . ."

6. Karl Barth, "Das Schriftprinzip der reformierten Kirche," *Zwischen den Zeiten* 3 (1925): 215–245 223.

7. For a representative example, see above all P. Hacker, *Das Ich im Glauben bei Martin Luther* (1966), who presents a sort of compendium of the traditional accusations of subjectivism by the Catholic tradition.

8. Ambrosius Catharinus, *Corpus Catholicorum* 27, ed. J. Schweizer (1956).

9. "Only Martin, a new theologian, a new Daniel, an expert in the new learning and especially in the new interpretation of the Holy Scriptures, which he begins to deny in part, to destroy in part by manifestly new and unheard of meanings, dares to pronounce heretical [the common teaching that the sacraments of the new law give justifying grace to those who do not place an obstacle]. How can one dispute with a man of such authority and liberty?" *Corpus Catholicorum* 27:286, 27–32.

10. "For it was necessary that he act so [i.e., by starting to deny the canonicity of James]. Nor will this be sufficient unless he also denies the letters of Paul and the four holy gospels of God, against which he contends no less." *Ibid.*, lines 1–3.

11. Cf. the programmatic study by N. Appel, *Kanon und Kirche. Die Kanonkrise im heutigen Protestantismus als kontroverstheologisches Problem*, Konfessionskundliche und Kontrovers-theologische Studien 9 (1964).

12. Cf. the discussion contributions by A. Kolping, J. Hamer, J. de Fraine, A. Fetcher, K. Adam and R. Marlé in *Kerygma und Mythos* 5 (1955); further Appel, *Kanon und Kirche* and G. H. Tavard, *Holy Writ and Holy Church. The Crisis of the Protestant Reformation* (1959).

13. Cf. my "Mitte des Evangeliums"—Om reformasjonens teologiske prinsipp som økumenisk problem, *SvTK* (1973): 153–161.

14. Albrecht Ritschl, "Über die beiden Prinzipien des Protestantismus," published originally in *Zeitschrift für Kirchengeschichte* 1 (1876), 397–413, then in *Gesammelte Aufsätze* 1 (1893), 234–247.

15. In this form the expression probably appears in A.D.C. Twesten, *Vorlesungen über die Dogmatik der Evangelisch-Lutherischen Kirche* 1 (1826) and gains a set place in the subsequent dogmatic presentations.

16. Cf. the evidence in my work *"Kanon im Kanon." Zum dogmatischen Grundlagenproblem des neutestamentlichen Kanons*, Forschungen zur Geschichte und Lehre des Protestantismus 10, Series B. 43 (1972), 194ff. (hereafter cited as "Kanon im Kanon").

17. Thus the line of development Chemnitz/Flacius-Wigand-Selneccer-Schröder, cf. *ibid.*, 200ff.

18. Shaped above all by J. Gerhard, *ibid.*, 206ff.

19. As in Quenstedt and Hollaz, see Hollaz's judgment: "But since today all evangelical teachers assign divine authority to both kinds of canonical books, this distinction in no way seems necessary." *Examen Theologicum Acroamaticum*, Q. 39 (1718), 146.

20. The Augsburg Confession and the later confessional writings in the Lutheran tradition have no definition of Holy Scripture. Considering the intensive discussion on the canon in the sixteenth century and the repercussions of this at Trent and in the Reformed and the Anglican confessions of the period, this is to be seen as a significant silence.

21. Cf. "Kanon im Kanon," 263ff.

22. This argument is already inchoately in Cochläus. It becomes full blown in the 1530s and 40s; cf. "Kanon im Kanon," 173ff.

23. Cf. the analysis of Luther's position in "Kanon im Kanon," 72ff., for the complex of questions dealing with Spirit/Letter in the Old and New Testaments; *ibid.*, above all 138ff.

24. This argumentation appears already in Chemnitz: "But history has shown what is principally to be observed with judgment, that God has not only instituted, but also by his own act and example, when he at the first wrote the words of the Decalogue, initiated, dedicated, and consecrated that way and method that through the divinely inspired Scriptures the purity of the heavenly doctrine be conserved and retained." *Examen Concilii Tridentini*, ed. E. Preuss, 1861, 9; English translation by Frederick Hassold (St. Louis: Lutheran Church—Missouri Synod, 1964, Microfilm), 20–21.

25. Cf. my "The Holy Scriptures" in V. Vajta, ed. *The Lutheran Church Past and Present* (Minneapolis: Augsburg, 1977), 110ff.

26. Luther matter of factly identifies theology and study of the Scripture. *LW* 34:283–288; *WA* 50:657–661.

27. Especially clear in "De servo arbitrio." Cf. G. Ebeling, *Luther. Einführung in sein Denken* (1965), 247, 253. Basic for the theme of the clarity of Scripture is F. Beisser, *Claritas scripturae bei Martin Luther,* Forschungen zur Kirchen und Dogmengeschichte 18 (1966).

28. *LW* 33:25–26; *WA* 18:606, 22–24, 30–37.

29. *LW* 33:25–26; *WA* 18:606, 24–29: "For what still sublimer thing can remain hidden in the Scriptures, now that the seals have been broken, the stone rolled from the door of the sepulcher and the supreme mystery brought to light, namely, that Christ the Son of God has been made man, that God is three and one, that Christ has suffered for us and is to reign eternally? Are not these things known and sung even in the highways and byways? Take Christ out of the Scriptures, and what will you find left in them?"

30. *LW* 33:91; *WA* 18:635,34f.: "We are obliged to begin by proving even that first principle of ours by which everything else has to be proved. . . ."

31. *LW* 33:91; *WA* 18:653, 31–35.

32. *LW* 33:91; *WA* 18:653, 28–31: "For it ought above all to be settled and established among Christians that the Holy Scriptures are a spiritual light far brighter than the sun itself, especially in things that are necessary to salvation."

33. *LW* 33:91; *WA* 18:653, 22–24.

34. *WA DB* 7:2, 14–15.

35. *WA DB* 7:384, 22–32; *LW* 35:396.

36. Cf. my "Petrus und Paulus." Gal. 2:11ff. als kontroverstheologisches Fundamentalproblem," *Studia Theologica* 24 (1970): 1–69; and "Kanon im Kanon," 144ff.

37. Cf. Lønning, "The Holy Scriptures," 86–87.

38. *WA DB* 6:2, 12–22.

39. "This report and encouraging tidings, or evangelical and divine news, is also called a New Testament. For it is a testament when a dying man bequeaths his property, after his death, to his legally defined heirs. And Christ, before his death, commanded that his Gospel be preached after his death in all the world...." *LW* 35:358f.; *WA DB* 6:4,12–17.

40. Cf. note 29.

41. *LW* 35:358; *WA DB* 6:4, 5–6.

42. *WA DB* 6:6, 22–24.

43. Cf. the role of this text in the Augsburg Confession, 7.

44. Cf. *LW* 34:285; *WA* 50:659, 5ff; and Lønning, "The Holy Scriptures," 99ff.

45. Cf. note 26.

46. Cf. above all the reflections on the temptation theme: *LW* 34, 286–7; *WA* 50:660,1ff., on the problem of certainty and the excerpts from *De servo arbitrio* given above.

47. Characteristically, in the "Large Commentary on Galatians, Gal. 1:9" we read: "Nevertheless, we are presented here with an example that enables us to know for a certainty that it is an accursed lie that the pope is the arbiter of Scripture or that the church has authority over Scripture." *LW* 26:57; *WA* 40 1,119, 23–26.

48. One must remember Augsburg Confession, 7, where this line of thought is expressed with exemplary clarity. Cf. the same line of thought in the Preface to the "Commentary on the Letter to Galatians" of 1519: "Therefore Paul is fighting against compulsion and on behalf of freedom. For faith in Christ is all that is necessary for our righteousness. Everything else is entirely without restriction and is no longer either commanded or forbidden." *LW* 27:213; *WA* 2:485,22ff.

49. Cf. E. Wolf, "Die Rechtfertigungslehre als Mitte und Grenze reformatorischer Theologie," *Peregrinatio* 2:11–21.

50. K. L. Schmidt, *Kanonische und apokryphe Evangelien und Apostelgeschichten* (1944), 30.

51. E. Käsemann, "Begründet der neutestamentliche Kanon die Einheit der Kirche?" (1951), *Exegetische Versuche und Besinnungen* 1:214–223.

52. Cf. "Kanon im Kanon," 226ff.

53. Cf. *Schrift und Tradition*, ed. K. E. Skydsgaard and L. Vischer (1963).

54. Cf. above all the works of J. R. Geiselmann: "Das Konzil von Trient über das Verhältnis der Heiligen Schrit und der nichtgeschriebenen Tradition" in *Die mündliche Überlieferung* (1957), 123–206; "Die Heilige Schrift und die Tradition," *Quaestiones disputatae* 18 (1962); "Zur neuesten Kontroverse über die Heilige Schrift und die Tradition," *Theologische Quartalschrift* (1964), 31–68; cf. also Y. M. J. Congar, *La Tradition et les Traditions. Essai historique* (1960); *La Tradition et les Traditions 2. Essai théologique* (1963).

55. Cf. the survey by I. Wikström, "Fundamentalkonsensus i dialogen mellan

romersk-katoliker och lutheraner?" *Meddelanden fran Stiftelsen för Abo Akademi Forskningsinstitut,* No. 73 (1982).

56. "The New Testament canon does not as such provide the basis for unity of the Church. As such, i.e. inasmuch as it is available to historians, it provides the basis for the multiplicity of confessions." These are the exact words of Käsemann's thesis in "Begründet der neutestamentliche Kanon," 221.

57. A. Harnack correctly points to the fact that the historical growing together of both Testaments "has introduced a healthy complication into the concept of the canon of the Scriptures" in *Beiträge zur Einleitung in das Neue Testament* 4 (1914), 82.

58. This also follows unambiguously from the introductory essay to the collection *Das Neue Testament als Kanon* (1970).

59. Cf. the examples in "Kanon im Kanon," 39ff.

60. H. Küng, "Der Frühkatholizismus im Neuen Testament als kontrovers-theologisches Problem," in *Kirche im Konzil* (1963), 125–155, 154.

61. Cf. note 55.

62. "The Gospel and the Church" (Malta Report), no. 26, speaks of the "far reaching consensus on the interpretation of justification"; no. 28 of "extensive agreement in the understanding of justification."

63. Cf. Wikström, "Fundamentalkonsensus," 382f.

64. Ibid., 288.

65. Cf. above all J. Lell, "Viva vox evangelii sive ecclesiae?" *Materialdienst des Konfessionskundlichen Instituts* (Bensheim) 23 (1972): 69–72; and Lønning, "Mitte des Evangeliums."

66. "The Gospel and the Church," no. 25.

67. Cf. Lønning, "Mitte des Evangeliums," 159f.

68. Cf. Wikström, "Fundamentalkonsensus," 179ff.

69. Cf. the conclusion in "The Gospel and the Church," no. 7, that it is no longer necessary to discuss the theological controversies of the sixteenth Century "as such."

70. For two representative examples, see "The Gospel and the Church," no. 15, and the "Leuenberg Concord," no. 5.

71. The question of the relative importance of the doctrine of justification is raised in "The Gospel and the Church," no. 28, and precisely as a limitation with regard to the previous statements about agreement on the doctrine of justification.

72. LW 33:24; WA 18:605, 32–34: "The Holy Spirit is no Skeptic, and it is not doubts or mere opinions that he has written on our hearts, but assertions more sure and certain than life itself and all experience."

The Diversity of Christian Witnessing in the Tension Between Subjection to the Word and Relation to the Context*

DOUGLAS JOHN HALL

THE TRUTH PROBLEMATIQUE IN CHRISTIAN FAITH AND THEOLOGY

There is a rudimentary problem lurking behind the rather complex title of this essay, and perhaps the most expeditious way of establishing contact with our subject is by identifying it straightway. The fact that it is rudimentary does not of course imply that it is a simple problem. Indeed it is not *a* problem at all but a whole cluster of problems subtly intermingled one with another; for this reason I prefer to allude to it through the use of the more cumbersome but also more descriptive word "problematique."

The problematique, then, into whose intricacies we are propelled by the terms of our title, expressed in its most elemental form, is Pilate's question, "What is truth?" What *is* truth? We are not being asked merely (!) what is *true*, or what is *the* truth, but what is *the nature of* truth. How does Christian faith conceive of "the truth"? Assuming that that to which the Christian community is called to bear its witness *is* the truth, how in the first place are we to conceive of this truth? Is it something eternal, immutable, always and everywhere the same, expressible in verbal forms which do not lose their essential validity with the passage of time? Then our testimony to it will certainly bear the marks of such permanency and homogeneity. Is the truth on the contrary something moving and alive, forever seeking expression in new forms but also transcending every form, defying containment, struggling to insert itself into the changing process of world history, and so forth? Then our witness to it will undoubtedly betray a similar quality of struggle— the struggle both to comprehend and to communicate this elusive thing that is no "thing."

Throughout the greater share of its history, the Christian Church has

---

*Since reference will be made occasionally to terms employed in the German title of this paper, of which the English title is only an approximation, it should be recorded here as well: "Die Vielgestaltigkeit christlichen Zeugnisses im Spannungsfeld zwischen Wortgebundenheit und Kontextbezogenheit."

inclined towards the assumption that the truth with which it had to do is of the first type. I do not of course mean that Christianity has suffered under a completely static conception of truth. The genuinely wise and pious have always understood that truth is larger than our grasp of it, and that error is the constant companion of all who try to understand what is. Whoever takes seriously even the first Commandment, not to mention the second, knows that the truth *of God* eludes our theology and that in consequence theology can only be "the most modest science."[1] Nevertheless, until the Modern period most Christians could take for granted that doctrinal formulations such as those of Nicaea or Chalcedon themselves not only contained truth but did so in language which, adequately translated and elucidated, was valid for every age and clime. Beyond that, current statistical data concerning the make-up of the Christian Church causes one to suspect that a majority even of contemporary Christians share this same preconception concerning the character of Christian truth.[2]

Modernity, however, discovered history: that is, from the Renaissance onwards Western peoples have all become far more aware than were our forebears of the influence of the particularities of the age upon the formulation of ideas. It belongs to contemporary consciousness, not so much as a matter of deliberate reflection as of an unconscious assumption, to suppose that the beliefs and behaviour of persons in the past were conditioned, as are ours, by the concrete situations in which they found themselves; that different socio-economic circumstances produce different accounts of reality; that given new scientific information, new technologies, new hopes and anxieties, new or at least altered expressions of truth are called for.

In the nineteenth century, this consciousness of the time-conditioned character of truth already introduced what was for many Christians the vexing problem of doctrinal relativity. What can be *true,* and what in consequence, could have any vital *authority* for religious faith, if everything— every doctrine, every theory and creed, every hymn, every translation of the Bible—is steeped in temporality? Against what was felt to be a slide towards "relativism," therefore, there emerged in the churches and elsewhere movements inspired by the need to return to fixed traditions. These were sometimes profound—I think there may be profundity behind the strong plea for "orthodoxy" expressed in these words of Cardinal Newman: "The Gospel faith is a definite deposit, a treasure common to all, one and the same in every age, conceived in set words, and such as admits of being received, preserved, transmitted."[3] One knows at least that such a polemic (for it is a polemic) was born of a deeply-felt anxiety concerning the religious and social chaos being courted by those who were ready to let go of every anchor in the tradition. More often, however, such polemics were (and still are) merely reactionary: like biblical fundamentalism, they purchase the tranquility of the absolute at the expense of losing touch with the ongoing and always unpredictable processes of life itself.[4]

Far from abating, the truth problematique of Christian faith and theology has been further compounded during the past decades by the growing recognition of many Christians that the historical character of the truth to which we bear witness means that our testimony must be not only *timely*, that is, addressed to the general character of the Age, but also explicit with respect to *place*. Especially has this insight made itself felt within the increasingly "independent" churches of the Third World. This is not accidental; for it has been in the Third World most dramatically that Christian conceptualization derived from the historical experiences of particular peoples (namely, the peoples of the *First* World) has played a very dubious role, not to say an oppressive one. Again and again, according to the critical analysis of theologians in these "younger" churches, what has been given off as "Christian Truth" ("one and the same in every age"!) has not only contained ideas and language totally alien to the experiences of Third World peoples, but has served to sustain social and political infrastructures that have prevented the majority from discovering the real liberty of the gospel. The struggle for what has come to be called *contextuality* in theology begins with this sense of inappropriateness and incongruity.[5]

Out of the search initiated by such a discovery has come some of the most exciting theology of our time. But it has also of course produced a further complication of the old problem. If what is true for West European Christians is not true for African or Latin American Christians but perhaps misleading, perhaps even demonic, then are we not teetering on the brink of ecumenical disaster? Are we not at very least evoking a situation in which truth, far from being "one," must eventually seem so fragmented that the church is in danger of becoming a veritable Tower of Babel, in which no "province" of Christendom really understands what the others are confessing?

One of the greatest contributions of Martin Luther to Christian understanding relates specifically to this "problematique of truth." Luther was a remarkable Christian in countless respects; but I doubt that he was anywhere more insightful than in connection precisely with this issue, and I suspect that much of our interest in him today stems from the fact that he—alone, I think, amongst the Reformers—anticipated in his own theological struggle the problematique which has become ours in the sense outlined above. Moreover, Luther not only faced this many-headed monster, but put forward an approach to living with it from which we can learn a great deal. Having said that, I hasten to add that in the following statement I shall regard it as my mandate not to exegete Luther but, using some of his ideas more or less illustratively, to address the problem as it seems to me to confront ecumenical Christianity today.

AUTHORITY, AUTHENTICITY, AND RELEVANCE OF CHRISTIAN WITNESS

FALSE RESOLUTIONS

Within the categories of Christian faith and theology, the truth problematique quite naturally and regularly "resolves itself" in two characteristic ways. On the one hand, faced by the prospect of the diversity *(Vielgestaltigkeit)* of Christian witnessing, and made nervous by this prospect, Christian groups and persons throughout the ages have found themselves turning towards the absolute, some absolute, and clinging to it in the face of every challenge. On the other hand, there have been movements within and alongside "official" Christianity which could apparently embrace diversity, and sometimes even delight in the seeming anarchy of ecstatic religious immediacy which had no thought for the morrow *or* for yesterday. We shall consider these in turn, for they clarify further the nature of the problematique, and can establish *via negativa* the parameters of our own handling of it.

Scripture and the Search for Absolutes

The history of the church could be written from the standpoint of its fevered search for absolutes. But when it came to the Protestant chapters of this long story one special object of that ancient conquest for finality would stand out: the Bible! The sacred scriptures have been regarded by all Protestants as the supreme witness to truth, and, given the historical basis of our faith, the rationale for such a high regard is manifest. But there is only a fine, razor's edge of a line between thinking the scriptures the supreme *witness* to the truth and construing them as if they were as such that truth; and as is demonstrated not only by the modern phenomenon of biblicism but also by its classical Protestant antecedents, the psychic demand for absolutes is powerful enough, apparently, to overlook and transgress this fine line with awesome regularity! The Reformation principle of *sola scriptura* has never been entirely free of peril in this respect.

The peril is a real one for reflective Protestantism. For, as Paul Tillich insisted, the very *essence* of the Protestant spirit lies in the "protest" against the substitution of finite, conditioned realities for the absolute.[6] If the *living God* is the one to whom ultimate trust and obedience are due, then to behave towards anything less than God as though it were worthy of unconditioned trust is to invite idolatry. Bibliolatry is no less idolatry than the worship of any other "thing" or creature. It is moreover an ironic form of idolatry, because when the Bible itself is listened to it always points away from itself towards the source to which it testifies and cannot contain. Too often, un-Protestant Protestantism has treated the Bible in a manner analogous to the treatment of the writings of Marx and Lenin by doctrinaire communists. It becomes for them a once-for-all statement of the truth, and so functions not merely as an authority for faith, but as *ideology:* that is, "a system of propositional truths independent of the situation, a superstructure no longer relevant to praxis, to the situation, to the real questions of life."[7] This is to resolve the truth problematique falsely, because to attribute ultimacy to the Bible as such is to violate the ultimate, to which the Bible itself bears witness.

Ecstatic Religion and Abandonment to the Moment

The other characteristic way in which Christians from the earliest times have thought to resolve the truth problematique inherent in the Faith is in a real sense the antithesis of the above; indeed, the two ways have frequently companioned each other historically, each driving the other to reactionary extremes in what we would now describe as the process of polarization. Over against the tendency to search for absolutes which can supposedly shelter us from the winds of uncertitude and disunity, this second posture throws itself upon the present, begging or wresting from the moment whatever truth it needs.

If the Bible has been the typical object of Protestant searchers after absolutes, those who have pursued truth in the moment have most frequently attributed their "resolution" of the truth problematique to . . . "the Spirit"! From the spiritualizers whom the author of the First Epistle of John had in mind when he cautioned his readers to "test the spirits" to the present-day charismatics, the promise of Jesus to send a "comforter" who would "lead you into all truth" has excited the souls of Christian enthusiasts. Revelation, insist the advocates of this path to certain truth, is after all not a thing of the past but an ongoing process. It is occurring *now!* The voice that addressed the prophets and apostles still speaks, and those who are open to the transcendent will *know,* when it is needful, what they are to believe, say, and do!

The falseness of this stance, however impressively pious it may be in "great spirits," is of course the one that the church already noticed with Montanism, that the Western Church feared when it insisted upon the *Filioque-* clause at Toledo, and that has been felt acutely by many contemporary congregations whose (no doubt half-hearted!) unity has been shattered by the inbreaking of factions possessed by "the Spirit." It is false, namely, because it only "resolves" the Christian truth problematique by eliminating one side of its dialectic, that is, the past and consistency with the past. Or rather, to speak more concretely, it virtually eliminates—by rendering secondary—the historical revelation given in Jesus as the Christ. Whatever our tradition has meant by the "finality" or "supremacy" of the revelation in and through Jesus of Nazareth, that is to say, always tends to be superceded in spiritualistic religion by "new truths" reputedly vouchsafed by the Spirit. Who can read the Scriptures intelligently and not discover that it is indeed "the voice" that faith is called to listen for? And yet, there are many voices;

and amongst them all the voice of the Good Shepherd may be "still and small" indeed! In fact, reading the history of Christianity under the impact of the *theologia crucis,* one might well conclude that the "hirelings" and "demons" normally speak with greater authority and influence than does the crucified Lord of the church! A Christian community that has lost touch with any hint of the "absolute" to which St. Paul referred when he cried, "I preach Jesus Christ and him crucified!"; a community which must move about in the world chartless and rudderless, may indeed be driven by a lively wind, but who is to say that it will be the *ruach* of God? The demons too breed ecstacy and certitude, and "No bad idea can be anything but worse when divine sanction is claimed for it!"[8]

LUTHER ON WORD AND SPIRIT

The reference to the "theology of the cross" brings us immediately to Luther's approach to this "problematique of Christian Truth"; for, in my opinion, it was precisely the spirit and method of reflection that Luther indicated through this peculiar nomenclature *(theologia crucis/theologia gloriae)* that provided the Saxon Reformer with his frame of reference for the question under discussion. For what it means that all our theology is done in the shadow of the cross *(crux sola nostra theologia)* is that the truth *is* given us, but always under the aspect of its apparent antithesis: it is given, but not impressively; it is given, but not to be possessed; it is given, but not as that which we ourselves entirely desired; it is given, but not to be used by us complacently or to achieve power over others; it is given, but never in such a form that it could permanently alter our condition as those who must beg for what we do not have. *Wir sind Bettler!* The lust to *have* the truth, as distinct from always receiving it as gift, is in fact born of "the theology of glory." The very attempt to *resolve* the problematique of truth is of the essence of Christian triumphalism. Luther's counsel is not to try to resolve it, but to live *between* and *in* the *tension* between what has been given and what is being given, what is and what is becoming, what is fixed and what is fluid . . . and so forth. (The terms *zwischen* and *Spannungsfeld* may thus be the most significant words of our title!) Faith is neither seeking refuge in what we have, what is fixed—the temptation of Lot's wife—nor thinking to possess already what we do not yet have—taking heaven by storm! Faith places itself willingly and with trust in the *present,* between past and future.

But we may state all this quite concretely along the lines of the foregoing discussion, because for Luther this "living between" means first of all living between the Word and the Spirit.

The Indispensability of the Word

There is no need to belabor the point that for Luther the Bible was of enormous importance, as it was for the other Reformers too. "Abandon scripture," warns Luther, "and God abandons us to the lies of men."⁹ On occasion, sentences stolen out of Luther's writings may even sound like the rantings of present-day television evangelists! But the larger context of Luther's thought reveals a mind *extremely* different from the spirit of biblicism. In my view it is a mind significantly different, even, from the minds of his fellow-Reformers, Calvin, Zwingli, and Philip Melanchthon. It is for one thing a still-medieval mind, that is to say, a mind capable of entertaining *mystery*, or, to state the matter more explicitly, a mind which in the tradition of late medieval mysticism (*not* of scholasticism) finds it essentially strange to think of truth as being capturable in propositions! Unlike the genuinely "modern" men who were his reforming co-workers, especially Zwingli, whose inability to comprehend Luther's view of the Eucharist must be traced to this same distinction,¹⁰ it was not the prospect of having "the original source" (the motivating drive of all the humanists!) that made Luther cherish the Scriptures so much as it was the (essentially mystical) belief that ineffable truth could breathe through these sometimes clearly inspired but nonetheless altogether human words. Since, in distinction from the modern spirit which from the outset tended to make history one-dimensional, Luther was still able to find the dimension of depth *in* the finite (*finitum capax infiniti*), he did not have to resort to Erasmus's philological purism or Calvin's doctrine of plenary inspiration in order to consider the Bible indispensable. These documents had been for the church—and above all for himself!—the medium of God's own address; one could therefore trust that they would again and again become the vehicles of communication between God and humanity.¹¹

All the same, Luther did not believe either that the Scriptures *necessarily* communicated truth (i.e., that their capacity for the infinite was inherent), or that what the church yesterday heard in and through the pages of this book would be obviously continuous with what the church today might have to hear! God himself remains the Lord of the Scriptures, and he will cause them to announce what must be announced, just as he caused Baalam's ass to speak, though it had no *natural* capacity for speech—and certainly not for *that* speech!

In short, for Luther the Bible cannot be called unambiguously "the Word of God." This betrays no disrespect for the Bible; what it demonstrates rather is Luther's very *high* respect for what the Bible itself calls "the *logos* of God": Jesus Christ, crucified, risen. If Luther permits himself to speak of God's Word in Scripture and also in preaching (which he does), then it is in a strictly dependent and derivative sense. That is, in the sense that here and there, now and then, the *Spirit* of God causes the words of the Bible and of the preacher to be bearers of the ultimate, convicting us of our sin, assuring us of our justification. What must be heard by us is "the Word," not just "the Bible." There is even a sense in which "the Bible" can get in the way of our hearing of "the Word"—not because the Bible itself is a barrier (though in some of its *parts* it is, for Luther, almost that!) so much as on account of our too close attention to it, our desire to "have" the Word in black and white! But "The Holy Spirit doesn't let himself be bound by words but makes the content known."[12]

This same thought is sometimes expressed by Luther in terms of the Augustinian distinction between "the outward Word and the inward Word":

> The outward Word is the Word of Scripture (or *verbum vocale*, of the sacrament), the inward Word is God's own voice by his Spirit. Without this inner Word of God the outward Word remains a letter, the word of man. Luther often uses 1 Cor. 3:7 in this connection. God alone can give increase to the Word. The outward Word is only the means which God uses when he writes his own living Word into the heart. Man is able to bring the Word to the ear, but not into the heart. This work belongs to God.[13]

There is here a parallel between Luther's concept of the Eucharist and his view of hearing the gospel: as the elements are only bread and wine, so the biblical words are only words; both become bearers of the Infinite only when they are visited and changed *pro nobis* by the presence and indwelling of the divine Spirit.

This is contrary to every propensity, open or covert, to assign to the Bible itself the colour of the absolute. God's lordship of the Scriptures means, as is well known, that Luther can be wonderfully playful or nonchalant with respect to the Bible (biblicists would say "disrespectful"!). This is because, unlike literalism of every variety, Luther does not consider it an insult to the infinite to think the Apocalypse of John confusing or the Epistle of James shallow. It is after all not the Bible as such that must prove itself "holy"; its holiness is borrowed from "the voice" that can and does use it.[14]

The Grounding of the Spirit

At the same time, it is hardly necessary to remind the reader that Luther was by no means prepared to cast in his lot with those contemporaries of his who regarded themselves as the great adherents of "the voice," those "prophetic" and "inspired" souls who were so carried away by their own religious experiences that they were ready to abandon every external authority and cling to the Spirit alone. It is against *these* interpreters (and here too we can discern Luther's essentially *contextual* approach to theological discourse) that he most often addressed the *sola scriptura* dogma. In his reaction to these evangelical "radicals" we hear again the grave warning of 1 John: "*Test the Spirits* to see whether they be of God. Not every spirit is of God, but only that spirit which confesses Jesus as the Christ. . . ." John's formula seems an almost precise statement of Luther's pneumatology. The Reformer was convinced of the indispensability of the Spirit—no spiritualist could be more convinced! At the same time, he was well aware of the pitfalls of Spirit-religion: its tendency towards erratic and unreasoned enthusiasm; its division of the church; its vulnerability to "every wind of doctrine," and so forth. In Luther's theology, therefore, the Spirit is carefully, almost painstakingly tied to the Word.

Now the Word, as we have seen, means first of all "the Word made flesh"; and therefore let no one leap to the conclusion on the basis of this affirmation of the Spirit's "grounding" that Luther was after all biblicistic! The Scriptures are nonetheless a *normative* witness to the Word made flesh, and therefore the *kerygma* that only the Holy Spirit can cause the church to hear must also always seek authentication by reference to the Scriptures. Against biblicism Luther warns that the letter kills; against spiritism he warns that the voice does not speak *independently* of the letter.[15]

The Significance of the Context in the Hearing of the Word

In sum, what Luther was about in this methodological reflection which occurred continuously throughout his ministry was the enucleation of a theological hermeneutic in which there is and must be a continuing, *unresolved* dialogue between the (relatively!)[16] fixed source of theological truth and authority (the Scriptures) and the ongoing, existential-spiritual authority of the triune God. Faith exists *between* Word and Spirit. But neither category—and this applies especially to "the Spirit" on account of the almost inevitable "mystification" of this third person of the Trinity!—should be understood in a merely religious, otherworldly manner, if we are to be true to Luther. To listen for the voice and Spirit of God did not mean for him what it meant and still means for pietistic spiritualism—the cultivation of a life of religious devotion far from the noise and bluster of the world, and so forth. Luther's pneumatology pictures a divine Spirit still brooding over the creation, disturbing the course of events, penetrating the chaos and darkness of history. Living between the testimony of the Bible and the witness of the Holy Spirit then means at the same time living between Scripture *and world*, between the tradition of Jerusalem and the ongoing, changing, never-easily-decipherable situation in which the *koinonia* must make its present witness. Karl Barth's metaphor is entirely appropriate here: it means having "the Bible in one hand the newspaper in the other." There can be no genuine discernment of the truth which is not simultaneously a struggle to "discern the signs *of the times.*" As Gerhard Ebeling has written, "This striving for a true understanding of the scripture, with its concern for the Spirit, *is of necessity concerned with the present existential situation.*" And he continues:

> For the Holy Spirit is a present and life-giving Spirit, by contrast to the letter,

which owes everything to the past. Thus in [an] early lecture, does Luther not merely sharply criticize the historical understanding of the Psalms as practised, for example, by Nicholas of Lyra in the fourteenth century, following rabbinic exegesis. The hermeneutic principle from which Luther starts, with its antithesis between the letter and the Spirit, also leads him to the realization that the understanding of Scripture is a continuous task which can never be brought to a conclusion. For there is a constant threat that an understanding once achieved will cease to be the Spirit, and return to being the mere letter, unless it is constantly attained anew and made one's own. Thus unceasing progress is necessary in understanding the Scripture. The Spirit turns into the letter; but the letter must in its turn constantly become the Spirit once again. One stage of understanding is always the letter from which the Spirit comes in the next stage. This reveals an astonishing insight into the historical limitations of our understanding.[17]

It also, I should say, reveals an equally "astonishing insight" into the nature of truth in the prophetic tradtion! Living in the *Spannungsfeld* between Word and Spirit, which is at the same time the tension between tradition and world, faith through grace discerns in the moment the Truth that it requires for its prophetic witness. The truth is dialogical, and therefore unresolved. That is, it never comes to the point where the community of faith or the individual believer (acting let us say the part of systematic theologian!) can decree once and for all that such-and-such is "the truth." It is not accidental that Luther, unlike Calvin, did not become a systematizer. Even if he had had the leisure to do so I am convinced that he would have found the approach incompatible. Whilst Calvin worked for twenty-six years polishing and rounding out his impeccable *Institutes*, Luther moved from issue to issue—not without consistency, but certainly without the systematizer's compulsive need to weave a seamless robe! The reason for this should not be attributed simply to Luther's preoccupation with the affairs of church and society. It is a concomitant of his deepest theological understanding. For him, God is alive and the world is "in process," changing and being changed. True theology has to do with the meeting of these two dynamic centers, creator and creation; and therefore to devise a "permanently true" theology is to substitute for the living God and his living creation an artificial construct. There may be comfort in such constructs, but there cannot be truth in them, for truth lives. Truth, finally, is for Luther nothing more and nothing less than the one who declares "I *am* the truth."

Thus for Luther, the important thing for theology is not to be "correct" but to be "obedient"—to achieve consistency, not with what has been regarded at this or that juncture as "orthodoxy," but to be consistent with the living truth who is Lord. Amongst historic theologians he is first in applying the *ethical* category of "obedience" to the dimension of *thought,* specifically to theology. This constitutes his permanent offense to Protestant Orthodoxy, which, try as it might, was never able to contain Martin Luther in its systems! To state the same thing in different words, theology for Luther is first of all confession. Confession cannot be reduced to doctrine, nor can it be all worked out a priori. It must occur as the *appropriate* witness, as "the Word," "the Word from the Lord." It is faith's witness to the truth that is struggling to be born at that time, in that place. Hence theology is always, as we may say, *strategic* theology. But Luther himself, as usual, puts the matter more concretely than any of his commentators:

> If I profess with the loudest voice and clearest exposition every portion of the truth of God except precisely that little point which the world and the devil are at that moment attacking, I am not *confessing* Christ, however boldly I may be *professing* him. Where the battle rages, there the loyalty of the soldier is proved, and to be steady on all the battlefield besides is mere flight and disgrace if he flinches at that point.[18]

CONTEXTUAL THEOLOGY

There could scarcely be a more precise definition of the spirit of contextuality in theology than is contained in the foregoing quotation. Let me use it, together with other aspects of the previous discussion, to elaborate briefly the principal points of contextual theology as these are expressing themselves in a great variety of contemporary theological moods and movements.

Theology as Confession

Contextual theology means theology as confession. The act of confession presupposes the coming together of the two realities which are kept apart in the false resolutions of the truth problematique: on the one hand, the reality of the Christian tradition, especially though not exclusively in its biblical expression, and, on the other hand, the reality of the historical situation of the confessing community. Without the remembrance of the tradition the church has nothing to confess, and may end by doing nothing more than offering stained-glass versions of contemporary "values." (Much present-day charismatic spiritualism is plainly a religious version of the same escapist and narcissistic inwardness that Christopher Lasch has identified as the *Zeitgeist* of a society "in an age of diminishing expectations.")[19] But without immersion in the situation, what the church says and does, though it may be very correct according to this or that form of "orthodoxy," can never make itself felt as *gospel*. Gospel is discovered by the church, not possessed by it. It is discovered, always anew, in the confluence of these two realities. For the gospel is not a formula or manifesto or list of "fundamentals"; it is not *theologia eterna*. Gospel is the Word of God which the church is enabled to hear only as it permits itself to enter with sufficient courage the darkness peculiar to its own historical moment. Only in that darkness can it expect to receive the light of the gospel.[20] Recalling Luther's metaphor, what the church hears is only *gospel* if it enables it to join battle with the world at that "little point" where the battle rages. The task of all theology, including "professional" theology, is to assist the witnessing community to discern that little point and thus to position itself for the hearing of the appropriate Word.

Openness to Word and World

The condition without which this confessional theology cannot occur is, accordingly, a twofold openness: openness on the one hand to the tradition (especially the biblical beginnings), and on the other hand openness to the human situation. We need to consider carefully what is meant here by openness.

With respect to the tradition, to be open means that the theological community is and must continually become a community of disciplined and meditative reflection upon scripture and the church's historic confessions, creeds, theological statements, and so forth. *Wortgebundenheit* graphically describes such openness, with its suggestion of the church's being at the same time free for the Word and constrained by it. In this connection we should notice that Luther's critical allusion to "profession" does not constitute a rejection of the activity signified by that term; on the contrary, on the basis of his own vocation as "professor," one must certainly assume that he takes it for granted that the Christian community will also be a *pro*fessing community.

But he rightly declares that such profession of faith is not to be confused with the end to which the church is called. It is not the business of this community to pursue historical theology or the history of doctrine or even scriptural exegesis as ends in themselves. They are, at most, means. The end towards which the whole disciplined life of theological scholarship is directed and without which it is an exercise in pride and futility is the ongoing discovery of the *appropriate* Word. Not every word that could be uttered out of the rich, perhaps too rich, Christian tradition is appropriate . . . *ever!* The church has indeed found no better way of *avoiding* the appropriate word than by attempting to say everything all at once—"the whole gospel," as it is sometimes euphemistically called! Gospel is perhaps never—or only seldom—"whole." Normally it is intensely *partial*. At very least, the *kerygma* is never a matter of everything being said at once—judgement, reconciliation, cross, resurrection, Pentecost, guilt, redemption, the kingdom of heaven, and so forth, and so forth! For as Qoheleth wisely stated it long ago, "There is a time . . . and a time . . . " (Ecclesiastes 3). The "gospel" of everything-at-once is no gospel but an ideology which keeps the church from discovering the "little point." The gospel truth that ought to have been proclaimed in Europe in the 1930s (said a perceptive German theologian), was "Jesus Christ was a Jew!" No doubt other things should eventually have to be said about the identity of the Christ; but to say "all," always to announce "everything," is in fact to proclaim nothing. "The whole" becomes a convenient ideological fence upon which Christians may sit so as to avoid participation in the world's battles. The point of *knowing, studying,* and "professing" the *whole* tradition is to be able, under the changing conditions of historical existence, to discern what *part* of the whole requires emphasis. Profession serves confession, not vice versa.

But, secondly, such a confession cannot occur, no matter how "professional" one may be with respect to Christian scripture and tradition, unless the theological community is also *open to the situation*. This, it seems to me, is where historic Christendom must be taken to task most severely. For too frequently the very "wholeness" of the tradition has provided the church with the illusion that it could discover nothing new in the world's marketplace; that it already knows beforehand what human and earthly wickedness is capable of; that in any case all of that is passing, transient, and a matter of *tentatio*. Unlike the prophetic tradition of Israel (which is certainly the *locus classicus* for Luther's conception of the lively "Word of God"), Christianity has too consistently acted as if it professed the truth and too seldom assumed the ongoing cost of receiving it. Paraphrasing Bonhoeffer, one may say that the Christian religion in its major historical manifestations has been built upon "cheap truth": truth without suffering. The suffering upon which the church has prided itself, when it has not been frankly enjoying its privileged position in society, has been that of a body thinking itself in possession of the truth and suffering on account of its possession. We have known very little of the suffering entailed in the hearing and discernment of God's truth![21] Openness to the human situation means experiencing the suffering of those who not only do not *have* the truth and can only hunger and thirst for it, but who for the most part actually prefer to live the lie. The Spirit imparts its truth only in the wilderness. For the theological community this means that it must again and again be exposed to the lie that it, too, harbors; again and again denied the certitude and comfort of false absolutes; again and again thrust into the wilderness of the present, historical moment (sometimes a very arid wilderness indeed).

In the Introduction to the second volume of his *Systematic Theology*, Tillich offers a poignant statement of the meaning of openness to one's context *(Kontextbezogenheit)* and of the suffering that is entailed in this openness. The theologian, he says, must always work at the formulation of "the question" to which the Christian message then may speak as "answer":

> In order to do so, he must participate in the human predicament, not only actually—as he always does—but also in conscious identification. He must participate in man's finitude, which is also his own, and in its anxiety as though he had never received the revelatory answer of "eternity." He must participate in man's estrangement, which is also his own, and show the anxiety of guilt as though he had never received the revelatory answer of "forgiveness." The

theologian does not rest on the theological answer which he announces. He can give it in a convincing way only if he participates with his whole being in the situation of the question, namely, the human predicament. In the light of this demand, the method of correlation [Tillich's own theological method] protects the theologian from the arrogant claim of having revelatory answers at his disposal. In formulating the answer, he must struggle for it.[22]

This, I judge, is a methodological and existential statement in the tradition of Luther's *theologia crucis*. Behind its more technical language, one can hear of the same struggle that Luther—the victim of *Anfechtungen*—frequently experienced. Whether all this is adequately captured in the German word *Kontextbezogenheit* I am not competent to say. I do not know precisely what *coloring* this word takes on for those whose native tongue is German; in translation it seems to me too weak. To be "open to the context," in order to find out where the "little point" of fiercest battle is located, means not only to allow oneself to think about one's society at the level of academic or pragmatic reflection ("How can we best understand this moment in order to devise a persuasive apologetic?"). It is rather to "participate" in one's sociological context existentially, to be oneself a child of the age, to be tempted by its temptations and its despair, to dream its dreams, to believe its story. Theology which is confession and not just the reiteration of *doctrina* is what happens when God's story of the world meets and does battle with humanity's story—the one that is current then and there. And the theological community, if it is genuine, is the place where that meeting occurs. It cannot occur without suffering. This too is what it means to do theology under the sign of the cross.

THE DANGERS OF CONTEXTUAL THEOLOGY AND THEIR ENGAGEMENT

Every faith-posture and the theological method belonging to it contains its peculiar dangers. There is no danger-free theology. The dangers of contextuality in theology are easily stated: that the social context may play a *too* decisive role; that the search for apologetic engagement (not to say "relevancy"!) may lead the Christian community to neglect the opposition to dominant social structures and values which is part of the prophetic tradition; and that the unity of the church will be threatened by the emergence of increasingly divergent interpretations of the meaning of the Christian message. The existence of such dangers ought, however, not to deter us. To "do theology" has in any case always been to "rush in where angels fear to tread"! Besides, the recognition of the dangers is always the first step towards meeting them. Beyond that, there are certain checks and balances which may be brought to bear against the three dangers named above:

1. Against the danger that the context may play too determinative a role in the discernment of theological truth, contextual theology which learns from

the tradition of Luther (not to mention the Scriptures, Augustine, and others from whom Luther himself learned!) will realize that the search for the genuinely *contextual* statement of Christian truth entails an equally serious and disciplined commitment to Bible and tradition *(Wortgebundenheit)*. It is a misrepresentation of responsible contextual thought to claim that attention to the context will necessarily end in neglect of the text. Certain popular types of "situationalism," particularly in the area of Christian ethics,[23] have undoubtedly erred in this direction; but the error is by no means inevitable. As even the language (in English) suggests, "text" and "context" belong together: the text is intended for the context, and the context evokes the text.

2. With respect to the danger of missing the prophetic critique on account of a too-rapt devotion to communication, this can become a *real* danger only where one makes the (quite unnecessary) assumption that contextual theology wants by definition to *commend itself* to its social context—that is, wishes to *appeal* to its host society by affirming what the society itself affirms, and so forth. This is an entirely erroneous assumption—as even a cursory glance at the course of Liberation Theology makes very clear. One may indeed say that contextual theology is a type of *apologetic* theology. Contrary to Barthian opinion, however, not all apologetic theology is merely commendatory! The kerygmatic element is very conspicuous in most contemporary forms of contextual theology. Indeed, Liberation and other types of theological witness concentrating upon the social context today have much in common with that intensely kerygmatic theology of the early part of this Century which in its initial phases was called "dialectical theology" and "the theology of crisis."[24] The point is not to *confirm* one's society but to *engage* it. The Tillichian "method of correlation," to which allusion has already been made, would state the matter in this way: the context (Tillich uses the term "situation") does not determine the *content* of the Christian message, but it does determine the *form*. The confession of faith must meet that "little point" where the battle is fiercest. This means that the "little point" is decisive for the character, emphasis, wording—in short, the form taken by the Christian *Zeugniss*. If a man is dying of cancer I do not speak to him about the opportunities of youth; analogously, if a society is full of anxiety about its future (as ours is!) I do not address it as though it were bursting with nineteenth-century industrial optimism! In neither case does this mean that what I *do* say (to the sick man, or to the society) will be what my hearer wants to hear!

3. The third danger—that of a diversification *(Vielgestaltigkeit)* of witness which may be destructive to Christian unity—requires a somewhat fuller commentary than the first two. Let me begin by suggesting that a certain amount of demythologization needs to inform our reflection upon this point. What passes for Christian "unity" is frequently a highly theoretical thing, and one which is by no means harmless. In the past, the unity of the church

has been sustained by many factors which, upon closer scrutiny, are quite extraneous to the gospel. Here I do not refer only to the structures of ecclesiastical government, which have sometimes been airtight enough to prevent any sort of diversification of witness; I refer also to the more subtle types of inauthentic unity created by the imposition of the theological struggles of a particular people upon the whole church.

Imposition is perhaps an imprecise word, for until rather recently the churches of the non-European world have gladly accepted the European experience and the theological conclusions wrested from that experience as if they were universally applicable. But they are not. They represent in fact an intensely *contextual* expression of the Christian message, but one that is hardly ever *acknowledged* as contextual. That is, they are derived from and addressed to the particularities of various European experiences over the centuries. The habit of considering these theological expressions (creeds, confessions, catechisms, liturgical forms, theological systems, etc.) *normative* is due entirely to mundane factors such as the long duration of Christianity in Europe, the contrasting brevity of the Christian experiences of people on other continents, and the general spread and influence of European culture throughout the Western world. I do not say that these "mundane factors" are wholly devoid of a providential dimension; but of this I feel quite certain—that the domination of European theological thought must not continue and will not continue in the church of the future.

It must not continue because when a people (such as the Christian community of Japan) allows, for example, German theologians an inordinate influence in the interpretation of the gospel, the Japanese church is not only asking for a reputation as a "Western" religion but it is avoiding what we identified in the discussion of Luther as "obedience." That is, it is failing to become a genuinely theological community; for it has accepted the struggles of another people, and the theological "answers" that have been derived from these struggles, instead of allowing the Spirit to lead it into its own wilderness.[25] Such a Christian community may be rich enough in "doctrine," but it will not be engaging in *theology*.

If this Euopean dominance *must* not continue, however, it is also important to add that it *will* not. For all over the globe today, Christians have begun to be aware of the need to enter into their own darkness, and to discover whatever light there may be in the tradition of Jerusalem for that darkness. This is one of the salutary effects of "the end of the Constantinian era."

Even in North America something like a process of indigenization is beginning to occur. I say "even" in North America because, more than any other continental province of the church, the North American church has been content for a very long time to accept its theology "ready-made" from the European mother- and fatherlands. Given our relatively long history (the first formal concert of classical music was given in my city of Montreal in 1535), we have produced very few indigenous expressions of theology.[26] We have been content to copy the parental culture at this as at almost every other level excepting technology, always looking to Europe for precedents, confirmation, and approval! As the Canadian political philosopher George Grant has expressed it ironically: "In a field as un-American as theology, the continually changing ripples of thought, by which the professionals hope to revive a dying faith, originate from some stone dropped by a European thinker."[27]

A personal statement may help to concretize the point, and at the same time further illustrate the nature of contextuality in theology. The realization of our North American theological dependency status came to me forcibly in the 1960s when, after a series of "theologies of," Jürgen Moltmann's *Theology of Hope* made its impact. I must insert here that I have no greater respect for any present-day European Christian thinker than for Moltmann; furthermore, I am quite sure that, had I been attempting to elaborate a theology in the West German situation of the post-war period I should have devised something very similar in emphasis, though not in brilliance, to his "theology of hope" in order if possible to combat the fatalism and "Nordic melancholy" (Barth) present in that context. But *that* context is not the North American context—as the fate of Moltmann's work in the United States and Canada proceeded to make abundantly plain. Moltmann's book was taken up by countless ministers and teachers of theology and journals on our side of the Atlantic and . . . I shall not say "read," because few were prepared to subject themselves to such heavy prose, but sloganized! The "Theology of Hope" became almost a byword, the title of thousands of sermons, seminars, talk-shows, youth rallies, and so forth, from coast to coast. The reason for this phenomenon was obvious to anyone who knew even a little of our continent's "spiritual" history as a European satellite. We were after all the *continent of hope*! The "New World"! Here, according to enlightened Europeans of the eighteenth century and the huddled masses of Europe over *many* centuries, the sins of the fathers would be set aside and a new day would dawn! But with Viet Nam, the environmental crisis, and the failure of our institutions (to mention only the *external* problems which surfaced in the 1960s), this New World hope was growing very thin (some think that it has since disappeared altogether!), and Moltmann's emphasis, lightly handled, was received with open arms. In Europe, especially in Germany, Moltmann's witness acted as a prophetic catalyst to waken many Christians from their "dogmatic slumbers." In North America it served the official religion in precisely Marx's sense, as an opiate. It did not make us more honest but less. It did not give us courage to face our truth, but provided us with yet another postponement. It became, in short, another, rather "catchy" statement of the official optimism that was our heritage from the European Enlightenment—that innocently positive outlook which, in the hands of a powerful people lacking in self-knowledge, can be devastating for the total world situation! Far from helping the North American middle class churches to discern the real signs of their times, this theology, simplistically interpreted, functioned as a comforting and repressive balm, giving us one more reason not to look for light for "our own darkness" (Eric Lincoln). Explicitly as it identified the target in Europe, it did not address the "little point" where *our* battle was raging. For our problem was not a lack of hope, but a surfeit of false hope![28]

It may be that in the next decades, Christian theology in Europe and North America will find expression in increasingly divergent forms. Europe, too, is changing, becoming conscious of itself as a sociological unit, and shaking off the vestiges of its economic and military dependence upon the United States. North Americans in the meantime are experiencing a *Götterdämmerung* of increasingly ubiquitous proportions: the "American Dream" is scarcely credible even to the alleged Silent Majority now. A consequence of these changing sociological factors may well be a growing cleavage between European and North American theology, because each of us has to deal with the specifics of our own situation. Meantime, this kind of diversification is happening even more dramatically in the churches whose context is the Third World, as well as in the churches of the Marxist bloc.

Does this mean a real division of the unity of the church and its gospel? Is it already questionable to speak of the unity of Christian truth, and may we expect Babel rather than Pentecost to characterize the church of the future?

Not necessarily. These currents may in fact lead to the working out of a *genuine* unity—a unity that is no longer merely formal, maintained by the power of ecclesiastical hierarchies, the weight of the Constantinian past, the imposition of doctrinal uniformity, or sheer inertia. Diversity there must be and will be. The truth for us in North America today must take the form of a critique of *power* such as we have never dreamt of in our Christian past on that continent. Meantime, the truth for many of our Third World Christian colleagues may well include the *discovery and use* of power, the throwing-off of the shackles of oppression, the taking of responsibility for their own destiny. Would this mean that we and they are therefore thrown into a state of alienation? It may well mean that we are alienated as citizens of this or that nation state. Professor Miguez Bonino and I find ourselves today on differing sides of a dispute that may take on very serious proportions. This "worldly" dividedness does not necessarily mean alienation as members of the body of Christ, however; for I understand perfectly well that for Professor Bonino and his people the gospel must mean a struggle against forms of oppression created, in part, by me and my people. I trust that he also can understand why my role within my own society may be quite different—in terms of its content, goals, and methods—from his. Similarly, the analysis of socio-economic conditions in one part of the world church may be more profitably undertaken with the help of Marxist categories than in other parts. Ecological concerns may dominate here, the distribution of wealth there, race relations in another arena, and the struggle against nuclear warfare in yet another. We are, to be sure, "one world," and therefore nothing that occurs here is irrelevant there. Yet as a member of a society that is only six percent of the globe's human population but consumes more than forty percent of its raw materials; a society whose leadership is making the threat of a nuclear confrontation daily more probable, I know that

> I am a man of unclean lips,
> and I dwell in the midst of
> a people of unclean lips;

I know this in a way that I do not expect my fellow-Christians in India or El Salvador to know this!

What it comes to then is surely this: that faithfulness to the Scriptures (*Wortgebundenheit*) and responsible participation in one's social context (*Kontextbezogenheit*) *necessarily* produces diversity (*Vielgestaltigkeit*) of Christian witness. In order for the ecumenical church to be faithful to its one Lord, its various parts must engage in different sorts of witness. Our Lord does not have the same tasks for each disciple-community any more than he had the same tasks for each of the original Twelve (See John 21:20 ff.!). He is a living Lord, not a dead one—a lively truth, not a doctrinal ideology. To confess him here is to say this and do this; to confess him there is something else again. What this diversity does mean, of course, is that there is today an even greater reason than there was in the earlier decades of this century for ecumenical dialogue, communication, and fellowship. It is no longer for the sake of creating denominational unity, but for the sake of comprehending each other's witness to the one truth, and therefore of keeping alive in a dangerously divided *world* the vision of a uniting truth which both transcends and informs our particularities.

NOTES

1. Karl Barth, *Evangelical Theology: An Introduction*, trans. Grover Foley (New York: Holt, Rinehart & Winston, 1963), 7.

2. According to the newly-published *World Christian Encyclopaedia*, the so-called "Evangelicals," most of whom accept the literal inerrancy of the Scriptures and/or cling to doctrinal absolutes, "command a healthy majority of Protestants in the world (157 million) as well as in the U.S. 59 million" (*Time Magazine*, 3 May 1982, 43). In short, Christianity in at least its "Protestant" expression is today in danger of being *defined* by those who use this concept of truth as a bulwark *against* Modernity.

3. Cardinal Newman, *Parochial and Plain Sermons*, 8 vols. (London, 1937), 2:22, 356.

4. Ironically, it is the strong psychic urge to escape precisely the "unpredictable

processes of life" that has lent power to such absolutist forms of religion today. The uncertain and even apocalyptic character of our era has created a climate in which many otherwise "realistic" people are willing to purchase "peace" at any price. But this is ironic when it occurs under the aegis of a religion of incarnation, i.e., a religion which desires the salvation *of the world*.

5. "Liberation Theology" is first and foremost a theology of contextual concern and reflection. One of the best, brief descriptions of the theology of liberation draws this out: "Instead of starting from eternal truths, which are then applied to the 'world-life situation,' the liberation theologians start with the reality in which the people are. This initial point illustrates the need for collaboration between the theologian and the social scientist." Lawrence A. Egan, in the Foreword to Ignacio Ellacuria, *Freedom Made Flesh* (New York: Orbis Books, 1976), vii.

6. Tillich in fact names this "The Protestant Principle." "Protestant theology protests in the name of the Protestant principle . . . against the identification of our ultimate concern with any creation of the church, including the biblical writings insofar as their witness to what is really ultimate is also a conditioned expression of their own spirituality." Paul Tillich, *Systematic Theology* (Chicago: University of Chicago Press, 1951), 2:37.

7. Dorothee Sölle, *Political Theology* (Philadelphia: Fortress Press, 1971), 23.

8. Robert McAfee Brown, *Issue*, No. 24 (1980):13 (Toronto, United Church of Canada).

9. *LW* 35:116.

10. The famous Marburg discussions of 1529 constitute one of the most notorious examples in history of parties talking past one another. It was the meeting of two ages, with some real but much merely superficial overlapping of concerns and presuppositions. It "contrasted two types of religious experience, the one [Luther] a mystical interpretation of the sacrament, the other [Zwingli] an intellectual interpretation." Paul Tillich, *A History of Christian Thought*, ed. Carl Braaten (New York: Simon & Schuster, 1967), 260.

11. Of course Luther believed in the inspiration of the Bible; and of course he was concerned about precision in translation—as his painstaking work of biblical translation readily demonstrates. But because his *primary* reverence for the Scriptures was grounded neither in an after all rather bizarre idea of unusual spiritual authorship nor in the humanist's notion of truth tied to "the original" but in the existential *experience* of "conviction by the Word," he neither struggled (as Calvin did) with the problem of verbal inspiration nor did he manifest Erasmus's *kind* of linguistic preciousness.

12. *LW* 54:353.

13. Regin Prenter, *Spiritus Creator: Luther's Concept of the Holy Spirit*, trans. J. M. Jensen (Philadelphia: Fortress Press, 1953), 102. "It is God who has the Scripture in his hand. If God does not infuse his Spirit the hearer of the Word is not different from the deaf man. No one can rightly understand the Word of God unless he receives it directly from the Holy Spirit. The sermon and the sacrament are here placed together with the Word of Scripture. They are all outward words which must necessarily wait upon the inward Word of God." Ibid., 103.

14. It is important in this connection to note that for Luther the *oral* dimension of the Word is the most important; so much so that he regards the description of the

New Testament as "gospel" to be erroneous, for the *gospel* is not something written. "The gospel should really not be something written, but a spoken word which brought forth the scriptures. . . ." *LW* 35:123.

15. "The Spirit is not bound *in* the Word. The Spirit is God's own high majesty and he has his own existence in God's eternal glory. . . . But as the revealing Spirit . . . he cannot be without the Word." Prenter, *Spiritus Creator*, 122.

16. I say "relatively" because quite clearly not even the Scriptures are *static* for Luther. Of course there is a "givenness" about the Bible, but its *meaning* is never permanently fixed. This is demonstrated by Luther's never-ending struggle to find just the right German words in his biblical translations. He did this, not out of academic, philological interest, but from the preacher's concern (the contextual concern!) to speak *to the situation*. Cf. Roland Bainton, *Here I Stand* (New York: Abingdon, 1950), ch. 19.

17. The examples Ebeling provides from Luther's own work are worth repeating here: "When the Psalmist prays: 'I am thy servant, give me understanding that I may know thy testimonies!' Luther's interpretation is as follows: 'The Psalmist prays for an understanding against the mere letter, for the Spirit is understanding. For as the years have passed on, so has the relationship grown closer between the letter and the Spirit. For what was a sufficient understanding in times past, has now become the letter to us. Thus at the present time, as we have said, the letter itself is more subtle in nature than before. And this is because of the progress of time. For everyone who travels, what he has left behind and forgotten is the letter, and what he is reaching forward to is the Spirit. For what one already possesses is always the letter, by comparison with what has to be achieved. . . .' And Luther is sufficiently bold to draw an example of this from traditional dogma: 'Thus the doctrine of the Trinity, when it was explicitly formulated at the time of Arius, was the Spirit, and only understood by a few; but today it is the letter, because it is something publicly known—unless we add something to it, that is, a living faith in it. Consequently we must always pray for understanding, in order not to be frozen by the letter that kills." Gerhard Ebeling, *Luther: An Introduction to his Thought*, trans. R. A. Wilson (Philadelphia: Fortress Press, 1977), 99–100.

18. Martin Luther, *Church Postil*, trans. and ed. John N. Lenker (Minneapolis: Lutherans in All Lands Co., 1903ff). Exact reference lost.

19. Christopher Lasch, *The Culture of Narcissism: American Life in an Age of Diminishing Expectations* (New York: W. W. Norton & Co., 1978).

20. Cf. Douglas J. Hall, *Lighten Our Darkness: Towards An Indigenous Theology of the Cross* (Philadelphia: Westminster Press), 1976.

21. "Because *we* live in a lie, the truth, when it shall come to us, must appear *adversaria specie*." Prenter, *Spiritus Creator*, 118–119.

22. Tillich, *Systematic Theology*, 2:15.

23. There is a world of difference, however, between Joseph Fletcher's "situation ethics" and Paul Lehmann's ethical contextualism.

24. In fact if one were looking for the modern historical antecedents of theological contextualism one would certainly have to pay close attention to the *early* Barth—the Barth before his "positivism of revelation" (Bonhoeffer) became dominant.

25. I do not single out Japan, of course. At the same time that country offers a very

instructive illustration of the problem under discussion. The Christianity first imposed upon Japan by Spanish and Portuguese Jesuits simply did not "take root" in that "swamp" (cf. the novel *Silence* by the Japanese Catholic author, Shusaku Endo). In the post-World War II period, Barth and Brunner became "interesting" to some Japanese Christians. But if Christianity survives in that culture, and can expect a future, it is because in the meantime an indigenous theological dialogue has sprung up in both Protestant and Catholic circles, one which seeks to engage Buddhism and other religious and secular influences native to the culture, and is assuming a color rather different from traditional Western Christian triumphalism, as the works of Endo, amongst many others, indicate.

26. The great exception is Reinhold Niebuhr.

27. George Grant, *Technology and Empire* (Toronto: House of Anansi, 1969), 16.

28. I discussed this subject at the time in "The Theology of Hope in the Officially Optimistic Society," *Religion in Life*, 40/3 (1971):376ff.

Responses

Response to the Problem of the Diversity of Christian Witnessing in the Tension between Text and Context

GERHARD HEINTZE

In this paper I will concentrate on the conflict between text and context as it is taken up by Professor Douglas Hall. I agree with him, that subjection to the Word and openness to the present belong together. ("It is a misrepresentation of responsible contextual thought to claim that attention to the context will necessarily end in neglect of the text. . . . 'Text' and 'context' belong together: the text is intended for the context, and the context evokes the text.") Hall has appropriately pointed to Luther's own dealing with Scripture, that is, his attachment to the Logos incarnated in Jesus Christ, which includes at the same time a certain liberty with the letter of Scripture: "God's lordship of the Scripture means, as is well known, that Luther can be wonderfully playful or nonchalant with respect to the Bible (biblicists would say 'disrespectful'!)." Hall gives as a proof Luther's harsh judgment on St. John's Book of Revelations and on James's Epistle—on which he nevertheless wrote a commentary—as well as Luther's reverence to the "living voice of the Gospel." Hall concludes: "It is after all not the Bible as such that must prove itself 'holy'; its holiness is borrowed from 'the voice' that can and does use it." I would like to investigate the association of the acceptance of the literal sense ("text") and openness to situations ("context") for the actual practical dissemination of the Word in my own country. I would then like to draw attention to some opportunities and dangers. We will first deal with the opportunities offered by a textual interpretation.

Now as before, our churches subsist on the powerful appeal to be bound to Jesus Christ, the only Word of God. This appeal was present in the Barmen Declaration of May 1934. (First Thesis: "Jesus Christ, such as he is shown in the Holy Scripture, is the only Word of God that we have to hear, in which we have to have faith in life and in death, and which we have to obey.") Although many Lutheran theologians of Germany at this time distanced themselves from the Declaration, it is in the Lutheran churches that the

Translated by Georges Herzog

declaration was very influential after 1945. As Lutherans, we also have reason to thankfully remember, in 1984, the fiftieth anniversary of the Barmen Declaration. Hall has documented in his paper Luther's attitude toward Scripture, that God's revelation in Jesus Christ, an event to which we are unconditionally attached, is not simply set on the same level as the Bible in the Barmen Declaration. Yet God's revelation is to be found in the Bible and nowhere else.

Therefore we have to greet any effort that contributes to the advancement of the meager biblical knowledge in our parishes. It is regrettable that, in the Germanic countries, the still incomplete revision of Martin Luther's translation of the Bible in a sense competes with an array of recent translations, and more particularly with the concerted ecumenical translation *The Good News: The Bible in Modern German,* which was introduced with pomp in the spring of 1982. Luther himself would certainly be troubled to hear that his translation is still used as the standard translation more than 400 years after his death and despite all the changes that have occurred.

The numerous ecumenical meetings of our present time, in particular the meetings between Protestants and Catholics, are a great help for a new, living approach to the Bible. These encounters are particularly fruitful when the parties of different churches meet for a common study of the Bible. The resulting closeness and mutual possibilities to understand each other are often truly surprising.

We should not underrate the fact that although there are no prescribed texts for preaching, the recommendations of the new *Lectionary* of the Lutheran-Liturgical Conference are widely followed, and that these accentuate better the diversity of biblical expression than the epistles and the gospel of the primitive church. The new liturgical ordinance for the ecclesiastical year constantly reminds us anew of the central biblical message, despite the differences to be found among individual churches.

We know also the dangers we can meet in our parishes because we are necessarily bound to the Word. No convincing way has yet been found to accept freely and openly, at the level of the parish, historico-critical research in biblical studies and yet to have it serve our bondage to the Word. In our dealing with historico-critical research we also often advance beyond Luther's knowledge. The history of exegesis of the last two-hundred years should certainly not be neglected. The fear of historico-critical research, and the fear of a hasty accommodation to the desires and demands of the environment, often lead to a biblicism which is also called a heresy in Hall's presentation. There are not only the vocal principles of biblical fundamentalism, but more commonly a factual biblicism in the praxis of the parish in order to preserve the parish from the uncertainties of the impact of historico-critical dealings on Scripture. It would be helpful to take more seriously concrete representation of the incarnation, in the same vein as Luther saw the letters of scripture as "diapers" and "manger" of the gospel. Few consequences have been drawn from many widely accepted results of historical criticism in the liturgy (for example, the different appreciation between epistles and gospels in the liturgy of the main services).

I find Hall's reference to the easy confusion between "to have" and "to desire" in the interpretation of the Scripture very important, for it enables him to rightly draw conclusions from Luther's nuanced antithesis of *theologia crucis* and *theologia gloriae*. ("Truth *is* given us, but always under the aspect of its apparent antithesis: it is given, but not impressively; it is given, but not to be possessed. . . . *Wir sind Bettler!* The lust to *have* the truth, as distinct from always receiving it as a gift, is in fact born of 'the theology of glory.' ") We can compare this to what Paul said in Phil. 3:12, at the end of his life, of his own process of faith. We can also remember Bonhoeffer's advice that we are today completely thrown back to the beginning of faith and understanding. We have to fear less a principled use of theology, in the spirit of a *theologia crucis* convinced of having the truth, than a practical usage of the Scripture in which we naturally "possess" the Word without any expectation of ever being spoken to differently by it, or questioned by it. Those who preach regularly fall particularly easily into this temptation, more precisely when they are only preoccupied with the question of transmission to others, and when J. A. Bengel's advice is no longer followed in practice: "Te totum applica ad textum. Rem totam applica ad te" ("Apply yourself totally to the study of the text. Apply the text totally to yourself").

A particular danger of our times is the noticeable decline of basic knowledge of the Bible in the parishes and even among theology students and ministers. Efforts to provide, despite the limitation of time, a religious and catechetical education that is complete and appropriate, particularly when compared to previous methods of teaching, have led to the opposite result that there is in general no longer any really deep and intensive dealing with the Bible. The dying out of traditional Bible study groups is another alarming sign. This is a reason to encourage any effort that would bring a new interest in Bible study through the aid of modern methods of communication. Ecumenical groups of research, whose goals are the common study of the Bible, open the door to new opportunities. Much depends on whether the preaching is open to the questions of the audience yet takes its message clearly from adherence to God's revelation in Jesus Christ, as it is transmitted to us through the witness of Scripture—in the same sense as Hall's comment in reference to Paul Tillich about the relation between question and answer.

In view of openness to the actual situation following the concrete bondage to the Word, I believe that there is a particular opportunity to come to the presently important and concrete point, especially if we follow Hall who insisted in his presentation on the necessary renunciation of the desire to exhaust the subject, and advocated a direct approach: "The church has indeed found no better way of *avoiding* the appropriate word than by attempting to say everything all at once—'the whole gospel,' as it is sometimes euphemistically called! Gospel is perhaps never—or only seldom—'whole.' Normally it is intensely *partial*." Luther's own manner of preaching can teach us many things on this subject. Luther refused to take everything out of a text, but abstracted what concerned him and his listeners at the time. The introduction to our sermons should contain the warning that a complete study of all aspects of the text can be a wrong approach.

Hall warns strongly against false efforts "to express the whole gospel" through examples, since these same examples expressing the gospel so well can be very restrictive in a radically different situation. I refer somewhat to what he said about Jürgen Moltmann's "theology of hope" in the European post-war horizon and in the North American context. In the European postwar situation, the biblical theme of "hope" was an effective help in dealing with rampant fatalism and "Nordic" melancholy. But in North America which, because of its history, has a confident optimism in human capability, the Moltmannian concept can become a superficial declaration and act as "opium" in Marx's sense instead of allowing one to know oneself and recognize one's sins. This is similar to what Hall said in his presentation about the differences between our Western and the "Third World situation."

In all our preaching we have to be aware, more than we generally do, of the concrete situations in which we talk, and of the listener's unquestioned acceptance of what we try to say.

The dangers of many representations of the common witnessing of Christ due to the contextual differences in time and place are certainly well known and are also often mentioned by Hall. It can result in a hasty accommodation to what is pleasing and supportive to the listener. In this manner, the "German Christians" exaggerated and betrayed the real call of Christ's mission, as it was then strongly expressed in the Barmen Declaration for the sake of the historical "moment." Also today we have the possibility to simply read what others have perhaps expressed better than one's own Christian confession. Even in our participation—made necessary by the gospel—in the debate for peace or in the debate about the utilization of future sources of energy there can be only an adaptation and therefore only a superficial "speaking with the tongue only." When we think of the variety of facets, commanded by the situation, of the actual Christian witness, we realize above all the great danger of relativism, where the resulting monotony is broken by the particular, and where a common Christian confession of faith seems utterly impossible.

The memory of the common Christian tradition, as it happened for example last year in the celebration of the sixteen hundredth anniversary of the Nicea-Constantinople Creed, could be a great help. The fact that Christians of all different regions and different faiths participate again and again in common church services represents an effective counterbalance to the threat of relativism. The question of the still not realised community in the Lord's Supper over confessional boundaries represents a particular problem that we will presently not address in more detail.

I found very useful Hall's words in relation to Luther's on the exhortation to be obedient in the dealing with Scripture: "Thus for Luther the important thing for theology is, not to be 'correct,' but to be 'obedient'—to achieve consistency, not with what has been regarded at this or that juncture as 'orthodoxy,' but to be consistent with the living truth who is the Lord . . . confession cannot be reduced to doctrine, nor can it be all worked out a priori. It must occur as the appropriate witness, as the 'Word,' 'the Word from the Lord.'" The difference between current, concrete confessions of faith and learned assertions is justified. I wonder, for example, if the direction of the United Evangelical Lutheran Church of Germany has considered enough this distinction in the concept of witnessing in its latest rejection of the confessionally founded declaration of the World Alliance of Reformed Churches about the necessity to reject dissuasion through atomic weapons.

What, finally, justifies the hope that, despite all the contextual situations we have to account for, we might nevertheless achieve a common Christian confession, is the fact that truth is no ideology or mere dogmatic teaching. Truth is rather identical to the living Lord, whose assembly transcends every border and who leads to the obedient confession of Him as *the* path, as *the* truth and as *the* life (John 14:6).

Response to Professor Douglas Hall

HENRY S. WILSON

Professor Douglas Hall raises the question of the often-mentioned tension between understanding the "truth" as "something eternal, immutable, always and everywhere the same" versus truth as "something moving and alive, forever seeking expressions in new forms, struggling to insert itself into the changing process of world history." He also points out the increasing awareness in the West from the time of the Renaissance of the "influence of the particularities of the age upon the formulations of ideas" and the "vexing problems of doctrinal relativity" in the West from the nineteenth century. However, he notes that theological developments in the Third World speak not only to their *people* but also to the *times* they are living in. Therefore he raises the following pertinent question: "If what is true for West European Christians is not true for African and Latin American Christians," are we not in danger of "becoming a veritable Tower of Babel, in which no 'province' of Christians really understands what the others are confessing?"

I would like to respond by touching on four points: 1) The problem of "truth"; 2) The relation between text and context; 3) diversity in expression of faith and possible "religious and social chaos"; 4) contextual theologies and the unity of Christians everywhere.

1. Should "truth" be understood or discussed only in terms of *absolute* and *relative*? Can there not be a third alternative? Can one not say that it is only in the end that "truth" will be fully disclosed or discerned; that "truth" is an *emergent process* that reveals itself in the given context. The question of truth is not a quality of propositions, but for us in the Third World "truth" is that which effects salvation and hence, it is salvific. Third World theologians often point out that in their context, truth is not just a logical quality of statement but it is an existential issue of understanding and interpreting the Scripture.

2. In the Third World, the relation between the text and the context is much more dynamic than just a literary activity. The text is not understood as a *constant* which needs to be applied to the *changing* context. Even the text has to open up in the context. Text by itself is dead and can be treated as a linguistic object till it becomes a living text as it opens up in the context. It is the context which opens up the positive revelatory aspect of the text. So we have to say that it is not the content (text) but only God and/or the Word that is unchangeable. The Word being unchangeable can break through the text and give new forms and content which speak to the context. So we have to talk not merely in terms of text and context but in terms of Word—text (Word of God)—context. Only the Word has to be understood as transcendent truth if we are to be true to Luther's theology.

> Somebody asked, "Doctor [Luther], is the Word that Christ spoke when he was on earth the same in fact and in effect as the Word preached by a minister?" The doctor replied, "Yes, because he said, 'He who hears you hears me' (Luke 10:16). And Paul calls the Word 'the power of God' (Rom. 1:16)." Then the inquirer asked, "Doctor, isn't there a difference between the Word that became flesh (John 1:14) and the Word that is proclaimed by Christ or by a minister?" "By all means!" he replied. "The former is the incarnate Word, who was true God from the beginning, and the latter is the Word that's proclaimed. The former Word is in substance God; the latter Word is in its effect the power of God, but isn't God in substance, for it has a man's nature, whether it's spoken by Christ or by a minister."[1]

> We must make a great difference between God's Word and the word of man. A man's word is a little sound, that flies into the air, and soon vanishes; but the Word of God is greater than death and hell, for it forms part of the power of God, and endures everlastingly. . . ."[2]

Luther's confrontation with the Enthusiasts led him to uphold the responsibility Jesus Christ entrusted to the Apostles to bear witness to him and also to greatly stress the importance of the Bible written according to him by the

Apostles. "The Apostles themselves considered it necessary to set down the New Testament and hold it fast in the Greek language. . . . They knew that if it was left exclusively to men's memory, wild and fearful disorder and confusion and a host of varied interpretations, fancies, and doctrines would arise in the Christian church, and that this could not be prevented and simple folk protected unless the New Testament were set down with certainty in written language."[3] The problem with the Enthusiasts was that they ignored the apostolic witness and emphasized direct revelation from above. So over against the Enthusiasts' teaching of the inner Word, that is, the immediate utterance of the Holy Spirit in the soul, Luther affirms the revelation of God through the Bible, the written and external Word. This does not mean that Luther reduced Christianity to a "religion of the book" and the Christian congregation to "a reading circle."[4] Since he viewed and understood the Word of God not as a static but as an active, dynamic and creative power, "the Bible is Word of God to Luther only in a derived sense. The Word of God is a much broader concept than just the Bible. It is the whole activity of God in the redemption of humanity. So it is proper to say that the Word of God is *in* the Scripture but to draw the relationship closer than that would probably be offensive to Luther."[5] Therefore the mere repetition of the biblical verses is not the Word of God. Rather it has to become a living Word to speak to people in their context.

3. Diverse expressions do not lead to religious and social chaos, rather insisting on the inherited expressions and formulations of faith and giving them the status of "immutable truth" with thought to the present contributes to chaos among people who have to face present realities and find appropriate answers to their challenges. In this search for understanding and expressing our faith we face truth transcending every form and expression whether traditional or historical. Therefore, giving finality to one way of expression necessarily means giving finality to the sphere of thought and mode of expression in which it is given.[6]

Not only the context of the *people* but also the *time* is very significant. If we believe that the plurality we inherited is not only a historical occurrence but also a gift of God, there is no escape from taking the given plurality seriously and giving it due consideration in our witness, faith articulation and formulation of theologies. One should not forget that all theological articulations have socio-political, cultural elements deeply embedded in them. Christianity's historical association with the colonial powers of the West has clearly shown how the theology they possessed and professed helped them to dominate and oppress the colonized people in the name of the "once for all given and unchanged" theology and faith.

Hall rightly gives due credit to the challenges the liberation theology of Latin American poses to the theology which came from the West and developed in their colonized countries. I must add here that ever since

Protestant Christianity appeared in India in the eighteenth century, there have been continual attempts by Indian Christians as well as Hindus to challenge Western formulations and presentations of Christianity. They tried to construct what we call Indian Christian theology to address our people from their own religious-cultural point of view. Most of you are familiar with such people as K. C. Sen, Brahmabandhav Upadhyaya, A. J. Appasamy and others. But their attempts were prevented in the name of the universality of the gospel and the permanency and homogeneity of Christian witness both by Western missionaries and Indian Christians. Today we realize that this was a mistake on the part of the Indian Church.

4. Let me also comment on the fear that unity of the church is in jeopardy if we contextualize theology. The Christianity and theology in our Asian countries originated in Western Europe and North America. It is a "potted plant" Christianity, to use the expression of D. T. Niles, which needs to be protected from its natural surroundings in the name of the unchangeable given truth. The result is that such a plant will remain "alien" to its immediate environment without any marked interaction. What we are longing for is that this potted plant should take root where it is placed. Whether in such a process it will wither away or not is what we Christians have to face in our situation.

A similar question can be raised to the Western churches. If the Western churches today try to take their present context seriously they also need to contextualize their theology. The Western churches perhaps may have a greater need for this than we in the Third World. Does nineteenth-century or even early twentieth-century European theology really speak to the present? This question is for the European churches to answer. I would say that in this common search we already have an expression of unity.

One also has to raise the question: Why do we need church unity? Church unity should not be an end in itself. The goal of church unity must be the unity of humankind. Further, the unity we seek is not merely unity in doctrine, but of discipleship. In following Christ and continuing in his mission we have the unity which we seek to fulfill.

I would say that the expressions "openness to the world" and "immersion in the situation" need further clarification. In our struggle to take context seriously we are not just turning to the world and people in general. Faithfulness to the gospel in our countries demands that we give special attention to marginalized people, the weak, the oppressed, the suffering and the victims of all our modern progress in the name of "development." This special bias cannot escape the challenge of developing contextual theology in Third World countries. Giving heed to the context, therefore, is not an option but an essential element of our Christian witness.

Finally, I would say that whatever is the truth today for North American and West European Christians could also be discovered in some form or other by listening to the people in the developing Third World and by participating in their struggle to live the command of the gospel. I conclude, therefore, that the tension in our Christian witness is not just between subjection to the Word and relation to the context. The tension also occurs when comfortable dogmas and doctrines are challenged by the changing situation, its demands and needs.

NOTES

1. *LW* 54:394; *WA TR* 4:695-696.
2. William Hazlitt, trans. and ed., *The Table Talk of Martin Luther* (London: Bell & Sons, 1890), 20.
3. *LW* 45:360; *WA* 15:38.
4. K. E. Skydsgaard, "Tradition and God's Word," *Studia Theologia* 19 (1965):222.
5. H. S. Wilson, *The Speaking God: Luther's Theology of Preaching* (Madras: Tranquebar Publishing House, 1982), 25.
6. D. J. C. Duraisingh, "Alternate Modes of Theologizing Now Prevalent in India," *Religion and Society*, 27/2 (1980):85.

The Exercise of Theology: The Conciliation of Literal Sense with Its Context

YOSHIKAZU TOKUZEN

Luther wrote, in the disputation theses for his students of 1536:

41. And scripture must be understood not contrary but rather for Christ, thus it must either lead to him or not be true Scripture.

49. We shall elevate Christ above Scripture, even if our adversaries had elevated Scripture above Christ.[1]

Luther insisted, through these provocative and easily misunderstandable declarations, that theology doesn't deal with letters but only with the real subject, that is, Christ. Luther wanted also to ascertain and proclaim in this declaration that Christ is at the center of Scripture.

Yet at the same time, Luther tries to integrate the subject in its context and to interpret it accordingly. His proclamation of the Word was always taken in context.

One of the explanations of this attitude could perhaps be found in the fact that, contrary to the other Reformers, Luther belonged to the monastic tradition and not to the tradition of cathedral schools. Luther was not a

Translated by Georges Herzog

theoretical and philosophical theologian, but exercised theology both in conjunction with a life of monastical piety (he said that for the true exercise of theology, there is a need of *oratio, meditatio,* and *tentatio*), and in close contact with the life of his city. In this sense we can speak of Luther's fight for the liberation of theology from philosophy.

His effort to be simultaneously bound by the Word and to operate in context is exemplified in his extraordinary talent and in his efforts to use the German language in his theology. As an example I would like to point to his use of the word *frum* (pious). *Frum* was certainly not a theoretical and philosophical concept, but belonged to the popular vocabulary. *Iustitia* was, however, as a theological *terminus technicus*, too complex and formal to be employed in popular explanations. This compelled Luther to take the common word *frum*, to transpose it in a context of faith, and to understand and to use it in the sense of being *frum* before God. Luther was a genius in such linguistic contextualizations.

In his efforts to render *iustus, iustitia* with *frum, frumkeit* we can see, in my opinion, how Luther left the medieval Latin language that was so static and burdened with substantives, to enter a new language that was primarily dynamic, and possessed precise expressions through its use of verbs. He no longer spoke of justice as such but of *Gerechtmachen* (to justify), *Gerechtgemacht-werden* or *Frum-werden* (to be justified). Through this technique Luther succeeded in presenting to us God's work properly. His fidelity to the Word and his attention to the context are united in him in this manner.

Luther's message is that we too have to accept the literal sense while understanding it in relation to our context. Different approaches provide us with different possibilities of interpretation that demonstrate nevertheless the same point. These different interpretations can unlock and convey a diversified and rich presentation of faith, provided that despite their differences, they concentrate on one point, Christ as the center of Scripture.

Kitamori published his book *Theology of the Pain of God*[2] in 1946, at a time when the topic of discussion was the *impassibilitas Dei*, that is, God's incapability to suffer. He was widely criticized and his theology was considered patripassianist. The catastrophic war and the post-war period were, materially and spiritually, Kitamori's *Sitz im Leben*. Having been influenced by Luther's *theologia crucis*, Kitamori tried, from and in this context, to express the main theme of Scripture, the *solus Christus*. Many theologians, such as Jürgen Moltmann and others, speak now of a crucified and suffering God.

According to such an interpretation, it is possible to make, from our own particular experience, contributions that will provide stimulations in other situations. In the same way as George Forell could write a work like *Ethics of Decision*,[3] I could interpret Luther in the sense of an "ethic of decidedness" from my culture and mentality.

RESPONSE—HENRY S. WILSON

I have the impression (to give only an example) that there is a certain restraint and helplessness when occidental interpreters have to translate or explain the concept of *posteriora Dei* of which Luther speaks in the Heidelberg Disputation.[4] I have to date found only one author who interpreted the text positively and developed a personal opinion on it.[5] In a society of "indirect communication" as in Japan, and perhaps particularly in the Far East, it is certainly easier to understand what Luther meant when he spoke of *posteriora Dei* than in Western society where people are exclusively used to a "direct," face to face, mode of communication.

Theology means to practice theology. The practice of theology can only be realized when one tries, from the context, and in the context to practice the main point, that is Christ. We are all urged to do this.

NOTES

1. WA 39:1,47.
2. Kitamori, *Theology of the Pain of God* (1946).
3. George Forell, *Ethics of Decision: An Introduction to Christian Ethics* (Philadelphia: Fortress Press, 1955).
4. *LW* 31:40; WA 1:362.
5. Paul G. Bretscher, *The Holy Infection: The Mission of the Church in Parish and Community* (St. Louis: Concordia Publishing House, 1969), 28ff.

Summary

DAVID W. PREUS

The relationship between text and context is an issue which has preoccupied contemporary theology, particularly with the development of Liberation Theology. Partly for this reason, and also due to the fact that panelists had received a copy of Douglas Hall's paper well in advance, it is not surprising that the discussion in this group focused on that paper, and its attempt to show that Luther was a contextual theologian who was always engaged in the process of relating the fixed source of theology to his context. Inge Lønning's paper, which also dealt with Luther's approach to Biblical interpretation, provided a helpful complement. The two Asian panelists, Tokuzen and Wilson, were appreciative of his approach to Luther. It was noted that a recognition of Luther's sensitivity to his context implies that the Reformer may make a contemporary contribution to the development of an indigenous theology in cultural settings that do not share Western history. This appreciation of Luther's contextual approach led virtually all the participants to reflect on how the gospel might be contextualized in their setting.

There was general agreement among participants about the contextual character of Luther's theology. Debate centered on two issues: (1) The adequacy of Hall's portrayal of Luther to account for Christian truth-claims; and (2) Whether Luther was self-consciously contextual in his approach.

In regard to the first point, while all agreed to the need for theology to be contextual, several participants thought they saw a tendency in the paper to make the context a norm for Christian truth, akin to the Method of Correlation approach in Tillich's theology, which might weaken the claims of truth. The exponents of contextuality, with Hall in the lead, were careful to respond that their concerns for contextuality would not lead to a relativizing of truth.

Some attempts were made to offer a synthesis between Hall's vision of Christian truth and a more static, fixed understanding of doctrinal truth. There was general agreement that truth must be formulated in sentences, even though such true sentences are not to be identified with Absolute Truth. Attention was also drawn to the importance of unchanging theological formulations as was the case, for example, during the gnostic crisis. A few participants held that this was also Luther's position.

It was noted by one participant that the group's discussion of the nature of Christian truth, and its relation to changing contexts, was a rehearsal of the debate between Otto Pesch and Peter Manns on the possibility of doctrinal development and the nature of truth. This observation was confirmed when Pesch agreed that Luther was a contextual theologian in seeking to overcome a late scholasticism that had obscured the truth. He doubted, however, whether Luther knew he was a contextual theologian and whether he was aware of the great difference between the scholastic context and his own. This led to a general discussion of the question of the sense in which Luther was a contextual theologian.

Pesch also clarified his statement from a previous day that matters not considered Catholic at one time were considered Catholic at a later time. He wanted it understood that it was not the truth that changed, but the recognition of it that changed.

In his response to the discussion, Lønning acknowledged that good theology is always contextual. That refers both to the context of the text and the context of today. The authority and clarity of Scripture, however, cannot be dealt with simply by saying that Christ is the meaning of the Scripture. We must face the fact that we ask questions with sentences, and speak the truth in sentences. We have to take great care with words as vehicles of truth even as we acknowledge that truth is a person who can never be absolutely embodied in words.

We cannot make a dichotomy of truth as statements or truth as person. St. John's statement of Jesus, "I am the truth," is a doctrinal statement. Then other doctrinal statements must be made that say who Jesus is. We cannot make the person true and the statements false. They go together. The opposition of static and dynamic views of truth is unacceptable. There is only one gospel, not several. The one gospel may be expressed in various ways. That does not diminish the truth of any one of such ways. The truth of the church and the unity of the church are two sides of the same matter. This is the essential point we can learn from Luther.

Hall indicated his frustration at not having time to respond to a wide range of issues that had been raised. He limited himself to general responses to a few of the issues. He expressed his doubts that contextual theologizing had become commonplace. Invoking Buber, he pointed out that all formulations are incapable of encompassing the "thou" in themselves. The truth cannot be "possessed." The "Protestant principle," as expressed by Tillich, indicates the Protestant "protest against the substitution of any finite, conditioned realities for the Absolute." Hall maintained his original paper had already dissociated contextuality from a number of the criticisms that have been registered in the discussion: relativizing of truth; an uncritical acceptance of the context; and an inability to make clear-cut affirmations.

In conclusion, it can be noted that, of all the discussions, this one was preoccupied with questions related to contemporary theological method. Given the dual focus of the consultation, both to investigate the resources in Luther's thought for overcoming church division and to ascertain the contribution Luther might offer the catholic church's ministry today, this attention to contemporary theological questions is not inappropriate to the study of Luther. The second focus of concern, ascertaining Luther's contribution to the church's contemporary witness, necessarily leads interpreters of Luther to consider questions about the most appropriate theological method of presentation, as well as about Luther's own method as a possible paradigm for contemporary theology. In view of Western society's pervasive relativism, which often challenges the credibility of the church's ministry today, the group's attention to the question of how best to present Luther's insights as "truth" is a most relevant concern for contemporary ministry.

Summary of the Consultation

REINHARD FRIELING

The concluding discussion provided the opportunity to gather and summarize the remarks concerning the main theme of the Consultation. What is to be hoped for in the future by an ecumenical engagement with Luther? Do we need an ecumenical "Lutherology" (Frieling)?

The Consultation and the concluding discussion revealed much common ground but also different accents. Daniel Olivier named an entire list of themes delivered to Christendom by Luther. "The unique authority of Holy Scripture, justification by faith without works, the priesthood of all believers as a question to the ordained priesthood, the theology of the cross as a measure and critique of the theology of the Church. Who else but Luther can be our master in these questions?"

The various accents were received by the Consultation in part as "tensions": Some were clearly interested in the historical Luther and his significance especially for Protestant-Catholic dialogue and the overcoming of the controversial questions of the sixteenth century. Others, on the other hand, were more concerned about the contemporary human situation. Does Luther have anything essential to say to us today? How do we see contemporary issues, for instance the human image, human rights, conscience and freedom, in light of Luther's theology?

The discussion showed that there is no presuppositionless exegesis of Luther. The interest is, among other things, always confessionally stamped: unconsciously apologetic or distancing itself from apologetic. The difficulty of the approach partly was in that the *entire* Luther was not sufficiently known. Why are often only the polemical writings of Luther made available while only the experts take notice of the rest of his work (Vilmos Vajta)? It is also to be noticed that we today hardly still live in the spirituality which for Luther was a matter of course. However, Catholic Christians are perhaps closer to him in spirituality than are Protestants, and accordingly Roman Catholic Luther research discovers dimensions of the faith which evangelicals overlook or do not see (Vajta). It could be a help toward the ecumenical disclosure of Luther if there were engagement with his hymns and catechisms in parishes and ecumenical circles (Heinz Schütte).

The disclosure of Luther is also determined by the good 450 years of

Translated by Carter Lindberg

church history since the Reformation. The Roman Catholic Church has experienced three influential Councils and proclaimed two Marian dogmas. Since Vatican II it has entered into ecumenical dialogue conscious of these developments. Without doubt its Luther research has enriched Luther research as a whole concerning many aspects and insights, even if unanimous judgments on the disclosure of the "Catholic" and the "reformatory" Luther have not yet been reached (Grote).

Access to Luther seems to be especially complicated for the Lutheran Church. At times it sounded in the Consultation—as in a "zero hour"—as if Luther must be engaged entirely anew, whereby one view considered the "Catholic" Luther as a sound bridge for ecumenism today, while the other experienced exactly in the "reformatory" Luther the most important help and challenge. The decisive questions, however, will be how Luther, the Reformation, and the way of the Reformation Church in general will be seen in the context of the saving history of God (Grote and Vajta in connection to Congar). Luther did not desire to be a founder of a church but nevertheless actually became one (Geoffrey Wainwright), while in the course of the development of the Reformation Churches they called upon him and do to some extent bear his name. What does an ecumenical disclosure of Luther mean before the background of the contemporary discussion of such models of unity as "reconciled diversity," *unitatis redintegratio,* and "conciliar fellowship"?

It became clear during the discussion that Luther does not belong to the Lutheran Churches alone (Georg Kretschmar). For the Lutherans this is not only a delightful experience, for at the same time it poses the question of what then is still their "Lutheran identity."

During the Consultation these questions were not expressly dealt with but rather were touched on in individual themes. Indeed, they arose as well in light of the tradition which Luther had consciously received in his time but which in the meantime, at least in part of Lutheranism, has atrophied or been lost (Metropolitan John of Helsinki), as also in view of Luther's judgment of others which Lutherans today no longer carry out: for example—apart from Luther's coarseness in general—his position toward the Anabaptists and his statements on the pope and the papacy as "Antichrist" (Kretschmar). Precisely in relation to these problems the question is posed of the possible "painful consequences" of an ecumenical disclosure of Luther for Lutheranism (Kretschmar). In any case, the way those of the Orthodox and Free churches see Luther merits more attention than granted up to now.

Luther's ecumenical significance was also seen with regard to his effect of loosening up church doctrine as well as church structure (Gottfried Maron). Nevertheless, Luther's relationship to "doctrine" was judged differently. Some emphasized that for Luther everything depended on "pure doctrine," which is a form of the gospel that is distributed in Word and sacrament.

Therefore it may not be said that the Lord desires "unity in discipleship but not unity in doctrine"; for according to Luther "the way of the Christian and of the church" remains "the way under the gospel and therefore also under pure doctrine" (Kretschmar). If Luther has become here "alien" to a part of Protestantism, then it is the ecumenical task to break through this alienation. Others emphasized that Luther stood apart from all stereotypedness of "doctrine" and often expressed himself very differently on one and the same issue. He was nothing short of a "genius of multiplicity," occasionally at the cost of verbal clarity (Maron). His essential intention was not the fixation of ecclesial doctrine but rather the quickening of faith by the sermon as the *viva vox evangelii*. Inasmuch as Luther has actually meant the end of the history of dogma on the evangelical side, "confession" then is something specifically other than "dogma." The progress of the history of dogma on the Roman Catholic side could also not exist in Luther's sense for it means an advancing fixation of the ecclesial-confessional *fides quae*. It is therefore ecumenically significant that Vatican II consciously did not continue this line and pronounced no new dogma (Maron).

Unanimity ruled in the conception that Luther is a common teacher of all Christians when it concerns the testimony that Jesus Christ is the starting and end point for all Christian thinking. Luther's fundamental perception was: "The *Deus loquens* lives!" (Peter Manns). It would be a fundamental error in ecumenism to believe that we could manipulate the truth-question instead of listening to the *Deus loquens*. It is important in this connection to learn the "gift of distinction" from Luther. "Every Christian theology must learn from Luther how to correctly distinguish between law and gospel, letter and Spirit, inner and outer person, cross and lordship, faith and works. We are working today—without great profit—with many distinctions. Luther's distinctions on the contrary bring forth genuine Christian preaching, the 'Christum-Treiben.' In Luther's school one learns what determines a real theological statement" (Olivier).

In this connection, Luther's "double-faceted concept of the church" was once more addressed. Next to the basic question of how the concept of the "spiritual-sacramental fellowship" (Vajta) relates to the thesis that no more can be said of the church than of Christians, namely that it is *simul iusta et peccatrix* (Reinhard Frieling), there was above all the theological meaning of church structure and office in Luther. On the one hand, Luther's "unheard-of unconcern" with regard to absolutizing and establishing ecclesial administration was discussed (Maron). The church for him is not primarily something of the eyes and security, but rather a thing of faith and Christian certainty. From this perspective Luther's thought of the hiddenness of the church should not be too quickly brushed aside, for it is worth serious ecumenical reflection.

On the other hand, such "unconcern" on Luther's part for church administration was challenged. Here again there broke open the question of the "Catholic" and the "reformatory" Luther. Is there not today a too one-sided adherence to the "reformatory" Luther? Do Lutherans have anxiety that the "Catholic Luther" could be the "true" Luther (Manns)?

In conclusion, the comprehensive questions were again posed concerning what, then, Luther could mean ecumenically. Olivier said:

> When we speak of Luther's ecumenical significance, we hardly think of Luther, for instance like Francis of Assisi, as a person who is a universal Christian ideal.
>
> Every Christian confessional family has its Patres Ecclesiae, and in this sense Luther belongs to the Lutherans.
>
> What he personally was and did during his life will long remain controversial. However, his writings have a universal significance in themselves as a remaining monument of Christian thought.
>
> Here, in his theological achievement, appears to me above all where Luther's ecumenical significance resides.

The International Consultation of Theologians on Disclosing Luther's Ecumenical Significance left many questions open and set forth many new ecumenical tasks. It was important that bishops and church leaders were included as participants in the Consultation and that from the beginning the Consultation stood in the context of the official dialogues being lead among the churches. The critical contributions of Catholics, Orthodox, Anglicans, Reformed, Methodists, Baptists, Mennonites, and those of the Union churches are altogether indispensable for Luther research, the Lutherans, and also for the ecumene.